# WHAT STUDENTS ARE SAYING ABOUT WESTEN . . .

**In the first edition of Westen's *Psychology: Mind, Brain, and Culture*, we invited students to e-mail their comments about the book to the author. Here is what they were moved to write after reading it.**

"This was one of the rare books that kept to its format throughout the entire text. The main issues were presented in easy to read columns before each chapter, readdressed in exact order within the text, and highlighted in summary at the end of the chapter. Finally, a text that is clear and true to its aim!"
—John J. Lagos, *Framingham State College*

"Your book TRULY held my interest. For the first time, I felt that the author wanted me to understand the material. So often I feel that the authors of my textbooks assume that I'm already familiar with the subject, or that they just want to flaunt their intelligence by using complicated words and the like. The examples you used were helpful and interesting, they really made the different concepts clearer. I just had to let you know that you've made me happy—at least I know that there's ONE textbook out there in the American educational system that is informative and, at the same time, engaging. If only all books could be like that!"
—Rachel Healy, *Fordham University*

"I want to compliment you on your book, *Psychology: Mind, Brain, & Culture*. I have always had a difficult time comprehending information through reading but I have found that your method of summarizing the chapters has been extremely helpful in allowing me to recall and understand what I have read."
—Roberta Myer, *University of California-Davis*

"I just wanted to compliment you on how well you wrote your textbook. I feel it is the most easy to read text that I have come across yet. Everything in your book flows and is so easy to understand. A job well done."
—Gregg McAuliffe, *JRI Health*

"I have been meaning to write to you to express my appreciation ever since I started starring and tallying up the funny yet subtle 'ha-has' and witty remarks you sprinkled your book with . . . This book was direct and understandable, despite the 'complex' and highly interpretive nature of this subject matter. I often found myself reading random chapters and picture captions for the simple sake of enjoyment and enrichment, even when I should have been doing something else, like reading the assigned pages . . . I felt compelled to inform you of how useful, applicable, and entertaining (the funnies 'rocked my psyche') I found your book. I'm not even going to sell it back to the bookstore after our exam, I like it so much."
—Marlena Marie Wojcik, *Northwestern University*

"I wanted to let you know that I am thoroughly enjoying reading your book. It is very organized, so I can easily follow the format and you have used language that is easy to understand (which is refreshing). I like that you begin each chapter with a real life story or example. It immediately draws the reader in. Also, all of the examples and anecdotes you provide add a lot to the book and make it easier to understand. I have frequently come up with examples in my own life that support the ideas that you have presented. I appreciate your subtle humor."
—Elizabeth Chiarello, *Trinity College*

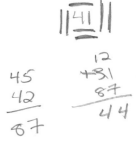

# PSYCHOLOGY

## MIND, BRAIN, & CULTURE

### SECOND EDITION

## DREW WESTEN
### HARVARD UNIVERSITY

## JOHN WILEY & SONS, INC.

New York     Chichester     Weinheim     Brisbane     Singapore     Toronto

# DEDICATION

*To Laura*

EXECUTIVE EDITOR     Christopher Rogers
SENIOR MARKETING MANAGER     Charity Robey
SENIOR PRODUCTION EDITOR     Elizabeth Swain
DESIGN SUPERVISORS     Ann Marie Renzi/Kevin Murphy
TEXT DESIGN     Nancy Field
SENIOR PHOTO EDITOR     Hilary Newman
PHOTO RESEARCHER     Jennifer Atkins
FINE ART CONSULTANT     Steven Diamond
ILLUSTRATION COORDINATOR     Anna Melhorn
COVER ART © Therese May, "Therese," 1969, 72" x 90", fabric, machine, applique. Photo by Sharon Risedorph.

This book was set in 10/12 Palatino by Ruttle, Shaw & Wetherill, Inc. and printed and bound by Von Hoffmann, Inc. The cover was printed by Phoenix.

This book is printed on acid-free paper.

Recognizing the importance of preserving what has been written, it is a policy of John Wiley & Sons, Inc. to have books of enduring value published in the United States printed on acid-free paper, and we exert our best efforts to that end.

The paper on this book was manufactured by a mill whose forest management programs include sustained yield harvesting of its timberlands. Sustained yield harvesting principles ensure that the number of trees cut each year does not exceed the amount of new growth.

*Library of Congress Cataloging in Publication Data:*
Westen, Drew, 1959–
    Psychology : mind, brain & culture / Drew Westen. — 2nd ed.
      p.     cm.
    Includes bibliographical references and index.
    ISBN 0-471-24049-4
    ISBN 0-471-31706-3 (five-chapter preview)
    1. Psychology.
    BF121.W44 1998
    150—dc21                    97-51291
                                        CIP

Printed in the United States of America

10 9 8 7 6 5 4 3 2 1

*Psychology: Mind, Brain, & Culture* emerged from my several years of teaching introductory psychology at the University of Michigan. My goal was to try to translate a style of teaching into the written word, a style that is at once personal and informal—engaging students by presenting material relevant to their own concerns and interests—yet highly conceptual and scientifically rigorous. Translating a lecture style into a book is no easy task because so much of effective teaching happens through interaction, eye contact, and humor, which all too often elude capture on the written page. So this has been quite a challenge.

## WRITING FOR A BROAD RANGE OF STUDENTS

In moving to a second edition, another challenge emerged. Over the last three years, I have received dozens of e-mails from around the world—many from professors who are using the book, but even more from their students. (These e-mails have been truly a pleasure to read and have reminded me of the importance of intermittent reinforcement, especially while in the midst of expending the thousand or so hours necessary to update the book for the second edition!) Aside from an occasional e-mail from some perceptive reader informing me that I had confusingly labeled the axes of some figure (thanks, by the way), perhaps the most striking thing about these e-mail messages has been the range of colleges and universities from which they have come.

I had hoped to write a book with the scientific rigor and conceptual complexity to be used at some of the top universities in the world; judging from the list of professors and universities who have adopted the book, that seems to have happened. But I also wanted to write a book that students would actually enjoy reading, and I hoped the book might find its way into the hands of students from a broad spectrum of colleges and universities, whose professors had faith in their ability to do what most cognitive-developmentalists suggest is optimal for learning: to tackle material at the top of their capacity instead of a level or two down. Some of the most rewarding e-mails have, in fact, come from some of the most unlikely places, including some junior colleges where professors who were willing to take a gamble thought the writing style might compensate for the high conceptual level of the book. But some professors who wanted to use the book have worried about the bottom third of their classes, who may need more guidance as they are reading to be sure they get the gist.

So the question was how to revise the book so that it could reach the widest audience without "dumbing it down" or killing perhaps the most distinctive feature of the book, the writing. So in careful consultation with both my editors at Wiley and a number of professors who are currently using the book, I decided to add two features, which have turned out, I think, to be helpful to students at every level: Interim Summaries, which periodically provide students with the gist of what they have just read; and an advanced discussion that appears in many chapters, called "One Step Further," which professors can choose either to assign or instruct students to ignore, depending on their interests. In addition, I have added more subheads to the text to help the students organize the concepts as they read.

## KEEPING PACE WITH EMERGING KNOWLEDGE

The other major change in the second edition is content. The first edition was written and rewritten from 1986 through 1995, with round after round of reviews and constant updating to keep up with the field. It was thus a very up-to-date book, with an organization that fit the 1990s. Nevertheless, some subfields—particularly those in which neuroscience is prominent—are moving so quickly that even a book crafted in the mid-1990s is behind the times. So I have substantially rewritten and reorganized several chapters, most of them in the first third of the text, to be sure that this book brings students forward into the 21st century instead of backward into the late 19th. Professors who have used the book will find this most apparent in Chapter 3 on the biological bases of psychology; in Chapter 4, on sensation and perception; in Chapter 5, on learning; in chapters 6 and 7, on memory and cognition; and in Chapter 17, on attitudes and social cognition.

In all of these cases, new data simply made parts of the old organization problematic. For example, the study of stereotypes (Chapter 17) has become one of the hottest, most fascinating areas of social psychology, with work by Claude Steele and his colleagues showing that an intervention as seemingly harmless as asking participants to report their race along with other demographic data will decrease the performance of individuals from groups stereotypically viewed as less competent.

The other major difference in the two editions is my better understanding of the history of the discipline and the recurrence and revision of ideas over time. Between this edition and the last, I added more on the history of psychology, and I now offer a broader view of where we have come from and where we are going.

## AIMS AND CORRESPONDING FEATURES

I set out in the first edition to write a textbook with five objectives: to focus on both the biological basis of psychology and the role of culture in shaping basic psychological processes; to provide a conceptual orientation that would capture the excitement and tensions in the field; to help students understand the logic of scientific discovery and hypothesis-testing as applied to psychological questions; to suggest ways of integrating psychological theories and knowledge across subfields; and to employ a language that would be sophisticated but engaging. A sixth aim, more clearly articulated in the second edition, is to find ways to help students who need more structure in learning the material without placing barriers in the way of students who like to read a good story and don't want the narrative disrupted with pedagogical devices. The features of the book follow from these six aims.

## BIOLOGY AND CULTURE: A MICRO TO MACRO APPROACH

A consistent theme of the book, introduced in the first chapter, is that biology and culture form the boundaries of psychology: Understanding people means attending simultaneously to biological processes, psychological experience, and the cultural and historical context. The focus on biological and neural underpinnings echoes one of the major trends in contemporary psychological science, as technological developments allow progressively more sophisticated understanding of the neural substrates of psychological experience. The focus on culture has been a central feature of this book since I began work on it in 1987. *Cross-cultural material is not tacked onto this book; it is integral to it.* My first book, *Self and Society* (1985), was on culture and personality, and a background in anthropology and sociology informs my understanding of the way people think, feel, learn, behave, and develop.

Each chapter of this book contains two extended discussions that show the way psychological experience is situated between the nervous system and cultural experience.

## FROM MIND TO BRAIN

- "From Mind to Brain" integrates concepts and findings from biopsychology and the neurosciences, discussing such issues as the way damage to the brain can alter personality. The latest research in neuroscience is integrated throughout the text.

## GLOBAL VISTA

- "A Global Vista" uses ethnographic examples and cross-cultural studies to explore psychological phenomena in other cultures, with an eye to addressing the universality or culture-specificity of psychological theories and observations. For example, menopause has a very different meaning, and hence different symptoms, in a Mayan village than it does in North America, and parenting styles fostering autonomy that are adaptive in Western, technologically developed societies are not necessarily optimal everywhere. In addition, cross-cultural research is integrated into the structure of each chapter, so that students do not balkanize cross-cultural issues as distinct from the "psychology of white people" but instead ask cross-cultural questions from the start.

These special features flow integrally from the text and are not presented as isolated "boxes." In this way, students will not get the message that the biological and cultural material is somehow superfluous or added on. In this edition, we have screened these features with color to highlight their importance and to help break up what can otherwise seem like a sea of words, without compromising their content or flow with the rest of the narrative.

## CONCEPTUAL ORIENTATION

The book is conceptually oriented. It attempts, within the limits of my objectivity and expertise, to give a fair and compelling account of the different perspectives psychologists take in understanding psychological phenomena. I have a healthy respect for each approach and assume that if thousands of my colleagues find an approach compelling, it contains something that students should know. Feedback from professors who have used the book over the past three years has been extremely helpful in alerting me to places in which my biases did creep in. The coverage in this edition is more balanced.

- From the start, students are challenged to think about psychological phenomena from multiple perspectives. Chapter 1 is not perfunctory; it introduces four perspectives—*psychodynamic, behavioral, cognitive,* and *evolutionary*—in enough depth to allow students to begin conceptualizing psychological data rather than simply memorizing a list of facts, names, or studies. Based on feedback from professors, I have expanded the evolution-ary coverage in the first chapter of this edition, so that students can get a firmer grasp of how evolutionary thinking can be applied across the range of psychological phenomena and how it can be tested empirically.

- At the same time, I have avoided slavishly introducing paragraphs on each perspective in every chapter, since some perspectives obviously apply better to certain phenomena than to others. For example, Chapter 6 on memory is organized primarily around cognitive information-processing models. It does, however, conclude with an evolutionary perspective which, like many contemporary cognitive models, challenges the view of an all-purpose, gen-eral processing brain, suggesting that the brain may have modules that process very specific information relevant to survival and reproduction.

- Although I have made every effort to present controversies in a balanced and dispassionate way, the danger in doing so is that one loses one's voice, and the last thing I wanted to write was a book with intellectual laryngitis. Thus, in "Commentary" sections, I periodically comment on issues of method that bear on the conclusions being reached. Unlike many texts, after presenting both sides of a debate, I let the reader know where I stand on controversial issues, such as the existence of repressed memories of sexual abuse. I have presented versions of some of these commentaries on National Public Radio's "All Things Considered."

## RESEARCH FOCUS

This book takes psychological science seriously. A student should come out of an introductory psychology class not only with a sense of the basic questions and frameworks for answering them but also with an appreciation for how to obtain psychological knowledge. Thus, Chapter 2 is devoted to research meth-ods; the style reflects an effort to engage, not intimidate, so students may see how methods actually make a difference. The statistical supplement that imme-diately follows it, which even the most seriously math-phobic can understand, is included in the body of the text rather than cast off at the end as an impene-trable appendix. In addition, throughout each chapter, students read about spe-cific studies so that they can learn about the logic of scientific investigation. In this edition I have done this earlier in the text, beginning in the first chapter, and continuing with the detective stories that constitute good research in Chapter 3 (on the biological basis of mental processes and behavior) and Chapter 4 (on sensation and perception). By providing the details of experimental design (e.g., how does imaging research really work?), the more biological chapters in partic-ular can read more like a story about living, evolving subdisciplines.

The research presented in this book is also up to date. Like Sisyphus, I have been pushing the boulder of citations up the hill every year, updating and re-thinking as it acquires new weight. At the same time, I have included many clas-sic citations and have tried to convey the way theories and hypotheses have evolved, not just their latest renditions for the sake of appearing current.

## INTEGRATIVE APPROACH

Solo-authoring an introductory text is probably presumptive evidence of men-tal instability (and is clearly a cause of it as well), but I could not have pro-duced this book any other way because my aim was to engage students in the enterprise of thinking about the whole person, not just the parts. As one psychologist put it (Holt, 1976), the human psyche is not the handiwork of an obsessive-compulsive god who created cognition on one day, affect on another, motivation on another, and so forth, and made sure they all stayed neatly in their own territories. Too often our efforts to classify and label lead us to try to separate the inseparable. The integrative bent of the book stems primarily from my own work as a researcher, which has focused on integrating clinical and experimental perspectives as well as concepts and methods from different psychological traditions.

Wherever possible, this book tries to delineate some of the links that our best intellectual efforts often obscure. For example, Chapter 7 presents connectionist models in some detail, linking them to concepts of association described in Chapter 1, Chapter 5 on associative learning, and Chapter 6 on associative memory. Chapter 11 on emotion, stress, and coping concludes by asking how we might begin to pull together the "cold" cognitive models presented in the chapters on learning, memory, thought, and intelligence with the "hot" models of emotion, stress, and motivation presented in the chapters that immediately follow them. The result is a modified information-processing model that describes the operation of implicit and explicit memory, thought, emotion, and motivation.

## LANGUAGE

Above all, I wanted to avoid writing in "textese," a language that presents dry summaries of data for students to memorize instead of engaging them in *thinking* about psychology. *Psychology: Mind, Brain, & Culture* offers a solid and comprehensive account of the principles of psychology in what I hope is an accessible, lively, and thought-provoking style.

- Throughout the book, I aim at clarity and introduce terminology only when it enlightens, not obscures. I am not shy about using metaphor or weaving a narrative, but not a single term in this book is defined by context alone. If students need to understand a concept, they will see the definition in the same sentence in which the word is boldfaced. I have also tried to keep the language at a level appropriate to college students, but if they have to look up an occasional word, I will not lose sleep over it. (I had to look up a few in writing it!)

- As a teacher and writer, I try to make use of one of the most robust findings in psychology: that memory and understanding are enhanced when target information is associated with vivid and personally relevant material. Each chapter begins, then, with an experiment, a case, or an event that lets students know why the topic is important and why anyone might be excited about it. None of the cases is invented; this is real material, and the questions raised in the opening study or vignette reemerge throughout each chapter. Chapter 2, for example, begins with the case of a young women who lost her entire family in a car accident and found herself suddenly contracting one minor ailment after another until finally starting to talk about the event with a psychologist. I then present an experiment by James Pennebaker on the influence of emotional expression on physical health to show how a researcher can take a striking phenomenon or philosophical question (the relation between mind and body) and turn it into a researchable question. A major change in this edition can be seen in the way I raise fundamental issues in each subfield at the beginning of the chapter, gradually address them as the chapter proceeds, and return to them in a more systematic way in the conclusion.

## PEDAGOGICAL FEATURES

I have tried to avoid pedagogy that is condescending or unnecessary. One student complained to me in an e-mail message that her biggest problem with the book was that her roommate kept stealing it from the bookshelf and reading it! In my experience students never follow up on annotated recommendations for future reading, so I have not cluttered the ends of chapters with them. Similarly, because all terms are defined in the text, there is no need to list key terms at the end of the chapter; students can use the index and the glossary if they have trouble locating them. On the other hand, students do need some guidance in studying the material. Three features address this issue: interim summaries, chapter summaries, and a new feature called "One Step Further."

**INTERIM SUMMARIES**   In this edition I have added interim summaries at the end of major sections. Their aim is to recap the "gist" of what has been presented, not only to help students consolidate their knowledge of what they have read but also to alert them if they didn't get something important. The inclusion of these summaries reflects both feedback from professors and the results of research, which suggests that distributing conceptual summaries throughout a chapter and presenting them shortly after students have read the material is likely to optimize learning.

## CHAPTER SUMMARIES

As in the first edition, each chapter concludes with a summary of the major points, organized under the headings in which they were presented. These summaries are essentially an outline of the chapter. Student feedback on their organization and level of detail has been very positive.

## ▶ ONE STEP FURTHER

In this edition I have added a new feature, called "One Step Further." Like the other recurring features in the book, these discussions flow naturally from the text but are highlighted in color. Generally, these are advanced discussions of some aspect of the topic, usually with a strong methodological, conceptual, or neuroscientific focus. These sections are intended to be assigned by professors who prefer a high-level text, or to be read by students who find the topic intriguing and want to learn even more about it even if it isn't assigned. Highlighting these sections gives professors—and students—some choice about what to read or not to read. For example, in Chapter 3, this feature describes some of the latest research on non-motor functions of the cerebellum. In Chapter 4, it addresses signal detection theory, which some professors consider central to introductory coverage of sensation and perception, whereas others consider this material too advanced. In Chapter 5, this feature addresses the theoretical question, "What makes reinforcers reinforcing?" and integrates Gray's work on affect-mediated systems of approach and avoidance, Davidson's work on cortical pathways involved in approach and avoidance, and integrative theories of emotion and reinforcement stemming back to Dollard and Miller. In each case, the material can be skipped without any break in the narrative if the professor chooses not to assign it.

## ORGANIZATION

I tried to organize **Psychology:** *Mind, Brain, & Culture* in a way that would be convenient for most instructors yet follow a coherent design. Of course, different instructors organize things differently, but I do not think many will find the organization idiosyncratic.

Teaching the material in the order presented is probably optimal, for chapters do build on each other. For example, the consciousness chapter presupposes knowledge of the distinction posed in Chapter 6 between implicit and explicit memory. However, if instructors want to rearrange the order of chapters, they can certainly do so, as material mentioned from a previous chapter is cross-referenced so that students can easily find any information they need.

## ILLUSTRATION AND DESIGN

When I began this enterprise, I had no idea what it meant to put together a whole textbook. As a person with minimal use of his right hemisphere, I assumed that some editorial type would come up with figures and tables. This assumption was obviously an example of a well-known psychological phenomenon, wishful thinking. After ten years of working on this project, I think I finally figured out how to educate the right hemisphere, even if mine does not work so well. I took tremendous care to select and design only figures and tables that actually add something and that do not just make the pages look less ominous. Additionally, in this edition, the illustrations were designed with a more vibrant, bolder color palette and larger, bolder labels for better clarity and legibility. The same is true of photo selection, which involved collaboration of the author, editors, and a very talented photo research department committed to finding images that would provide thought and not simply provide momentary respite from the prose. We also worked with the best designers in the business to create a design that is sophisticated and readable, adding the color background screens to the three categories of embedded essays (From Mind to Brain, A Global Vista, and One Step Further) and a bolder, more dynamic palette to their design elements.

## SUPPLEMENTARY MATERIALS

Accompanying the text is an integrated supplements package that includes the following components.

### For Instructors

**Test Bank and Instructor's Manual:** The new edition of the test bank has been written by *The Princeton Review,* the leading publisher of course-preparation materials, and reviewed by Professor Runi Mukerji of the State University of New York at Old Westbury. Known for getting excellent results through their test-preparation publications and courses, *The Princeton Review* and John Wiley & Sons provide instructors with carefully edited materials and techniques that will help them most effectively test students who use the Westen text and in turn achieve positive results with their own students. The *Instructor's Manual* has been written by The Princeton Review and Professor Paul Wellman of Texas A&M University, and reviewed by Professor Dean McKay at Fordham University, and contains cross-references to the text, the *Test Bank,* and *Study Guide* as well as links found in the *On-Line Guide* with tips for instructors on how to incorporate the Web material found on these sites into the classroom.

**Computerized Test Bank:** All of the paper *Princeton Review Test Bank* questions are incorporated into this easy-to-use software program that enables instructors to create, save, customize, and print exams.

**Instructor's Resource CD-ROM:** Created and developed by Professor Paul Wellman of Texas A&M University, this CD includes digital slide shows of 450 original lecture slides and 215 art slides that can be sequenced and customized by instructors to fit any lecture. It also includes the complete *Instructor's Manual* and entire *Test Bank,* and a *Science News* archive containing the most important and current articles on psychology research from 1997 to the present. These *Science News* research pieces will be updated bi-weekly on the new Web site.

**Transparencies:** Full-color traditional acetates of illustrations from the text will be provided in special cases for those who cannot use the slides on our CD.

**The Psychology Web Site for Instructors:** The new Web site includes a Listserve that instructors can join to receive updates every two weeks about new Web links, new technology and how to integrate it into the classroom, new search engine information, and continually updated information on new images available for lecture presentations. An exciting new Web feature will be *In the News,* a unique feature organized and updated bimonthly by Paul Wellman, which will contain news stories from *Science News* magazine and discussion questions that tie each article directly to related material in the Westen text. The site also contains useful tips on creatively using the *Instructor's Resource CD* and the digital slide presentations, and describes the changes made to the new edition of the text. Instructors will also have access to the Wiley Course Management Software through this site that will enable them to give on-line quizzes with automatic scoring, post messages and syllabi to students, and take class polls.

**For Students:**

**Art Notebook:** Packaged with every text, this notebook contains all of the art illustrations in *Psychology: Mind, Brain, and Culture* that students will see in lecture from the art slides and transparencies. Students can easily take notes in class on the illustrations contained in the slide shows on the *Instructor's Resource CD-ROM* without having to bring their text to class, and then use this notebook to study for exams.

**The Psychology Web Site for Students:** Packaged with every text will be a password that will be the students' key to the new Web site. Here students will have access to the latest research through *Science News* articles, updated biweekly and specifically tied into each of the chapters they study. Over 100 Web sites with descriptions researched and written by Paul Wellman will be included on the site, separated by text chapter, that will guide students through the most useful and accurate information available on the Web. Students can take practice quizzes here, written by Professor Runi Mukerji, that are scored and also can be sent directly to their instructors.

**Study Guide:** Written by Alastair Younger at the University of Ottawa, and edited and reviewed by *The Princeton Review* so it ties in well with the *Test Bank* and *Instructor's Manual,* the study guide offers students a great way to review the material in the text and test their knowledge. Each chapter in the text has a corresponding chapter in the study guide. Six tools help students master the material: chapter outlines, learning objectives, key terms, fill-in exercises, critical thinking exercises, and sample test questions with answers.

**On-Line Guide:** This paperback Web guide will be included with every copy of the text and covers the basics of student use of the Internet and how to most efficiently use search engines to find the exact information you're looking for. A special chapter covering *Mental Health Net* is included and also a complete section of URLs relating Web links to topics in each chapter of the Westen text.

**Videos:** There are a number of videotapes available to adopters of the Westen text that are new to this edition. Please contact your local Wiley representative for details of this exciting new program.

# Acknowledgments

This project began many years ago—in 1987—and several people have played important roles in getting it off the ground. The initial plan for the book was to co-write it with a very talented writer, Jean Stein, who helped draft the first draft of the first half of the first edition. (Hopefully my writing is a little more clear in the text.) Her involvement ended a year after the project began, and the writing and content are now very different because of the many rounds of revisions the book has undergone since then. Nevertheless, many flashes of sparkle, felicitous turns of phrase, and clear passages remain from her efforts, for which I am extremely grateful. Several other people also contributed in the early stages, notably Judy Block, Barbara Misle, Carol Holden, and Karen Schenkenfeldter. Like Jean, they helped lay the foundations, and their efforts, too, are greatly appreciated. Since then, I have gained from the work of multiple research assistants, including (but not limited to) Lauren Korfine, Patricia Harney, Colleen Coffey, and Michelle Levine. To all of them I am very grateful.

## REVIEWERS

Over the past ten years, this book has been shaped by the insightful comments of dozens of colleagues and would look nothing like it does now without their tireless efforts. In particular, I would like to thank Walt Lonner of Western Washington University, who advised me on cross-cultural coverage for many chapters and gave feedback on several, and Paul Watson of the University of Tennessee for his uncanny ability throughout the years to notice where my prose was getting sloppy, my thoughts confused, or my coverage idiosyncratic.

### General Reviewers, Second Edition

Eugene Aidman, University of Ballarat

Joanna Boehnert, University of Guelph

Douglas A. Bors, University of Toronto at Scarborough

James Butler, James Madison University

Simone Buzwell, Swinburne University of Technology

Hank Davis, University of Guelph

Richard Eglsaer, Sam Houston State University

Nellie Georgiou, Monash University

Linda Hort, Griffith University

Robert F. Mosher, Northern Arizona University

Andrew Neher, Cabrillo College

Dorothy C. Pointkowski, San Francisco State University

Laura Reichel, Metropolitan State College of Denver

Paul Roberts, Murdoch University

Hillary Rodman, Emory University

Alexander Rothman, University of Minnesota

David A. Schroder, University of Arkansas

Norm Simonson, Univeristy of Massachusetts

Paul Stager, York University Toronto, Canada

David Uttal, Northwestern University

Paul J. Watson, University of Tennessee at Chattanooga

Paul Waxer, York University

In this edition, a special team of reviewers with expertise related to specific chapters took time to provide especially thorough reviews and critiques of chapters in their area of expertise:

## Expert Reviewers, Second Edition

**Chapter 3:**

John D. Bonvillian, University of Virginia
Bruce Bridgeman, University of California, Santa Cruz
Hillary Rodman, Emory University

**Chapter 4:**

Hillary Rodman, Emory University
Richard Schiffman, Rutgers University
Billy Wooten, Brown University

**Chapter 5:**

Leonard Green, Washington University

**Chapter 6:**

Douglas Herrmann, Indiana State University
Alan Searlman, St. Lawrence University

**Chapter 7:**

John D. Bonvillian, University of Virginia

**Chapter 8:**

John D. Bonvillian, University of Virginia

**Chapter 9:**

William Domhoff, University of California, Santa Cruz
David M. Wulff, Wheaton College

**Chapter 11:**

Randy J. Larsen, The University of Michigan

**Chapter 12:**

David M. Wulff, Wheaton College

**Chapter 13:**

John D. Bonvillian, University of Virginia

**Chapter 14:**

Toon Cillessen, University of Connecticut

**Chapter 18:**

John B. Nezlek, College of William and Mary

In addition, prior to publication of this edition and the last, a growing body of introductory psychology professors from around the world with a wide range of areas of expertise have provided detailed reviews of every chapter of the book. Their comments have shaped every aspect of it. Special thanks go to the following:

## GENERAL REVIEWS FOR PRIOR DRAFTS

Gordon Allen, Miami University
Harvard L. Armus, University of Toledo
Robert Batsell, Southern Methodist University
Carol M. Batt, Sacred Heart University
Col. Johnson Beach, United States Military Academy-West Point
John B. Best, Eastern Illinois University
John Bonvillian, University of Virginia

Robert Brown, Georgia State University
Mark Byrd, University of Canterbury (New Zealand)
Barbara K. Canaday, Southwestern College
George A. Cicala, University of Delaware
John M. Clark, Macomb Community College
Margaret Cleek, University of Wisconsin-Madison

James Dalziel, University of Sydney

Peter Ditto, Kent State University

Allen Dobbs, University of Alberta

Eugene B. Doughtie, University of Houston

J. Gregor Fetterman, Arizona State University

Nelson Freedman, Queens University

Herbert Friedman, The College of William and Mary

Mauricio Gaborit, S. J., St. Louis University

Adrienne Ganz, New York University

Mark Garrison, Kentucky State University

Marian Gibney, Phoenix College

William E. Gibson, Northern Arizona University

Marvin Goldfried, State University of New York-Stony Brook

Mary Alice Gordon, Southern Methodist University

Charles R. Grah, Austin Peay State University

Mary Banks Gregerson, George Washington University

Timothy Jay, North Adams State College

James Johnson, Illinois State University

Lance K. Johnson, Pasadena City College

Lynne Kiorpes, New York University

Stephen B. Klein, Mississippi State University

Keith Kluender, University of Wisconsin-Madison

James M. Knight, Humboldt State University

James Kopp, University of Texas-Arlington

Emma Kraidman, Franciscan Children's Hospital, Boston

Philip Langer, University of Colorado-Boulder

Peter Leppmann, University of Guelph

Alice Locicero, Tufts University

Richard M. Martin, Gustavus Adolphus College

Donald McBurney, University of Pittsburgh

Eleanor Midkift, Eastern Illinois University

David Mitchell, Southern Methodist University

David I. Mostofsky, Boston University

John Mullennix, Wayne State University

John Nezlek, The College of William and Mary

J. Faye Pritchard, La Salle University

Freda Rebelsky, Boston University

Bradley C. Redburn, Johnson County Community College

Daniel Roenkert, Western Kentucky University

Lawrence Rosenblum, University of California-Riverside

Kenneth W. Rusiniak, Eastern Michigan University

Ina Samuels, University of Massachusetts-Boston

Karl E. Scheibe, Wesleyan University

Richard Schiffman, Rutgers University

Robert Sekuler, Brandeis University

Norman Simonson, University of Massachusetts-Amherst

Steven Sloman, Brown University

J. Diedrick Snoek, Smith College

Sheldon Solomon, Skidmore College

Perry Timmermans, San Diego City College

D. Rene Verry, Millikin University

Paul Watson, University of Tennessee-Chatanooga

Russell H. Weigel, Amherst College

Joel Weinberger, Adelphi University

Cheryl Weinstein, Harvard Medical School

Paul Wellman, Texas A & M University

Macon Williams, Illinois State University

Jeremy M. Wolfe, Massachusetts Institute of Technology

Todd Zakrajsek, Albion College

Thomas Zentall, University of Kentucky

## STUDENT FOCUS GROUPS

We also benefitted considerably from student response in focus groups. Many thanks to the faculty members and graduate students who coordinated them, as well as to the students who provided their feedback.

- **Canisius College**   *Coordinator:* Harvey Pines
- **Johnson County Community College**   *Coordinator:* Tody Klinger
- **Ohio State University**   *Faculty Coordinator:* Alexis Collier
- **Southern Illinois University-Carbondale**   *Coordinator:* Gordon Pitz
- **University of Minnesota-Minneapolis**   *Coordinator:* Gail Peterson
- **University of New Mexico-Albuquerque**   *Coordinator:* Robert J. Sutherland
- **University of Oklahoma-Norman**   *Coordinator:* Richard Reardon
- **University of Tennessee-Knoxville**   *Coordinator:* William H. Calhoun

Finally, I'd like to offer my deep appreciation to the extraordinary team at Wiley. Foremost, Chris Rogers has shepherded this project for several years and helped elaborate its vision. He has been a wonderful friend and editor, a rare combination of scholar, businessman, and empathic soul who understands the torment of textbook authorship (when he isn't, by virtue of his role, contributing to it). In this edition, Rachel Nelson assumed much of the editorial responsibility for the project and did a superb job. In this edition and the last, Harriett Prentiss went through every word of every paragraph and probably taught me more about writing than anyone since my twelfth-grade English teacher. Anna Melhorn and Hilary Newman have done a superb job developing the art work and photography programs, respectively. They performed an impressive balancing act in giving me autonomy while sharing their expertise whenever my defective right hemisphere led me astray. My thanks also go to Art Ciccone, who helped render accurate technical illustrations in the first edition; the artists at J. A. K. Graphics, who did an extraordinary job of turning my sketches into illustrations that are both aesthetically appealing and edifying; Ann Marie Renzi, who supervised the design; Elizabeth Swain, who carefully oversaw production; Kristen Karyczak and Caroline Ryan, who helped pull the final project together; and Charity Robey, Senior Marketing Manager. More generally, I couldn't ask for a better publisher, from the extraordinary efforts of a gifted editorial and production staff, to the marketing and sales force who put this book in your hands, and to a CEO, Will Pesce, and a Chairman of the Board, Brad Wiley, II, who are committed to publishing textbooks that edify and excite rather than just sell.

# *About the Author*

*Drew Westen*

Drew Westen is Associate Professor of Psychology at the Harvard Medical School and Chief Psychologist at the Cambridge Hospital, in Cambridge, Massachusetts. He received his undergraduate degree from Harvard, an M.A. in Social and Political Thought from the University of Sussex (England), and a Ph.D. in Clinical Psychology from the University of Michigan, where he taught introductory psychology for several years. While at the University of Michigan, he was honored two years in a row by the *Michigan Daily* as the best teaching professor at the university, and was the recipient of the first Golden Apple Award for outstanding undergraduate teaching. His major areas of research are personality disorders, emotion regulation, implicit processes, and adolescent psychopathology. Much of his theoretical work has attempted to bridge cognitive, behavioral, psychodynamic, and evolutionary perspectives. His series of videotaped lectures on abnormal psychology, called *Is Anyone Really Normal?*, was published by the Teaching Company, in collaboration with the Smithsonian Institution. He also provides psychological commentaries on political issues for "All Things Considered" on National Public Radio. His main love outside of psychology is music. He writes comedy music and has performed as a stand-up comic in Boston.

# Contents in Brief

# Contents

Glenys Barton, "Three Faced Head 1990, Small Madonna 1990." Courtesy Angela Flowers Gallery, London.

# CHAPTER 1

# Psychology: The Study of Mental Processes and Behavior

A 15-year-old girl we will call Susan was hospitalized in a psychiatric unit because of severe adjustment problems. The most notable characteristic of her case was a dramatic change in her IQ score, which had dropped 50 points in less than five years, from 120 to 70. IQ is a measure of intelligence, and 120 is quite high, whereas 70 is on the border of mental retardation. As IQ scores in adolescence and adulthood typically remain fairly stable, a change of even 10 or 15 points in such a short time span is remarkable.

Susan had a poorly controlled case of epilepsy, a disorder characterized by abnormal patterns of electrical activity in the brain. In epilepsy, nerve cells in the brain discharge, or "fire," without appropriate stimulation. This leads to alterations in consciousness and behavior called *seizures*, characterized by brief periods of psychological "absence" from reality or violent muscle movements. Epilepsy can usually be controlled with medication (Smith & Darlington, 1996), but Susan was one of the unfortunate minority for whom nothing seemed to work.

Susan was peculiar in a number of ways. She was extremely egocentric, focusing only on her own perspective and interrupting conversations with her own concerns. She had difficulty sticking to the subject and would often blurt out inappropriate thoughts. When asked questions, she would often delay for up to a minute before answering. Finally, she was overly preoccupied with religion, a phenomenon observed in a small percentage of people with epilepsy (Daiguji, 1990; Tucker et al., 1987).

According to Susan, her only problem was that her mother no longer lived with her; Susan's mother had abandoned the family five years earlier, and Susan had never recovered emotionally. As soon as her mother returned, she insisted, she would be fine again. However, the medical team treating Susan—I was part of that team—had a different prognosis. We suspected Susan had a degenerative brain disease—a deteriorating brain—that was responsible for both the epilepsy and her plummeting IQ score.

Several months after her release from the hospital, something strange happened: Susan's IQ rose almost 30 points, her social and academic difficulties diminished somewhat, and her seizures decreased in frequency. She would never return to normal, but the change was extraordinary. When I heard of this dramatic improvement, I presumed that her doctors had probably hit upon a new medication, but like many psychological hypotheses, this one turned out to be wrong. In fact, what had prompted Susan's dramatic improvement was just what she had predicted: Her mother had returned.

Susan's case is unusual because rarely does an environmental change lead to such a remarkable improvement in brain functioning. Yet it illustrates a central issue that has vexed philosophers for over two millennia and psychologists for over a century—namely, the relation between mental and physical events, between meaning and mechanism.

Humans are complex creatures whose psychological experience lies at the intersection of biology and culture. To paraphrase one theorist, Erik Erikson (1963), psychologists must practice "triple bookkeeping" to understand an individual at any given time, simultaneously tracking biological events, psychological experience, and the cultural and historical context. Susan had **lesions,** or damaged areas, throughout her brain, but she also had emotional "lesions"—a broken heart as well as a broken brain. Together these misfortunes created a syndrome that probably neither alone would have produced. Yet even this interaction of mind and brain does not fully account for Susan's syndrome, for in most cultures throughout human history, people have lived in small communities with their extended families, and mothers have not had the option of moving far away from their children. Had she lived in another place or another time, Susan may not have experienced either a rapid decline or a remarkable recovery.

At this intersection of biology and culture lies **psychology,** *the scientific investigation of mental processes and behavior*. All psychological processes occur through the interaction of cells in the nervous system, and all human action occurs in the context of cultural beliefs and values that render it meaningful. Psychological understanding thus requires a constant movement between the micro-level of biology and the macro-level of culture. But psychology is not simply about cells or societies. It is simultaneously about mind, brain, and culture.

This chapter begins by exploring the biological and cultural boundaries and borders that frame human psychology. We then examine the theoretical perspectives that have focused, and often divided, the attention of the scientific community for a century.

INTERIM SUMMARY    **Psychology** is the scientific investigation of mental processes and behavior. Understanding a person requires attention to the individual's biology, psychological experience, and cultural context.

## THE BOUNDARIES AND BORDERS OF PSYCHOLOGY

Biology and culture establish both the possibilities and the constraints within which people think, feel, and act. On the one hand, the structure of the brain sets the parameters, or limits, of human potential. Most ten-year-olds cannot solve algebra problems because the neural circuitry essential for abstract thought has not yet matured. Similarly, the capacity for love has its roots in the innate tendency of infants to develop an emotional attachment to their caretakers. These are biological givens.

On the other hand, most adults throughout human history would find algebra problems as mystifying as would a preschooler because their culture never provided the groundwork for this kind of reasoning. And though love may be a basic potential, the way people love depends on the values, beliefs, and practices of their society. In some cultures, people seek and expect romance in their marriages, whereas in others, they do not select a spouse based on affection or attraction at all.

## FROM MIND TO BRAIN

### THE BOUNDARY WITH BIOLOGY

The biological boundary of psychology is the province of **biopsychology** (or **behavioral neuroscience**), which investigates the physical basis of psychological phenomena such as memory, emotion, or stress. Instead of studying thoughts, feelings, or fears, behavioral neuroscientists (some of whom are physicians or biologists rather than psychologists) investigate the electrical and chemical processes in the nervous system that underlie these mental events. Their aim is to link mind and body, psyche and brain.

The connection between mind and brain became increasingly clear during the nineteenth century, when doctors began observing patients with severe head injuries. Language and memory were often greatly curtailed in these patients, who might also show dramatic alterations in their personalities. A socially appropriate, genteel businessman and devoted father could suddenly become lewd and cantankerous and lack affection for loved ones following a severe blow to the head. These observations led researchers to experiment by *producing* lesions surgically in animals in different neural regions to observe the effects on behavior. This method is still used today, as in research on emotion, which has begun to identify the neural pathways involved in fear reactions (LeDoux, 1995). In this research, psychologists lesion one brain structure at a time along pathways hypothesized to be involved when rats learn to fear an object associated with pain. When a lesion disrupts learning, the researcher knows that the lesioned area, or other areas connected to it, is involved in fear.

Since its origins in the nineteenth century, one of the major issues in behavioral neuroscience has been **localization of function,** or the extent to which different parts of the brain control different aspects of functioning. In 1836, a physician named Marc Dax presented a paper in which he noted that lesions on the left side of the brain were associated with *aphasia,* or language disorders. The notion that language was localized to the left side of the brain (the left hemisphere) developed momentum with new discoveries linking

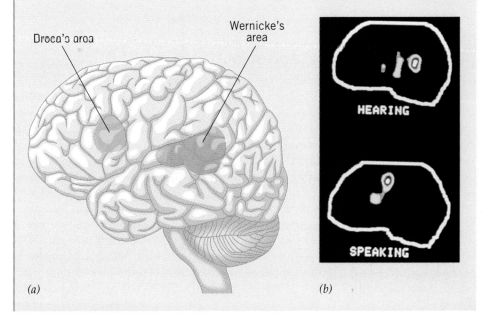

**FIGURE 1.1**
Broca's and Wernicke's areas. (*a*) Discovery of different effects of lesions to Broca's and Wernicke's areas led to increased sophistication about localization of function. Broca's aphasia involves difficulty producing speech, whereas Wernicke's aphasia typically involves difficulty comprehending language. (*b*) A positron emission tomography (PET) scan is a computerized imaging technique that allows researchers to study the functioning of the brain as the person responds to stimuli. The PET scans here show activity in Wernicke's and Broca's areas.

specific language functions to specific regions of the left hemisphere. Paul Broca (1824–1880) discovered that brain-injured people with lesions in the front section of the left hemisphere were often unable to speak fluently but could comprehend language. Carl Wernicke (1848–1904) showed that damage to an area a few centimeters behind the section Broca had discovered could lead to another kind of aphasia, in which the person can neither understand language nor speak comprehensibly (Figure 1.1). Individuals with this form of aphasia may speak fluently, apparently following rules of grammar, but the words they utter make little sense ("I saw the bats and cuticles as the dog lifted the hoof, the pauser").

One of the metaphors that underlies neuropsychological thinking compares the brain to an electronic machine with a complex series of circuits. Particular experiences or behaviors reflect patterns or sequences in the activation of cells that are "wired" together. To offer an analogy, no single point on a television screen means anything on its own because each pixel or dot can be used in millions of different configurations. The *pattern* in which that dot is activated gives it meaning, just as the pattern of firing cells determines the meaning of a neural event.

Contemporary neuroscientists no longer believe that complex psychological functions "happen" exclusively in a single localized part of the brain. Rather, the circuits for psychological events, such as emotions or thoughts, are distributed throughout the brain, with each part contributing to the total experience. A man who sustains lesions to one area may be unable consciously to distinguish his wife's face from the face of any other woman—a disabling condition indeed—but may react physiologically to her face with a higher heart rate or pulse (Bruyer, 1991; Young, 1994). Technological advances over the last two decades have allowed researchers to pinpoint lesions precisely, and even to watch computerized portraits of the brain light up with activity (or fail to light up, in cases of neural damage) as people perform psychological tasks (Alivisatos & Petrides, 1997; Nadeau & Crosson, 1995).

## A GLOBAL VISTA

### THE BOUNDARY WITH CULTURE

Humans are not only collections of cells; they are also themselves the "cells" of larger groups, such as tribes or nations, which similarly impose their stamp on psychological functioning. The emergence of agriculture and cities, generally known as *civilization*, occurred less than ten thousand years ago. Before that time, and until well into the twentieth century in much of this planet's southern hemisphere, humans lived in small bands composed largely of their kin. Several bands often joined together into larger tribes in order to trade mates, protect territory, wage war on other groups, or participate in communal rituals.

The anthropologists who first studied these "exotic" cultures in Africa, Australia, North America, and elsewhere were struck by their differentness from their own cultures. Their observations raised a central issue that psychology has been slow to address: To what extent do cultural differences create psychological differences? What can we make of someone who becomes terrified because he believes that a quarrel with kin has offended the forest and may bring disaster upon his family? Does he share our psychological nature, or does each society produce its own psychology?

The first theorists to address this issue were psychologically sophisticated anthropologists like Margaret Mead and Ruth Benedict, who were interested in the relation between culture and personality (LeVine, 1982). Impressed with the wide variation of cultural beliefs and practices across the globe, they argued that individual psychology is fundamentally shaped by cultural values, ideals, and ways of thinking. As Benedict put it, "The life history of the individual is first and foremost an accommodation to the patterns and standards traditionally handed down in the community" (1934, p. 2). As children develop, they learn to behave in ways that conform to cultural standards. The openly competitive, confident, self-interested style generally rewarded in North American society would be unthinkable in Japan, where communal sentiments are much stronger. Japanese manufacturing companies do not lay off workers during economic downturns as do their North American and European counterparts because they believe corporations are like families and should treat their employees accordingly. Even ways of thinking—using witchcraft to explain disease or manipulating things that do not exist in reality, such as negative numbers—are shaped through interactions with others and become woven into the individual's own psychological fabric (Vygotsky, 1978; Wertsch & Kanner, 1992).

In the middle of the twentieth century, **psychological anthropologists,** who study psychological phenomena in other cultures by observing people in their natural settings (see Bock, 1988; Mathews & Moore, 1998; Suarez-Orozco et al., 1994), turned their interest to the way economic realities shape childrearing practices, which in turn mold personality (Kardiner, 1945; Whiting & Child, 1953). Then, as now, people in much of the Third World were leaving their ancestral homelands seeking work in large cities. Working as a laborer in a factory requires different attitudes toward time, mobility, and individuality than farming or foraging. A laborer must be able and willing to punch a time clock, move where the work is, work for wages, and spend all day away from kin (see Inkeles & Smith, 1974). Notions we take

*Margaret Mead was a leading figure among anthropologists and psychologists trying to understand the relation between personality and culture. Here she is pictured among the Manus of Micronesia in the late 1920s.*

*Working in a factory requires attitudes, behaviors, and personality traits such as punctuality that require years, if not generations, to form.*

for granted—such as arriving to work within a prescribed span of minutes—are not "natural" to human beings. Punctuality is necessary for shiftwork in a factory or for changing from class to class in a modern school, and we consider it an aspect of character or personality. Yet punctuality was probably not even recognized as a dimension of personality in most cultures before the contemporary era and was certainly not a prime concern of parents in rearing their children.

After the 1950s, interest in the relation between culture and psychological attributes waned for decades. Within psychology, however, a small group of researchers developed the field of **cross-cultural psychology,** which attempts to test psychological hypotheses in different cultures (Berry et al., 1992, 1997; Lonner & Malpass, 1994; Triandis, 1980, 1994). Interest in cross-cultural psychology has blossomed recently as issues of diversity have come to the fore in the political arena. Psychologists have now been reflecting more carefully on the extent to which decades of research on topics such as memory, motivation, psychological disorders, or obedience have yielded results about *people* or about a particular *group* of people. Do individuals in all cultures experience depression? Do toddlers learn to walk and talk at the same rate cross-culturally? Do people dream in all cultures, and if so, what is the function of dreaming? Only cross-cultural comparisons can distinguish between universal and culturally specific psychological processes.

**INTERIM SUMMARY** **Biopsychology** (or **behavioral neuroscience**) examines the physical basis of psychological phenomena such as motivation, emotion, and stress. Although different neural regions perform different functions, the neural circuits that underlie psychological events are distributed throughout the brain and cannot be "found" in one location. At one other boundary of psychology, cross-cultural investigation is essential to try to distinguish psychological processes that are universal from those that are more specific to particular cultures.

## FROM PHILOSOPHY TO PSYCHOLOGY

Questions about human nature, such as whether psychological attributes are the same everywhere, were once the province of philosophy. Early in this century, however, philosophers entered a period of intense self-doubt, wrestling with the limitations of what they could know about topics like morality, justice, and the nature of knowledge. At the same time, psychologists began to apply the methods and technologies of natural science to psychological questions. They reasoned that if physicists can discover the atom and industrialists can mass-produce automobiles, then psychological scientists can uncover basic laws of human and animal behavior.

## Philosophical Roots of Psychological Questions

The fact that psychology was born from the womb of philosophy is of no small consequence. Many of the issues at the heart of contemporary psychological research and controversy are classic philosophical questions. One of these is whether human action is the product of **free will** or **determinism**—that is, whether we freely choose our actions or whether our behavior is really caused, or determined, by things outside our control. Those who champion free will follow in the footsteps of seventeenth-century French philosopher Rene Descartes (1596–1650), who contended that human action follows from human intention—that people choose a course of action and act on it. In contrast, proponents of determinism, from the Greek philosopher Democritus onward, assert that behavior follows lawful patterns like everything else in the universe, from falling rocks to planets revolving around the sun. Psychological determinists believe that the actions of humans and other animals are determined by physical forces, internally by genetic processes and externally by environmental events.

This issue has no easy solution. Subjectively, we have the experience of free will. I could choose to stop writing—or you to stop reading—at this very moment. Yet here we are, continuing into the next sentence. Why? What determined our choice to forge ahead? And how can mental processes exercise control over physical processes such as moving a pen or turning a page? Humans are material beings, part of nature, like birds, plants, and water. When we choose to move, our limbs exert a force that counters gravity and disturbs molecules of air. How can a nonmaterial force—will—displace material forces? No one has ever proposed a satisfactory solution to the **mind–body problem,** the question of how mental and physical events interact. However, psychological phenomena such as the decline and subsequent rise of Susan's IQ put the mind–body problem in a new light by drawing specific attention to the way psychological meaning (despair at her mother's absence) can become transformed into mechanism (physiological events such as seizure activity).

Psychologists do not tackle philosophical issues such as free will directly, but these classic philosophical questions reverberate through many contemporary psychological discussions. Research into the genetics of personality and personality disturbances provides an intriguing, if disquieting, example. People with antisocial personality disorder have minimal conscience and a tendency toward aggressive or criminal behavior. In an initial psychiatric evaluation one man boasted about the way he had terrorized his former girlfriend for an hour by brandishing a knife and telling her in exquisite detail the ways he intended to slice her flesh. This man could undoubtedly have exercised his free will to continue or discontinue his behavior at any moment and hence was morally (and legally) responsible for his acts. He knew what he was doing, he was not hearing voices commanding him to behave aggressively, and he thoroughly enjoyed his victim's terror. A determinist, however, could offer an equally compelling case. Like many violent men, he was the son of violent alcoholic parents, who had beaten him severely as a child. Both physical abuse in childhood and parental alcoholism (which can exert both genetic and environmental influences) render an individual more likely to develop antisocial personality disorder (see Cadoret et al., 1995;

*People who deliberately inflict injury on others for political purposes that seem bizarre but were fully aware of what they were doing press the limits of what we mean by free will or personal responsibility. The Unabomber, who embarked on a 20-year killing spree to protest modern technology, was surely emotionally unstable, although his disorder did not meet the legal criteria for insanity.*

**TABLE 1.1 PHILOSOPHICAL ISSUES AND PSYCHOLOGICAL QUESTIONS**

| PHILOSOPHICAL ISSUE | EXAMPLES OF CONTEMPORARY PSYCHOLOGICAL QUESTIONS |
|---|---|
| *Free will versus determinism:* Do people make free choices or are their actions determined by forces outside their control? | What causes patients with antisocial personality disorder to produce criminal behavior? |
| *Nature versus nurture:* To what extent do psychological processes reflect biological or environmental influence? | To what extent is intelligence inherited, and how do genes and environment interact to influence intellectual functioning? |
| *Rationalism versus empiricism:* To what extent does knowledge about the world come from observation and experience or from logic and reasoning? | How do children come to understand that other people have thoughts and feelings? |
| *Reason versus emotion:* To what extent are people guided by their knowledge or by their feelings (and to what extent should they be)? | Should people choose their mates based on "gut" feelings, or should they carefully weigh a potential partner's costs and benefits if they want to have a happy, long-lasting marriage? |
| *Continuity versus discontinuity with other animals:* To what extent are humans similar to other animals (that is, to what extent is human psychology continuous with the psychology of other animals)? | To what degree can studying fear responses in rats inform psychologists about the nature of human emotions? |
| *Individualism versus relationality:* To what extent are humans fundamentally self-interested or oriented toward relating to and helping other people? | Do people ever really help others without any benefit to themselves or are they motivated by other considerations, such as desires to feel good about themselves or avoid guilt? |
| *Conscious versus unconscious:* To what extent are people conscious of the contents of their minds and the causes of their behavior? | Can people describe themselves accurately, or are they unaware of many aspects of their personality? |

Zanarini et al., 1990). In the immediate moment, perhaps, he had free will, but over the long run, he may have had no choice but to be the person he was.

Other philosophical questions set the stage for psychology and remain central to contemporary psychological theory and research. Many of these questions, like free will versus determinism, take the apparent form of choices between polar opposites, neither of which can be entirely true. Does human behavior reflect nature (biology) or nurture (environmental influence)? Does knowledge come from observing the world or from thinking about it? Several of these fundamental questions are summarized in Table 1.1.

## From Philosophical Speculation to Scientific Investigation

Philosophical arguments have thus set the agenda for many of the issues confronting psychologists, and in our lifetimes, psychological research may shed light on questions that have seemed unanswerable for 2500 years. The fact that psychology was born from the womb of philosophy, however, has had another monumental influence on the discipline. Philosophers searched for answers to questions about the nature of thought, feeling, and behavior in their minds, using

*Wilhelm Wundt is often called the "father of psychology" for his pioneering laboratory research. This portrait was painted in Leipzig, where he founded the first psychological laboratory.*

logic and argumentation. By the late nineteenth century an alternative viewpoint emerged: If we want to understand the mind and behavior, we should investigate it scientifically, just as physicists study the nature of light or gravity through systematic observation and experimentation. Thus, in 1879, Wilhelm Wundt (1832–1920), often described as the "father of psychology," founded the first psychological laboratory in Leipzig, Germany.

Wundt hoped to use scientific methods to uncover the elementary units of human consciousness that combine to form more complex ideas, much as atoms combine into molecules in chemistry. One of the major methods he and his students used was **introspection,** the process of looking inward and reporting on one's conscious experience. The kind of introspection Wundt had in mind, however, was nothing like the introspection of philosophers, who tended to speculate freely on their experiences and observations. Instead, Wundt trained observers to report verbally everything that went through their minds when presented with a stimulus or task. By varying the objects presented to his observers and recording their responses, he concluded that the basic elements of consciousness are sensations (such as colors) and feelings. These elements combine into more meaningful perceptions (such as of a face or a cat), which can be combined into still *more* complex ideas by focusing attention on them and mentally manipulating them.

Wundt never believed that experimentation was the only route to psychological knowledge. Experimentation is essential for studying the basic elements of mind, he argued, but other methods—such as the study of myths, religion, and language in various cultures—are essential for understanding higher mental processes. The next generation of experimental psychologists, however, took a different view, motivated by their wish to divorce themselves from philosophical speculation and to establish a fully scientific psychology. Wundt's student, Edward Titchener (1867–1927), advocated the use of introspection in experiments in hopes of devising a periodic table of the elements of human consciousness, much like the periodic table discovered by chemists. Because of his interest in studying the structure of consciousness, the school of thought he initiated was known as **structuralism.** Unlike Wundt, Titchener believed that experimentation was the only appropriate method for a science of psychology and that concepts such as "attention" implied too much free will to be scientifically useful. As we will see, the generation of experimental psychologists who followed Titchener went even further, viewing the study of consciousness itself as unscientific because the data—sensations and feelings—could not be observed by anyone except the person reporting them.

Structuralism was one of two competing schools of thought that dominated psychology in its earliest years. The other was functionalism. Instead of focusing on the *contents* of the mind, **functionalism** emphasized the role—or *function*—of psychological processes in helping individuals adapt to their environment. A functionalist would not be content to state that the idea of running tends to come into consciousness in the presence of a bear showing its teeth. From a functionalist perspective, it is no accident that this particular idea enters consciousness when a person sees a bear but not when he sees a flower.

One of the leaders of functionalism, Harvard psychologist William James (1842–1910), penned the first textbook in psychology in 1890. (If you think *this* one is long, try reading James's 1400-page, two-volume set.) James was more comfortable with philosophical arguments than Titchener, and he believed that experimentation was only one path to psychological knowledge. Knowledge about human psychology, he argued, could come from many sources, including not only introspection but also the study of children, other animals (whose introspective reports may not be very useful), and people whose minds do *not* function adequately (such as the mentally ill). James viewed the structuralists' attempt to catalog the elements of consciousness as not only misguided but profoundly boring.

Consciousness exists because it serves a function, and the task of the psychologist is to understand that function. James was interested in explaining, not simply describing, the contents of the mind. As we will see, functionalism bore the clear imprint of the evolutionary theory of Charles Darwin, whose work has once again begun to play a central role in psychological theory a century later.

Structuralism and functionalism were two early "camps" in psychology that attracted passionate advocates and opponents. As we will see, they were not the last.

**INTERIM SUMMARY** Although many contemporary psychological questions derive from age-old philosophical questions, by the end of the nineteenth century psychology emerged as a discipline, which aimed to answer questions about human nature through scientific investigation. Among the earliest schools of thought were **structuralism** and **functionalism.** Structuralism attempted to use **introspection** to uncover the basic elements of consciousness and the way they combine. Functionalism attempted to explain psychological processes in terms of the role, or function, they serve.

## PERSPECTIVES IN PSYCHOLOGY

A tale is told of several blind men in India who came upon an elephant. They had no knowledge of what an elephant was, and eager to understand the beast, they reached out to explore it. One man grabbed its trunk and concluded, "An elephant is like a snake." Another touched its ear and proclaimed, "An elephant is like a leaf." A third, examining its leg, disagreed: "An elephant," he asserted, "is like the trunk of a tree."

Psychologists are in some ways like those blind men, struggling with imperfect instruments to try to understand the beast we call human nature and typically touching only part of the animal while trying to grasp the whole. Structuralism and functionalism provided the earliest perspectives in psychology. In this

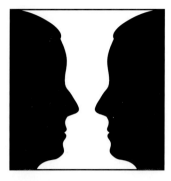

**FIGURE 1.2**
An ambiguous figure. The indentation in the middle could be either an indentation in a vase or a nose. In science, as in everyday perception, knowledge involves understanding "facts" in the context of a broader interpretive framework.

chapter and throughout the book, we examine four perspectives that guide current psychological thinking, offering sometimes competing and sometimes complementary points of view on phenomena ranging from antisocial personality disorder to the way people make decisions when choosing a mate.

These perspectives are similar in many respects to the intuitive perspectives people take in daily life. The importance of perspective can be illustrated by a simple perceptual phenomenon. Consider Figure 1.2. Does it depict a vase? The profiles of two faces? The answer depends on one's perspective on the whole picture.

This picture was used by a German school of psychology in the early twentieth century, known as **Gestalt psychology.** The Gestalt psychologists argued that perception is not a passive experience through which people take photographic snapshots of details of the world around them. Rather, they argued, perception is an active experience of imposing order on an overwhelming panorama of details by seeing them as parts of larger wholes (or *gestalts*).

On simple perceptual tasks, then, the way people understand specific details depends on their interpretation of the object as a whole. This is equally true of complex scientific observations, which always occur within the context of a broader view, a theoretical perspective. To take a clinical example (an example from the therapeutic practice of psychology), a patient with an irrational fear, or *phobia*, of elevators may be told by one psychologist that her problem stems from the way thoughts and feelings were connected in her mind as a child. A second psychologist informs her that her problem results from an unfortunate connection between something in her environment, an elevator, and her learned response— avoidance of elevators. A third—examining the same data, no less—concludes that she has faulty wiring in her brain that leads to irrational anxiety.

What can we make of this state of affairs, in which experts disagree on the meaning and implications of a simple symptom? And what confidence could anyone have in seeking psychological help? The alternative is even less attractive: A psychologist with no perspective at all would be totally baffled and could only recommend to this patient that she take the stairs. Perspectives are like imperfect lenses through which we view some aspect of reality. They are frequently too convex or too concave, and they often leave their wearers blind to data on the periphery of their understanding. Without them, however, we are totally blind.

## PARADIGMS AND PSYCHOLOGICAL PERSPECTIVES

Thomas Kuhn, a philosopher of science, studied the history of science to learn about the relationship between scientific "facts" and scientists' interpretations. Kuhn (1970) observed that science does not progress through the accumulation of facts, as many had believed. Rather, scientific progress depends on the development of better and better paradigms. A **paradigm** is a broad system of theoretical assumptions that a scientific community uses to make sense of a domain of experience. For example, the scientific community of physicists develops paradigms to make sense of the domain of the physical world; economists develop paradigms to explain market forces.

A paradigm has several key components. First, it includes a set of theoretical assertions that provide a **model,** or abstract picture, of the object of study. In economics, this model includes laws of supply and demand. Second, a paradigm includes a set of shared metaphors that compare the object under investigation to another that is readily apprehended (such as "the mind is like a computer"). Metaphors provide mental models for thinking about something that may be unfamiliar in a way that seems more familiar and understandable. Third, a paradigm includes a set of methods that members of the scientific community agree will, if properly executed, produce valid and useful data. Astronomers, for example, agree that telescopic investigation provides a window to events in space.

According to Kuhn, the social sciences and psychology differ from the older natural sciences (like physics and biology) in that they lack an accepted paradigm upon which most members of the scientific community agree. Instead, he proposes, these young sciences are still splintered into several schools of thought, or what we will call **perspectives.** The four psychological perspectives we examine offer the same kind of broad orienting approach as a scientific paradigm, and they share its three essential features. Focusing on these particular perspectives does not mean that other, less comprehensive approaches have not contributed to psychological knowledge or that nothing can be studied without them. A researcher interested in a specific question, such as whether preschool programs for economically disadvantaged children will improve their functioning later in life (Reynolds et al., 1995), does not need to endorse a broader outlook. But perspectives generally guide psychological investigations.

In the following sections we examine the **psychodynamic, behaviorist, cognitive,** and **evolutionary perspectives.** In many respects, these perspectives have evolved independently, and each places at its center phenomena that others tend to ignore.

**INTERIM SUMMARY**    A **paradigm** is a broad system of theoretical assumptions employed by a scientific community that includes shared models, metaphors, and methods. Psychology lacks a unified paradigm but has a number of schools of thought, or **perspectives,** that can be used to understand psychological events.

## THE PSYCHODYNAMIC PERSPECTIVE

A friend has been dating a man for five months and has even jokingly tossed around the idea of marriage. Suddenly, her boyfriend tells her he has found someone else. She is shocked and angry and cries uncontrollably but a day later asserts that "he didn't mean that much to me anyway." When you try to console her about the rejection she must be feeling, she says, "Rejection? Hey, I don't know why I put up with him as long as I did," and jokes that "bad character is a genetic abnormality carried on the Y chromosome" (more on that later). You know she really cared about him, and you conclude that she is being defensive—that she really feels rejected. You draw these conclusions because you have grown up in a culture influenced by the psychoanalytic theory of Sigmund Freud.

In the late nineteenth century, Sigmund Freud (1856–1939), a Viennese physician, developed a theory of mental life and behavior and an approach to treating psychological disorders known as **psychoanalysis.** Since then, many psychologists have maintained Freud's emphasis on **psychodynamics,** or the dynamic interplay of mental forces. Psychodynamic psychologists make several basic assumptions. First, people's actions are determined by the way thoughts, feelings, and wishes are connected in their minds. Second, many of these mental events occur outside of conscious awareness. And third, these mental processes may conflict with one another, leading to compromises among competing motives. Thus, people are unlikely to know precisely the chain of psychological events that leads to their conscious thoughts, intentions, feelings, or behaviors.

### Origins of the Psychodynamic Approach

Freud originated his theory in response to patients whose symptoms, although real, were not based on physiological malfunctioning. At the time, scientific think-

*Sigmund Freud poring over a manuscript in his home office in Vienna around 1930.*

ing had no way to explain patients who were preoccupied with irrational guilt after the death of a parent or were so paralyzed with fear that they could not leave their homes. Freud made a deceptively simple deduction, but one that changed the face of intellectual history: If the symptoms were not consciously created and maintained, and if they had no physical basis, only one possibility remained: Their basis must be unconscious.

Just as people have conscious motives or wishes, Freud argued, they also have powerful unconscious motives that underlie their conscious intentions. The reader has undoubtedly had the infuriating experience of waiting for half an hour as traffic crawls on the highway, only to find that nothing was blocking the road at all—just an accident in the opposite lane. Why do people slow down and gawk at accidents on the highway? Is it because they are concerned? Perhaps. But Freud would suggest that people derive an unconscious titillation or excitement, or at least satisfy a morbid curiosity, from viewing a gruesome scene, even though they may deny such socially unacceptable feelings.

## Metaphors of the Psychodynamic Approach

Freud likened the relation between conscious awareness and unconscious mental forces to the visible tip of an iceberg and the vast, submerged hulk that lies out of sight beneath the water. Before Freud's time, most people believed that their own and others' actions were directed by their conscious wishes and beliefs. In contrast, Freud argued that these conscious desires themselves may reflect *unconscious* conflicts and compromises.

One patient, for example, came to a psychotherapist because she was always choosing men who were unobtainable. She explained that she was only attracted to men who were exciting, charismatic, and ultra-successful. As she explored her dating history in therapy, a pattern emerged: If she could actually win these "special" men, she became disinterested. Exploring her childhood history revealed that her father was a flashy, charismatic, and highly successful businessman whose love and respect she felt she never could obtain. As an adult, she was attracted to men much like her father, but she was also afraid that they would reject her as her father had in many ways. As a result, she was caught in an impasse, looking for men like her father but rejecting them as soon as they showed interest. Recent research in fact supports the view that the relationship between children and their parents is crucial in shaping later social relationships, and that these patterns of relating may be transmitted from generation to generation through parent–child interactions beginning in infancy (Bretherton, 1990; Main, 1995; Main, Kaplan, & Cassidy, 1985; van IZjendoorn, 1995).

Another psychodynamic metaphor compares the mind to a battleground in which warring factions struggle for expression. Imagine a young man growing up in a culture such as our own, which views homosexuality with considerable hostility. The young man has sexual feelings only toward other males, but these feelings conflict with societal norms and with his conscience, which has been shaped by social and parental attitudes. The high suicide rate among homosexual teenagers attests to the intensity of the pain this conflict can produce (Hartstein, 1996).

One option for this man is to acknowledge his homosexual feelings and ultimately accept them, a path that increasing numbers of gay men and lesbian women are now choosing. Alternatively, he may resolve the conflict unconsciously. For instance, he might **repress** his wishes, that is, keep himself unaware of them to avoid emotional distress. Freud maintained, however, that things are rarely that simple. Unconscious motives may be out of sight, but they are not out of mind. They will continue to press for satisfaction, and the stronger their force, the more intense the efforts to deny them may be. Thus, the man might convince himself that he is not really homosexual and join a crusade against homosexuality. In doing so, he exerts considerable effort trying to eradicate the homosexuality outside of him, when his real aim is to stifle the homosexual feelings and impulses within. Interestingly, recent experimental research finds that homophobic men—men who report particularly negative attitudes toward homosexuality—show heightened sexual arousal when viewing photos of homosexual intercourse in comparison to their less homophobic peers (Adams et al., 1996).

## Methods and Data of the Psychodynamic Perspective

The methods used by psychodynamic psychologists flow from their aims. Psychodynamic understanding seeks to *interpret meanings*—to infer underlying wishes, fears, and patterns of thought from an individual's conscious, verbalized thought and behavior. Accordingly, a psychodynamic clinician observes a patient's dreams, fantasies, posture, and subtle behavior toward the therapist. The psychodynamic perspective thus relies substantially on the *case study* method, which entails in-depth observation of a small number of people (Chapter 2).

The data of psychoanalysis can be thoughts, feelings, and actions that occur anywhere, from a vice president jockeying for power in a corporate boardroom to a young child biting his brother for refusing to vacate a hobbyhorse. The use of any and all forms of information about a person reflects the psychodynamic assumption that people reveal themselves in everything they do (which is why psychoanalysts may not always be the most welcome guests at dinner parties).

Psychodynamic psychologists have typically relied primarily on clinical data to support their theories. Because clinical observations are open to many alternative interpretations, this has led to skepticism about psychodynamic ideas among many research psychologists. However, a growing number of researchers who are both committed to scientific method and interested in psychodynamic concepts have subjected these concepts to experimental tests (see Fisher & Greenberg, 1985, 1996; Shedler et al., 1993; Westen, 1990, in press). For example, several studies have now documented that people who avoid conscious awareness of their negative feelings are at increased risk for a range of health problems such as asthma, heart disease, and cancer (Weinberger, 1990). One recent study found that individuals who chronically remain unaware of unpleasant feelings tend to have high levels of a hormone that suppresses the body's capacity to fight disease (Brown et al., 1996).

INTERIM SUMMARY    The **psychodynamic perspective** proposes that people's actions reflect the way thoughts, feelings, and wishes are associated in their minds; that many of these processes are unconscious; and that mental processes can conflict with one another, leading to compromises among competing motives. Although psychodynamic psychologists are making increasing use of experimental methods, their primary method is the analysis of case studies, since their primary goal is to interpret complex meanings hypothesized to underlie people's actions.

## THE BEHAVIORIST PERSPECTIVE

You are enjoying an intimate dinner at a little Italian place on Main Street when your partner springs on you an unexpected piece of news: The relationship is over. Your stomach turns and you leave in tears. One evening a year or two later, your new flame suggests dining at that same restaurant. Just as before, your stomach turns and your appetite disappears.

The second broad perspective that developed in psychology early in this century, **behaviorism,** argues that the aversion to that quaint Italian cafe, like many

Unbeknownst to most students of psychology, Pavlov's first experiment was to ring a bell and cause his dog to attack Freud's cat.

*Animals of many species can learn to strike some "unnatural" poses.*

reactions, is the result of *learning*—in this case, instant, one-trial learning. Whereas the psychodynamic perspective emphasizes internal mental events, behaviorism focuses on the relation between objects or events in the environment **(stimuli)** and an organism's response to those events. Indeed, John Watson (1878–1958), a pioneer of American behaviorism, considered mental events outside the province of a scientific psychology altogether, and B. F. Skinner (1904–1990), who developed behaviorism into a full-fledged perspective years later, stated, "There is no place in a scientific analysis of behavior for a mind or self" (1990, p. 1209).

### Origins of the Behaviorist Approach

At the same time Freud was developing psychoanalytic theory, Ivan Pavlov (1849–1936), a Russian physiologist, was conducting experiments on the digestive system of dogs. During the course of his experiments, Pavlov made an important and quite accidental discovery: Once his dogs became accustomed to hearing a particular sound at mealtime, they began to salivate automatically whenever they heard it, just as they would salivate if food were presented. The process that had shaped this new response was learning. Behaviorists argue that human and animal behaviors—from salivation in Pavlov's laboratory to losing one's appetite upon hearing the name of a restaurant associated with rejection—are largely acquired by learning. Psychologists today have even begun to identify the biochemical changes in brain cells and the neural circuits involved as humans and other animals learn (Lavond, Kim, & Fitzgerald, 1993; Martinez & Derrick, 1996).

The behaviorist perspective, particularly as it developed in the United States, sought to do away with two ideas propounded by the philosopher Descartes. Descartes stressed the role of reason in human affairs; he believed that thought can generate knowledge that is not derived from experience. To be human is to reflect upon one's experience, and to reflect is to create new insights about oneself and the world. Descartes also proposed a dualism of mind and body, in which mental events and physical events can have different causes. The mind, or soul, is free to think and choose, while the body is constrained by the laws of nature.

Behaviorists asserted that the behavior of humans, like other animals, can be understood entirely without reference to internal states such as thoughts and feelings. And they attempted to counter **Cartesian dualism** (the doctrine of dual spheres of mind and body) by demonstrating that human conduct follows laws of behavior, just as the law of gravity explains why things fall down instead of up.

The task for behaviorists was to discover the ways in which environmental events, or stimuli, control behavior. John Locke (1632–1704), a seventeenth-century British philosopher, had contended that at birth the mind is a *tabula rasa*, or blank slate, upon which experience writes itself. In a similar vein, John Watson later claimed that if he were given 12 healthy infants at birth, he could turn them into whatever he wanted, doctors or thieves, regardless of any innate dispositions or talents, simply by controlling their environments (Watson, 1925).

### The Environment and Behavior

The dramatic progress of the natural sciences in the nineteenth century led many psychologists to believe that the time had come to wrest the study of human nature away from philosophers and put it into the hands of scientists. For behaviorists, psychology is the *science of behavior*, and the proper procedure for conducting psychological research should be the same as that for other sciences—rigorous application of the scientific method, particularly experimentation.

Scientists can directly observe a rat running a maze, a baby sucking on a plastic nipple to make a mobile turn, or even the rise of a rat's heart rate at the sound of a bell that has previously preceded a painful electric shock. But no one can directly observe unconscious motives. Science, behaviorists argued, entails making observations on a reliable and calibrated instrument that others can use to make precisely the same observations. If two observers can view the same data very differently, as often occurs with psychodynamic inferences, then prediction and hypothesis testing are impossible.

According to behaviorists, psychologists cannot even study *conscious* thoughts in a scientific way because no one has access to them except the person reporting them. Structuralists like Titchener had attempted to understand the way conscious sensations, feelings, and images fit together, using introspection as their primary method. Behaviorists like Watson questioned the scientific value of this research, since the observations on which it relied could not be independently verified. They proposed an alternative to psychodynamic and introspective methods: Study observable behaviors and environmental events and build a science around the way people and animals *behave*. Hence the term *behaviorism*. In recent years, some behaviorists have been more comfortable acknowledging the existence of mental events but do not believe such events play a *causal* role in human affairs; they tend to see mental processes as byproducts of environmental stimulation, not as independent causes of behavior.

Perhaps the most systematic behaviorist approach was developed by B. F. Skinner. Building on the work of earlier behaviorists, Skinner observed that the behavior of organisms can be controlled by environmental consequences that either increase *(reinforce)* or decrease *(punish)* their likelihood of occurring. Subtle alterations in these conditions, such as the timing of an aversive consequence, can have dramatic effects on behavior. Most dog owners can attest that swatting a dog with a rolled-up newspaper after it grabs a piece of steak from the dinner table can be very useful in suppressing the dog's unwanted behavior, but not if the punishment comes an hour later. Researchers from a behaviorist perspective have discovered that this kind of learning-by-consequences can be used to control some very unlikely behaviors in humans. For example, by presenting people with feedback on their biological or physiological processes *(biofeedback)*, psychologists can help them learn to control "behaviors" such as headaches, chronic pain, and blood pressure (Arena & Blanchard, 1996; Lisspers & Ost, 1990; Paran, Amir, & Yaniv, 1996).

*B. F. Skinner offered a comprehensive behaviorist analysis of topics ranging from animal behavior to language development in children. In* Walden Two, *he even proposed a utopian vision of a society based on behaviorist principles.*

## Metaphors, Methods, and Data of Behaviorism

A primary metaphor of behaviorism is that humans and other animals are like machines. Just as pushing a button starts the coffee maker brewing, presenting food triggered an automatic or reflexive response in Pavlov's dogs. Similarly, opening this book probably triggered the learned behavior of underlining and note taking. Some behaviorists also view the mind as a "black box" whose mechanisms can never be observed. A stimulus enters the box, and a response comes out; what happens inside is not the behaviorist's business. Other behaviorists are interested in what might occur in that box but are not convinced that current technologies render this information accessible to scientific investigation. They prefer to study what *can* be observed—the relation between what goes into it and what comes out.

The primary method of behaviorism is experimental. The experimental method entails framing a hypothesis, or prediction, about the way certain environmental events will affect behavior and then creating a laboratory situation to test that hypothesis. Consider two rats placed in simple mazes shaped like the letter T, as shown in Figure 1.3. The two mazes are identical in all respects but one: Pellets of food lie at the end of the left arm of the first rat's maze but not of the second. After a few trials (efforts at running through the maze), the rat that obtains the reward will be more likely to turn to the left and run the maze faster. The ex-

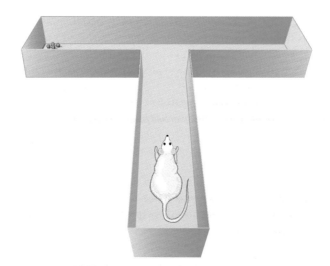

**FIGURE 1.3**
A standard T-maze from a behaviorist experiment. The experimenter controls the rat's behavior by giving or eliminating rewards in one arm or the other of the T.

perimenter can now systematically modify the situation, again observing the results over several trials. What happens if the rat is rewarded only every third time? Every fourth time? Will it run faster or slower? Because these data can be measured quantitatively, experimenters can test the accuracy of their predictions with great precision, and they can apply them to practical questions, such as how an employer can maximize the rate at which employees produce a product.

Behaviorism was the dominant perspective in psychology, particularly in North America, from the 1920s to the 1960s. In its purest forms it has lost some favor in the last two decades as psychology has once again become concerned with the study of mental processes. Many psychologists have come to believe that thoughts *about* the environment are just as important in controlling behavior as the environment itself (Bandura, 1977, 1991; Mischel, 1990; Mischel & Shoda, 1995; Rotter, 1966, 1990), and some contemporary behaviorists define behavior broadly to include thoughts as private behaviors. Nevertheless, traditional behaviorist theory continues to have widespread applications, from helping people quit smoking or drinking to enhancing children's learning in school.

**INTERIM SUMMARY**    The **behaviorist perspective** focuses on learning and studies the way environmental events control behavior. Behaviorists reject the concept of "mind" or view mental events as the contents of a black box that cannot be known or studied scientifically. Scientific knowledge comes from studying the relation between environmental events and behavior using experimental methods.

## THE COGNITIVE PERSPECTIVE

In the past 30 years psychology has undergone a "cognitive revolution." Today the study of **cognition,** or thought, dominates psychology in the same way that the study of behavior did in the middle of the twentieth century. Indeed, when chairpersons of psychology departments were asked to rank the ten most important contemporary psychologists, eight were cognitive psychologists (Korn, Davis, & Davis, 1991). One could argue that the history of psychology has seen a shift from the "philosophy of mind" of the Western philosophers, to the "science of the mind" in the work of the structuralists, to the "science of behavior" in the research of the behaviorists, to the "science of behavior and mental processes" in contemporary, cognitively informed psychology.

Cognitive psychology has roots in experiments conducted by Wundt and others in the late nineteenth century, which examined phenomena such as the influence of attention on perception and the ability to remember lists of words. Gestalt psychology, too, was arguably a cognitive psychology, in its focus on the way people organize sensory information into meaningful units. In large measure, though, the cognitive perspective owes its contemporary form to a technological development—the computer. Many cognitive psychologists use the metaphor of the computer to understand and model the way the mind works. From this perspective, thinking is **information processing:** The environment provides inputs, which are transformed, stored, and retrieved using various mental "programs," leading to specific response outputs. Just as the computer database of a book store may code its inventory according to topic, title, author, and so forth, human memory systems encode information in order to store and retrieve it. The coding systems we use affect how easily we can later access information. Thus, most people would find it hard to name the forty-second president of the United States (but easy to tell which recent president came from Arkansas) because they do not typically code presidents numerically.

To test hypotheses about memory, researchers need ways of measuring it. One way is simple: Ask a question like, "Do you remember seeing this object?" A second method is more indirect: See how quickly people can name an object they saw some time ago. Our memory system evolved to place frequently used and more recent information in the front of our memory "files" so that we can get to it faster. This makes sense, since dusty old information is less likely to tell us about our immediate environment. Thus, *response time* is a useful measure of memory.

For example, one investigator used both direct questions and response time to test memory for objects seen weeks or months before (Cave, 1997). In an initial session, she exposed undergraduate participants in the study to over 100 drawings presented rapidly on a computer screen and asked them to name them as quickly as they could. That was their only exposure to the pictures. In a second session, which occured weeks or months later, she mixed some of these drawings in with other drawings the students had not previously seen and asked them either to tell her whether they recognized them from the earlier session or to name them. When asked directly, participants were able to distinguish the old pictures from new ones with better-than-chance accuracy as many as 48 weeks later; that is, they correctly identified which drawings they had seen previously more than half the time. Perhaps more striking, as Figure 1.4 shows, they were also faster at naming the pictures they had seen previously than those they had not seen almost an entire year later! Thus, exposure to a visual image appears to keep it toward the front of our mental "files" for a very long time.

The cognitive perspective is useful not only in examining memory but also in understanding processes such as decision making. When people enter a car showroom, they have a set of attributes in their minds: smooth ride, sleek look, good gas mileage, affordable price, and so forth. At the same time, they must process a great deal of new information (the salesman's description of one car as a "real steal," for instance) and match it with stored linguistic knowledge. This allows them to comprehend the meaning of the dealer's speech, such as the connotation of "real steal" (from both his viewpoint and theirs). In making a decision, they must process the information they are receiving, taking into account both the importance of particular attributes and the quality of each car on those dimensions.

## Origins of the Cognitive Approach

The philosophical roots of the cognitive perspective lie in a series of questions about where knowledge comes from that were first raised by the ancient Greek philosophers and later pondered by British and European philosophers over the last four centuries (see Gardner, 1985). Descartes, like Plato, reflected on the remarkable truths of arithmetic and geometry and noted that the purest and most

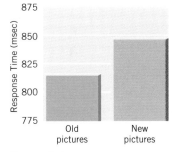

**FIGURE 1.4**
Response time in naming drawings 48 weeks after initial exposure. This graph shows the length of time participants took to name drawings they saw 48 weeks earlier ("old" drawings) versus similar drawings they were seeing for the first time. Response time was measured in milliseconds (thousandths of a second). As can be seen, at 48 weeks—nearly a year—participants were faster at naming previously seen pictures.

*People categorize an object that resembles a dog by comparing it to examples of dogs, generalized views of dogs, or characteristic features of dogs stored in memory.*

useful abstractions—such as a circle, a hypotenuse, pi, or a square root—could never be observed by the senses. Rather, this kind of knowledge appeared to be generated by the mind itself. Other philosophers, however, emphasized the role of experience in generating knowledge. Locke proposed that complex ideas emerge from the mental manipulation of simple ideas; these simple ideas are products of the senses, of observation.

The behaviorists roundly rejected Descartes's view of an active, reasoning mind with knowledge that can be independent of experience. Cognitive psychologists, in contrast, have shown more interest in questions raised by Descartes and other **rationalist** philosophers, who emphasized the role of reason in creating knowledge. For example, cognitive psychologists have studied the way people form abstract concepts or categories. These concepts are derived in part from experience, but they often differ from any particular instance the person has ever perceived, which means that they must be mentally constructed (Medin et al., 1997; Smith, 1995). Children can recognize that a bulldog is a dog even if they have never seen one before because they have an abstract concept of "dog" stored in memory that goes beyond the details of any specific dogs they have seen.

### Metaphors, Methods, and Data of Cognitive Psychology

Both the cognitive and behaviorist perspectives view organisms as machines that respond to environmental input with predictable output. Some cognitive theories even propose that a stimulus evokes a series of mini-responses inside the head, much like the responses the behaviorist studies outside the head (Anderson, 1983). But the metaphors used by cognitive psychologists differ from those of behaviorists. As noted earlier, some behaviorists view the mind as a black box whose contents are unobservable and therefore problematic for a scientific psychology; most actually object entirely to the concept of mind. The cognitive perspective, in contrast, has filled the box with software—mental programs that produce output. In fact, the cognitive perspective is often more interested in how mental programs operate than in either the particular stimulus or the end result.

Recently, cognitive psychologists have begun to use the brain itself as a metaphor for the mind (McClelland, 1995; Rumelhart, McClelland & PDP Research Group, 1986). According to this view, an idea can be conceived as a network of brain cells that are activated together. Thus, whenever a person thinks of the concept "bird," a set of nerve cells becomes active. When confronted with a stimulus that resembles a bird, part of the network is activated, and if enough of the network becomes active, the person concludes that the animal is a bird. From this point of view, a person is likely to recognize a robin as a bird quickly because it resembles most other birds and hence activates most of the "bird" network immediately. Correctly classifying a penguin takes longer because it is less typically "birdlike" and activates less of the network.

Like behaviorism, the primary method of the cognitive perspective is experimental, but with one important difference: Cognitive psychologists use experimental procedures to infer mental processes at work. For example, when people try to retrieve information from a list (such as the names of states), do they scan all the relevant information in memory until they hit the right item? One way psychologists have explored this question is by presenting subjects with a series of word lists of varying lengths to memorize, such as those in Figure 1.5. Then they ask the participants in the study if particular words were on the lists. If participants take longer to recognize that a word was *not* on a longer list—which they do—they must be scanning the lists sequentially (that is, item by item), because additional words on the list take additional time to scan (Sternberg, 1975).

Cognitive psychologists originally tended to study processes such as memory and decision making that had little to do with emotion or motivation. In more recent years, however, some have attempted to use cognitive concepts and metaphors to explain a much wider range of phenomena (Cantor & Kihlstrom, 1987; Sorrentino & Higgins, 1996). Cognitive research on emotion, for example, documents that the way people think about events plays a substantial role in generating emotions (Lazarus, 1993; Roseman et al., 1995). For example, people are more likely to become angry when they perceive a situation as negatively affecting their goals, perceive someone else as the cause, and have difficulty imagining a way out of it (Smith et al., 1993).

| LIST A | LIST B |
| --- | --- |
| Nevada | Texas |
| Arkansas | Colorado |
| Tennessee | Missouri |
| Texas | South Carolina |
| North Dakota | Alabama |
| Nebraska | California |
| Michigan | Washington |
| Rhode Island | Idaho |
| Massachusetts | |
| Idaho | |
| New York | |
| Pennsylvania | |

**FIGURE 1.5**
Two lists of words used in a study of memory scanning. Presenting participants in a study with two lists of state names provides a test of the memory-scanning hypothesis. Iowa is not on either list. If an experimenter asks whether Iowa was on the list, participants take longer to respond to list A than to list B because they have to scan more items in memory.

**INTERIM SUMMARY**   The **cognitive perspective** focuses on the way people process, store, and retrieve information. Cognitive pyschologists are interested in questions such as how memory works and how people solve problems and make decisions. The primary metaphor underlying the cognitive perspective is the mind as computer. In recent years, many cognitive psychologists have begun to turn to the brain itself as a source of metaphors. The primary method of the cognitive perspective is experimental.

## THE EVOLUTIONARY PERSPECTIVE

- The impulse to eat in humans has a biological basis.
- The sexual impulse in humans has a biological basis.
- Caring for one's offspring has a biological basis.
- The fact that most males are interested in sex with females, and vice versa, has a biological basis.
- The higher incidence of aggressive behavior in males than in females has a biological basis.
- The tendency to care more for one's own offspring than for the offspring of other people has a biological basis.

Most people fully agree with the first of these statements, but many have growing doubts as the list proceeds. The degree to which inborn processes determine human behavior is a classic issue in psychology, called the **nature–nurture controversy.** Advocates of the "nurture" position maintain that behavior is primarily learned and not biologically ordained. Other psychologists, however, point to the similarities in behavior between humans and other animals, from chimpanzees to birds, and argue that some behavioral similarities are so striking that they must reflect shared tendencies rooted in biology. Indeed, anyone who believes the sight of two male teenagers "duking it out" behind the local high

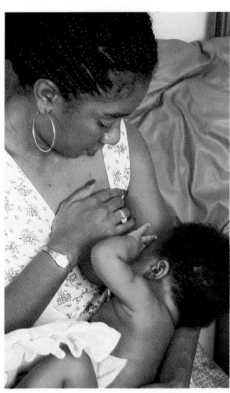

*The notion that birds instinctively care for their children (a) is widely accepted, but the corresponding claim that humans have innate mechanisms that elicit caretaking behavior (b) is more controversial.*

(a)                                                    (b)

school for the attention of a popular girl is distinctively human should observe the behavior of rams and baboons. As we will see, many, if not most, psychological processes reflect an *interaction* of nature and nurture, as in the case of Susan's epileptic seizures, which waxed and waned with her mother's presence. Human life is like a gray fabric, with strands of genetics (white) and environmental influence (black) so tightly interwoven that one can rarely discern the separate threads (Kagan & Snidman, 1991).

The evolutionary perspective argues that many behavioral proclivities, from the need to eat to concern for our children, became prevalent in human populations because they helped our ancestors survive and rear healthy offspring. Why, for example, was Susan, whose case opened this chapter, so devastated by her mother's absence? From an evolutionary perspective, a deep emotional bond between parents and children prevents them from straying too far from each other while children are immature and vulnerable. Breaking this bond leads to tremendous distress.

Like the functionalists at the turn of the century, evolutionary psychologists believe that most enduring human attributes at some time served a function for humans as biological organisms (Buss, 1991). They argue that this is as true for physical traits—such as the presence of two eyes (rather than one), which allows us to perceive depth and distance—as for cognitive or emotional tendencies such as the child's distress at the absence of her caregivers. The implication for psychological theory is that understanding human mental processes and behaviors requires insight into their evolution.

### Origins of the Evolutionary Perspective

The evolutionary perspective is rooted in the writings of Charles Darwin (1859). Darwin did not invent the concept of evolution, but he was the first to propose a mechanism that could account for it—**natural selection.** Darwin argued that nat-

*Similar behavior in humans and other animals may suggest common evolutionary roots.*

ural forces select traits in organisms that are **adaptive,** that is, that help them adjust to and survive in their environment. This occurs naturally because organisms endowed with fewer features that help them adapt to their particular environmental circumstances, or *niche,* are less likely to survive and reproduce; in turn, they have fewer offspring who survive and reproduce.

A classic example of natural selection occurred in Birmingham, Liverpool, Manchester, and other industrial cities in England (Bishop & Cook, 1975). A light-colored variety of peppered moth common in rural areas of Britain also populated most cities, but as England industrialized in the nineteenth century, light-colored moths became scarce in industrial regions and dark-colored moths predominated.

How did this happen? With industrialization, the air became sooty, darkening the bark of the trees on which these moths spent much of their time. Light-colored moths were thus easily noticed and eaten by predators. Prior to industrialization, moths that had darker coloration were selected *against* by nature because they were conspicuous against light-colored bark. Now, however, they were *better* able to blend into the background of the dark tree trunks (Figure 1.6). As a result, they

*Charles Darwin revolutionized human self-understanding in 1859 by rewriting the family tree.*

*(a)*                    *(b)*

**FIGURE 1.6**
The natural selection of moth color. As environmental conditions changed in industrial England, so, too, did the moth population. In (*a*), where two pepper moths rest on the dark bark of an oak tree in Manchester, the darker moth is better camouflaged. With industrialization, darker moths were better adapted to their environments. In contrast, (*b*) shows a light-colored oak bark typical of rural Wales, where the light moth is extremely difficult to see and hence better able to evade its predators.

survived to pass on their coloration to the next generation. Over decades, the moth population changed to reflect the differential selection of light and dark varieties. Since England has been cleaning up its air through more stringent pollution controls in the past 30 years, the trend has begun to reverse.

The peppered moth story highlights a crucial point about evolution: Because adaptation is always relative to a specific niche, evolution is not synonymous with progress. A trait or behavior that is highly adaptive can suddenly become maladaptive in the face of even a seemingly small change in the environment. A new insect that enters a geographical region can eliminate a flourishing crop, just as the arrival of a warlike tribe (or nation) into a previously peaceful region can render prior attitudes toward war and peace maladaptive. People have used Darwinian ideas to justify racial and class prejudices ("people on welfare must be naturally unfit"), but sophisticated evolutionary arguments contradict the view that adaptation or fitness can ever be absolute. Adaptation is always relative to a niche.

### Ethology, Sociobiology, and Evolutionary Psychology

If Darwin's theory of natural selection can be applied to characteristics such as the color of a moth, can it also apply to behaviors? It stands to reason that certain behaviors, such as the tendency of moths to rest on trees in the first place, evolved because they helped members of the species to survive. In the middle of the twentieth century the field of **ethology,** which studies animal behavior from a biological and evolutionary perspective (Hinde, 1982), began to apply this sort of evolutionary approach to understanding animal behavior. For example, several species of birds emit warning cries to alert their flock about approaching predators; some even band together to attack. Konrad Lorenz, an ethologist who befriended a flock of black jackdaws, was once attacked by the flock while carrying a wet black bathing suit. Convinced that the birds were not simply offended by the style, Lorenz hypothesized that jackdaws have an inborn, or *innate*, tendency to become distressed whenever they see a creature dangling a black object resembling a jackdaw, and they respond by attacking (Lorenz, 1979).

If animal behaviors can be explained by their adaptive advantage, can the same logic be applied to human behavior? Just over two decades ago, Harvard biologist E. O. Wilson (1975) christened a new, and controversial, field called **sociobiology,** which explores possible evolutionary and biological bases of human social behavior. Sociobiologists and **evolutionary psychologists,** who apply evolutionary thinking to a wide range of psychological phenomena, note that genetic transmission is not limited to physical traits such as height, body type, or vulnerability to heart disease. Parents also pass onto their children behavioral and mental tendencies. Some of these are universal, such as the need to eat and sleep or the capacity to perceive certain wavelengths of light to which the eye is attuned. Others differ across individuals. As we will see in later chapters, recent research in **behavioral genetics**—a field that examines the genetic and environmental bases of differences among individuals on psychological traits—suggests that heredity is a surprisingly strong determinant of many personality traits and intellectual skills. The tendencies to be outgoing, aggressive, or musically talented, for example, are all under partial genetic control (Loehlin, 1992; Loehlin et al., 1988; Plomin et al., 1997).

Perhaps the fundamental concept in all contemporary evolutionary theories is that evolution selects organisms that maximize their reproductive success. **Reproductive success** refers to the capacity to survive and produce offspring. Over many generations, organisms with greater reproductive success will have many more descendants because they will survive and reproduce more than other organisms, including other members of their own species. Central to evolutionary

▶ It is seldom that I laugh at an animal, and when I do, I usually find out afterwards that it was at myself, at the human being whom the animal has portrayed in a more or less pitiless caricature, that I have laughed. We stand before the monkey house and laugh, but we do not laugh at the sight of a caterpillar or a snail, and when the courtship antics of a lusty greylag gander are so incredibly funny, it is only [because] our human youth behaves in a very similar fashion.

(LORENZ, 1979, P. 39)

psychology is the notion that the human brain, like the eye or the heart, has evolved through natural selection to solve certain problems associated with survival and reproduction, such as selecting mates, using language, competing for scarce resources, and cooperating with kin and neighbors who might be helpful in the future (Tooby & Cosmides, 1992).

For example, we take for granted that people usually tend to care more about, and do more for, their children, parents, and siblings than for their second cousins or nonrelatives. Most readers have probably received more financial support from their parents in the last five years than from their aunts and uncles. This seems natural—and we rarely wonder about it—but *why* does it seem so natural? And what are the causes of this behavioral tendency? From an evolutionary perspective, individuals who care for others who share their genes will simply have more of their genes in the gene pool generations later. Thus, evolutionary theorists have expanded the concept of reproductive success to encompass **inclusive fitness,** which refers not only to an individual's own reproductive success but also to her influence on the reproductive success of genetically related individuals (Daly & Wilson, 1983; Hamilton, 1964).

According to the theory of inclusive fitness, natural selection should favor animals whose concern for kin is proportional to their degree of biological relatedness. In other words, animals should devote more resources, and offer more protection, to close relatives than to more distant kin. The reasons for this are strictly mathematical. Imagine you are sailing with your brother or sister and with your cousin, and the ship capsizes. Neither your sibling nor your cousin can swim, and you can save only one of them. Whom will you save?

Most readers, after perhaps a brief, gleeful flicker of sibling rivalry, will opt for the sibling—because first-degree relatives such as siblings share much more genetic material than more distant relatives such as cousins. Siblings share half of their genes, whereas cousins share only one-eighth. In crass evolutionary terms, two siblings are worth eight cousins. Evolution selects the neural mechanisms that make this preference feel natural—so natural that psychologists have rarely even thought to explain it.

At this point the reader might object that the real reason for saving the sibling over the cousin is that you know the sibling better; you grew up together, and you have more bonds of affection. This poses no problem for the evolutionary theorist, since familiarity and bonds of affection are probably the psychological mechanisms selected by nature to help you in your choice. When human genes were evolving, close relatives typically lived together. People who were familiar and loved were more often than not relatives. Humans who protected others based on familiarity and affection would be more prevalent in the gene pool thousands of years later because more of their genes would be available.

## Metaphors, Methods, and Data of the Evolutionary Perspective

Darwin's theory of natural selection is part of a tradition of Western thought since the Renaissance that emphasizes individual self-interest and competition for scarce resources. Its major metaphor is borrowed from another member of that tradition, the sixteenth-century philosopher Thomas Hobbes (1538–1679): Wittingly or unwittingly, we are all runners in a race, competing for survival, sexual access to partners, and resources for ourselves and our kin.

Evolutionary methods are frequently deductive; that is, they begin with an observation of something that already exists in nature and try to explain it with logical arguments. For instance, evolutionary psychologists might begin with the fact that people care for their kin and try to deduce an explanation. This method is very different from experimentation, in which investigators create circumstances in the laboratory and test the impact of changing these conditions on behavior.

Many psychologists have challenged the deductive methods of evolutionary psychologists, just as they have criticized psychodynamic explanations of individual cases. They argue that predicting behavior in the laboratory is much more difficult and convincing than explaining what has already happened.

Evolutionary psychologists are increasingly making use of experimental and other procedures that involve prediction of responses in the laboratory (Buss et al., 1992). For example, two recent studies, one from the United States and one from Germany, have used evolutionary theory to predict the extent to which grandparents will invest in their grandchildren (DeKay, 1998; Euler & Weitzel, 1996). According to evolutionary theory, one of the major problems facing males in many animal species, including our own, is paternity uncertainty—the lack of certainty that their presumed offspring are really theirs. Female primates (monkeys, apes, and humans) are always certain that their children are their own because they bear them. Males, on the other hand, can never be certain of paternity because their mate could have copulated with another male. (Psychological language is typically precise but not very romantic.)

If a male is going to invest time, energy, and resources in a child, he wants to be certain that the child is his own. Not surprisingly, males of many species develop elaborate ways to try to minimize the possibility of accidentally investing in another male's offspring, such as guarding their mates during fertile periods and killing off infants born too close to the time at which they began copulating with the infants' mother. In humans, infidelity (and suspicion of infidelity) is one of the major causes of spouse battering and homicide committed by men cross-culturally (Daly & Wilson, 1988).

Evolutionary psychologists have used the concept of paternity uncertainty to make some very specific, and novel, predictions about patterns of *grandparental* investment in children. As can be seen in Figure 1.7*a*, the father's father is the least certain of all grandparents that his grandchildren are really his own, since he did not bear his son, who did not bear *his* child. The mother's mother is the most certain of all grandparents because she is sure that her daughter is hers, and her daughter is equally certain that she is the mother of *her* children. The other two grandparents (father's mother and mother's father) are intermediate in certainty. This analysis leads to a hypothesis about the extent to which grandparents will invest in their grandchildren: The greatest investment should be seen in maternal grandmothers, the least in paternal grandfathers, and intermediate levels in paternal grandmothers and maternal grandfathers.

To test this hypothesis, in one study U.S. college students ranked their grandparents on a number of dimensions, most notably level of emotional closeness and amount of time and resources their grandparents invested in them (DeKay, 1998). On each of these dimensions, the pattern was as predicted: Maternal grandmothers, on the average, were ranked as the most invested of all four grandparents and paternal grandfathers as the least invested. Figure 1.7*b* shows the percent of college students who ranked each grandparent a 1—that is, most invested or most emotionally close. A similar pattern emerged in a German study (Euler & Weitzel, 1996). Although a critic could generate alternative explanations, these studies are powerful because the investigators tested hypotheses that were not intuitively obvious or readily predictable from other perspectives.

INTERIM SUMMARY    The **evolutionary perspective** argues that many human behavioral tendencies evolved because they helped our ancestors survive and reproduce. Psychological processes have evolved through the natural selection of traits that help organisms adapt to their environment. Evolution selects organisms that maximize their reproductive success, defined as the capacity to survive and reproduce as well as to maximize the reproductive success of genetically related individuals. Although the primary methods of evolutionary theorists have traditionally been deductive and comparative, evolutionary psychologists are making increasing use of experimental methods.

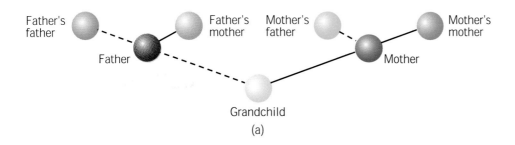

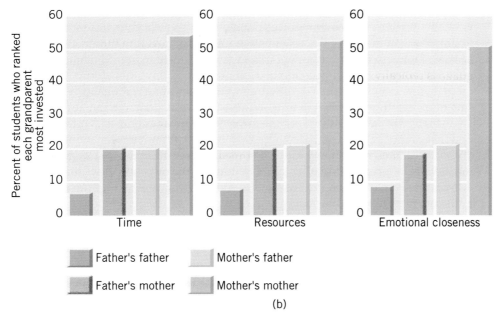

**FIGURE 1.7**

(*a*) Certainty of genetic relatedness. Dashed lines indicate uncertainty of genetic relatedness, whereas solid lines indicate certainty. As can be seen, the father's father is least certain that his presumed grandchild is his own (dashed lines between both himself and his son and his son and the son's child), whereas the mother's mother is most certain. Each of the other two grandparents are sure of one link but unsure of the other. (*b*) Rankings of grandparental investment. This graph shows the percent of participants in the study who ranked each grandparent the highest of all four grandparents on two kinds of investment and on emotional closeness to them. Students ranked their maternal grandmothers most invested and close and their paternal grandfathers least invested and close on all three dimensions. Similar findings emerged when participants were asked to rate each grandparent on the same dimensions using a 1–7 scale. (Based on DeKay, 1998.)

## PUTTING PSYCHOLOGICAL PERSPECTIVES IN PERSPECTIVE

We have seen that what psychologists study, how they study it, and what they observe reflect not only the reality "out there" but also the conceptual lenses they wear. In many cases adherents of one perspective know very little—and may even have stereotypic views or misconceptions—about other perspectives. The reader will no doubt be tempted at times to conclude that a particular perspective is the right one. This condition unfortunately afflicts most of us who make our careers donning a set of theoretical lenses and then forgetting that we are bespectacled. Before succumbing to this fate, be forewarned that the different perspectives often contribute in unique ways depending on the object under investigation. Deciding that one perspective is valid in all situations is like choosing to use a telescope in-

*Behavior that seems "natural" to us, like the bond between grandparent and grandchild, may well be the handiwork of natural selection.*

stead of a microscope without knowing whether the objects of study are amoebas or asteroids.

## Contributions of Each Perspective

Psychologists disagree on the relative merits of the different perspectives, but each has made distinctive contributions. Philosophers have long speculated about the relative value of "reason" and "passion" in human life; the psychodynamic perspective focuses above all on the passionate—on motivation and emotion. From a psychodynamic standpoint, people rarely associate anyone or anything of any importance with just one feeling, which means that we are likely to find ourselves at times in conflict, and recent research supports this view (Caccioppo et al., 1997). Perhaps the most important legacy of the psychodynamic perspective is its emphasis on the pervasive role of unconscious processes in human life. The existence of unconscious processes was once rejected by many psychologists but has now gained widespread acceptance as technologies have developed that allow the scientific exploration of cognitive, emotional, and motivational processes outside of conscious awareness (Bargh, in press; Schacter, 1992; Westen, in press).

Among the contributions of the behaviorist perspective to psychology are two that cannot be overestimated. The first is its focus on learning and its postulation of a *mechanism* for many kinds of learning: reward and punishment. Behaviorists have offered a fundamental insight about the psychology of humans and other animals that can be summarized in a simple but remarkably important formula: *Behavior follows its consequences.* The notion that the consequences of our actions shape the way we behave has a long philosophical history, but the behaviorists were the first to develop a sophisticated, scientifically based set of principles about the way environmental events shape behavior. This leads to the second major contribution of the behaviorist approach, its emphasis on **empiricism**—the belief that the path to scientific knowledge is systematic observation and, ideally, experimental observation.

The cognitive perspective focuses on the *reason* pole of the reason–passion dichotomy. Most of what is distinctive about *Homo sapiens*—and what lent our species its name (*sapiens* means "knowledge" or "wisdom")—is our extraordinary capacity for thought and memory. This capacity allows actors to perform a two-hour play without notes, three-year-old children to create grammatical sentences they have never heard before, and scientists to develop vaccines for viruses that cannot be seen with the naked eye. In only three decades since the introduction of the first textbook on cognition (Neisser, 1967), the cognitive perspective has transformed our understanding of thought and memory in a way that 2500 years of philosophical speculation could not approach. Like the behaviorist perspective, the contributions of the cognitive perspective reflect its commitment to empiricism and experimental methods.

Finally, the evolutionary perspective asks a basic question about psychological processes that directs our attention to phenomena we might easily have taken for granted: *Why* do we think, feel, or behave the way we do as opposed to some other? Although many psychological attributes are likely to have developed as accidental byproducts of evolution with little adaptive significance, the evolutionary perspective forces us to examine *why* we feel jealous when our lovers are unfaithful, *why* we are so skillful at recognizing the emotions people are feeling just by looking at their faces, and *why* children are able to learn new words so rapidly in their first six years that if they were to continue at that pace for the rest of their lives they would scoff at *Webster's Unabridged.* In each case, the evolutionary perspective suggests a single and deceptively simple principle: We think, feel, and behave these ways because doing so helped our ancestors adapt to their environments and hence to survive and reproduce.

## TABLE 1.2 MAJOR SUBDISCIPLINES IN PSYCHOLOGY

| SUBDISCIPLINE | EXAMPLES OF QUESTIONS ASKED |
| --- | --- |
| *Biopsychology:* investigates the physical basis of psychological phenomena such as thought, emotion, and stress | How are memories stored in the brain? Do hormones influence whether an individual is heterosexual or homosexual? |
| *Developmental psychology:* studies the way thought, feeling, and behavior develop through the lifespan, from infancy to death | Can children remember experiences from their first year of life? Do children in daycare tend to be more or less well adjusted than children reared at home? |
| *Social psychology:* examines interactions of individual psychology and group phenomena; examines the influence of real or imagined others on the way people behave | When and why do people behave aggressively? Can people behave in ways indicating racial prejudice without knowing it? |
| *Clinical psychology:* focuses on the nature and treatment of psychological processes that lead to emotional distress | What causes depression? What impact does childhood sexual abuse have on later functioning? |
| *Cognitive psychology:* examines the nature of thought, memory, and language | What causes amnesia, or memory loss? How are people able to drive a car while engrossed in thought about something else? |
| *Industrial/organizational (I/O) psychology:* examines the behavior of people in organizations and attempts to help solve organizational problems | Are some forms of leadership more effective than others? What motivates workers to do their jobs efficiently? |
| *Educational psychology:* examines psychological processes in learning and applies psychological knowledge in educational settings | Why do some children have trouble learning to read? What causes some teenagers to drop out of school? |
| *Experimental psychology:* examines processes such as learning, sensation, and perception in humans and other animals | How often should a rat, pigeon, or human be rewarded to produce optimal learning? Do braille readers have heightened abilities to perceive with their fingers than people who read with their eyes? |
| *Health psychology:* examines psychological factors involved in health and disease | Are certain personality types more vulnerable to disease? What factors influence people to take risks with their health, such as smoking or not using condoms? |

## Applying and Integrating the Perspectives

Psychology has a number of subfields (Table 1.2), and the perspectives psychologists take tend to differ among (and even within) these areas of investigation. For example, *developmental psychology* studies the way thought, feeling, and behavior develop through the lifespan, from infancy to death. Developmental psychologists researching the influence of television on children's aggressive behavior tend to take a cognitive or an integrated cognitive-behavioral approach, guided by the hypothesis that what children observe influences the way they behave (Hughes & Hasbrouck, 1996; Singer, 1986). Research on the close ties that form between infants and their parents, on the other hand, has drawn heavily on the work of John Bowlby (1969, 1988), who was both a psychoanalyst and an ethologist. *Social psychology* examines interactions of individual psychology and social

*How might a psychologist from each of the four perspectives explain why a soldier would go off for war, leaving behind loved ones and risking his life for his country?*

phenomena. Social psychologists study phenomena such as prejudice, mob violence, peer pressure, and the way people process information about themselves and others. Social psychology has been increasingly influenced in recent years by the cognitive perspective (Markus & Zajonc, 1985), as researchers have tried to understand how the way people process information can lead them to discriminate against members of minority groups, behave aggressively, or respond to people who behave in ways that seem unjust (Berkowitz, 1993; Darley, 1990; Devine, 1989).

Although the different perspectives have often developed in isolation from one another, some attempts at integration have occurred, particularly in clinical work, where the goal of helping patients has at times been strong enough to induce psychologists to cross territorial lines. For example, many psychologists who treat patients are **cognitive-behavioral,** accepting the behaviorist principle that learning is the basis of behavior but also emphasizing the role of mental processes in determining the way individuals respond to their environment (Bandura, 1977, 1986; Goldfried & Davison, 1994; Meichenbaum, 1977). Thus, a person who is terrified of speaking in a group may not only have an automatic fear reaction every time he considers saying something but may also be inhibited from speaking by beliefs that he will look stupid or that people will not like him. A small group of psychologists have taken an even more integrative stance, bringing together aspects of cognitive-behavioral and psychodynamic theory (Arkowitz, 1997; Wachtel, 1997). These therapists might attend not only to the person's conscious thoughts and fears in groups but also to less conscious beliefs, fears, or conflicting motives that might be triggered outside of conscious awareness. For example, alongside one patient's fear of saying something "dumb" was an equally strong fear that what he had to say might actually be *too smart,* so that speaking would make him feel guilty that he was outdoing or humiliating other people in the room.

INTERIM SUMMARY    Although the different perspectives tend to offer radically different ways of approaching psychology, each has made distinctive contributions. These perspectives have often developed in mutual isolation, but efforts to integrate aspects of them are likely to continue to be fruitful, particularly in clinical psychology.

## COMMENTARY

### *How to Grasp an Elephant from Trunk to Tail Without Getting Skewered on the Tusks*

Many readers may have wondered, in reading about the perspectives described in this chapter, where the author stands on them. Does he see vases, profiles, or simply random collections of white and black dots? Forewarned is forearmed: The best way to inoculate oneself against the subtle intrusions of an author's biases in any field is to know what they are.

My own point of view reflects, and is shaped by, the fact that I am both a researcher and a clinician. Much of my research has been at the intersection of cognitive science and psychodynamic psychology, since I believe the former offers insight into the dynamics of thought and memory, whereas the latter delves into the dynamics of motivation and emotion. My understanding of motivation and emotion has also been heavily influenced by evolutionary and behaviorist principles, particularly the idea that human emotions have evolved to regulate our behavior in adaptive ways, by rewarding or punishing different courses of action. As a freshman in college I took a year-long course on the evolutionary bases of human social behavior taught by one of the leaders of that emerging approach, which forever sensitized me to questions about the adaptive functions and evolution of psychological processes. Thus, I am a hybrid—in the vernacular, a mutt—and the words "psychodynamic," "behavioral," "cognitive,"and "evolutionary" have all appeared in the titles of articles I have written for professional journals.

An advantage of being a mutt is recognizing some of the limitations of the pure-bred positions and the impact that inbreeding can have on the health of a perspective. I sometimes find my fingers tapping impatiently when psychoanalysts or evolutionary psychologists spin elaborate theoretical yarns without subjecting their hypotheses to rigorous scientific scrutiny. I am sometimes struck, as well, by the problems that can occur when studies of cognitive processes neglect or minimize the role of emotion and motivation. When people think about issues that matter to them, which is most of the time, their thinking is frequently biased toward the conclusions they want to reach, as when fans on opposite sides of a college football stadium see a pass-interference call entirely differently or lovers fail to see each others' foibles and failings—until they are ready to break up, at which point they may see *nothing but* foibles and failings. I have trouble with the underlying assumptions of the behaviorist perspective, or at least of its most radical proponents, because experimental studies on thought and memory and my patients' life stories have impressed me with the richness and importance of the thoughts, feelings, and personal meanings that guide human action. At the same time, I believe the principles of learning elucidated by behaviorists must be at the heart of any theory of mind and behavior, and as a clinician, I consider the therapeutic contributions of the behaviorist perspective among the most important of any theoretical perspective. I once even attended the annual conventions of both the Association for the Advancement of Behavior Therapy and the American Psychoanalytic Association in the same year!

Being a mutt requires a high tolerance for ambiguity and conflict. However, the obvious contributions of each of the perspectives, despite their often contradictory assumptions, will likely motivate me for the rest of my career to search for ways to integrate aspects of them, as I believe a whole elephant is more valuable than part of one. ∎

## SUMMARY

### THE BOUNDARIES AND BORDERS OF PSYCHOLOGY

1. **Psychology** is the scientific investigation of mental processes and behavior. Understanding a person means practicing "triple bookkeeping": simultaneously examining the person's biological makeup, psychological experience and functioning, and the cultural and historical moment.

2. **Biopsychology** (or **behavioral neuroscience**) examines the physical basis of psychological phenomena such as motivation, emotion, and stress. **Cross-cultural psychology** attempts to test psychological hypotheses in different cultures. Biology and culture form the boundaries, or constraints, within which psychological processes operate.

3. A classic question inherited from philosophy is whether human action is characterized by **free will** or **determinism,** that is, whether people freely

choose their actions or whether behavior follows lawful patterns. A related issue is the **mind–body problem**—the question of how mental and physical events interact—a contemporary version of which addresses the genetics of personality.

4. The field of psychology began in the late nineteenth century as experimental psychologists attempted to wrest questions about the mind from philosophers. Most shared a strong belief in the scientific method as a way of avoiding philosophical debates about the way the mind works. Among the earliest schools of thought were structuralism and functionalism. **Structuralism,** developed by Edward Titchener, attempted to use introspection as a method for uncovering the basic elements of consciousness and the way they combine with one another into ideas (that is, the *structure* of consciousness). **Functionalism** looked for explanations of psychological processes in their role, or *function,* in helping the individual adapt to the environment.

## PERSPECTIVES IN PSYCHOLOGY

5. A **paradigm** is a broad system of theoretical assumptions employed by a scientific community to try to make sense of a domain of experience. Psychology lacks a unified paradigm but has a number of schools of thought, or **perspectives,** which are broad ways of understanding psychological phenomena. A psychological perspective, like a paradigm, includes theoretical propositions, shared metaphors, and accepted methods of observation.

6. The **psychodynamic perspective** originated with Sigmund Freud. From a psychodynamic perspective, conflict is central to mental life, as are unconscious processes. Thus, the mind is like a battleground, and consciousness is like the tip of an iceberg. Because a primary aim is to interpret the underlying meanings or motives behind human behavior, psychodynamic psychologists tend to rely on case studies as a method for investigating the mind.

7. The **behaviorist perspective** focuses on the relation between environmental events (or **stimuli**) and the responses of the organism. Skinner proposed that all behavior can ultimately be understood as learned responses and that behaviors are selected on the basis of their consequences. A primary metaphor underlying behaviorism is the machine; many behaviorists have also considered the "mind" to be an unknowable black box, whose contents cannot be studied scientifically. The primary method of behaviorists is laboratory experimentation.

8. The **cognitive perspective** focuses on the way people process, store, and retrieve information. **Information processing** refers to taking input from the environment and transforming it into meaningful output. The metaphor underlying the cognitive perspective is the mind as computer, complete with software. In recent years, however many cognitive psychologists have used the brain itself as a metaphor for the way mental processes operate. The primary method of the cognitive perspective is experimental.

9. The **evolutionary perspective** argues that many human behavioral proclivities exist because they helped our ancestors survive and produce offspring that would likely survive. It proposes the mechanism of **natural selection,** through which natural forces select traits in organisms that are adaptive in their environmental niche. The basic notion of evolutionary theory is that evolution selects organisms that maximize their **reproductive success,** defined as the capacity to survive and reproduce. The primary methods are de-

ductive and comparative, although evolutionary psychologists are increasingly relying on experimental methods.

10. Although the four major perspectives largely developed independently, each has made distinctive contributions, and some areas of integration have occurred, particularly in clinical psychology. The **cognitive-behavioral** approach accepts many behaviorist principles but emphasizes as well the role of thought processes, such as expectations, in learning.

Jacob Lawrence, "The Library," 1960. National Museum of American Art, Smithsonian Institution/Art Resource, NY."

CHAPTER *2*

# Research Methods in Psychology

*S*andra was 19 years old when she received a call that would change her life forever. Her parents and only brother had been killed in an automobile accident. Like most people, Sandra initially reacted with shock and tremendous grief, but over the course of the next year, she gradually regained her emotional equilibrium. Sometimes when she would think of her family her eyes would well up, but as the months passed, she knew she had little choice but to go on.

About a year after the accident, though, Sandra noticed that something was different. She was constantly ill with one cold, sore throat, or flu after another. After a few trips to the health service, an astute doctor asked her if anything out of the ordinary had happened in the last year. When she mentioned the death of her family, the doctor recommended she see a psychologist. She did—and was free from physical illness for over a year from the day she entered the psychologist's office.

Was it an accident that Sandra's health improved just as she began expressing her feelings about the loss of her family with a psychologist? Research by James Pennebaker and his colleagues (1990) suggests that the timing may not have been coincidental. In one study, they demonstrated this relationship using a stressful experience much less calamitous than Sandra's: the transition to college. For most people, entering college is an exciting event, but it can also be stressful, since it often means leaving home, breaking predictable routines, finding a new group of friends, and having to make many more decisions independently.

To assess the impact of emotional expression on health, Pennebaker and his colleagues assigned college freshmen to one of two groups. Students in the first group were instructed to write for 20 minutes on three consecutive days about "your very deepest thoughts and feelings about coming to college," including "your emotions and thoughts about leaving your friends or your parents—or even about your feelings of who you are or what you want to become." Students in the other group were asked "to describe in detail what you have done since you woke up this morning"; they were explicitly instructed *not* to mention their emotions, feelings, or opinions.

The results were dramatic (Figure 2.1). Students in the emotional expression group made significantly fewer visits to the health service in the following two to three months than those who simply described what they had done that day. The effect largely wore off by the fourth month, but it was remarkable given how seemingly minor the intervention had been.

Philosophers have speculated for centuries about the relation between mind and body. Yet here, psychologists were able to demonstrate empirically—that is, through observation—how a psychological event (in this case, simply expressing

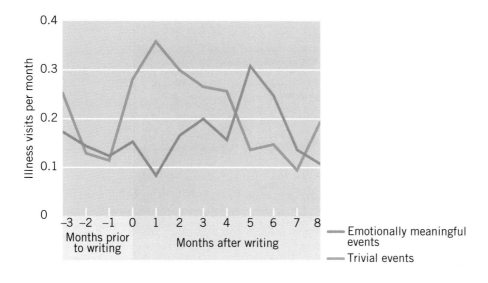

**FIGURE 2.1**
Emotional expression and health. The figure shows the number of visits to the health service per month for students writing about emotionally meaningful or trivial events. In the three months prior to writing, students in the two groups showed no clear differences in number of visits to the health center. Directly following writing (month 0), however, students who wrote about trivial events were much more likely to seek medical attention. Thus, expressing feelings has an impact on health, although without continued attention to emotion, the impact disappears. *Source:* Adapted from Pennebaker et al., 1990, p. 533.

feelings about a stressful experience) can affect the body's ability to protect itself from infection. The methods psychologists use to address issues ranging from the relation between mind and body to the impact of daycare on children are the topic of this chapter. We begin by describing the features of good psychological research. How do researchers take a situation like the sudden improvement in Sandra's health upon entering therapy and turn it into a researchable question? How do they know when the findings apply to the real world? Then we describe three major types of research: experimental, descriptive, and correlational. Next, we discuss how to distinguish a good research study from a bad one. We conclude by returning to some central questions worth bearing in mind throughout the chapter: How do the theoretical perspectives psychologists adopt affect the methods they choose? What methods—or combination of methods—provide the most conclusive results? What do we gain and what do we lose when we "domesticate" a psychological phenomenon and bring it into the laboratory? And how do we know when we have asked the right questions in the first place?

## CHARACTERISTICS OF GOOD PSYCHOLOGICAL RESEARCH

The tasks of a psychological researcher trying to understand human nature are in some respects similar to the tasks we all face in our daily lives as we try to predict other people's behavior. For example, a student named Elizabeth is running behind on a term paper. She wants to ask her professor for an extension but does not want to risk his forming a negative impression of her. Her task, then, is one of prediction: How will he behave?

To make her decision, she can rely on her observations of the way her professor normally behaves, or she can "experiment," by saying something and seeing how he responds. Elizabeth has observed her professor on many occasions, and her impression—or theory—about him is that he tends to be rigid. She has noticed that when students arrive late to class he looks angry and that when they ask to meet with him outside of class he often seems inflexible in scheduling appointments. She thus expects—hypothesizes—that he will not give her an extension. Not sure, however, that her observations are accurate, she tests her hypothesis by speaking with him casually after class one day. She mentions a "friend" who is

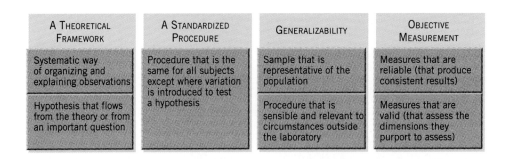

**FIGURE 2.2**
Characteristics of good psychological research. Studies vary tremendously in design, but most good research shares certain attributes.

having trouble finishing the term paper on time, and she carefully observes his reaction—his facial expressions, his words, and the length of time he takes to respond. The professor surprises her by smiling and advising her that her "friend" can have an extra week.

In this scenario, Elizabeth is doing exactly what psychologists do: observing a psychological phenomenon (her professor's behavior), constructing a theory, using the theory to develop a hypothesis, measuring psychological responses, and testing the hypothesis. Psychologists are much more systematic in applying scientific methods, and they have more sophisticated tools, but the logic of investigation is basically the same.

Like an architect or carpenter, researchers have a number of tools at their disposal. Just as a carpenter would not use a hammer to turn a screw or loosen a bolt, a researcher would not rely exclusively on any single method to lay a solid empirical foundation for a theory. Nevertheless, most of the methods psychologists use—the tools of their trade—share certain features: a theoretical framework, standardized procedures, generalizability, and objective measurement (Figure 2.2). We examine each of these in turn.

## THEORETICAL FRAMEWORK

Psychologists study some phenomena because of their practical importance. They may, for example, conduct studies on the impact of divorce on children (Kalter, 1987, 1990; Wallerstein, 1988, 1991) or the effect of the human immunodeficiency virus (HIV), which causes acquired immunodeficiency syndrome (AIDS), on the nervous system (Kelly et al., 1996). In most cases, however, research is grounded firmly in theory.

A **theory** is a systematic way of organizing and explaining observations; it includes a set of propositions, or statements, about the relations among various phenomena. For example, a theory might propose that having a pessimistic attitude promotes poor physical health, for two reasons: Pessimists do not take good care of themselves, and pessimism taxes the body's defenses against disease by keeping the body in a constant state of alert. People frequently assume that a theory is simply a fact that has not yet been proven. As suggested in Chapter 1, however, a theory is always a mental construction, an imperfect rendering of reality by a scientist or community of scientists, which can have more or less evidence to support it. The scientist's thinking is the mortar that holds the bricks of reality in place.

In most research, theory provides the framework for the researcher's specific hypothesis. A **hypothesis** is a tentative belief or educated guess about the relationship between two or more variables. A **variable** is any phenomenon that can differ, or vary, from one situation to another or from one person to another; in other words, it is a characteristic that can take on different values (such as IQ scores of 115 or 125). Researchers measure variables they believe have important connections with each other. For example, a research team interested in the links between optimism and health decided to test the hypothesis that optimism (variable 1) is related to speed of recovery from heart surgery (variable 2). The researchers found that patients undergoing coronary artery bypass operations who are optimistic are quicker to recover than people who are pessimistic (Scheier & Carver, 1993).

In this case, optimism and health are variables because different people are more or less optimistic (they vary on degree of optimism) and recover more or less quickly (they vary on recovery rate). A variable that can be placed on a continuum—such as degree of optimism, intelligence, shyness, or rate of recovery—is called a **continuous variable.** In contrast, some variables are comprised of groupings or categories, such as gender, species, or whether a person has *had* a heart attack. A **categorical variable** of this sort cannot easily be placed on a continuum; people are either male or female and cannot usually be located on a continuum between the two.

## STANDARDIZED PROCEDURES

In addition to being grounded in theory, good psychological research uses **standardized procedures;** that is, it exposes the participants in a study to as similar procedures as possible. For example, in the study of emotional expression and health that opened this chapter, the experimenters instructed students to write for 20 minutes a day for three days. If instead they had let the students write as long as they wanted, students in one group might have written more, and the experimenters would not have been able to tell whether differences in visits to the health service reflected the *content* of their writing or simply the *quantity.*

## GENERALIZABILITY FROM A SAMPLE

Psychological research typically studies the behavior of a subset of people in order to learn about a larger **population.** The population might be as broad as all humans or as narrow as preschool children with working mothers. A **sample** is a subgroup of the population that is likely to be **representative** of the population as a whole—that is, similar enough to other members of the population that conclusions drawn from the sample are likely to be true of the rest of the population. The individuals who participate in a study are called **participants** (or **subjects**).

A representative sample contributes to the generalizability of a study's conclusions. **Generalizability** refers to the applicability of the findings to the entire population of interest to the researcher. Participants in the study of emotional expression and health were U.S. college students. Would the study have had the same results in a sample of soldiers who might consider writing about feelings weak or sentimental? Would the results have been different in a culture that discourages expression of unpleasant feelings?

For a study to be generalizable, its procedures must also be sound, or **valid.** To be valid, a study must meet two criteria. First, it must employ methods that convincingly test the hypothesis. This is often called **internal validity**—validity of the design itself. If a study has fatal flaws—such as an unrepresentative sample, or a failure to standardize aspects of the design that could affect the way participants respond—its internal validity is jeopardized. Second, the study must establish **external validity,** which means that the findings can be generalized to situations outside, or external to, the laboratory. Does expressing feelings on paper for three days in a laboratory simulate what happens when people express feelings in their diary or to a close friend? Often researchers must strike a balance between internal and external validity, because the more tightly a researcher controls what participants experience, the less the situation may resemble life outside the laboratory.

**INTERIM SUMMARY**   Psychological research is generally guided by a **theory**—a systematic way of organizing and explaining observations. The theory helps generate a **hypothesis,** or tentative belief about the relationship between two or more variables. **Variables** are phenomena that differ or change across circumstances or individuals; they can be either **continuous** or **categorical,** depending on whether they form a continuum or are comprised of categories. **Standardized procedures** expose participants in a study to as similar procedures as possible. Although psychologists are typically interested in knowing something about a **population,** to do so they usually study a **sample,** or subgroup, that is likely to be representative of the population. To be **generalizable,** a study must have both **internal validity** (a valid design) and **external validity** (applicability to situations outside the laboratory).

## OBJECTIVE MEASUREMENT

As in all scientific endeavors, objectivity is an important ideal in psychological research. The reader of a study wants to be confident that the results are not simply the experimenter's subjective impression. Variables must therefore be defined in a way that enables researchers to quantify or categorize them. For example, one research team wanted to learn about the friendship patterns of children who had been physically abused by their parents (Parker & Herrera, 1996). Does abuse at home tend to disrupt the ability to form close friendships? Based on the theory that abuse makes children more aggressive and less trusting, the researchers hypothesized that abused children would show more conflict and less intimacy than nonabused children when interacting with a friend.

To test this hypothesis, the researchers had to overcome two major hurdles: how to distinguish abused from nonabused children and how to measure variables such as degree of conflict. To identify abused children, the investigators received permission from the state agency charged with the protection of children to locate children whose parents had beaten or kicked (or in one case, burned) them in the past 2.5 years to such a degree that the state had had to intervene. Nonabused children were recruited from flyers posted in similar neighborhoods, and their records were checked with the protective services agency to make sure they had no reported histories of abuse.

To assess friendship patterns, the researchers asked the children to nominate their closest friend and obtained parental permission to bring the children and their best friend into the laboratory for a two-hour session. In the laboratory, the children interacted with their friend in a standardized series of tasks, ranging from chatting with each other while the experimenter allegedly worked on some paperwork to playing particular games that allowed the opportunity for cooperation, conflict, competition, negotiation, and generosity between the partners. The researchers wanted to see how the children interacted on several different types of tasks to increase the likelihood that they would observe the way the children actually behave in many situations.

The interactions between the pairs of children were videotaped and later rated on several dimensions such as conflict and intimacy. For example, each segment of the laboratory session was rated on a conflict scale based on the presence of disagreements, insults, and fights, ranging from 0 *(no conflicts)* to 3 *(five or more conflicts).* Each segment was also rated for intimacy, defined as disclosure of personal or private information involving sharing of thoughts and feelings, on a scale from 1 *(little or no disclosure)* to 4 *(extensive discussion of feelings or discussion of things that could lead to considerable vulnerability).* In terms of variables, the researchers were interested in the relation between a categorical variable (whether

| TABLE 2.1 | INTIMACY AND CONFLICT IN THE FRIENDSHIPS OF ABUSED AND NONABUSED CHILDREN | |
| --- | --- | --- |
| VARIABLE | ABUSED | NONABUSED |
| Intimacy | 2.39 | 2.87 |
| Conflict | .72 | .25 |

*Source:* Adapted from Parker and Herrera, 1996.

*Note:* For intimacy, the table shows the average intimacy rating across all tasks on which the children interacted. For conflict, the two groups differed only in the amount of conflict shown during the game-playing task. The table shows the average amount of conflict during that task. Other differences between abused and nonabused children's friendships were specific to one gender or the other. For example, abused girls showed less positive emotion in their interactions with their friends than nonabused girls, whereas boys showed more negative emotion in interactions with their friends than nonabused boys. Thus, abuse seems to take some of the pleasure out of girls' friendships but to increase the hostility in boys'.

or not the pair included an abused child) and two continuous variables (degree of conflict and degree of intimacy). As can be seen in Table 2.1, the friendships of abused children showed more conflict and less intimacy than those of nonabused children.

To study a variable, then, the researcher must first devise a technique to measure it. A **measure** is a concrete way of assessing a variable, a way of bringing an often abstract concept down to earth, such as coding intimacy between children on a 1–4 scale. In the research linking optimism to health, the investigators used a questionnaire to measure optimism. The questionnaire included items such as "I hardly ever expect things to go my way" and "In uncertain times, I usually expect the best." The investigators measured recovery from heart attack by assessing concrete behaviors, such as how quickly the patients began to sit up in bed, walk around the hospital room after surgery, or return to work. In the study of emotional expression and health, the investigators obtained actual records of visits from the campus health service as a rough measure of illness. This was a better measure than simply asking people how often they got sick, since people may not be able to remember or report illness objectively. (One person's threshold for being "sick" might be much lower than another's.)

For some variables, measurement is not a problem. Researchers typically have little difficulty distinguishing males from females. However, for some characteristics, such as conflict in friendships, optimism, and health, measurement is much more complex. In these cases, researchers need to know two characteristics of a measure: whether it is reliable and whether it is valid.

## Reliability

**Reliability** refers to a measure's ability to produce consistent results. Using a measure is like stepping on a scale: The same person should not register 145 pounds one moment and 152 a few minutes later. Similarly, a reliable psychological measure does not fluctuate substantially despite the presence of random factors that may influence results, such as whether the participant had a good night's sleep or who coded the data. Reliability in this technical sense is not altogether different from reliability in its everyday meaning: A test is unreliable if we cannot count on it to behave consistently, just as a plumber is unreliable if we cannot count on him consistently to show up when he says he will. An unreliable measure may sometimes work, just as an unreliable plumber may sometimes work, but we can never predict when either will perform adequately.

Three kinds of reliability are especially important. **Test–retest reliability** refers to the tendency of a test to yield relatively similar scores for the same individual over time. If a measure is reliable, people who are retested should receive scores close to their initial scores, unless they have changed dramatically. Another kind of reliability is **internal consistency.** A measure is internally consistent if several ways of asking the same question yield similar results. For example, suppose a researcher asks two questions designed to assess self-esteem: "Do you like yourself?" and "Do you think you are a good person?" If people who answer "yes" to the first question are very likely to answer "yes" to the second, then the test is internally consistent; that is, the two items are assessing the same underlying dimension. A third kind of reliability is **inter-rater reliability.** If two different interviewers rate an individual on some dimension, both should give the person similar scores. To make sure that a test has inter-rater reliability, raters must be trained to use precise definitions of the phenomena they are measuring. When the researchers studying abused children's friendships rated conflict and intimacy, they thus used very specific definitions of each (defining intimacy, for example, in terms of disclosure of personal information and putting a premium on discussion of feelings and information that would make the children vulnerable to their friends.) Obtaining inter-rater reliability on data of this sort often requires developing detailed coding procedures to guarantee that different raters are similarly "calibrated," like two thermometers recording temperature in the same room.

The distinctions among these kinds of reliability can be clarified by returning to the plumbing analogy. A plumber establishes his *test–retest* reliability by showing up when he says he will on different occasions and by performing competently on each occasion. He establishes *internal consistency* by fixing an overflowing commode with as much dispatch as he would a stopped-up sink. He can boast *inter-rater reliability* if his customers agree in their assessment of his work. If he fails any of these reliability tests, he is unlikely to be called again, just as an unreliable measure will not be used in another study.

## Validity

When the term **validity** is applied to a psychological measure, it refers to the measure's ability to assess the variable it is supposed to measure. For example, readers are all familiar with IQ tests, which are supposed to measure intelligence. One way psychologists have tried to demonstrate the validity of IQ test scores is to show that they consistently predict other phenomena that require intellectual ability, such as school performance. As we will see in Chapter 8, IQ tests and similar tests such as the Scholastic Aptitude Test (the SAT) are, in general, highly predictive of school success (Anastasi & Urbina, 1997), although they are not without their critics (Elliott, 1988). Some of the measures people intuitively use in their daily lives have much less certain validity, as when Elizabeth initially presumed that her professor's inflexibility in arranging meetings with students was a good index of his general flexibility (rather than, say, a tight schedule).

To ensure the validity of a psychological measure, researchers conduct validation research. **Validation** means demonstrating that a measure consistently relates to some objective criterion or to other measures that have themselves already demonstrated their validity. For example, the Affect Intensity Measure (AIM) is a self-report measure of emotional intensity on which people report how strongly they typically experience their emotions (Larsen & Diener, 1987). To assess the validity of the instrument, the psychologists who developed the AIM measured the extent to which study participants responded physiologically to emotion-arousing events in the laboratory, by examining variables such as heart rate. They also measured the extent to which participants' moods actually fluctuated in daily life by having them carry beepers and record the intensity of their feelings when beeped periodically. Participants who described themselves as emotionally intense on the AIM tended to be the most physiologically reactive in the laboratory and reported more intense emotions when their emotional experiences were monitored at various times throughout a normal day. These findings supported the validity of the AIM.

### Multiple Measures

One of the best ways to obtain an accurate assessment of a variable is to employ multiple measures of it. **Multiple measures** are important because no psychological measure is perfect. A measure that assesses a variable accurately 80 percent of the time is excellent—but it is also inaccurate 20 percent of the time. In fact, built into every measure is a certain amount of **error,** or discrepancy between the phenomenon as measured and the phenomenon as it really is. For example, IQ is a good predictor of school success *most* of the time, but for some people it overpredicts or underpredicts their performance. Multiple measures therefore provide a safety net for catching errors. The study of abused children's friendships, for example, used several measures of intimacy: global intimacy, peak intimacy (highest recorded level of intimacy across all tasks), amount of "relationship talk," and physical closeness and positive touching. Global intimacy proved the best measure, although taking the average of multiple measures often produces the most reliable results.

Virtually all good psychological studies share the ingredients of psychological research outlined here: a theoretical framework, standardized procedures, generalizability, and objective measurement. Nevertheless, studies vary considerably in design and goals. The following sections examine three broad types of research (Table 2.2): experimental research, which tries to demonstrate cause-and-effect relationships; descriptive research, which attempts to describe psychological phenomena; and correlational research, which attempts to assess the relations among variables such as IQ and school achievement. As we will see, the lines among these types are not hard and fast. Many studies categorized as descriptive, such as studies of small numbers of patients with brain lesions that affect their ability to recognize people's faces, actually include experimental components, and correlational questions are often built into experiments. The aim in designing research is scientific rigor and practicality, not purity; the best strategy is to use whatever systematic empirical methods are available to explore the hypothesis.

**INTERIM SUMMARY** Just as researchers take a sample of a population, they similarly take a "sample" of a variable—that is, they use a **measure** of the variable, which provides a concrete way of operationalizing it. A measure is **reliable** if it produces consistent results— that is, if it does not show too much random fluctuation. A measure is **valid** if it accurately assesses or "samples" the construct it is intended to measure. Because every measure includes some component of error, researchers often use **multiple measures** of the same construct (in order to assess more than one sample of the relevant behavior).

## EXPERIMENTAL RESEARCH

In **experimental research,** investigators manipulate some aspect of a situation and examine the impact on the way participants respond. Experimental methods are particularly important because they can establish cause and effect— *causation*—directly. An experiment can demonstrate causation by proving that manipulating one variable leads to predicted changes in another. The researchers studying the impact of emotional expression on health could be confident that

**TABLE 2.2    COMPARISON OF RESEARCH METHODS**

| METHOD | DESCRIPTION | USES AND ADVANTAGES | POTENTIAL LIMITATIONS |
|---|---|---|---|
| Experimental | Manipulation of variables to assess cause and effect | • Demonstrates causal relationships<br>• Replicability: study can be repeated to see if the same findings emerge<br>• Maximizes control over relevant variables | • Generalizability outside the laboratory<br>• Many complex phenomena cannot be tested<br>• Does not offer insight into personal meanings |
| Descriptive | | | |
|    Case study | In-depth observation of a small number of cases | • Reveals individual psychological dynamics<br>• Allows study of complex phenomena not easily reproduced experimentally<br>• Provides data that can be useful in framing hypotheses | • Generalizability to the population<br>• Replicability: study may not be repeatable<br>• Researcher bias<br>• Cannot establish causation |
|    Naturalistic observation | In-depth observation of a phenomenon as it occurs in nature | • Reveals phenomena as they exist outside the laboratory<br>• Allows study of complex phenomena not easily reproduced experimentally<br>• Provides data that can be useful in framing hypotheses | • Generalizability to the population<br>• Replicability<br>• Observer effects: the presence of an observer may alter the behavior of the participants<br>• Researcher bias<br>• Cannot establish causation |
|    Survey research | Asking people questions about their attitudes, behavior, etc. | • Reveals attitudes or self-reported behaviors of a large sample of individuals<br>• Allows quantification of attitudes or behaviors | • Self-report bias: people may not be able to report honestly or accurately<br>• Cannot establish causation |
| Correlational | Examines the extent to which two or more variables are related and can be used to predict one another | • Reveals relations among variables as they exist outside the laboratory<br>• Allows quantification of relations among variables | • Cannot establish causation |

writing emotionally about a stressful experience *caused* better health because participants who did so were subsequently healthier than those who did not.

The emphasis on experimentation as a way of understanding nature derives in part from Sir Francis Bacon (1561–1626), a British philosopher who was writing as England took its first steps into the modern age in the sixteenth century. According to Bacon, the best way to test our understanding of nature is to bend it to do something it normally does not do (Smith, 1992). Scientists who understand the laws of physics—or behavior—ought to be able to "bend nature" in a laboratory to do something scientifically interesting or practically useful. College students do not typically write for 20 minutes a day for three consecutive days about the experience of beginning college, but when researchers bent nature this way, they found some very practical, and theoretically interesting, impacts on physical health.

The logic of experimentation is much more straightforward and intuitive than many people think. Elizabeth used it implicitly when she tested her professor's flexibility, as we all do multiple times a day in one situation after another. An experimenter manipulates variables that are outside the participants' control, independent of their actions; these are known as **independent variables.** The aim is to assess the impact of these manipulations on the way participants subsequently respond. Because participants' responses depend on both the participant and the independent variable, they are known as **dependent variables.** The independent variable, then, is the variable the experimenter manipulates; the dependent variable is the one the experimenter measures to see if the manipulation has had an effect.

To assess cause and effect, experimenters present participants with different possible variations, or **conditions,** of the independent variable and study the way participants react. In the study of emotional expression and health, the experimenters used an independent variable (emotional expression) with two conditions (express or do not express). They then tested the impact on health (dependent variable).

Consider a series of classic studies conducted in the 1950s by Harry Harlow and his colleagues (Harlow & Zimmerman, 1959). They were interested in determining which of two theories better explained why infant monkeys become emotionally attached to their mothers. One theory hypothesized that the basis for this attachment was the mother's role as the source of food. An alternative theory suggested that infant monkeys are drawn by the security and comfort mothers provide their young. To test these two hypotheses, the researchers conducted an experiment in which infant monkeys were separated from their mothers and raised in social isolation. Each monkey shared its cage with two surrogate or replacement "mothers," one made of wire and the other also made of wire but covered with terrycloth (and hence softer).

The independent variable—the variable manipulated by the researchers—was the placement of the milk bottle. In one experimental condition, a bottle was attached to the wire mother, whereas in the other condition it was attached to the cloth mother (Figure 2.3). The dependent variable was the infant monkeys' response, notably the amount of time they spent holding onto each of the two mothers and which mother they turned to when frightened. The researchers found that whether the wire or the cloth surrogate was the source of milk did not matter: The infants showed a clear preference for the cloth surrogate. Harlow and his colleagues concluded that security and comfort were more important than simple nourishment in the development of attachment to the mother.

Experiments vary widely in both their designs and their goals, but the steps in conceiving and executing them are roughly the same, from the starting point of framing a hypothesis to the ultimate evaluation of findings (Figure 2.4). Although these steps relate specifically to the experimental method, many apply to descriptive and correlational methods as well.

**FIGURE 2.3**
Surrogate mother in Harlow's monkey studies. Monkeys were separated from birth from their mothers and given the choice of spending time with a wire mother or a terrycloth mother. Regardless of which "mother" fed the baby monkey, it preferred the soft terrycloth mother, suggesting that security, not nourishment, is the basis of attachment in monkeys.

INTERIM SUMMARY    In **experimental research,** psychologists manipulate some aspect of a situation (the **independent variables**) and examine the impact on the way participants respond (the **dependent variables**). This allows researchers to assess cause and effect.

## STEP 1: FRAMING A HYPOTHESIS

The first step in constructing an experiment is to develop a hypothesis that predicts the relationship between two or more variables. For example, Gordon Bower and his associates have investigated the impact of mood on memory (Bower, 1981, 1989; Gilligan & Bower, 1984). Based on a cognitive theory of the way people store

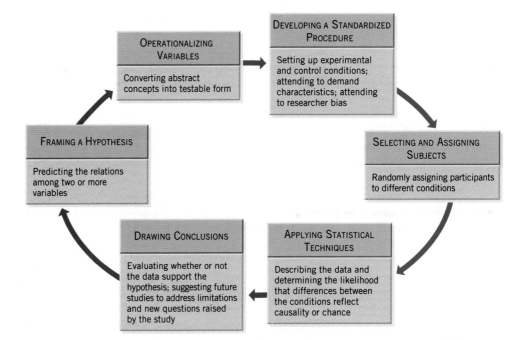

**FIGURE 2.4**

Conducting an experiment requires systematically going through a series of steps, from the initial framing of a hypothesis to drawing conclusions about the data obtained. The process is circular, as the conclusion of one study is generally the origin of another.

and retrieve memories, they hypothesized that people who are in a positive mood while learning information will be more likely to remember pleasant aspects of that information. Conversely, people in a negative mood while learning will be more likely to remember negative information. This hypothesis states a relationship between two variables: *mood state* when learning material (the independent variable) and later ability to *recall* that material (the dependent variable).

## STEP 2: OPERATIONALIZING VARIABLES

The second step in experimental research is to operationalize the variables. **Operationalizing** means turning an abstract concept into a concrete variable defined by some set of actions, or operations. Bower operationalized the independent variable, mood state, by hypnotizing participants to feel either happy or sad (the two conditions of the independent variable). He then had participants read a psychiatric patient's descriptions of various happy and sad memories. Bower operationalized the dependent variable—the ability to recall either positive or negative information—as the number of positive and negative memories the participant could recall 20 minutes later.

## STEP 3: DEVELOPING A STANDARDIZED PROCEDURE

The next step in constructing an experiment is to develop a standardized procedure, so that the only things that vary from participant to participant are the independent variables and participants' performance on the dependent variables. Standardized procedures maximize the likelihood that any differences observed in participants' behavior can be attributed to the experimental manipulation, allowing the investigator to draw inferences about cause and effect.

In Bower's study, the experiment would have been *contaminated,* or ruined, if different participants had heard different stories or varying numbers of positive and negative memories. These differences might have influenced the number of positive and negative memories participants would later recall. Bower's method of inducing happy or sad mood states also had to be standardized. If the experimenter induced a negative mood in one participant by hypnotizing him and in another by asking him to try to imagine his mother dying, differences in recall could stem from the different ways mood was induced.

## Control Groups

Experimental research typically involves dividing participants into groups who experience different conditions of the independent variable and then comparing the responses of the different groups. In Bower's experiment, the two groups consisted of participants who were hypnotized to be in a happy mood in one group and those who were hypnotized to be in a sad mood in the other. Experiments often include another kind of group or condition, called a control group. Instead of being exposed to the experimental manipulation, participants in the **control group** experience a neutral condition. Although Bower's experiment did not have a control group, a control condition for this experiment could have been a group of participants who were brought under hypnosis but were not given any mood induction. By comparing participants who were induced to feel sad while reading the story with those who were not induced to feel anything, Bower could have seen whether sad participants recall more sad memories (or fewer happy ones) than neutral participants. Examining the performance of participants who have not been exposed to the experimental condition gives researchers a clearer view of the impact of the experimental manipulation.

## Protecting Against Bias

Researchers try to anticipate and control the many sources of bias that can affect the results of a study. Investigators must sometimes ensure that participants do not know too much about the study because this knowledge could influence their performance. Some participants try to respond in the way they think the experimenter wants them to respond. (They are nice people but lousy participants.) The ways participants' perceptions of the researcher's goals influence their responses are known as the **demand characteristics** of a study. To prevent demand characteristics from biasing the results, psychologists sometimes conduct **blind studies,** in which participants are kept unaware of, or blind to, important aspects of the research. If participants in the study of emotional expression and health had known why their subsequent health records were important, they might have tried to avoid the doctor as long as possible if they were in the experimental group. If they believed the hypothesis, they might even have been less likely to *notice* when they were sick.

Blind studies are especially valuable in researching the effect of interventions such as medications on psychological symptoms. Researchers in these studies have to contend with **placebo effects,** in which giving a participant a pill, for example, produces an effect because participants *believe* it will produce an effect. Participants who think they are taking a medication often find that their symptoms disappear after they have taken what is really an inert, or inactive, substance such as a sugar pill (a placebo). Simply believing that a treatment is effective can sometimes prove as effective as the drug itself. In a **single-blind study,** participants are kept blind to crucial information, such as the condition to which they are being exposed (in this case, placebo versus medication). In this case, the participant is blind, but the experimenter is not.

The design of an experiment should also guard against researcher bias. Experimenters are usually committed to the hypotheses they set out to test, and, being human, they might be predisposed to interpret their results in a positive

*An Italian faith healer works miracles—a likely example of the powerful effect of a placebo.*

light. An experimenter who expects an anti-anxiety medication to be more effective than a placebo may inadvertently overrate improvement in participants who receive the medication. Experimenters may also inadvertently communicate their expectations to participants—by probing for improvement more in the medication group than in the control group, for example. The best way to avoid the biases of both participants and investigators is to perform a **double-blind study.** In this case, both participants *and* researchers who interact with them are blind to the experimental condition to which each participant has been exposed until the research is completed.

## STEP 4: SELECTING AND ASSIGNING PARTICIPANTS

Having developed standardized procedures, the researcher is now ready to find participants who are representative of the population of interest. Experimenters typically place participants randomly in each of the experimental conditions (such as sad mood, happy mood, or neutral mood). Random assignment is essential for internal validity; it minimizes differences between participants in different groups that cannot be attributed to the independent variable. If all participants in the sad condition were male and all those in the happy condition were female, Bower could not tell whether his participants' responses were determined by mood or by sex. In this case the sex of the participants would be a **confounding variable,** a variable that could produce effects that are confused, or confounded, with the effects of the independent variable. The presence of confounding variables compromises the internal validity of a study by making inferences about causality impossible.

Ideally, the samples psychologists use to test general hypotheses about mental and behavioral processes should be representative of the human population as a whole. From a practical point of view, however, collecting data on participants from multiple cultures, or even from a true cross section of a single society, is very difficult. Because so many researchers are based on college campuses, the most frequently studied population is largely white, middle-class, 18- to 20-year-old Americans—a fact that led one somewhat cynical observer to call psychology the "science of the behavior of the college sophomore" (Rubenstein, 1982). Although this constraint is too seldom acknowledged in research studies, it undoubtedly limits the generalizability of many research findings.

Should one therefore discount all North American or European psychological research because it depends on student participants? To do so, a critic would need a good reason to believe that people in other cultures or other age groups would respond differently on the particular task at hand. In the case of Bower's research, for example, there is little reason to suspect that the relation between mood state and recall would differ from a Canadian college student to an Australian aborigine, although the only way to know is to test the hypothesis cross-culturally.

In contrast, consider the findings of a remarkable study that examined genetic influences on the tendency to become divorced (Jockin, McGue, & Lykken, 1996). Using methods that will be described in Chapter 3, the researchers were able to determine that more than one-third of the tendency to become divorced can be explained by genetic influences on personality, and that this was especially true for women. Of particular importance in accounting for the finding is that the tendency to become upset, which is heavily influenced by genes, is also associated with increased risk for divorce. As we will see, the link between genes and emotional distress is probably universal across cultures, but the link to divorce is not. Many cultures do not permit divorce, and women in many cultures have not been allowed to initiate divorce. Even where divorce is permitted, divorce rates vary substantially. If only 10 percent of couples divorce, findings from a U.S. sample, where 50 percent of marriages end in divorce, may not be applicable, because divorce would presumably occur in only the most extremely distressed couples. This could either increase or decrease the role of genetically influenced traits such as negative emotionality; the only way to know is to *replicate,* or repeat, the study cross-culturally.

## STEP 5: APPLYING STATISTICAL TECHNIQUES TO THE DATA

Once an investigator has selected participants and conducted an experiment, the next step is to analyze the data. When psychologists present and analyze data, they are typically confronted with two tasks. First, they must describe the findings in a way that summarizes their essential features **(descriptive statistics)**; second, they must draw inferences from the sample to the population as a whole **(inferential statistics).** Descriptive statistics are a way of taking what may be a staggeringly large set of observations, sometimes made over months or years, and putting them into a summary form that others can comprehend in a table or graph.

Almost *any* time two groups are compared, differences will appear between them simply because no two groups of people are exactly alike. The task for the researcher is to try to infer whether the differences that do emerge are meaningful or simply random. This is the job of inferential statistics. In experimental research, the goal is to test for differences between groups or conditions to see if the independent variable really had an impact on the way participants responded. Figure 2.5 shows the results of Bower's study in which participants heard about the psychiatric patient while they were either happy or sad. As this figure reveals, the average number of positive and negative memories recalled by participants varied according to mood. Happy participants recalled almost eight happy story incidents but fewer than 6.5 sad ones, whereas sad participants recalled over eight sad but fewer than six happy incidents. The supplement that immediately follows this chapter addresses descriptive and inferential statistics in enough detail to allow the reader to make sense of most articles in psychological journals. (Fight the urge to skip it—it is comprehensible even to the seriously math phobic and is even occasionally interesting.)

## STEP 6: DRAWING CONCLUSIONS

The final step in experimental research, drawing conclusions, involves evaluating whether or not the hypothesis was supported, that is, whether the independent and dependent variables were related as predicted. It also entails interpreting the findings in light of the broader theoretical framework of the study and assessing their generalizability to phenomena outside the laboratory. Most studies conclude by acknowledging their limitations and pointing toward future research that might address unanswered questions. The findings of the study of emotional expression and health, for example, raised an intriguing question: What if people think about a stressful event but do not focus on their feelings about it? In fact, subsequent studies showed that focusing on the feelings is essential to reaping the health rewards of thinking about stressful or distressing experiences (Pennebaker, 1990).

INTERIM SUMMARY    Conducting a study, particularly an experiment, entails a series of steps. The first is framing a hypothesis that predicts the relations among two or more variables. The second is to **operationalize** variables—to turn abstract constructions into concrete form defined by a set of actions or operations. The third step is to develop a standard-

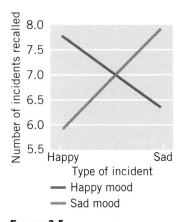

**FIGURE 2.5**
The influence of mood on memory. Happy participants stored and later retrieved more happy incidents, whereas sad participants were more likely to recall sad incidents. *Source:* Bower, 1981.

ized procedure, so that only the variables of interest vary. In experimental research, researchers often divide participants into different groups, who experience different conditions of the independent variable; some participants are often assigned to a **control group**—a neutral condition against which participants in various experimental conditions can be compared. The fourth step is to select samples that are as representative as possible of the population of interest. The fifth step is to analyze the data using statistical techniques. The final step is to draw conclusions from the data to help assess whether the hypothesis was supported and whether the results are likely to generalize.

## LIMITATIONS OF EXPERIMENTAL RESEARCH

Because experimenters can manipulate variables one at a time and observe the effects of each manipulation, experiments provide the "cleanest" findings of any method in psychology. No other method in psychological research can determine cause and effect so unambiguously. Furthermore, experiments can be replicated, or repeated, to see if the same findings emerge with a different sample; the results can thus be corroborated or refined.

Experimental methods do, however, have their limitations. First, for both practical and ethical reasons, many complex phenomena cannot be tested in the laboratory. A psychologist who wants to know whether divorce has a negative impact on children's intellectual development cannot manipulate people into divorcing in order to test the hypothesis. Researchers frequently have to examine phenomena as they exist in nature.

When experiments are impractical, psychologists sometimes employ **quasi-experimental designs,** which share the logic and many features of the experimental method but do not afford the experimenter as much control over all relevant variables, such as random assignment of participants to different conditions (Campbell & Stanley, 1963). An experimenter interested in the impact of divorce on memory, for example, might compare the ability of children from divorced and nondivorced families to retrieve positive and negative memories. The researcher would also test to be sure the two groups did not differ on variables that could potentially influence the results, such as age, gender, and socioeconomic status (social class). Although quasi-experimental designs cannot provide the degree of certainty about cause-and-effect relationships that experiments offer, they are probably the most common designs used in psychology. Reality, unfortunately, is both the object of scientific inquiry and its major impediment.

A second limitation of the experimental method centers on the problem of external validity. Researchers can never be certain how closely the phenomena observed in a laboratory parallel their real-life counterparts. In some instances, such as the study with which this chapter opened, the implications seem clear: If briefly writing about stressful events can improve health, imagine what talking about them with a professional over time might do. And in fact, research shows that people who get help for *psychological* problems through psychotherapy tend to make fewer trips to the doctor for *medical* problems (Gabbard et al., 1996). In other cases, external validity is more problematic. Do the principles that operate in a laboratory study of memory apply when a person reflects on past events to decide whether or not to stay in a relationship (Ceci & Bronfenbrenner, 1991; Neisser, 1976; Rogoff & Lave, 1984)?

A third limitation is emphasized by psychologists who take an **interpretive** (also called *hermeneutic*) stance on methodology (Messer et al., 1988). They argue that the aim of a science of human mental life and behavior is not *predicting* behavior but *understanding* the highly idiosyncratic personal meanings that lead to an individual's actions. One person may commit suicide because he feels he is a failure; another may kill himself to get back at a relative or spouse; another may do so to escape intense or chronic psychic pain; still another individual might take his life because cultural norms demand it in the face of a wrongdoing or humiliation. From an interpretive point of view, explaining a behavior such as suicide means understanding the subjective meanings behind it, not predicting it from some combination of variables. Interpreting meanings of this sort typically requires in-depth interviewing that is beyond what can be accomplished in an experiment.

Despite its limitations, the experimental method is the bread and butter of psychology. No method in psychology is more definitive than a well-executed experiment. Nevertheless, few would desire a steady diet of bread and butter, and scientific investigation is nourished by multiple methods and many sources of data.

INTERIM SUMMARY   Experiments are the only methods in psychology that allow researchers to draw unambiguous conclusions about cause and effect. The limits of experimental methods are the difficulties of bringing some complex phenomena into the laboratory, the question of whether the results apply to phenomena outside the laboratory, and the problem of exploring idiosyncratic personal meanings that may lead to an individual's actions.

## DESCRIPTIVE RESEARCH

The second major type of research, **descriptive research,** attempts to describe phenomena as they exist rather than to manipulate variables. Do people in different cultures use similar terms to describe people's personalities, such as "outgoing" or "responsible" (Paunonen et al., 1992)? Do members of other primate species compete for status and form coalitions against powerful members of the group whose behavior is becoming oppressive? Do young women with anorexia have personality characteristics that distinguish them from their peers (Bruch, 1973; Vitousek & Manke, 1994)? To answer such questions, psychologists use a variety of descriptive methods, including case studies, naturalistic observation, and survey research. Table 2.2 summarizes the major uses and limitations of these descriptive methods as well as the other methods psychologists use.

### CASE STUDY METHODS

A **case study** is an in-depth observation of one person or a small group of individuals. Case study methods are useful when trying to learn about complex psychological phenomena that are not yet well understood and require exploration or that are difficult to produce experimentally. Some of the most famous case studies in psychology are Sigmund Freud's studies of his early patients. Freud sought to discover the origin of his patients' symptoms (such as a little boy's fear of horses or a physically healthy woman's inability to breastfeed her baby) in their past experiences. Researchers tend to describe cases they believe are representative of a population, much as Freud used the case of the little boy who was afraid of horses to set forth some hypotheses about the origins of phobias. Single-case designs can also be used in combination with quantitative or experimental procedures (Kazdin & Tuma, 1982). For example, some researchers assess change in patients over time by coding videotaped psychotherapy sessions for qualities such as emotion, self-esteem, or defensiveness (Hilliard, 1993).

Case studies are often useful when large numbers of subjects are not available, either because they do not exist or because obtaining them would be extremely difficult. For example, extensive case studies of patients who have undergone surgery to sever the tissue connecting the right and left hemispheres of the brain (in order to control severe epileptic seizures) have yielded important information about the specific functions of the two hemispheres (Chapter 3).

A major limitation of case study methods is their small sample size. Because case studies examine only a small group of participants, generalization to a larger population is always uncertain. An investigator who conducts intensive research on one young woman with anorexia and finds that her self-starvation behavior is strongly tied to her wishes for control might be tempted to conclude that control issues are central in cases of this disorder. They may well be, but they may also be idiosyncratic to this particular person. One way to minimize this limitation is to use a multiple-case-study method (Rosenwald, 1988), extensively examining a small sample of people individually and drawing generalizations across them.

A second limitation of case studies is their susceptibility to researcher bias. Investigators tend to see what they expect to see. A psychotherapist who believes that anorexic patients have conflicts about sexuality will undoubtedly see such conflicts in her anorexic patients because they are operative in everyone. In writing up the case, she may select examples that demonstrate these conflicts and miss other issues that might be just as salient to another observer. Because no one else is privy to the data of a case, no other investigator can examine the data directly and draw any different conclusions unless the therapy sessions are videotaped; the data are always filtered through the psychologist's theoretical lens.

Case studies are probably most useful at either the beginning or end of a series of studies that employ quantitative methods with larger samples. Exploring individual cases can be crucial in deciding what questions to ask or what hypotheses to test because they allow the researcher to immerse herself in the phenomenon as it appears in real life. A case study can also flesh out the meaning of quantitative findings by providing a detailed analysis of representative examples.

## NATURALISTIC OBSERVATION

A second descriptive method, **naturalistic observation,** is the in-depth observation of a phenomenon in its natural setting. For example, Frans de Waal, a primatologist (researcher who studies primates, such as humans and chimpanzees), has spent years both in the wild and at zoos observing the way groups of apes or monkeys behave. de Waal (1989) describes an incident in which a dominant male chimpanzee in captivity made an aggressive charge at a female. The troop, clearly distressed by the male's behavior, came to the aid of the female and then settled into an unusual silence. Suddenly, the room echoed with hoots and howls, during which two of the chimps kissed and embraced. To de Waal's surprise, the two chimps were the same ones who had been involved in the fight that had set off the episode! After several hours of pondering the incident, de Waal suddenly realized that he had observed something he had naively assumed was unique to humans: reconciliation. This led him to study the way primates maintain social relationships despite conflicts and acts of aggression. His research led him to conclude that for humans, as for our nearest neighbors, "making peace is as natural as making war" (p. 7).

Psychologists also observe humans "in the wild" using naturalistic methods, as in the classic studies of Genevan school children by the Swiss psychologist Jean Piaget (1926). Piaget and his colleagues conducted their research in playgrounds and classrooms, taking detailed notes on who spoke to whom, for how long, and on what topics. Piaget found that young children often speak in "collective monologues," talking all at once; they may neither notice whether they are being listened to nor address their comments to a particular listener. An advantage of nat-

*Naturalistic observation can lead to novel insights, such as the importance of peacemaking in primates.*

uralistic observation over experimental methods is that its findings are clearly applicable outside the laboratory.

Most people behave somewhat differently when they are aware that someone is watching them; thus, a limitation of observational methods is that the very fact of being watched may influence behavior, if only subtly. Researchers often try to minimize this bias in one of two ways. One is simply to be as inconspicuous as possible—to blend into the woodwork. The other is to become a participant-observer, interacting naturally with subjects in their environment. Naturalistic observation shares other limitations with the case study method, such as the problem of generalizability. When can a psychologist conclude that after she has seen one baboon troop, she has seen them all? Researcher bias can also pose limitations since observers' theoretical biases can influence what they look for and therefore what they see. As with case studies, this limitation can be minimized by observing several groups of participants or by videotaping interactions, so that more than one judge can independently rate the data.

Finally, like other descriptive studies, naturalistic observation primarily *describes* behaviors; it cannot demonstrate *why* they take place. Based on extensive observation, a psychologist can make a convincing *argument* about the way one variable influences another, but this method does not afford the luxury of doing something to participants and seeing what they do in response, as in experimental designs.

*Jean Piaget observes children on a playground.*

## SURVEY RESEARCH

A third type of descriptive research, **survey research,** involves asking a large sample of people questions, usually about their attitudes or behaviors. For instance, in 1976, a team of researchers embarked on a massive study of over 2200 Americans to see whether conceptions of mental health and attitudes about treatment for emotional problems had changed since the administration of a similar survey 20 years earlier (Veroff et al., 1981). Survey research can yield rigorous quantitative findings by attaching numbers to participants' responses. The researcher might ask people how many times they saw a mental health professional in the last year or to rate the extent to which they believe that seeing a therapist is a sign of weakness on a seven-point scale (where 1 = strongly disagree and 7 = strongly agree). The two most frequently used tools of survey researchers are **questionnaires,** which participants fill out by themselves, and **interviews,** in which researchers ask questions using a standard format.

Selection of the sample is extremely important in survey research. For example, pollsters want to be sure that their predictions of election results accurately reflect a large and heterogeneous population. Researchers typically want a **random sample,** a sample selected from the general population in a relatively arbitrary way that does not introduce any systematic bias. A researcher seeking a random sample of residents of Montreal, for instance, might choose names out of the phone book.

Random selection, however, does not always guarantee that a sample will accurately reflect the **demographic characteristics** (such as gender, race, and socioeconomic status) of the population in which the researcher is interested. A telephone survey based on a random sample of Montreal residents listed in the phone book may overrepresent people who happen to be home answering the phone during the day, such as older people (and underrepresent poor people who do not have a phone). Where proportional representation of different subpopulations is important, researchers select a stratified random sample. A **stratified random sample** specifies the percentage of people to be drawn from each population

**THE FAR SIDE** By GARY LARSON

"So, you're a *real* gorilla, are you? Well, guess you wouldn't mind munchin' down a few beetle grubs, would you? ... In fact, we wanna see you chug 'em!"

category (age, race, etc.) and then randomly selects participants from *within* each category. Researchers often use census data to provide demographic information on the population of interest and then match this information as closely as possible in their sample. The 1976 mental health study was stratified along a number of lines, including age, sex, race, marital status, geographical region, and education.

The major problem with survey methods is that they rely on participants to report on themselves truthfully and accurately. Unfortunately, most people tend to describe their behaviors and attitudes in more flattering terms than others would use to describe them (Greenwald, 1984; John & Robins, 1994). How many people are likely to admit their addiction to *General Hospital* or *Leave It to Beaver* reruns? In part, people's answers may be biased by their conscious efforts to present themselves in the best possible light. They may also unconsciously shade the truth because they want to feel intelligent or psychologically healthy (Shedler, Mayman, & Manis, 1993). In addition, participants may honestly misjudge themselves. Measuring people's attitudes toward the disabled by questionnaire typically indicates much more positive attitudes than does measuring how far they *sit* from a disabled person when entering a room (see Wilson, 1996).

**INTERIM SUMMARY**    **Descriptive methods** describe phenomena as they already exist rather than manipulate variables. A **case study** is an in-depth observation of one person or a group of people. Case studies are useful in generating hypotheses, exploring complex phenomena that are not yet well understood or difficult to examine experimentally, or fleshing out the meaning of quantitative findings. **Naturalistic observation** is the in-depth observation of a phenomenon in its natural setting. It is useful for describing complex phenomena as they exist outside the laboratory. **Survey research** involves asking a large sample of people questions, usually about their attitudes or behavior, through **questionnaires** or **interviews.** By obtaining **random** or **stratified random samples,** psychologists can gain substantial information about a representative sample of the population. Unlike experiments, descriptive methods cannot unambiguously establish cause and effect.

# CORRELATIONAL RESEARCH

The aim of **correlational research** is to determine the degree to which two or more variables are related, so that knowing the value (or score) on one allows prediction of the other. Correlational analyses can be applied to data from experiments, case studies, or naturalistic observation, but most often, correlational designs rely on survey data such as self-reports. Do children who are shy, fearful, and inhibited in the second year of life remain similarly timid and socially uncomfortable when they are older (Schwartz, Snidman, & Kagan, 1996)? Are people who are highly prejudiced more likely to think simply than less prejudiced people, or are prejudice and intellectual sophistication unrelated to each other? These are the kinds of questions that can be addressed using correlational designs.

For example, one study examined the extent to which people who frequently experience one emotion, such as guilt, experience others, such as shame (Izard et al., 1993). Participants completed questionnaires asking them to rate how frequently in their lives they experience various emotions, on a scale from 1 *(never)* to 5 *(very often).* Do people who frequently feel guilty also often feel ashamed, fearful, or angry? To answer this question, the researchers correlated guilt with other emotions. To **correlate** two variables means to assess the extent to which being high or low on one measure predicts being high or low on another. The statistic that allows a researcher to do this is called a correlation coefficient. A **correlation coefficient** measures the extent to which two variables are related (literally,

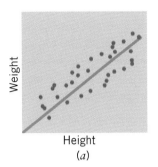 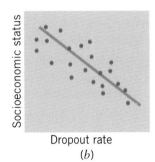 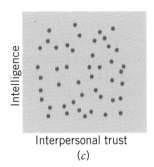

| Height | Dropout rate | Interpersonal trust |
| (a) | (b) | (c) |

**FIGURE 2.6**

(a) Positive, (b) negative, and (c) zero correlations. A correlation expresses the relation between two variables. The panels depict three kinds of correlations on hypothetical scatterplot graphs, which show the way data points fall (are scattered) on two dimensions. Panel (a) shows a positive correlation, between height and weight. A comparison of the dots (which represent individual participants) on the right with those on the left shows that those on the left are lower on both variables. The dots scatter around the line that summarizes them, which is the correlation coefficient. Panel (b) shows a negative correlation, between socioeconomic status and dropout rate from high school. The higher the socioeconomic status, the lower the dropout rate. Panel (c) shows a zero correlation, between intelligence and the extent to which an individual believes people can be trusted. The dots are randomly distributed across the diagram, indicating that being high on one dimension predicts nothing about whether the participant is high or low on the other.

*co-related,* or related to each other). A correlation can be either positive or negative. A **positive correlation** means that the higher individuals measure on one variable, the higher they are likely to measure on the other. This also means, of course, that the lower they score on one variable, the lower they will score on the other. A **negative correlation** means that the higher participants measure on one variable, the *lower* they will measure on the other. Correlations can be depicted on **scatterplot graphs,** which show the scores of every participant along two dimensions (Figure 2.6).

Correlation coefficients vary between +1.0 and –1.0. A strong correlation—one with a value close to either positive or negative 1.0—means that a psychologist who knows a person's score on one variable can confidently predict that person's score on the other. For instance, one would expect a strong negative correlation between level of alcohol in a person's blood and his ability to recite the alphabet backward; the higher the alcohol level, the fewer letters accurately recited backward. A weak correlation hovers close to zero, either on the positive or the negative side. Variables with a correlation close to zero are unrelated and thus cannot be used to predict one another, such as adult weight and IQ score.

To return to the study of emotions, one might hypothesize that people who tend to feel one unpleasant emotion also tend to feel others. That is, guilt, fear, and shame should all be positively correlated with one another. Table 2.3 presents the correlations among various emotions as a **correlation matrix**—a table presenting the correlations among a number of variables. The strongest positive correlation (.61) is between shame and guilt: People who tend to feel guilty also tend to feel ashamed. The negative correlations between joy and the unpleasant emotions are all relatively weak (–.14 to –.30). This suggests, somewhat counterintuitively, that people who frequently experience unpleasant feelings do not necessarily tend to lack positive feelings.

The virtue of correlational research is that it allows investigators to study a whole range of phenomena that vary in nature—from personality characteristics to attitudes—but cannot be produced in the laboratory. Like other nonexperimental methods, however, correlational research can only *describe* relationships among variables (which is why it is actually sometimes categorized as a descriptive method, rather than placed in its own category). When two variables corre-

**TABLE 2.3    CORRELATIONS AMONG VARIOUS EMOTIONS**

|         | GUILT | SHAME | FEAR | JOY |
|---------|-------|-------|------|-----|
| Guilt   | —     | .61   | .54  | −.23 |
| Shame   |       | —     | .51  | −.30 |
| Fear    |       |       | —    | −.14 |
| Joy     |       |       |      | —   |

*Source:* Adapted from Izard et al., 1993.

*Note:* The dashes represent correlations between a variable and itself (e.g., fear with fear), which by definition are 1.0 (a perfect correlation). Note that only half a table is needed to present a correlation matrix because any correlations below the dashes would be redundant, having already been presented elsewhere in the table.

late with each other, the researcher must infer the relation between them: Does one cause the other, or does some third variable explain the correlation?

Media reports on scientific research often disregard or misunderstand the fact that *correlation does not imply causation*. If a study shows a correlation between drug use and poor grades, the media often report that "scientists have found that drug use leads to bad grades." That *may* be true, but an equally likely hypothesis is that some underlying aspect of personality (such as alienation) or home environment (such as poor parenting, abuse, or neglect) produces both drug use *and* bad grades (Shedler & Block, 1990). Similarly, in 1986 the Meese Commission, established by President Ronald Reagan, reviewed the evidence (most of it correlational) linking pornography to violence, particularly crimes against women, and concluded that pornography leads to rape. Just because rapists read pornography, however, does not prove that pornography *leads to* rape. Many people who do not commit rapes also read pornography. In rapists, both pornographic viewing and violent sexual behavior may reflect a third variable, disturbed sexuality (see Mould, 1990).

**INTERIM SUMMARY**    **Correlational research** assesses the degree to which two variables are related; a **correlation coefficient** quantifies the association between two variables. Correlational research can shed important light on the relations among variables, but correlation does not demonstrate causation.

## FROM MIND TO BRAIN

### RESEARCHING THE BRAIN

The methods psychologists use are only as powerful as the technologies and statistical tools that support them. For example, the invention of a seemingly simple mathematical device—the correlation coefficient—set the stage for psychologists to begin answering questions about the influence of heredity on traits such as intelligence, anxiety, and shyness that were previously mere topics of speculation. In the last two decades, a new set of technologies has emerged in one area of psychology that has revolutionized our understanding of human thought and memory: the study of the brain (Barinag, 1997; Posner & Raichle, 1996). Advances in these technologies are proceeding at such a bewildering rate that the next decade may well yield as much new knowledge about the basic mechanisms of human thought, feeling, and behavior as humans have accumulated since the dawn of civilization.

Scientists began studying the functioning of the brain by examining patients who had sustained damage or disease (lesions) to particular neural regions. As noted in Chapter 1, physicians discovered the promise of *lesion studies* in the mid-nineteenth century when they observed patients with left-hemisphere damage who had speech or language impairments. They reasoned that one way to infer what a neural structure normally does is to see what happens when it is *not* working. Experimental psychologists subsequently discovered that they could learn about the function of a particular region by *creating* a lesion in an animal and examining the effects.

In the middle of the present century, neurosurgeons began to learn about the functions of different parts of the brain in humans by stimulating them during surgery using a mild electrical current. This procedure was necessary to "map" the brain of a given patient to avoid damaging essential regions, such as those involved in language. Observing that stimulation of certain regions seemed to yield similar effects *across* patients, researchers began to use this method to learn about the functions of particular neural structures.

Another major advance in understanding the brain came in the 1930s, with the development of the **electroencephalogram,** or **EEG.** The EEG capitalizes on the fact that every time a nerve cell fires it produces a measurable quantity of electrical activity. Researchers can measure this activity in a region of the brain's outer layers by placing electrodes on the scalp. The EEG is frequently used to diagnose disorders such as epilepsy as well as to study neural activity during sleep. It has also been used to examine questions such as whether the two hemispheres of the brain respond differently to stimuli that evoke positive versus negative emotions, which they do (Davidson, 1996).

A major step forward occurred when scientists discovered ways to use X-ray technology and other methods to produce pictures of soft tissue (rather than the familiar bone X-rays), such as the living brain. These **imaging techniques** use computer programs to convert the data taken from brain-scanning devices into visual images of the brain. One of the first such

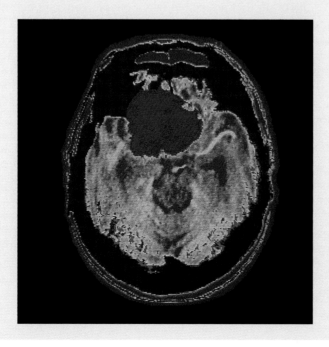

*A CT scan of a patient with a tumor (shown in purple).*

techniques to be developed was **computerized axial tomography,** commonly known as a **CT scan** or **CAT scan.** A CT scanner rotates an X-ray tube around a person's head, producing a series of X-ray pictures. A computer then combines these pictures into a composite visual image. CT scans can pinpoint the location of abnormalities such as neuronal degeneration and abnormal tissue growths (tumors). A related technology, **magnetic resonance imaging (MRI),** can accomplish similar tasks without using X-rays.

A quantum leap forward has occurred with the development of two imaging techniques that actually allow researchers to observe the brain in action rather than simply to detect neural damage. These techniques rely on properties of cells in the brain, such as the amount of blood that flows to cells that have just been activated, that can be measured using sophisticated instruments designed by physicists and engineers. By having participants perform tasks such as solving mathematical problems, watching images, or retrieving memories, researchers are able directly to observe the links between mind and brain. One technique, **positron emission tomography (PET),** requires injection of a small quantity of radioactive glucose (too small a dose to be dangerous) into the bloodstream. Nerve cells use glucose for energy, and they replenish their supply of glucose from the bloodstream. As these cells make use of glucose that has been radioactively "tagged," a computer produces a color portrait of the active parts of the brain. Researchers and clinicians can thus examine ongoing activity in various regions in patients suffering from disorders such as schizophrenia, yielding clues to the structures and pathways in the brain that underlie the symptoms of these diseases (Buchsbaum et al., 1996; Holcomb et al., 1996).

Another technique, called **functional magnetic resonance imaging (fMRI),** uses MRI to watch the brain as the individual carries out tasks such as recognizing an object visually or looking at emotionally evocative pictures (Breiter et al., 1996; Puce et al., 1996). Functional MRI works by exposing the brain to pulses of a phenomenally strong magnet (strong enough to lift a truck) and measuring the response of chemicals in blood cells going to and from various regions, which become momentarily "lined up" in the direction of the magnet. For example, one research team used fMRI to study the parts of the brain that are active when people generate mental images, such as of a horse, an apple, or a house (D'Esposito et al., 1997). When we conjure up a picture of a horse in our minds, do we activate different parts of the brain than when we simply hear about an object but do not picture it? In other words, how are memories *represented* in our brains? Do we actually form visual images, or do we really think in words?

The investigators set out to answer this question by asking seven participants to carry out two tasks with their eyes closed, while their heads were surrounded by the powerful magnet of the MRI scanner. In the first experimental condition, participants listened to 40 concrete words and were asked to try to picture them in their minds. In the second condition, they listened to 40 words that are difficult to picture (such as "treaty" and "guilt") and were asked simply to listen to them. (This is called a *within-subjects* experimental design, because instead of placing each subject in one condition or the other, each subject is exposed to *both* conditions. Differences in the way subjects respond to the two conditions are then compared within, rather than across, subjects.) The experimenters then used fMRI to measure whether the same or different parts of the brain were activated under the two conditions. They hypothesized that when people actually picture objects, their brains would show activity in regions involved in forming and remembering visual images and their meanings, regions that are also acti-

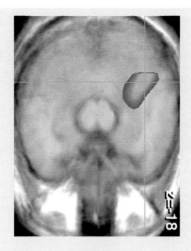

**FIGURE 2.7**
The figure shows an averaged view of the brains of participants in the study using fMRI. The red area indicates the region of the brain that, on average, showed the highest activation in the visual imagery condition after subtracting out activation that occurred in the non-imagery condition; in other words, this region showed significantly more activation while participants were forming mental images than when performing a control task.

vated when people actually see an object, such as a horse. When people just hear words, in contrast, these vision centers should not be active. That is precisely what the investigators found, as can be seen in Figure 2.7.

Researchers are still a long way from mapping the micro-details of the brain. The *resolution*, or sharpness, of the images produced by most scanning techniques is still too fuzzy to allow psychologists to pinpoint, for example, the different neural networks activated when a person feels guilty versus sad or angry. Further, people's brains differ, so that a single map will not work precisely for every person; averaging the responses of several participants can thus sometimes lead to imprecise results. Nevertheless, if progress made in the last decade is any indication, imaging techniques will continue to increase in precision at a dazzling pace, and so will our knowledge of mind and brain.

## A GLOBAL VISTA

### CROSS-CULTURAL RESEARCH

To some degree, human nature is the same everywhere because the brain and its genetic blueprints are so similar. But the *expression* of those blueprints can be as varied as an adobe hut and a high-rise apartment. Determining the extent to which psychological findings in one culture apply to people around the globe presents challenges as important and difficult as brain mapping.

Like anthropological fieldwork, in which an investigator lives in another culture and observes daily events, many cross-cultural investigations involve naturalistic observation, usually supplemented with quantitative methods. For example, when Western researchers wanted to explore the origins of social behavior in infants reared in a culture very different from their own, they studied Efe pygmies in the tropical rain forests of Zaire, who survive by hunting, gathering food, and trading with neighboring agricultural peoples (Tronick et al., 1992). The Efe establish camps composed of huts arranged in a semicircle, usually consisting of about 20 people. Researchers armed with laptop computers recorded minute-by-minute observations of the social life of Efe infants and toddlers in the camps. They found that, unlike Western children, who are groomed for independence, Efe children are

*Among the Efe, as in many cultures, children are rarely alone.*

surrounded by other people virtually every hour of their lives, preparing them well for a communal lifestyle as adults.

Other researchers rely on correlational and experimental methods to investigate psychological phenomena across cultures. In the 1940s anthropologists created the Human Relations Area Files, a database on hundreds of cultures taken from detailed observations by anthropologists. The information is indexed under categories such as supernatural beliefs, treatment of outsiders, rituals, infant care, and childrearing practices. This allows researchers to test hypotheses by correlating variables with each other across cultures, asking questions such as, "Do cultures that treat children harshly tend to have physically violent adults?" (Ember, 1997; Naroll et al., 1976). Studies since the 1950s have examined the correlations between various childrearing variables and cultural practices (Whiting & Child, 1953). For example, harsh childhood discipline correlates with beliefs in evil deities (Rohner, 1986). Apparently, cultural views of the gods are not independent of children's views of the godlike figures in their lives—their parents. Cross-cultural psychologists have also applied experimental procedures in other countries to test whether the findings of Western studies on phenomena replicate cross-culturally (see Berry et al., 1992, 1997; Triandis, 1994).

Psychologists interested in the cross-cultural validity of their theories face many difficulties, however, in transporting research from one culture to another. The same stimulus may mean very different things to people in different cultures. How might people from Bali, whose culture emphasizes *control* of emotions in the face of events such as grief, respond to instructions to describe a stressful event in full emotional detail in a study of emotional expression and health? Would they comply, or would this experimental situation itself be stressful because it forced them to violate a cultural norm? Or how might people from a culture like the Efe, who have had minimal exposure to photographs, respond to a study asking them to judge what emotion people are feeling from pictures of faces? Creating an equivalent experimental design often requires using a *different* design, but then is it really the same experiment?

Similarly, when employing a questionnaire cross-culturally, researchers must be very careful about translation because even minor changes or ambiguities could make cross-cultural comparisons invalid. To minimize distortions in translation, researchers use a procedure called back-translation, in which a bilingual speaker translates the items into the target language, and another bilingual speaker translates it back into the original language (usually English). The speakers then repeat the process until the translation back into English matches the original. Even this procedure is not always adequate; sometimes concepts simply differ too much across cultures to make the items equivalent. Asking a participant to rate the item "I have a good relationship with my brother" would be inappropriate in Japan, where speakers distinguish between older and younger brothers and lack a general term to denote both (Brislin, 1986). Once again reality poses obstacles to research, but we have to try to hurdle them if we want to learn about the psychology of *people* rather than of particular *peoples*.

**INTERIM SUMMARY**     Researchers study the relation between mental and neural processes using a number of methods, including case studies of patients with brain damage, experimental lesion studies with animals, **electroencephalograms (EEGs),** and computerized **imaging techniques** that allow researchers to study the brain in action, such as **CT, PET,** and **fMRI.** The aim of cross-cultural research is to assess the extent to which psychological processes vary across cultures. Researchers studying psychological phenomena cross-culturally use a variety of methods, including naturalistic observation, correlational studies linking one cultural trait to another, and experiments.

# HOW TO EVALUATE A STUDY CRITICALLY

Having explored the major research designs, we now turn to the question of how to be an informed consumer of research. In deciding whether to "buy" the results of a study, the same maxim applies as in buying a car: *caveat emptor,* let the buyer beware. The popular media often report that "researchers at Harvard have found . . ." followed by conclusions that are tempting to take at face value. In reality, most studies have their limitations. To evaluate a study critically, the reader should examine the research carefully and attempt to answer seven broad questions (Figure 2.8).

## DOES THE THEORETICAL FRAMEWORK MAKE SENSE?

The first step in evaluating a study is to consider whether the theory and the specific hypothesis to be tested make sense. Do the authors specify precisely what they mean by the concepts they use? Do all definitions of a key concepts refer to the same thing? For example, if the study explores the relation between social class and intelligence, does the article explain why social class and intelligence should have some relationship to each other? Do the authors clearly and consistently define both social class and intelligence?

## IS THE SAMPLE ADEQUATE AND APPROPRIATE?

The next step is to examine the sample and determine if it adequately represents the population from which it is drawn. If researchers want to know about emotional expression and health in undergraduates, then a sample of undergraduates is perfectly appropriate. If they want to generalize to other populations, however, they need to use other samples, such as adults drawn from the local community, or people from Bali, to see if the effects hold. Another important issue is whether

1. Assess the study's theoretical framework.

   Does the theory make sense?
   Does the hypothesis make sense?
   Are terms defined logically and consistently?

2. Assess the adequacy and appropriateness of the sample.

   Is it representative of the population of interest?
   Is it of sufficient size to test the hypothesis?

3. Assess the adequacy of the measures and procedures.

   Are the measures reliable and valid?
   Did the investigators properly control confounding
      variables?

4. Examine the data.

   Do the data demonstrate what the authors claim?
   Could the data be explained some other way?

5. Examine the conclusions drawn by the investigators.

   Do the conclusions follow from the data?
   Does the study have limitations that affect the
      interpretation or generalizability of the findings?
   Can the findings be understood in the context of
      previous research?

6. Consider the meaningfulness of the study.

   Does the study pass the "so what" test?
   Do the theory and data shed any new light on the
      phenomenon under investigation?

7. Evaluate the ethics of the study.

   Did the costs outweigh the benefits?
   Did the investigators carefully consider the welfare
      of human and animal subjects?

**FIGURE 2.8**
Steps in evaluating a study critically. Examining a study critically means considering every aspect of the investigation, from the theory underlying it to its ethics.

the sample is large enough to allow for adequate statistical tests of the findings' significance (Chapter 2 Supplement).

### WERE THE MEASURES AND PROCEDURES ADEQUATE?

The third broad question is whether the measures and procedures were well suited to the hypothesis being tested. Do the measures assess what they were designed to assess? Were proper control groups chosen to rule out alternative explanations and to assure the validity of the study? Did the investigators fail to notice any confounding variables that might have influenced the results? For example, if the study involved interviewing participants, were some of the interviewers male and some female? If so, did the gender of the interviewer affect how participants responded?

### ARE THE DATA CONCLUSIVE?

Another step in evaluating a study is to examine the data presented. Do they demonstrate what the author claims? Typically, data in research articles are presented in a section entitled "Results," usually in the form of graphs, charts, or tables. In evaluating a study critically, the reader should carefully examine the data presented in these figures and ask whether any alternative interpretations could explain the results as well as or better than the researcher's explanation. Often, data permit many interpretations, and the findings may fit a pattern that the researcher rejected or did not consider.

### ARE THE BROADER CONCLUSIONS WARRANTED?

Still another question is whether the researcher's broad conclusions fit both the theory presented and the data of the study. Does the study have limitations that render the conclusions invalid or applicable only under certain circumstances? An experiment may nicely test a phenomenon in a very specific domain, but then the investigator may try to generalize the findings to other areas with different properties. A reader should be wary of a research article that describes the effects of overcrowding on rats and then tries to draw broad conclusions about the need for human population control.

## DOES THE STUDY SAY ANYTHING MEANINGFUL?

The sixth question in evaluating a study is the "so what?" test: Are the results meaningful? Does the study tell us anything we did not already know? Does it lead to questions for future research? The meaningfulness of a study depends in part on the importance, usefulness, and adequacy of the theoretical perspective from which it derives. Important studies also tend to produce findings that are in some way surprising or help choose between theories that offer opposing predictions.

## IS THE STUDY ETHICAL?

A final question concerns ethics. If the study uses human or animal subjects, does it treat them humanely, and do the ends of the study—the incremental knowledge it produces—justify the means? The study of emotional expression and health required that the investigators have access to participants' medical records. Given the unreliability of self-reports of doctor visits, this seems justified, but the researchers no doubt took extra measures to assure confidentiality, such as requesting permission from participants to find out the *number* of visits but not specific details.

Individual psychologists were once free to make ethical determinations on their own, and the vast majority have always carefully considered the welfare of participants in designing studies. Today, however, the American Psychological Association (APA) publishes guidelines that govern psychological research practices (APA, 1973, 1997), and universities and other institutions have boards that review proposals for psychological studies, with the power to reject them on ethical grounds.

▶ ONE STEP FURTHER

### *Ethical Questions Come in Shades of Gray*

The ethical issues involved in research are not always black and white. For example, in 1991, Jacob, Krahn, and Leonard published a study of problem solving in alcoholic fathers and their adolescent children. Participants were offered a sizable honorarium, or payment, to participate in the study ($400). During one procedure, alcoholic beverages were made available to participants in order to explore the impact of alcohol consumption on the parent–child interaction. Not surprisingly, the alcoholics availed themselves of this opportunity, with a mean consumption of 3.4 ounces.

The study itself was very strong methodologically and overcame numerous problems of previous research. For instance, many studies have used college students as participants. Yet even college students who display symptoms of alcohol abuse may not be a representative sample. Some students abuse alcohol during college because of its novelty, peer pressure, and cultural norms of college behavior but later have normal drinking patterns. Studies that *have* used actual alcoholics as participants have often relied on self-reports. Unfortunately, self-reports of alcohol consumption are notoriously unreliable among alcoholics, who may be unwilling or unable (because of denial or memory lapses) to provide accurate information. Thus, Jacob and colleagues could argue that their study was of particular value in offering new insights into an important topic.

Other psychologists, however, expressed concerns about the ethics of the research. The study essentially paid alcoholics to drink, thereby colluding in a disorder that has substantial negative consequences for families (Koocher, 1991; Stricker, 1991). As one commentator noted, $400 is a substantial payment for participation in a study, especially since roughly one-quarter of the participants were unemployed (Koocher, 1991). Jacob and colleagues responded that they had safeguarded the welfare of the participants in a number of ways, such as sending them home in taxis to prevent them from driving under the influence (Jacob & Leonard, 1991). Furthermore, most participants drank less than two drinks during the procedure, hardly an amount likely to influence the lives of men who had been drinking heavily for 10 to 20 years. Nevertheless, this example demonstrates the ambiguity that sometimes arises when researchers are confronted with ethical decisions.

## Deception in Psychological Research

Many studies keep participants blind to the aims of the investigation until the end; some even deceive participants, giving them a "cover story" so that demand characteristics will not bias their responses. For example, in one experiment researchers wanted to study the conditions under which people can be induced to make false confessions (Kassin & Kiechel, 1996). They led college student participants to believe that they would be taking a typing test with another participant, who was really an accomplice, or *confederate*, of the experimenters. The experimenters explicitly instructed the participants not to touch the ALT key on the computer, since that would allegedly make the computer crash, and all data would be lost. Sixty seconds into the task, the computer seemed to stop functioning, and the experimenter rushed into the room accusing the participant of having hit the forbidden key. To assess whether false incriminating evidence could convince people that they had actually done something wrong, in one condition the confederate (allegedly simply waiting to take the test herself) "admitted" having seen the participant hit the ALT key; in a control condition, the accomplice denied having seen anything. The striking finding was that in the experimental condition about half of the participants came to believe that they *had* hit the key and destroyed the experiment. Obviously, if they had known what the experiment was really about, the experiment would not have worked.

From an ethical standpoint, the use of deception raises questions about **informed consent**—the participant's ability to agree (or refuse) to participate in an informed manner. Can individuals really give informed consent to participate in a study whose aims they do not know? Some psychologists argue that "the use of intentional deception in the research setting is unethical, imprudent, and unwarranted scientifically" (Baumrind, 1985). Others, however, point to evidence demonstrating that participants in deception experiments actually tend to enjoy the experience more, learn more from their participation, and rarely object to the deception when they are "debriefed" at the end (Christensen, 1988).

Only a small proportion of experiments actually involve deception, and APA guidelines permit deception only if a study meets four conditions: (1) The research is of great importance and cannot be conducted without the use of deception; (2) participants can be expected to find the procedures reasonable once they are informed of them after the experiment is completed; (3) participants can withdraw from the experiment at any time; and (4) experimenters debrief the participants afterward, explaining the purposes of the study and removing any stressful aftereffects. Many universities address the issue of deception by asking potential participants if they would object to being deceived temporarily in a study. That way, any participant who is deceived by an experimenter has given prior consent to be deceived.

### Ethics and Animal Research

A larger ethical controversy concerns the use of nonhuman animals for psychological research (Bowd & Shapiro, 1993; Ulrich, 1991). By lesioning a region of a rat's brain, for example, researchers can sometimes learn a tremendous amount about the function of similar regions in the human brain. Such experiments, however, have an obvious cost to the animal, raising questions about the moral status of animals, that is, whether they have rights (Plous, 1996; Rollin, 1985). Again the issue is how to balance costs and benefits: To what extent do the costs to animals justify the benefits to humans? The problem, of course, is that, unlike humans, animals cannot give informed consent.

To what extent can humans use, and even breed, other sentient creatures (that is, animals who feel) to satisfy intellectual or other human interests? Groups such as Mobilization for Animals (1984) argue that animal research in psychology has produced little of value to humans, especially considering the enormous suffering animals have undergone. Most psychologists dispute this claim (Miller, 1985). They note that animal research has led to important advances in behavioral therapy, biofeedback, and potential treatments for serious disorders such as Alzheimer's disease (a degenerative brain illness that ultimately leads to death). Animal research has also contributed to the understanding of such phenomena as stress, weight gain, and the effects of aging on learning and memory. The difficulty lies in balancing the interests of humans with those of other animals and advancing science while staying within sensible ethical boundaries (Bowd, 1990). Accordingly, institutional review boards examine proposals for experiments with nonhuman animals as they do with human participants and may similarly veto proposals they deem unethical.    ◄

**INTERIM SUMMARY**    To evaluate a study, a critical reader should ask a number of broad questions, including whether the study's theoretical framework makes sense and the hypotheses flow sensibly from it, the sample is appropriate, the measures and procedures are valid and reliable, the data fit the theory, and the results are meaningful. An additional concern is whether the study is ethical. Whether a study entails deception or poses potential harm to humans or other animals, the ethical question is one of weighing potential costs against benefits.

## SOME CONCLUDING THOUGHTS

As we have seen, psychological research has the power to tackle questions that have seemed unanswerable for centuries. Can talking about unpleasant experiences reduce the risk of illness? Yes. Is the brain equipped to produce mental images that people can generate from memory and scan as they try to find their way around a new city? Yes. Is psychology essentially the same cross-culturally, or do humans think, feel, and behave in entirely different ways depending on their culture? Neither. These are solid answers that only solid empirical procedures could have provided.

At the outset we posed a series of questions. How do the theoretical perspectives psychologists adopt affect the methods they choose? What methods—or combination of methods—provide the most conclusive results? What do we gain and what do we lose when we "domesticate" a psychological phenomenon and bring it into the laboratory? And how do we know when we have asked the right questions in the first place?

Psychologists with a behavioral or cognitive orientation are almost uniformly committed to experimental investigation. The philosopher of science Karl Popper (1963), among others, has argued that the criterion that distinguishes science from other practices (and from mere speculation) is the formulation and evaluation of testable hypotheses that can be refuted if they are untrue. Preferably, these hypotheses should not be intuitively obvious, so they can put a theory to the test. From this standpoint, the behaviorist and cognitive perspectives have the greatest scientific support, although psychodynamic and evolutionary psychologists are increasingly relying on experimental methods.

The phenomena that most readily lend themselves to experimental investigation, however, are not necessarily the most important to study. For instance, as we saw in Chapter 1, researchers have offered competing theories for over a century about the extent to which specific parts of the brain perform specific functions. We now know that many functions are, in fact, localized to specific structures and pathways, although most functions are distributed across circuits in many parts of the brain, not just a single region. The question of how the brain is organized was no less important before the advent of brain imaging techniques than after, and researchers did the best they could with the technologies available, such as lesion and EEG studies. Similarly, based on case studies, psychodynamic theorists have asserted for a century that much of human mental life is unconscious. We did not have the technologies to test that proposition adequately, either, until the last 15 years, but it turned out to be correct.

Should a hypothesis be discarded simply because it is difficult to assess? To do so would confuse the truth-value of a hypothesis with its testability. A sophisticated theory of human nature may include many accurate propositions that are difficult to test empirically precisely because humans are complex creatures, and psychology is only a century old. Science, like all human cognition, involves constructing a story, or a map, of a phenomenon we want to understand, using all the information at our disposal. That means tentatively accepting hypotheses supported by our strongest methods, even more tentatively holding other theoretical beliefs that have *some* basis in more limited methods, and gradually weeding out those beliefs that do not withstand closer scientific scrutiny when the technologies are available to test them.

In its broadest sense, a scientific, empiricist attitude in psychology means keeping one's eyes wide open in as many settings as possible and constantly testing what one believes. Philosophers of science sometimes distinguish between the **context of discovery** (in which phenomena are observed, hypotheses are framed, and theories are built) and the **context of justification** (in which hypotheses are tested empirically). Case studies, naturalistic observation, and surveys are often most useful in the context of discovery precisely because the investigator is *not* structuring the situation. The more experimenters exert control, the less they see unconstrained behavior—behavior as it occurs in nature. Descriptive methods often foster the kind of exploration that leads researchers to ask the right questions. In the context of justification, where hypotheses are put to the test, the best designs are experimental, quasi-experimental, and sometimes correlational. By using inferential statistics, researchers can assess the likelihood that their theories and hypotheses have merit.

The road to psychological knowledge is paved in many directions. Just as an optimal study uses multiple measures, so an optimal science of mental life and behavior uses multiple methods of observation. The remainder of this text examines the discoveries to which the various methods have led, beginning with the biological bases of mental processes and behavior.

**INTERIM SUMMARY**    Descriptive methods tend to be most useful in the **context of scientific discovery,** whereas experimental methods tend to be most useful in the **context of justification.** A scientific, empiricist attitude means using whatever methods one can to study a phenomenon, continually testing one's hypotheses, and applying experimental and quasi-experimental methods wherever possible to assess cause and effect.

# SUMMARY

## CHARACTERISTICS OF GOOD PSYCHOLOGICAL RESEARCH

1. Good psychological research typically has a number of features: a theoretical framework, standardized procedures, generalizability, and objective measurement.

2. A **theory** is a systematic way of organizing and explaining observations that includes a set of propositions about the relations among various phenomena. A **hypothesis** is a tentative belief or educated guess that purports to predict or explain the relationship between two or more **variables;** variables are phenomena that differ or change across circumstances or individuals. A variable that can be placed on a continuum is a **continuous variable.** A variable comprised of groupings or categories is a **categorical variable.**

3. A **sample** is a subgroup of a **population** that is likely to be **representative** of the population as a whole. **Generalizability** refers to the applicability of findings based on a sample to the entire population of interest. For a study's findings to be generalizable, its methods must be sound, or **valid.**

4. A **measure** is a concrete way of assessing a variable. A good measure is both reliable and valid. **Reliability** refers to a measure's ability to produce consistent results. The **validity** of a measure refers to its ability to assess the construct it is intended to measure.

## EXPERIMENTAL RESEARCH

5. In **experimental research,** investigators manipulate some aspect of a situation and examine the impact on the way participants respond in order to assess cause and effect. **Independent variables** are the variables the experimenter manipulates; **dependent variables** are the participants' responses, which indicate if the manipulation had an effect.

6. Conducting a study entails a series of steps: framing a hypothesis, operationalizing variables, developing a standardized procedure, selecting participants, testing the results for statistical significance, and drawing conclusions. **Operationalizing** means turning an abstract concept into a concrete variable defined by some set of actions, or operations.

7. A **control group** is a neutral condition of an experiment in which participants are not exposed to the experimental manipulation. Researchers frequently perform **blind studies,** in which participants are kept unaware of, or "blind" to, important aspects of the research. In a **single-blind study,** only participants are kept blind; in **double-blind studies,** participants and researchers alike are blind.

8. A **confounding variable** is a variable that could produce effects that might be confused with the effects of the independent variable.

9. Limitations of experimental studies include the difficulty of bringing com-

plex phenomena into the laboratory, the question of external validity (applicability of the results to phenomena in the real world), and limited possibility of exploring personal meanings. An **interpretive** stance on methodology argues that the aim of a science of human action is not the *prediction* of behavior but the *understanding* of the highly idiosyncratic personal meanings that lead to an individual's actions.

## DESCRIPTIVE RESEARCH

10. Unlike experimental studies, **descriptive** methods cannot unambiguously demonstrate cause and effect. They describe phenomena as they already exist rather than manipulate variables to test the effects. Descriptive methods include case studies, naturalistic observation, and survey research.

11. A **case study** is an in-depth observation of one person or a small group of people. **Naturalistic observation** is the in-depth observation of a phenomenon in its natural setting. Both case studies and naturalistic observation are vulnerable to researcher bias—the tendency of investigators to see what they expect to see. **Survey research** involves asking a large sample of people questions, often about attitudes or behaviors, using **questionnaires** or **interviews.**

## CORRELATIONAL RESEARCH

12. **Correlational research** assesses the degree to which two variables are related, in an effort to see whether knowing the value of one can lead to prediction of the other. A **correlation coefficient** measures the extent to which two variables are related; it may be positive or negative. A **positive correlation** between two variables means that the higher individuals measure on one variable, the higher they are likely to measure on the other. A **negative correlation** means that the higher individuals measure on one variable, the lower they will measure on the other, and vice versa. *Correlation does not demonstrate causation.*

13. Researchers studying the relation between mental and neural processes use a number of methods, including case studies of patients with brain damage, experimental lesion studies with animals, **electroencephalograms (EEGs),** and computerized **imaging techniques,** such as **CT, PET,** and **fMRI.**

14. Researchers studying psychological phenomena cross-culturally use a variety of methods, including naturalistic observation, correlational studies linking one cultural trait to another, and experiments.

## HOW TO EVALUATE A STUDY CRITICALLY

15. To evaluate a study, a critical reader should answer several broad questions: (1) Is the study's theoretical framework sensible, and do the hypotheses flow sensibly from it? (2) Is the sample adequate and appropriate? (3) Were the measures and procedures valid and reliable? (4) Are the data conclusive? (5) Are the broader conclusions warranted? (6) Does the study say anything meaningful? (7) Is the study ethical?

## SOME CONCLUDING THOUGHTS

16. Where they can be used, experimental methods are the strongest, but the optimal path to psychological knowledge is through the use of multiple methods.

# Statistical Principles In Psychological Research

---

Statistics are far more intuitive than most people believe, even to people who do not consider mathematics their strong suit. As described in Chapter 2, psychologists use descriptive statistics to summarize quantitative data in an understandable form. They employ inferential statistics to tell whether the results reflect anything other than chance. We discuss each in turn.

## SUMMARIZING THE DATA: DESCRIPTIVE STATISTICS

The first step in describing participants' responses on a variable is usually to chart a frequency distribution. A **frequency distribution** is exactly what it sounds like—a method of organizing the data to show how frequently participants received each of the many possible scores. In other words, a frequency distribution represents the way scores were distributed across the sample. The kind of frequency distribution that a professor might observe on a midterm examination (in a very small class, for illustration) is shown in Table 2S.1 and again graphically in Figure 2S.1. The graph, called a **histogram**, plots ranges of scores along the $x$ axis and the frequency of scores in each range on the $y$ axis. The rounded-out version of the histogram drawn with a line is the familiar "curve."

### MEASURES OF CENTRAL TENDENCY

Perhaps the most important descriptive statistics are **measures of central tendency,** which provide an index of the way a typical participant responded on a

| TABLE 2S.1    DISTRIBUTION OF TEST SCORES ON A MIDTERM EXAMINATION |
|---|
| 98 |
| 92 |
| 87 |
| 87 |
| 84 |
| 78 |
| 74 |
| 70 |
| 60 |
| 730 |

$$\text{Mean} = \frac{730\,(\text{total of scores})}{9\,(\text{number of students})} = 81.1$$

*Note:* The mean is the average of all scores (in this case, 81.1). The mode is the most common score (87). The median is the score in the middle of the distribution, with half of all scores above it and half below it (84).

"How do you expect me to average 55 miles an hour if I don't speed?"

measure. The three most common measures of central tendency are the mean, the mode, and the median. The **mean** is simply the statistical average of the scores of all participants, computed by adding up all the participants' scores and dividing by the number of participants. The mean is the most commonly reported measure of central tendency and is the most intuitively descriptive of the average participant.

Sometimes, however, the mean may be misleading. For example, suppose as part of a larger study a team of researchers wanted to know how much money the typical rural family in Peru earns per year. Now suppose they found, in a sample of ten families, that eight earned $2000 per year, one earned $100,000 per year, and one earned $300,000 (Table 2S.2). Relying strictly on mean income as the measure of central tendency, the researcher would conclude that rural Peruvians are, on the average, a wealthy bunch, with a mean annual income of $41,600. However, this would obviously misrepresent the majority, whose meager incomes were averaged in with their wealthy landowning neighbors.

**FIGURE 2S.1**
Histogram showing a frequency distribution of test scores. A frequency distribution shows graphically the frequency of each score (how many times it occurs) distributed across the sample.

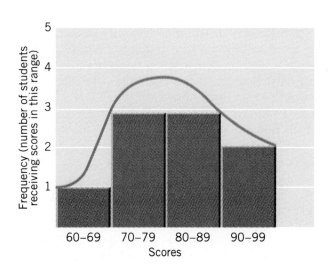

**TABLE 2S.2**    **WHEN A MEAN IS MISLEADING**

| FAMILY NUMBER | ANNUAL INCOME (IN DOLLARS) | | | |
|:---:|:---:|---|---|---|
| 1 | 2,000 | | | |
| 2 | 2,000 | | | |
| 3 | 2,000 | | | |
| 4 | 100,000 | | | |
| 5 | 2,000 | | | |
| 6 | 2,000 | | | |
| 7 | 2,000 | | | |
| 8 | 300,000 | | | |
| 9 | 2,000 | $\text{Mean} = \dfrac{\text{sum of all incomes}}{\text{number of families}} = \dfrac{\$416{,}000}{10} = \$41{,}600$ | | | |
| 10 | 2,000 | Mode = $2000 | | |

In this case, both the mode and the median would be more useful measures of central tendency, because a mean can be strongly influenced by extreme and unusual scores in a sample. The **mode** (or *modal score*) refers to the most *common* score observed in the sample. In this case, $2000 is the modal income because eight of ten families had an income of $2000. In Table 2S.1, the modal test score is 87, whereas the mean is 81.1. One or two students with particularly low scores pulled down the class mean. The mode, however, can be a misleading measure of central tendency if the sample has more than one frequent score and these frequent scores are far apart from one another. In the Peruvian example what if five families had an income of $2000 and four had an income of $40,000. The mode would be $2000 but would not really be representative of the whole sample.

The **median** refers to the score that falls in the middle of the distribution of scores, with half scoring below and half above it. Reporting the median essentially allows one to ignore extreme scores on each end of the distribution that

*In Peru as in much of Latin America, mean income is a misleading measure of central tendency.*

**TABLE 2S.3   THE STANDARD DEVIATION**

| SCORE | DEVIATION FROM THE MEAN | D² |
|-------|------------------------|-----|
| 98 | 98 – 91 = 7 | 49 |
| 94 | 94 – 91 = 3 | 9 |
| 91 | 91 – 91 = 0 | 0 |
| 87 | 87 – 91 = –4 | 16 |
| 85 | 85 – 91 = –6 | 36 |
| 455 | 0 | 110 |

$$\text{Mean} = 455/5 = 91$$

$$\text{Standard deviation} = \frac{\sqrt{\Sigma D^2}}{N} = \frac{\sqrt{110}}{5} = \frac{\sqrt{22}}{5} = 4.7$$

*Note:* The table presents the scores of five students on an examination (column 1). Computing a standard deviation is actually quite intuitive. The first step is to calculate the mean score, which in this case is 91. The next step is to calculate the difference, or deviation, between each participant's score and the mean score, as shown in column 2. The standard deviation is the average deviation of participants from the mean. The only complication is that taking the average of the deviations always produces a mean deviation of zero because the sum of deviations is by definition zero (see the total in column 2). Thus, the next step is to square the deviations (column 3). The standard deviation is then computed by taking the square root of the sum of all the squared differences, divided by the number of participants.

would bias a portrait of the typical participant. In the Peruvian example in which eight of ten families lived on $2000 per year, median income, like modal income, is $2000 because $2000 falls in the middle of the distribution. Half of the families sampled earn $2000 or less, and half earn $2000 or more, even though those who are wealthier earn *substantially* more. The median test score on the midterm examination in Table 2S.1 is 84; half the scores fall above and half below.

## VARIABILITY

As the above examples demonstrate, another important descriptive statistic is a measure of the **variability** of scores, that is, how much participants' scores differ from one another. Variability influences the choice of measure of central tendency. The simplest measure of variability is the **range** of scores, which refers to the difference between the highest and the lowest value observed on the variable. In the Peruvian case, values of the income variable run from $2000 to $300,000, for a range of $298,000.

The range can be a biased estimate of variability, however, in much the same way as the mean can be a biased estimate of central tendency. Income does range considerably in this sample, but for the majority of Peruvians studied, variability is minimal (ranging from $2000 to $2000—no variability at all). Hence, a more useful measure is the **standard deviation (SD),** which again is just what it sounds like: the amount that the average participant deviates from the mean of the sample. Table 2S.3 shows how to compute a standard deviation.

## THE NORMAL DISTRIBUTION

When researchers collect data on continuous variables (such as weight or IQ) and plot them on a histogram, the data usually approximate a normal distribution, like the distribution of IQ scores shown in Figure 2S.2. In a **normal distribution,**

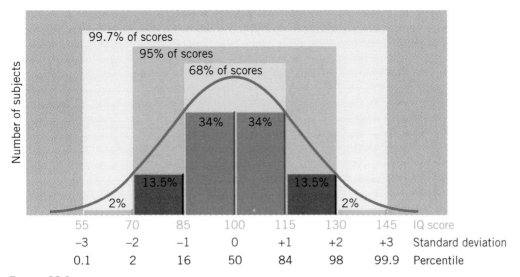

**FIGURE 2S.2**
A normal distribution. IQ scores approximate a normal distribution, which looks like a bell-shaped curve; 68 percent of scores fall within one standard deviation of the mean (represented by the area under the curve in blue). The curve is a smoothed-out version of a histogram. An individual's score can be represented alternatively by the number of standard deviations it diverges from the mean in either direction or by a percentile score, which shows the percentage of scores that fall below it (to the left on the graph).

the scores of most participants fall in the middle of the bell-shaped distribution, and progressively fewer participants have scores at either extreme. In other words, most individuals are about average on most dimensions, and very few are extremely above or below average. Thus, most people have an IQ around average (100), whereas very few have an IQ of 70 or 130. In a distribution of scores that is completely normal, the mean, mode, and median are all the same.

Participants' scores on a variable that is normally distributed can be described in terms of how far they are from average, that is, their deviation from the mean. Thus, a person's IQ could be described either as 85 or as one standard deviation below the mean, for the standard deviation in IQ is about 15. A participant two standard deviations below the mean would have an IQ of 70, which is bordering on mental retardation. For normal data, 68 percent of participants fall within one standard deviation of the mean (34 percent on either side of it), 95 percent fall within two standard deviations, and over 99.7 percent fall within three standard deviations. Thus, an IQ above 145 is a very rare occurrence.

Knowing the relation between standard deviations and percentages of participants whose scores lie within different parts of a distribution allows researchers to report **percentile scores,** which indicate the percentage of scores that fall below a score. Thus, a participant whose score is three standard deviations above the mean is in the 99.7th percentile, whereas an average participant (whose score does not deviate from the mean) is in the 50th percentile.

**INTERIM SUMMARY**     Descriptive statistics allows researchers to summarize data in a readily understandable form. The first step in describing the data is often to provide a **frequency distribution,** which shows how frequently participants received each of the many possible scores. The most important descriptive statistics are **measures of central tendency,** which provide an index of the way a typical participant responded on a measure. The **mean** is the statistical average of the scores of all participants; the **mode** is the most common score; the **median** is the score that falls in the middle of the distribution. Another important descriptive statistic is **variability,** which refers to the extent to which participants tend to differ from one another. The **standard deviation** describes how much the average participant deviates from the mean. When psychologists collect data on continuous variables, they often find that the data approximate a **normal distribution,** with most scores toward the middle. Participants' scores on a normally distributed variable can be described in terms of the number of standard deviations from the mean or as **percentile scores,** which indicate the percentage of scores that fall below them.

# TESTING THE HYPOTHESIS: INFERENTIAL STATISTICS

When researchers find a difference between the responses of participants in one condition and another, they must infer whether these differences likely occurred by chance or reflect a true causal relationship. Similarly, if they discover a correlation between two variables, they need to know the likelihood that the two variables simply correlated by chance. As the philosopher David Hume (1711–1776) demonstrated two centuries ago, we can never be entirely sure about the answer to questions like these. If someone believes that all swans are white and observes 99 swans that are white and none that are not, can the person conclude with certainty that the hundredth swan will also be white? The issue is one of probability: If the person has observed a representative sample of swans, what is the likelihood that, given 99 white swans, a black one will emerge next?

## STATISTICAL SIGNIFICANCE

Psychologists typically deal with this issue in their research by using tests of **statistical significance.** These procedures determine whether the results of a study are likely to have occurred simply by chance (and thus cannot be meaningfully generalized to a population) or whether they reflect true properties of the population. Statistical significance should not be confused with practical or theoretical significance. A researcher may demonstrate with a high degree of certainty that, on the average, females spend less time watching football than males, but who cares? Statistical significance means only that a finding is unlikely to be an accident of chance.

Beyond describing the data, then, the researcher's second task in presenting and analyzing data is to draw inferences from the sample to the population as a whole. Inferential statistics help sort out whether or not the findings of a study really show anything. Researchers usually report the likelihood that their results mean something in terms of a **probability value** (or **p-value**). A *p*-value represents the probability that any positive findings obtained with the sample (such as differences between two experimental conditions) were just a matter of chance. In other words, a *p*-value is an index of the probability that positive findings obtained would not apply to the population and instead reflect only the peculiar characteristics of the particular sample.

*How many swans must one observe before concluding that all swans are white?*

**TABLE 2S.4   CHILDREN'S PROSOCIAL RESPONSE TO ANOTHER PERSON'S DISTRESS DURING THE SECOND YEAR OF LIFE**

| | PERCENTAGE OF EPISODES IN WHICH THE CHILD BEHAVED PROSOCIALLY | | |
|---|---|---|---|
| TYPE OF INCIDENT | TIME 1 | TIME 2 | TIME 3 |
| Witnessed distress | 9 | 21 | 49 |
| Caused distress | 7 | 10 | 52 |

*Source:* Adapted from Zahn-Waxler et al., 1992.

To illustrate, one study tested the hypothesis that children increasingly show signs of morality and empathy during their second year of life (Zahn-Waxler et al., 1992). The investigators trained 27 mothers to dictate into a tape recorder reports of any episode in which their one-year-olds either witnessed distress (e.g., seeing the mother burning herself on the stove) or caused distress (e.g., pulling the cat's tail, teasing a sibling, or biting the mother's breast while nursing). The mothers dictated descriptions of these events over the course of the next year; each report included an account of the way the child responded to the other person's distress. Coders then rated the child's behavior using categories such as prosocial behavior, defined as efforts to help the person in distress.

Table 2S.4 shows the percentage of times the child behaved prosocially during these episodes at each of three periods: time 1 (13–15 months of age), time 2 (18–20 months), and time 3 (23–25 months). As the table shows, the percentage of times the child behaved prosocially increased dramatically over the course of the second year of life, regardless of whether the child witnessed or caused the distress. When the investigators analyzed the changes in percentages over time for both types of distress (witnessed and caused), they found the differences statistically significant. A jump from nine to 49 prosocial behaviors in 12 months was not likely to be accidental.

By convention, psychologists accept the results of a study whenever the probability of positive findings attributable to chance is less than 5 percent. This is typically expressed as $p < .05$. Thus, the smaller the $p$-value, the more certain one can feel about the results. A researcher would rather be able to say that the chances that her findings are spurious (that is, just accidental) are 1 in 1000 ($p < .001$) than 1 in 100 ($p < .01$). Nevertheless, researchers can never be *certain* that their results are true of the population as a whole; a black swan could always be swimming in the next lake. Nor can they be sure that if they performed the study with 100 different participants they would not obtain different findings. This is why replication—repeating a study to see if the same results occur again—is extremely important in science. For example, in his studies of mood and memory described in Chapter 2, Bower hit an unexpected black swan: His initial series of studies yielded compelling results, but some of these findings failed to replicate in later experiments. He ultimately had to alter parts of his theory that the initial data had supported (Bower, 1989).

The best way to ensure that a study's results are not accidental is to use a large sample. The larger the sample, the more likely it reflects the actual properties of the population. Suppose 30 people in the world are over 115 years old and researchers want to know about hearing ability in this population. If the researchers test 25 of them, they can be much more certain that their findings are generalizable to this population than if they study a sample of only two of them.

These two could have been born with hearing deficits that have no connection to their age or could be unusual in their hearing ability.

Most people intuitively understand the importance of large numbers in sampling, even if they do not realize it. For example, tennis fans recognize the logic behind matches comprised of multiple sets and would object if decisions as to who moves on to the next round were made on the basis of a single game. Intuitively, they know that a variety of factors could influence the outcome of any single game other than the ability of the players, such as fluctuations in concentration, momentary physical condition (such as a dull pain in the foot), lighting, wind, or which player served first. Because a single game is not a large enough set of observations to make a reliable assessment of who is the better player, many sports rely on a best-of-three, best-of-five, or best-of-seven series.

INTERIM SUMMARY    To assess whether the results of a study likely reflect anything other than chance, psychologists use inferential statistics, notably tests of **statistical significance.** They usually report a **probability value,** or *p*-**value,** which represents the probability that any positive findings obtained (such as a difference between groups, or a correlation coefficient that differs from zero) were accidental or just a matter of chance. By convention, psychologists accept *p*-values that fall below .05 (that have a probability of being accidental of less than 5 percent). The best ways to protect against spurious findings are to use large samples and to try to replicate findings in other samples.

## COMMON TESTS OF STATISTICAL SIGNIFICANCE

Choosing which inferential statistics to use depends on the design of the study and particularly on whether the variables assessed are continuous or categorical. If both sets of variables are continuous, the researcher simply correlates them to see whether they are related and tests the probability that a correlation of that magnitude could occur by chance. For many kinds of research, however, the investigator wants to compare two or more groups, such as males and females, or participants exposed to several different experimental conditions. In this case, the independent variables are categorical (male/female, condition 1/condition 2). If the dependent variables are also categorical, the appropriate statistic is a **chi-square** test (or $\chi^2$). A chi-square compares the observed data with the results that would be expected by chance and tests the likelihood that the differences between observed and expected are accidental. For example, suppose a researcher wants to know whether patients with antisocial personality disorder are more likely than the general population to have had academic difficulties in elementary school. In other words, she wants to know whether one categorical variable (a diagnosis of antisocial versus normal personality) predicts another (presence or absence of academic difficulties, defined as having failed a grade in elementary school). The researcher collects a sample of 50 male patients with the disorder (since the incidence is much higher in males and gender could be a confounding variable) and compares them with 50 males of similar socioeconomic status (since difficulties in school are correlated with social class). She finds that, of her antisocial sample, 20 individuals failed a grade in elementary school, whereas only two of the normals did (Table 2S.5). The likelihood is extremely small that this difference could have emerged by chance, and the chi-square test would therefore show that the differences are statistically significant.

In many cases, the independent variables are categorical, but the dependent variables are continuous. This was the case in the study of emotional expression described in Chapter 2, which placed participants in one of two conditions (writing about emotional events or about neutral events) and compared the number of visits they subsequently made to the health service (a continuous variable). The question to be answered statistically regards the likelihood that the mean number

**TABLE 2S.5 TYPICAL DATA APPROPRIATE FOR A CHI-SQUARE ANALYSIS**

|  |  | School Failure | |
|---|---|---|---|
|  |  | Present | Absent |
| Diagnostic Group | Antisocial | 20 | 30 |
|  | Normal | 2 | 48 |

*Note:* A chi-square is the appropriate statistic when testing the relation between two categorical variables. In this case, the variables are diagnosis (presence or absence of antisocial personality disorder) and school failure (presence or absence of a failed grade). The chi-square statistic tests the likelihood that the relative abundance of school failure in the antisocial group occurred by chance.

of visits to the doctor made by participants in the two conditions differed by chance. If participants who wrote about the transition to college made .73 visits to the health service on the average whereas those who wrote about a neutral event made 1.56, is this discrepancy likely to be accidental or does it truly depend on the condition to which they were exposed?

When comparing the mean scores of two groups, researchers use a *t*-test. A **t-test** is actually a special case of a statistical procedure called an **analysis of variance (ANOVA),** which can be used to compare the means of two or more groups. ANOVA assesses the likelihood that mean differences among groups occurred by chance. To put it another way, ANOVA assesses the extent to which variation in scores is attributable to the independent variable. Once again, a larger sample is helpful in determining whether mean differences between groups are real or random. If Pennebaker and his colleagues tested only two participants in each condition and found mean differences, they could not be confident of the findings because the results could simply reflect the idiosyncrasies of these four participants. If they tested 30, however, and the differences between the two conditions were large and relatively consistent across participants, the ANOVA would be statistically significant.

Chi-square, *t*-tests, and analysis of variance are not the only statistics psychologists employ. They also use correlation coefficients and many others. In all cases, however, their aim is the same: to try to draw generalizations about a population without having to study every one of its members.

**INTERIM SUMMARY** Whether one uses inferential statistics such as **chi-square** or **analysis of variance (ANOVA)** depends on the design of the study, particularly on whether the variables assessed are continuous or categorical.

## SOME CONCLUDING THOUGHTS

Inferential statistics are extremely important in trying to draw inferences from psychological research, but they are not fool-proof. In fact, some psychologists are now debating whether significance testing is really useful (see Abelson, 1997; Hunter, 1997; Shrout, 1997). One problem with significance testing is that *p*-values are heavily dependent on sample size. With a large enough sample, a tiny correlation will become significant, even though the relation between the two variables may be miniscule. Conversely, researchers often mistakenly infer from nonsignificant findings that no real difference exists between groups, when they simply have not used a large enough sample to know. If group differences *do* emerge, a *p*-value is meaningful because it specifies the likelihood that the findings could have occurred by chance. If group differences do *not* emerge, however, a *p*-value can be misleading because true differences between groups or experimental conditions may not show up simply because the sample is too small or the study is not conducted well enough.

For these reasons, some psychologists have called for other methods of reporting data that allow consumers of research to draw their own conclusions. For example, instead of reporting the size of the *p*-value, one approach is to report the size of the *effect* of being in one group or another, such as how much difference an experimental manipulation made on the dependent variable. *Effect size* can be reported as the number of standard deviations the average participant in one condition differs from the average participant in another on the dependent variable. For example, if participants who write about an emotional event for four days in a row go to the health service .73 times and those who write about a neutral event go 1.56 times, the meaning of that discrepancy is unclear unless we know the standard deviations of the means. If the SD is around .75, then students who write about emotional events are a full standard deviation better off than control subjects—which is definitely a finding worth writing home about. If the SD is .25, the effect size is *three* standard deviations, which means that writing about emotional events would put the average participant in the experimental condition in the 99th percentile of health in comparison with participants in the control condition, which would be an extraordinary effect. This example illustrates why researchers always report SDs along with means: .73 vs 1.56 is a meaningless difference if we do not know how much the average person normally fluctuates from these means.

In the final analysis, perhaps what statistics really do is to help a researcher tell a compelling story (Abelson, 1995). A good series of studies aims to solve a mystery, leading the reader step by step through all the possible scenarios, ruling out one suspect after another. Statistics can lend confidence to the conclusion, but they can never entirely rule out the possibility of a surprise ending.

## SUMMARY

### SUMMARIZING THE DATA: DESCRIPTIVE STATISTICS

1. The most important descriptive statistics are **measures of central tendency,** which provide an index of the way a typical participant responded on a measure. The **mean** is the statistical average of the scores of all participants. The **mode** is the most common or frequent score or value of the variable observed in the sample. The **median** is the score that falls right in the middle of the distribution of scores; half the participants score below it and half above it.

2. **Variability** refers to the extent to which participants tend to differ from one another in their scores. The **standard deviation** refers to the amount that the average participant deviates from the mean of the sample.

### TESTING THE HYPOTHESIS: INFERENTIAL STATISTICS

3. To assess the results of a study, psychologists use tests of **statistical significance** to determine whether positive results are likely to have occurred sim-

ply by chance. A **probability value,** or **_p_-value,** represents the probability that positive findings (such as group differences) were accidental or just a matter of chance. By convention, psychologists accept _p_-values that fall below .05 (that have a probability of being accidental of less than 5 percent). The best way to ensure that a study's results are not accidental is to use a large enough sample that random fluctuations will cancel each other out.

4. The choice of which inferential statistics to use depends on the design of the study, particularly on whether the variables assessed are continuous or categorical. Common statistical tests are **chi-square** and **analysis of variance (ANOVA).**

5. Tests of statistical significance are not without their limitations. With a large enough sample size, significant differences are likely to emerge whether or not they are meaningful, and _p_-values do not adequately reflect the possibility that _negative_ findings occurred by chance. Thus, some psychologists have begun to advocate the use of other methods for making inferences from psychological data, such as effect size. Statistical techniques are useful ways of making an argument, not fool-proof methods for establishing psychological truths.

© Jim Lange/Stockworks. Untitled.

# CHAPTER 3

# Biological Bases of Mental Life and Behavior

*I*n 1917, an epidemic broke out in Vienna that quickly spread throughout the world. The disease was a mysterious sleeping sickness called encephalitis lethargica. *Encephalitis* refers to an inflammation of the central nervous system that results from infection. (*Lethargica* simply referred to the fact that extreme lethargy, or lack of energy, was a defining feature of the disease.) The infection that led to the disease was thought to be viral, although the viral agent was never discovered. The epidemic disappeared as unexpectedly as it emerged, though not until 10 years had passed and 5 million people had fallen ill to it (Cheyette & Cummings, 1995; Sacks, 1993).

The acute phase of the illness, during which symptoms were most intense, was characterized by extreme states of arousal. Some patients were so under-aroused that they seemed to sleep for weeks; others became so hyperaroused they could not sleep at all (Sacks, 1973). Roughly one-third of those who contracted the disease died during its acute phase, but those who seemingly recovered did not know what would later hit them. Delayed-onset symptoms usually

arose five to ten years later and were remarkably diverse, including severe depression, mania (a state that often includes extreme grandiosity, extraordinarily high energy, and little need for sleep), sexual perversions, abnormal twitching movements, sudden episodes in which the person would shout obscenities, and severe conduct problems in children afflicted with the disorder (Cheyette & Cummings, 1995).

For most of the survivors of the epidemic, the most striking and tragic symptom was brain deterioration within the years following the acute phase of the illness, leaving many in a virtual state of sleep for almost 40 years. These survivors were aware of their surroundings, but they did not seem to be fully awake. They were motionless and speechless, without energy, motivation, emotion, or appetite. And they remained in that stuporous state until the development of a new drug in the 1960s. The drug, L-dopa, suddenly awakened many from their slumbers by restoring a chemical in the brain that the virus had destroyed.

Ms. B contracted a severe form of encephalitis lethargica when she was 18 (Sacks, 1973). Although she recovered in a few months, she began to show signs of the post-encephalitic disorder four years later. For almost half a century she was unable to perform any voluntary movements, to speak, or even to blink for long periods of time. Ms. B was not in a coma. She was aware of the events around her, but she could not react to them physically or emotionally.

Ms. B began to come alive within days of receiving L-dopa. After one week, she started to speak. Within two weeks she was able to write, stand up, and walk between parallel bars. Eventually her emotions returned, and she reestablished contact with her family—or what was left of it. She had fallen asleep a vibrant young woman of 22. She awakened a woman of 67.

To comprehend Ms. B's experience requires an understanding of the **nervous system**—the interacting network of nerve cells that underlies all psychological activity. At the time of the outbreak physicians had difficulty finding a link between many symptoms that seemed unrelated, such as the inability to move and the tendency to develop compulsions or scream obscenities. Only recently have researchers begun to understand how the damaged parts of the brain could produce such a seemingly incomprehensible picture.

We begin by examining the neuron, or nerve cell, and the way neurons communicate with one another to produce thought, feeling, and behavior. After briefly exploring the hormones that work with neurons to create psychological experience, we then consider the extraordinary organization of billions of neurons in the central nervous system (the brain and spinal cord) and in the peripheral nervous system (neurons in the rest of the body). We conclude with a brief discussion of the role of biology and genetics in understanding human mental life and behavior. Throughout, we wrestle with some thorny questions about how physical mechanisms are translated into psychological meanings and consider whether our subjective experience is little more than a shadow cast by our neurons, hormones, and genes.

## NEURONS: BASIC UNITS OF THE NERVOUS SYSTEM

Nerve cells, or **neurons,** are the basic units of the nervous system. Appreciating a sunset, swaying to music, pining for a lover 500 miles away, or praying for forgiveness—all of these acts reflect the coordinated action of thousands or millions of neurons. We do not, of course, *experience* ourselves as systems of interacting nerve cells, any more than we experience hunger as the depletion of sugar in the bloodstream. We think, we feel, we hurt, we want. But we do all these things through the silent, behind-the-scenes activity of neurons, which carry information from cell to cell within the nervous system as well as to and from muscles and organs.

No one knows how many neurons are in the nervous system; the best estimates range from 10 to 100 billion in the brain alone (Stevens, 1979). Some neurons connect with as many as 30,000 neurons, although the average neuron transmits information to about 1000 (Damasio, 1994).

The nervous system is composed of three kinds of neurons: sensory neurons, motor neurons, and interneurons. **Sensory neurons** (also called *afferent neurons*) transmit information from sensory cells called receptors (that is, cells that *receive* sensory information) to the brain, either directly or by way of the spinal cord. Thus, sensory neurons might send information to the brain about the sensations perceived as a sunset or a sore throat. **Motor neurons** (or *efferent neurons*) transmit commands from the brain to the glands and muscles of the body, most often through the spinal cord. Motor neurons carry out both voluntary actions, such as grabbing a glass of water, and vital bodily functions, such as digestion and heartbeat. **Interneurons** connect other neurons with one another and comprise the vast majority of neurons in the brain and spinal cord.

## ANATOMY OF A NEURON

No two neurons are exactly alike in form, size, and shape, but their cellular structure is basically the same. The main part of the neuron is the **cell body,** or *soma* (Figure 3.1). The cell body includes a nucleus that contains the genetic material of the cell (the chromosomes) as well as other structures vital to cell functioning. Like other cells, the neuron is surrounded by a membrane made of lipids (fats) and proteins that transport chemicals across the membrane and receive signals from other cells. Neurons are held in place in much of the nervous system by *glial cells* ("glial" means glue), which also insulate the neurons from messages not "intended" for them.

Branchlike extensions of the cell body, called **dendrites,** receive information from other cells. If a neuron receives enough stimulation through its dendrites and cell body, it passes information to other neurons through its axon. The axon is a long extension—occasionally as long as several feet—that frequently has two or more offshoots, or **collateral branches.**

The axons of all but the shortest neurons in the nervous system are covered with a **myelin sheath,** a tight coat of cells composed primarily of lipids. Myelinated axons give some portions of the brain a white appearance (hence the term *"white matter"*). The "gray matter" of the brain gets its color from cell bodies, dendrites, and unmyelinated axons.

The myelin sheath insulates the axon from chemical or physical stimuli that might interfere with the transmission of nerve impulses, much as the coating of a wire prevents electrical currents from getting crossed. The myelin sheath can also dramatically increase the speed of transmission of messages. It does this by capitalizing on the fact that between the cells that form the sheath are small spaces of "bare wire" called **nodes of Ranvier.** When a neuron **fires** (is activated enough to send information to other neurons), the electrical impulse is rapidly conducted from node to node, like an express train that does not have to stop at every station.

Not all axons are myelinated at birth. The transmission of impulses along these axons is slow and arduous, which helps explain why babies have such poor motor control. As myelination occurs in areas of the nervous system involved in motor action, an infant becomes capable of reaching and pointing. Such developmental achievements can be reversed in *demyelinating* diseases such as multiple sclerosis. In these disorders, degeneration of the myelin sheath on large clusters of axons can cause jerky, uncoordinated movement, although for reasons not well understood, the disease often goes into remission and the symptoms temporarily disappear. Multiple sclerosis and other diseases that progressively strip axons of their myelin may be fatal, particularly if they strike the neurons that control basic life-support processes such as the beating of the heart.

At the end of an axon are **terminal buttons,** which send signals from a neuron to adjacent cells and are triggered by the electrical impulse that has traveled down the axon. These signals are then typically received by the dendrites or cell bodies of other neurons, although they may also be received by muscle or gland cells. Connections between neurons occur at **synapses.** Two neurons do not actually touch at a synapse; instead, a space exists between the two, called the **synaptic cleft.** Not all synapses actually occur at terminal buttons at the end of an axon; in the brain, many synapses are located directly on it.

**INTERIM SUMMARY**    The nervous system is the interacting network of nerve cells that underlies all psychological activity. **Neurons** are the basic units of the nervous system. **Sensory neurons** carry sensory information from sensory receptors to the central nervous system. **Motor neurons** transmit commands from the brain to the glands and muscles of the body. **Interneurons** connect neurons with one another. Neurons generally have a **cell body, dendrites** (branchlike extensions of the cell body), and an **axon** that carries information to other neurons. Neurons connect at **synapses.**

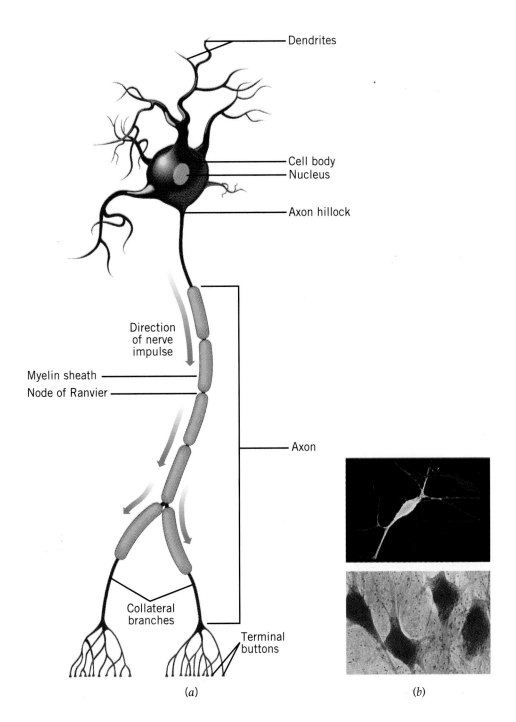

Dendrites

Cell body
Nucleus

Axon hillock

Direction
of nerve
impulse

Myelin sheath
Node of Ranvier

Axon

Collateral
branches

Terminal
buttons

(a)

(b)

**FIGURE 3.1**
The anatomy of a neuron. (*a*) The branched fibers called dendrites receive neural information from other neurons and pass it down the axon. The terminal buttons then release neurotransmitters, chemicals that transmit information to other cells. (*b*) As can be seen, actual neurons differ in their shape throughout the nervous system. The top photo shows a neuron in the most evolutionary recent part of the brain, the cerebral cortex, which is involved in the most complex psychological processes. The bottom photo shows neurons in the spinal cord, which is a much older structure. These images were magnified using an electron microscope.

## FIRING OF A NEURON

Most neurons communicate at the synapse through a process that involves electrical and chemical changes. To understand this process, we examine how neurons function in their normal resting state and the events that lead them to fire.

### Resting Potentials

When a neuron is "at rest," its membrane is *polarized*, like two sides of a battery: Inside the membrane is a negative electrical charge, whereas the fluid outside the cell has a positive charge. This polarized state reflects the fact that the cell membrane naturally lets some chemicals in, keeps others out, and actively pumps some in and out. (In a sense, neurons are never really at rest, since they use vast amounts of energy to pump chemicals across their membranes.)

A combination of chemicals normally exists inside and outside the membrane, the most important of which are sodium ($Na^+$), potassium ($K^+$), and chloride ($Cl^-$) ions. (An *ion* is an atom or small molecule that carries an electrical charge.) Outside the cell is a fluid much like the seawater within which the most primitive cells appear to have evolved millions of years ago. Thus, sodium and chloride ions tend to concentrate on the outside of the cell. (Sodium chloride, or NaCl, is salt.) The cell membrane of a neuron is typically not permeable to positively charged sodium ions; that is, these ions cannot easily get through the membrane, so they tend to accumulate outside the neuron. The membrane is also completely impermeable to a variety of negatively charged protein ions inside the cell that are involved in carrying out its basic functions. As a result, the electrical charge is normally more negative on the inside than on the outside of the cell.

This "resting" condition, in which the neuron is not firing, is called the **resting potential.** (It is called a *potential* because the cell has a stored-up source of energy, which has the potential to be used.) At its resting potential, the difference between the electrical charge inside and outside the neuron is about −70 millivolts (mV). (A volt is a standard unit of electricity, and a millivolt is one-thousandth of a volt.) Researchers discovered this by inserting tiny electrodes (materials that conduct electricity) on the inside and outside of the cell membrane of animals with the largest neurons they could find and measuring the electrical potential across the membrane.

### Graded Potentials

When a neuron is stimulated by another, one of two things can happen. The stimulation can reduce the membrane's polarization, decreasing the voltage discrepancy between the inside and the outside. For instance, the resting potential might move from −70 to −60 mV. Alternatively, stimulation from another neuron can *increase* polarization. Typically, a decrease in polarization (**depolarization)** stems from an influx of positive sodium ions. As a result, the charge inside the cell membrane becomes less negative. The opposite state of affairs—increasing the electrical difference between the inside and outside of the cell—is called **hyperpolarization.** This condition usually results from an outflow of potassium ions, which are also positively charged, or an influx of negatively charged chloride ions; as a result, the potential across the membrane becomes even more negative.

Most of these brief voltage changes occur at synapses along the neuron's dendrites and cell body; they then spread down the cell membrane like ripples on a pond. These spreading voltage changes, which occur when the neural membrane receives a signal from another cell, are called **graded potentials,** and they have two notable characteristics. First, their strength diminishes as they travel along the cell membrane away from the source of the stimulation, just as the ripples on a pond grow smaller with distance from a tossed stone's point of impact. Second, graded potentials are cumulative, or additive. If a neuron is simultaneously depolarized by +2 mV at one point on a dendrite and hyperpolarized by −2 mV at an adjacent point, the two graded potentials add up to zero and essentially cancel each other out. In contrast, if the membrane of a neuron is depolarized at multiple points, a progressively greater influx of positive ions occurs, producing a "ripple" all the way down the cell body to the axon.

### Action Potentials

If this cumulative electrical "ripple" crosses a certain threshold, depolarizing the membrane at the axon from its resting state of −70 mV to about −50 mV, a sudden

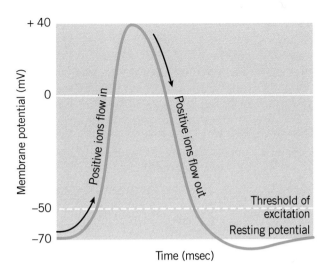

**FIGURE 3.2**
An action potential. This figure depicts the firing of a neuron as recorded by two electrodes, one inside the membrane of the axon and the other just outside the membrane. When a neuron is depolarized to about −50 mV (the threshold of excitation), an influx of positively charged ions briefly creates an action potential. An outpouring of positive ions then contributes to restoring the neuron to its resting potential. (This outpouring actually overshoots the mark briefly, so that for a brief instant after firing the potential across the membrane is slightly more negative than −70mV.)

change occurs. For a flicker of an instant, the membrane is totally permeable to positive sodium ions, which have accumulated outside the membrane. These ions pour in, changing the potential across the membrane to about +40 mV (Figure 3.2). Thus, the charge on the inside of the cell becomes momentarily positive. An outpouring of positive potassium ions then rapidly restores the neuron to its resting potential, rendering the charge inside the cell negative once again. This entire electrochemical process typically takes less than 2 milliseconds (msec, or thousandths of a second).

The shift in polarity across the membrane and subsequent restoration of the resting potential is called an **action potential,** or the "firing" of the neuron. The action potential rapidly spreads down the length of the axon to the terminal buttons. Unlike a graded potential, an action potential (or *nerve impulse*) is not cumulative. Instead, it has an **all-or-none** quality: It either occurs or does not. In this sense, the firing of a neuron is like the firing of a gun. Unless the trigger is pulled hard enough, the amount of pressure placed on the trigger below that threshold does not matter. Once the threshold is crossed, however, the trigger gives way, the gun fires, and the trigger springs back, ready to be pulled once more.

Although action potentials seem more dramatic, in many ways the prime movers behind psychological processes are graded potentials. Graded potentials create *new* information at the cellular level by integrating signals from multiple sources (multiple synapses). Action potentials, in contrast, can only pass along information already collected without changing it.

INTERIM SUMMARY    When a neuron is at rest (its **resting potential**), it is polarized, with a negative charge inside the cell membrane and a positive charge outside. When a neuron is stimulated by another, its cell membrane is either **depolarized** or **hyperpolarized.** The spreading voltage changes along the cell membrane that occur as one neuron is excited by other neurons are called **graded potentials.** If the cell membrane is depolarized by enough graded potentials, the neuron will fire. This is called an **action potential,** or nerve impulse.

## TRANSMISSION OF INFORMATION BETWEEN CELLS

When a nerve impulse travels down an axon, it sets in motion a series of events that can lead to transmission of information to other cells. Figure 3.3 presents a simplified diagram of a synaptic connection between two neurons. The neuron that is sending an impulse is called the **presynaptic neuron** (that is, *before* the synapse); the cell receiving the impulse is the **postsynaptic neuron.**

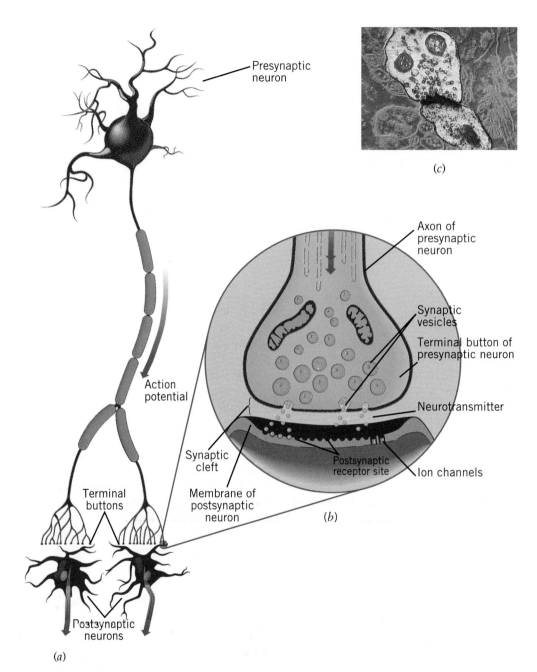

**FIGURE 3.3**

(*a*) Transmission of a nerve impulse. When an action potential occurs, the nerve impulse travels along the axon until it reaches the synaptic vesicles. The synaptic vesicles release neurotransmitters into the synaptic cleft. (*b*) The neurotransmitters then bind with postsynaptic receptors and produce a graded potential on the membrane of the postsynaptic neuron. Receptors are strings of amino acids (the building blocks of proteins) suspended in the fatty membrane of the postsynaptic neuron. Typically, several strands of these proteins extend outside the cell into the synapse, where they detect the presence of neurotransmitters and may transport them through the membrane. Other strands remain on the inside of the cell and send information to the nucleus of the cell, alerting it, for example, to open or close channels in the membrane (called ion channels) in order to let various ions in or out. (*c*) An electron micrograph of a synapse.

## Neurotransmitters and Receptors

Within the terminal buttons of a neuron are small sacs called **synaptic vesicles.** These sacs contain **neurotransmitters** (also called *transmitter substances*), chemicals that transmit information from one cell to another. When the presynaptic neuron fires, the synaptic vesicles in its terminal buttons move toward the cell's membrane (the presynaptic membrane). Some of them adhere to the membrane and break open, releasing neurotransmitters into the synaptic cleft.

Once in the synaptic cleft, some of these chemical molecules then bind with protein molecules in the *post*synaptic membrane called **receptors.** Receptors act like locks that can be opened only by particular keys. In this case, the keys are neurotransmitters in the synaptic cleft. When a receptor binds with the neurotransmitter that fits it—in both molecular structure and electrical charge—the chemical and electrical balance of the postsynaptic cell membrane changes, producing a graded potential—a ripple in the neuronal pond.

## The Effects of Neurotransmitters

Neurotransmitters can either *increase* or *decrease* neural firing. **Excitatory neurotransmitters** depolarize the postsynaptic cell membrane, making an action potential more likely. (That is, they *excite* the neuron.) In contrast, **inhibitory neurotransmitters** hyperpolarize the membrane (increase its polarization); this reduces the likelihood that the postsynaptic neuron will fire (or *inhibits* firing). Excitatory neurotransmitters thus grease the wheels of neural communication, whereas inhibitory neurotransmitters put on the brakes. A neuron can also release more than one neurotransmitter, affecting the cells to which it is connected in various ways.

Aside from being excitatory or inhibitory, neurotransmitters differ in another important respect. Some, like the ones we have been describing, are released into a specific synapse and only affect the neuron at the other end of the synaptic cleft (the postsynaptic neuron). Others have a much wider radius of impact and remain active considerably longer. Once released, they find their way into multiple synapses, where they can affect any neuron within reach that has the appropriate chemicals in its membrane. The primary impact of these transmitter substances, called *neuromodulators*, is to increase or decrease (that is, *modulate*) the impact of other neurotransmitters released into the synapse.

## Types of Neurotransmitters

A decade ago, researchers only knew of a handful of neurotransmitters. Progress in the understanding of neural transmission has proceeded so rapidly, however, that we now know of at least 75 substances that can transmit messages between neurons. For example, **epinephrine** and **norepinephrine** are involved in emotional arousal, particularly fear and anxiety. **Endorphins** are chemicals that elevate mood and reduce pain (Watkins & Mayer, 1982). Endorphins have a range of effects, from the numbness people often feel immediately after tearing a muscle (which wears off once these natural pain killers stop flowing), to the "runner's high" athletes sometimes report after a prolonged period of exercise (see Hoffman, 1997). The word "endorphin" comes from *endogenous* (meaning "produced within the body") and *morphine* (a chemical substance derived from opium that elevates mood and reduces pain). Opium and similar narcotic drugs kill pain and elevate mood because they stimulate receptors in the brain specialized for endorphins. Essentially, narcotics "pick the locks" normally opened by endorphins.

Table 3.1 describes some of the best-understood neurotransmitters, although our knowledge remains incomplete. We will briefly examine five of them: glutamate, GABA, dopamine, serotonin, and acetylcholine.

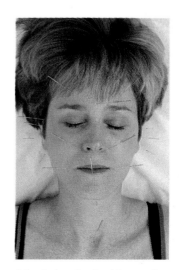

*Stimulation of endorphins may be responsible in part for the pain-killing effects of acupuncture.*

---

**TABLE 3.1    PARTIAL LIST OF NEUROTRANSMITTERS**

| TRANSMITTER SUBSTANCE | SOME OF ITS KNOWN EFFECTS |
|---|---|
| Glutamate | Excitation of neurons throughout the nervous system |
| GABA (gamma-aminobutyric acid) | Inhibition of neurons in the brain |
| Glycene | Inhibition of neurons in the spinal cord and lower brain |
| Dopamine | Emotional arousal, pleasure, and reward; voluntary movement; attention |
| Serotonin | Sleep and emotional arousal; aggression; pain regulation |
| Acetylcholine (ACh) | Learning and memory |
| Epinephrine and norepinephrine | Emotional arousal, anxiety, and fear |
| Endorphins and enkephalins | Pain relief and elevation of mood |

*Note:* The effect of a neurotransmitter depends on the type of receptor it fits. Each neurotransmitter can activate different receptors, depending on where in the nervous system the receptor is located. Thus, the impact of any neurotransmitter depends less on the neurotransmitter itself than on the receptor it unlocks; in fact, some neurotransmitters can have an excitatory effect at one synapse and an inhibitory effect at another.

---

**Glutamate and GABA    Glutamate** (glutamic acid) and **GABA** (gamma-aminobutyric acid) are two of the most widespread neurotransmitters in the nervous system. Glutamate can excite nearly every neuron in the nervous system, whereas GABA has the opposite effect in the brain, playing an inhibitory role. One of the reasons glutamate and GABA are so important is that they not only bind with specific receptors like other neurotransmitters but they also act directly on the axons of neurons, lowering or raising their threshold for firing.

Glutamate is involved in many psychological processes, but recent research suggests that it may play an important role in learning (Blokland, 1997; Izquierdo & Medina, 1997). Some people respond to the MSG (monosodium glutamate) in Chinese food with neurological symptoms such as tingling and numbing because this ingredient activates glutamate receptors.

Roughly one-third of all the neurons in the brain use GABA for synaptic communication (Petty, 1995). GABA is particularly important in the regulation of anxiety; drugs like valium and alcohol that bind with its receptors tend to reduce anxiety. Low levels of GABA may also be related to both severe depression and mania.

**Dopamine    Dopamine** has wide-ranging effects in the nervous system (Baldessarini & Tarazi, 1996). Some neural pathways that rely on dopamine are involved in the experience of pleasure and in the learning of behaviors associated with reward. Drugs ranging from marijuana to heroin increase the release of dopamine in these pathways; the addictive quality of many drugs is related in part to this effect (Wicklegren, 1996). Other dopamine pathways are involved in movement, attention, decision making, and other cognitive processes. Abnormally high levels of dopamine in some parts of the brain have been linked to schizophrenia (Chapter 15).

Degeneration of the dopamine-releasing neurons in a part of the brain called the *substantia nigra* (literally, "dark substance") causes **Parkinson's disease,** a disorder characterized by uncontrollable tremors, a general slowing down, and difficulty both initiating behavior (such as standing up) or stopping movements that are already in progress (such as walking forward). Physicians discovered the role of the substantia nigra in this disorder when they noticed the lack of this region's

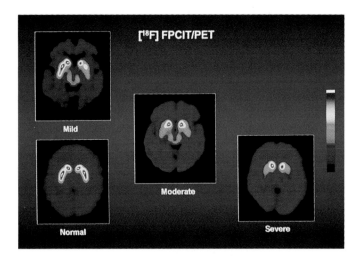

*These PET scans contrast the brain of a normal volunteer (left) with that of a patient with Parkinson's disease (center and right). Areas of the brain that normally use dopamine and control movement are less active in the Parkinsonian brain. Brighter areas indicate more activity.*

typical coloration in an autopsied Parkinson's patient; the dark color is normally a byproduct of chemical reactions involving dopamine. Although disordered movement is the most visible sign of Parkinson's disease, other symptoms can include depression and a general slowing of thought that parallels the slowing of behavior (Rao et al., 1992; Tandberg et al., 1996).

Because the victims of encephalitis lethargica described at the beginning of this chapter showed Parkinsonian symptoms, researchers believed the dopamine-rich neurons in the substantia nigra and areas of the brain connected to it had been destroyed; autopsies of patients with the disease corroborated this hypothesis. Physicians therefore tried treating these patients, who had virtually been asleep for decades, with L-dopa, a chemical that readily converts to dopamine and had recently proven effective in treating Parkinson's disease. Dopamine itself cannot be administered because it cannot cross the *blood–brain barrier*, which normally protects the brain from foreign substances in the blood. (The blood–brain barrier results from the fact that the cells in the blood vessels of the brain tend to be so tightly packed that large molecules have difficulty entering).

Unfortunately, only a small percentage of even L-dopa gets past the blood–brain barrier. The rest affects neurons in the rest of the body and can cause side effects such as nausea, vomiting, and shortness of breath. The L-dopa that *does* make its way into the brain can also have unwanted consequences because the brain uses dopamine for neural transmission in many regions and for different purposes. L-dopa can thus reduce Parkinsonian symptoms, but it can also produce disordered thinking (such as hallucinations) or movement disorders other than Parkinson's. For example, Ms. B, the victim of the 1917 encephalitis epidemic, developed a "touching tic," whereby she had to touch everything she passed. For many patients, however, symptoms such as tics were a minor price to pay for reawakening.

Serotonin    Like other neurotransmitters, **serotonin** serves a variety of functions. It appears to be involved in the regulation of mood, sleep, eating, arousal, and pain. Decreased serotonin in the brain is common in severe depression, which often responds to medications that increase serotonin activity. People who are depressed often have trouble sleeping and eating, in part because the disruption of serotonin activity that may accompany depression can also affect these other functions.

Serotonin plays an inhibitory role in most sites in the nervous system. For example, serotonin appears to inhibit neural circuits involved in aggression. Low serotonin levels have been found in aggressive rhesus monkeys (Higley et al., 1992) as well as in antisocial adult humans and delinquent children (Kruesi et al., 1992). Studies that have manipulated serotonin levels experimentally, using

**FIGURE 3.4**
Neural transplants and learning in aged rats. The investigators compared three groups: old rats without transplants, old rats with transplants, and unimpaired young rat controls. The investigators tested the rats' learning ability by seeing how long they would take to learn to swim to a platform submerged under water. Old rats given transplants showed remarkable improvements in their ability to learn this task compared to untreated old rats, as measured by their response time. *Source*: Adapted from Bjorklund & Gage, 1985.

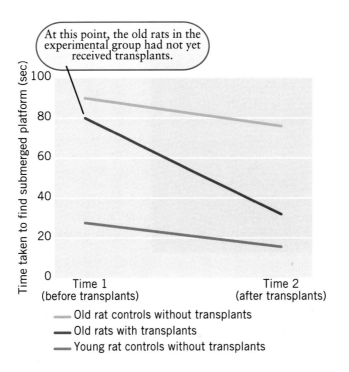

chemicals that affect the availability of serotonin in the brain, have similarly found an association between low serotonin and aggression, at least in males (Cleare and Bond, 1997).

**Acetylcholine**   Another neurotransmitter of considerable importance is **acetylcholine (ACh),** which is involved in learning and memory. For example, experiments have shown increased ACh activity in rats learning to discriminate one stimulus from another, in comparison to rats in control conditions that do not require learning (Butt et al., 1997).

A key piece of evidence linking ACh to learning and memory is the fact that patients with Alzheimer's disease, which destroys memory, show depletions in ACh. Transplanting tissue rich in ACh has led to markedly improved functioning in learning-impaired rats. The results of one such study are reproduced in Figure 3.4. In this study, old rats with neural transplants performed substantially better on a learning task than same-aged peers without the transplants (Bjorklund & Gage, 1985). Brain-grafting techniques of this sort hold the promise of helping patients with a variety of degenerative neurological disorders (such as Parkinson's disease), although their use in humans remains years away (Iwashita et al., 1994).

**INTERIM SUMMARY**   Within the terminal buttons of the **presynaptic neuron** are **neurotransmitters,** such as glutamate, GABA, dopamine, serotonin, and acetylcholine. Neurotransmitters transmit information from one neuron to another as they are released into the synapse from the synaptic vesicles. They bind with **receptors** in the membrane of the postsynaptic neuron, which produces graded potentials that can either excite or inhibit the postsynaptic neuron from firing.

# THE ENDOCRINE SYSTEM

Neurotransmitters are not the only chemicals that transmit psychologically significant messages. The **endocrine system** is a collection of glands that secrete chemicals directly into the bloodstream; these chemicals are called **hormones**

(Figure 3.5). Like neurotransmitters, hormones bind with receptors in cell membranes, but because they travel through the bloodstream, they can simultaneously activate many cells in the body as long as these cells are equipped with the right receptors. The chemical structure of some hormones is similar or even identical to that of some neurotransmitters. The hormone **adrenalin,** for example, is the same compound as the neurotransmitter epinephrine; similarly, the chemical structure of the hormone **noradrenalin** is the same as norepinephrine.

The endocrine system is thus a second system for intercellular communication, but it does not rely on the kind of intricate "wiring" between cells used by the nervous system. The difference between the methods of communication used by the two systems is like the difference between word of mouth—which requires transmission from one person to the next—and mass media—which can communicate information to millions of people at once. The endocrine system "broadcasts" its signals by releasing hormones into the bloodstream. Its messages are less specific but readily "heard" throughout the body.

In many instances the endocrine and nervous systems send simultaneous messages. When a person faces an emergency, the adrenal glands release adrenalin into the bloodstream. At the same time, neurons send "word-of-mouth" impulses by releasing epinephrine and its close cousin, norepinephrine, into synapses at strategic locations in the nervous system. These parallel actions ready the body for emergency in a variety of ways, such as increasing heart rate and diverting blood to the muscles and away from internal organs such as the stomach. People typically remain in a slightly aroused state and continue to feel jittery after a crisis (or a horror movie) is over because the bloodstream continues to contain elevated levels of adrenalin for minutes or even hours after the neurons have stopped firing.

Endocrine glands perform many functions other than readying the body for

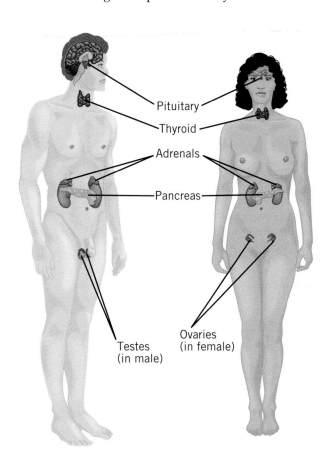

Pituitary
Thyroid
Adrenals
Pancreas
Testes
(in male)
Ovaries
(in female)

**FIGURE 3.5**

The major endocrine glands. The endocrine system is a series of glands that rely on hormonal communication to activate cells throughout the body.

emergency. The **pituitary gland** is an oval structure about the size of a pea that is located in the brain. It is often described as the "master gland" because some of the hormones it releases stimulate and regulate the other glands. The pituitary is connected more directly to the central nervous system than any of the other endocrine glands.

The **thyroid gland,** located in the neck, releases a hormone that controls metabolism (transformation of food into energy). The thyroid gland also affects energy levels and mood (Haggerty et al., 1993). People with **hypothyroidism,** or an underactive thyroid (*hypo* means "under"), sometimes require artificial replacement of thyroid hormones to relieve sluggishness and depression. One study found a 10 percent incidence of undiagnosed hypothyroidism in patients complaining of depression (Gold & Pearsall, 1983).

The **adrenal glands** are located above the kidneys. (The Latin *ad renal* means "toward the kidney.") These glands secrete adrenalin and other hormones during emergencies. Another endocrine gland, the **pancreas,** is located near the stomach and produces hormones that control blood-sugar level.

The **gonads** influence sexual development and behavior. The male gonads, or **testes,** are located in the testicles; the most important hormone they produce is **testosterone.** The female gonads, the **ovaries,** produce **estrogens.** In both sexes, these hormones control not only sex drive but also the development of secondary sex characteristics such as growth of breasts in females, deepened voice in males, and pubic hair in both sexes.

**INTERIM SUMMARY**   The **endocrine system** is a collection of glands that control various bodily functions through the secretion of **hormones.** The endocrine system complements the cell-to-cell communication of the nervous system by sending global messages through the bloodstream. Hormones are like neurotransmitters, except that they travel through the bloodstream and can thus activate many cells simultaneously.

# THE PERIPHERAL NERVOUS SYSTEM

Although the endocrine system plays an important role in psychological functioning, the center of our psychological experience is the nervous system. The nervous system has two major divisions, the central nervous system and the peripheral nervous system (Figures 3.6 and 3.7). The **central nervous system (CNS)** consists of the brain and spinal cord; the **peripheral nervous system (PNS)** consists of neurons that convey messages to and from the central nervous system. We begin with the peripheral nervous system, which has two subdivisions: the somatic and the autonomic nervous systems.

## THE SOMATIC NERVOUS SYSTEM

The **somatic nervous system** transmits sensory information to the central nervous system and carries out its motor commands. Sensory neurons receive information through receptors in the eyes, ears, skin, muscles, and other parts of the body such as the tongue. Motor neurons direct the action of skeletal muscles. Because the somatic nervous system is involved in intentional actions, such as standing up or shaking someone's hand, it is sometimes called the *voluntary nervous system.* However, the somatic nervous system also directs some involuntary or automatic actions, such as adjustments in posture or balance.

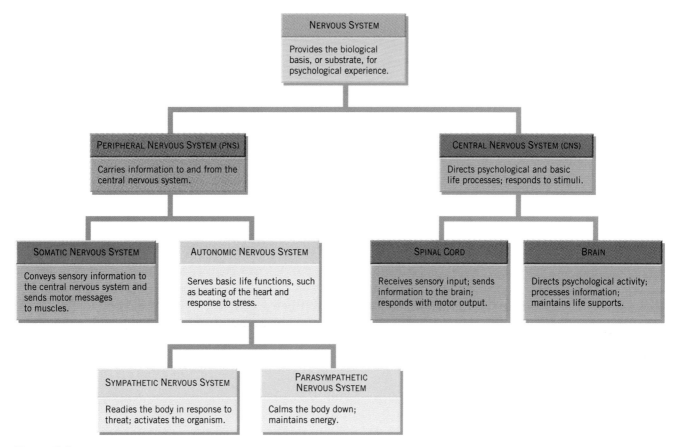

**FIGURE 3.6**
Divisions of the nervous system.

## THE AUTONOMIC NERVOUS SYSTEM

The **autonomic nervous system** conveys information to and from internal bodily structures that carry out basic life processes such as digestion and respiration. It consists of two parts: the sympathetic and the parasympathetic nervous systems. Although these systems work together, their functions are often opposed or complementary. In broadest strokes, one can think of the sympathetic nervous system as an emergency system and the parasympathetic nervous system as a "business-as-usual" system (Figure 3.8).

The **sympathetic nervous system** is typically activated in response to threats. Its job is to ready the body for fight or flight, which it does in several ways. It stops digestion, since diverting blood away from the stomach re-directs the blood to the muscles, which may need extra oxygen for an emergency response. It increases heart rate, dilates the pupils, and causes hairs on the body and head to stand erect. It is also involved in other states of intense activation, such as ejaculation in males.

By preparing the organism to respond to emergencies, the sympathetic nervous system serves an important adaptive function. Sometimes, however, the sympathetic cavalry comes to the rescue when least wanted. A surge of anxiety, tremors, sweating, dry mouth, and a palpitating heart may have helped prepare our ancestors to flee from a hungry lion, but they are less welcome when trying to deliver a speech. Similar physiological reactions occur in panic attacks, which include symptoms such as intense anxiety, tremors, and palpitating heart (Chapter 15).

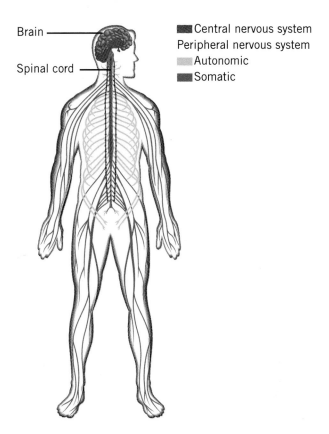

Brain

Spinal cord

■ Central nervous system
Peripheral nervous system
■ Autonomic
■ Somatic

**FIGURE 3.7**
The nervous system. The nervous system consists of the brain, the spinal cord, and the neurons of the peripheral nervous system that carry information to and from these central nervous system structures.

The **parasympathetic nervous system** supports more mundane, or routine, activities that maintain the body's store of energy, such as regulating blood-sugar levels, secreting saliva, and eliminating wastes. It also participates in functions such as regulating heart rate and pupil size. The relationship between the sympathetic and parasympathetic nervous systems is in many ways a balancing act: When an emergency has passed, the parasympathetic nervous system resumes control, reversing sympathetic responses and returning to the normal business of storing and maintaining resources.

A good illustration of the way these two systems interact—and how their interaction can be derailed—is sexual activity. In males, the parasympathetic nervous system controls the flow of blood to the penis; it is thus responsible for engorging the blood vessels that produce an erection. In females, parasympathetic processes are similarly involved in vaginal lubrication. Ejaculation, however, is controlled by the sympathetic nervous system, which is likely involved in female orgasms as well.

The capacity to become excited and experience orgasm thus depends on the synchronized activation of the parasympathetic and sympathetic nervous systems. If a man experiences sympathetic activation too early, he loses his capacity to sustain an erection and may ejaculate prematurely. Conversely, if he does not experience sympathetic activation, ejaculation will not take place (Kimble, 1992). In women, poor coordination of sympathetic and parasympathetic activity may inhibit vaginal lubrication and thus hinder sexual pleasure.

In a society that places a premium on sexual performance, a few disappointing sexual experiences can disrupt the delicate balance between sympathetic and parasympathetic activation. For example, a man who experiences a brief period of difficulty maintaining sexual excitement may begin to see himself as a failure sexually and become more anxious with each new encounter. The anxiety, in turn,

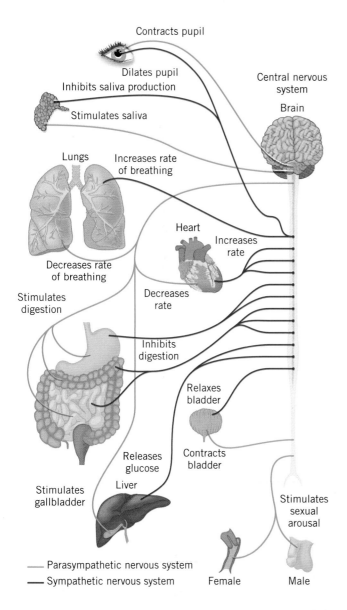

Contracts pupil

Dilates pupil

Inhibits saliva production

Stimulates saliva

Central nervous system

Brain

Lungs

Increases rate of breathing

Decreases rate of breathing

Heart

Increases rate

Decreases rate

Stimulates digestion

Inhibits digestion

Relaxes bladder

Contracts bladder

Releases glucose

Stimulates gallbladder

Liver

Stimulates sexual arousal

Female

Male

— Parasympathetic nervous system
— Sympathetic nervous system

**FIGURE 3.8**
The sympathetic and parasympathetic divisions of the autonomic nervous system.

*The sympathetic nervous system is involved in fight-or-flight responses in the face of threat.*

can inhibit the parasympathetic activation that normally leads to erection, setting in motion a cycle in which sympathetic activation and feelings of anxiety fuel each other and create a full-fledged problem in sexual functioning. This example illustrates the interaction of psychological experience, physiological processes, and culture. Based on cultural standards of sexual performance, a transitory dysfunction (failure to sustain an erection) leads the person to feel anxious and inadequate, which then exacerbates the initial psychobiological condition.

**INTERIM SUMMARY**   The nervous system consists of the **central nervous system (CNS)** and the **peripheral nervous system (PNS).** Neurons of the PNS carry messages to and from the central nervous system. The PNS has two subdivisions: the somantic nervous system and the autonomic nervous system. The **somantic nervous** system consists of sensory neurons that carry sensory information to the brain and motor neurons that direct the action of skeletal muscles. The **autonomic nervous system** controls basic life processes such as beating of the heart, workings of the digestive system, and breathing. It consists of two parts, the **sympathetic nervous system,** which is activated primarily in response to threats (but is also involved in general emotional arousal), and the **parasympathetic nervous system,** which is involved in more "mundane" activities such as maintaining the body's energy resources and restoring the system to an even keel following sympathetic activation.

# THE CENTRAL NERVOUS SYSTEM

The peripheral nervous system reflects a complex job of neural wiring, but the human central nervous system is probably the most remarkable feat of electrical engineering ever accomplished. Understanding the way it functions requires some knowledge of its evolution.

## EVOLUTION OF THE CENTRAL NERVOUS SYSTEM

If an engineer were to design the command center for an organism like ours from scratch, it would probably not look much like the human central nervous system. The reason is that, at every evolutionary juncture, nature has had to work with the *structures* (collections of cells that perform particular functions) already in place. The modifications made by natural selection have thus been sequential, one building on the next. For example, initially no organisms had color vision; the world of the ancestors of all contemporary sighted organisms was like a black-and-white movie. Gradually the capacity to perceive certain colors emerged in some species, conferring an adaptive advantage on organisms that could now, for instance, more easily distinguish one type of vegetation from another. The human central nervous system, like that of all animals, is like a living fossil record: The further down one goes (almost literally, from the upper layers of the brain down to the spinal cord), the more one sees ancient structures that evolved hundreds of millions of years ago and were shared—and continue to be shared—by most other vertebrates (animals with spinal cords).

It is tempting to think of nature's creatures as arranged on a scale from simple to complex, beginning with organisms like amoebas, then moving up the ladder perhaps to pets and farm animals, and on to the highest form of life, ourselves (see Butler & Hodos, 1996). And in a sense, there is something to this; after all, *we* can dissect the brain of a frog, but a frog cannot return the favor.

One must always remember, however, that natural selection is a process that favors *adaptation to a niche*, and different niches require different adaptations. I would not trade my brain for that of my dog, no matter how endearing he might be, because I would rather be the one throwing than fetching. But my dog has abilities I lack, either because we humans never acquired them or because over time we lost them as our brains evolved in a different direction. My dog can hear things I cannot hear, and he does not need to call out in the dark, "Who's there?" because his nose tells him. And anyone who thinks humans and insects are easy to place on a single, evolutionary scale has never stared a scorpion in the face and asked, "Who is better adapted, you or I?" (Do not try this experiment at home.)

## The Evolution of Vertebrates

Our understanding of the evolution of the human nervous system still contains heavy doses of guesswork, but a general outline looks something like the following (Butler & Hodos, 1996; Healy, 1996; Killacky, 1995; Kolb & Whishaw, 1996; MacLean, 1982, 1990). The earliest precursors to vertebrate animals were probably fishlike creatures whose actions were less controlled by a central "executive" like the human brain than by specific, or "local," reactions at particular points along the body. These organisims were likely little more than stimulus–response machines whose actions were controlled by a simple fluid-filled tube of neurons that evolved into the spinal cord. Sensory information from the environment entered the upper side of the cord, and neurons exiting the underside produced automatic responses (reflexes). Vision and smell were likely the first senses to develop and were shared by our most immediate prevertebrate ancestors.

Through evolution, the front end of the spinal cord became specialized to allow more sophisticated processing of information and more flexible motor responses (Figure 3.9). Presumably this end developed because our early ancestors moved forward, head first—which is why our brains are in our heads instead of our feet. The primitive vertebrate brain, or *brainstem*, appears to have had three parts. The foremost section, called the *forebrain*, was specialized for sensation at a very immediate level—smell, and eventually taste. The middle region, or *midbrain*, controlled sensation for distant stimuli—vision and hearing. The back of the brainstem, or *hindbrain*, was specialized for movement, particularly for balance

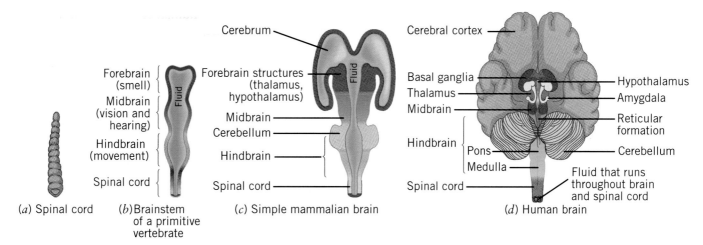

**FIGURE 3.9**

Evolution of the human brain. (*a*) The earliest central nervous system in the ancestors to contemporary vertebrates was likely a structure similar to the contemporary spinal cord. (*b*) The primitive brain, or brainstem, allowed more complex sensation and movement in vertebrates. (*c*) Among the most important evolutionary developments of mammals was the cerebrum. (*d*) The human brain is a storehouse of knowledge packed in a remarkably small container, the human skull. *Source:* Adapted from Kolb & Whishaw, 1990.

(Sarnat & Netsky, 1974). The hindbrain was also the connecting point between the brain and spinal cord, allowing messages to travel between the two. This rough division of labor in the primitive central nervous system still applies in the spinal cord and brainstem of humans. Many human reflexes, for example, occur precisely as they did, and do, in the simplest vertebrates: Sensory information enters one side of the spinal cord (toward the back of the body in humans, who stand erect), and motor impulses exit the other.

As animals, and particularly mammals, evolved, the most dramatic changes occurred in the hindbrain and forebrain. The hindbrain sprouted an expanded *cerebellum,* which increased the animal's capacity to put together complex movements and make sensory discriminations. The forebrain of contemporary mammals is also probably very different from that of its ancestors. It evolved many new structures, most notably those that comprise the **cerebrum,** the part of the brain most involved in complex thought, which greatly expanded the capacity for processing information and initiating movement (see Finlay & Darlington, 1995). Thus, even relatively simple mammals such as hedgehogs and opossums are able to discriminate and respond to more subtle features of the environment than most fish, whose less developed cerebrum renders them less "cerebral" (Diamond & Hall, 1969). In "brainier" mammals, and especially in humans, considerable evolution has occurred in the many-layered surface of the cerebrum known as the **cortex** (from the Latin word for "bark"). In fact, 80 percent of the human brain's mass is cortex (Kolb & Whishaw, 1996).

### The Human Nervous System

Although the human brain and the brains of its early vertebrate and mammalian ancestors differ dramatically, most of the differences are the result of additions to, rather than replacement of, the original brain structures. Two very important consequences flow from this. The first, as we have seen, is that many neural mechanisms are the same in humans and other animals; others differ across species that have evolved in different directions from common ancestors. Generalizations between humans and animals as seemingly different as cats or rats are likely to be more appropriate at lower levels of the nervous system, such as the spinal cord and brainstem, because these lower neural structures were already in place before these species diverged millions of years ago. The human brainstem (which includes most of the structures below the cerebrum) is almost identical to the brainstem of sheep (Kolb & Whishaw, 1996), but the two species differ tremendously in the size, structure, and function of their cortex. Much of the sheep's cortex is devoted to processing sensory information, whereas a greater part of the human cortex is involved in forming complex thoughts, perceptions, and plans for action.

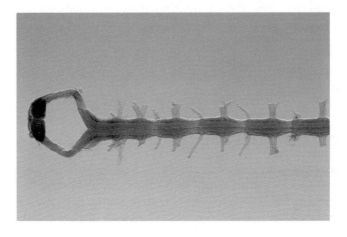

*The nervous system of the earthworm includes a spinal cord and a small, simple brain.*

**How the brain works.**

The second implication is that human psychology bears the distinct imprint of the same relatively primitive structures that guide motivation, learning, and behavior in other animals. This is a sobering thought, which led Darwin to place species on our family tree that we might consider poor relations; led Freud to view our extraordinary capacities to love, create, and understand ourselves and the universe as a thin veneer (only a few millimeters thick, in fact) over primitive structures that motivate our greatest achievements and our most "inhuman" atrocities; and led Skinner to argue that the same laws of learning apply to humans as to other animals.

The human nervous system is thus a set of hierarchically organized structures built layer upon layer over millions of years of evolution. The most primitive centers send information to, and receive information from, higher centers; these higher centers are in turn integrated with, and regulated by, still more advanced areas of the brain. Behavioral and cognitive precision progressively increases from the lower to the higher and more recently evolved structures (Luria, 1973). Thus, the spinal cord can respond to a prick of the skin with a reflex without even consulting the brain, but more complex cognitive activity simultaneously occurs as the person makes sense of what has happened. We reflexively withdraw from a pinprick, but if the source is a vaccine injection, we inhibit our response—though often milliseconds later, since information traveling to and from the brain takes neural time. Responding appropriately requires the integrated functioning of structures from the spinal cord up through the cortex.

Before discussing the major structures of the central nervous system, an important caveat, or caution, is in order. A central debate since the origins of modern neuroscience in the nineteenth century has centered on the extent to which certain functions are localized to specific parts of the brain. One of the most enlightening things about watching a brain scan in action as a person performs even a simple task is just how much of the brain actually "lights up" much of the time. Different regions are indeed specialized for different functions; a severe blow to the head that damages the back of the cortex is more likely to disrupt vision than speech. Knowing that a lesion at the back of the cortex can produce blindness thus suggests that this region is *involved in visual processing* and that it must be relatively intact for normal visual functioning to occur. But this does not mean that this region is the brain's "center" for vision. Every thought, feeling, or psychological attribute is always the result of a *network* of neurons acting in combination.

In the pages that follow, we describe a series of structures as if they were discrete entities. In reality, evolution did not produce a nervous system with neat boundaries. Distinctions among structures, of course, are not simply the whims of neuroanatomists; they are based on qualities such as the appearance, function, and cellular structure of adjacent regions. Nevertheless, where one structure ends and another begins is to some extent arbitrary. Axons from the spinal cord synapse with neurons far into the brain, so that parts of the brain could actually be called spinal. Similarly, progress in the understanding of the brain has led to increased recognition of different functions served by particular clumps of neurons or axons *within* a given structure. Where researchers once asked questions such as "What does the cerebellum do?" today they are more likely to ask about the functions of specific parts of the cerebellum.

**INTERIM SUMMARY**    The design of the human nervous system, like that of other animals, reflects its evolution. Early precursors to the first vertebrates (animals with spinal cords) probably had minimal centralized control over behavior and instead tended to react with reflexive responses to environmental stimulation at specific points of their bodies. As vertebrates evolved, the front end of the spinal cord became specialized to allow more complex sensory processing and movement. The most primitive vertebrate brain, or brainstem, included a **forebrain** (specialized for sensing nearby stimuli, notably smells and tastes), a **midbrain** (specialized for sensation at a distance, namely vision and hearing), and a **hindbrain** (specialized for control of movement). This rough division of labor persists in contemporary vertebrates, including humans. The forebrain of humans and other contemporary vertebrates includes an expanded **cerebrum,** with a rich network of cells comprising its outer layers or **cortex,** which allows much more sophisticated sensory, cognitive, and motor processes. The human nervous system is a hierarchically organized system with an overall structure that follows its evolution. Evolutionarily more recent centers control, rechannel, and receive feedback from many of the processes that begin at lower levels.

## THE SPINAL CORD

As in all vertebrates, neurons in the human spinal cord produce reflexes, as sensory stimulation activates rapid, automatic motor responses. In humans, however, the main function of the **spinal cord** is to transmit information between the brain and the rest of the body. The spinal cord sends information from sensory neurons in various parts of the body to the brain, and it relays motor commands back to muscles and organs (such as the heart and stomach) via motor neurons. In some animals, notably certain species of fish, the spinal cord is more autonomous from the brain. Swishing back and forth in water requires less subtle coordination of movements than walking or climbing, so the spinal cord in these animals can control movement without much involvement of the brain except under special circumstances, such as attack by a predator (Butler & Hudos, 1996).

The spinal cord in humans is segmented, with each segment controlling a different part of the body. By and large, the upper segments control the upper parts of the body and the lower segments the lower body (Figure 3.10). As in the earliest vertebrates, sensory information enters one side of the spinal cord (toward the back of the body), and motor impulses exit the other (toward the front). Outside the cord, bundles of axons from these sensory and motor neurons join together to form 31 pairs (from the two sides of the body) of **spinal nerves;** these nerves carry information to and from the spinal cord to the periphery. Inside the spinal cord, other bundles of axons (*spinal tracts*, which comprise much of the white matter of the cord) send impulses to and from the brain, relaying sensory messages and motor commands. (Outside the central nervous system, bundles of axons are usually called **nerves;** within the brain and spinal cord, they are called **tracts.**)

When the spinal cord is severed, the result is loss of feeling and paralysis at all levels below the injury, which can no longer communicate with the brain. Even with less severe lesions, physicians can often pinpoint the location of spinal damage from patients' descriptions of their symptoms alone. If a patient complains of a lack of feeling in the upper part of the foot and nerve damage to the foot or brain

*Actor Christopher Reeves, now an activist for research on spinal cord injuries, become a quadriplegic after breaking his neck, which severed the connection between the brain and all his muscles below the point of the injury.*

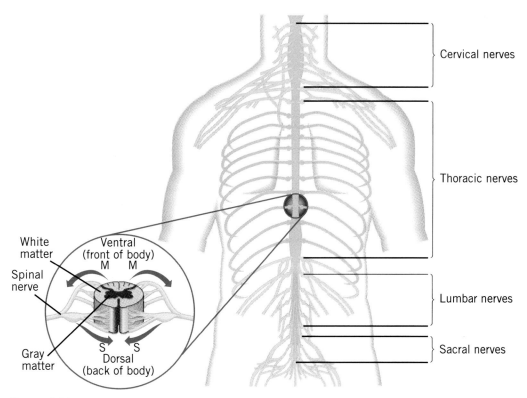

Cervical nerves

Thoracic nerves

Lumbar nerves

Sacral nerves

White matter

Ventral (front of body)
M    M

Spinal nerve

Gray matter

S    S
Dorsal (back of body)

**FIGURE 3.10**
The spinal cord. Segments of the spinal cord relay information to and from different parts of the body. Sensory fibers relay information to the back of the spine (dorsal), and motor neurons transmit information from the front of the spinal cord (ventral) to the periphery.

has been ruled out, the lowest segment of the spinal cord (the sacral segment) has probably been damaged (Figure 3.10).

INTERIM SUMMARY    The central nervous system (CNS) consists of the brain and spinal cord. The **spinal cord** carries out reflexes, transmits sensory information to the brain, and transmits messages from the brain to the muscles and organs. Each of its segments controls sensation and movement in a different part of the body.

## THE HINDBRAIN

Directly above the spinal cord in humans are several structures that comprise the **hindbrain:** the medulla oblongata, cerebellum, and parts of the reticular formation. Another small hindbrain region, the *pons,* is not yet well understood, although it may play some role in learning (Figure 3.11). As in other animals, hindbrain structures link the brain to the spinal cord, sustain life by controlling the supply of air and blood to cells in the body, and regulate arousal level. With the exception of the cerebellum, which sits at the back of the brain and has a distinct appearance, the structures of the hindbrain merge into one another and perform multiple functions as information passes from one structure to the next on its way to higher brain regions.

### Medulla Oblongata

Anatomically, the lowest brainstem structure, the **medulla oblongata** (or simply **medulla**), is actually an extension of the spinal cord. Although quite small—about an inch and a half long and three-fourths of an inch wide at its broadest part—the

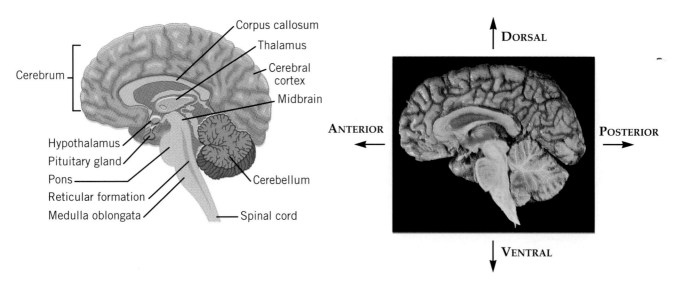

**FIGURE 3.11**

Cross-section of the human brain. The drawing and accompanying photo show a view of the cerebral cortex and the more primitive structures below the cerebrum. Not shown here are the limbic system and basal ganglia, which are structures within the cerebrum. Also marked on the photo are common terms used to describe location in the brain. For example, a structure toward the front of the brain is described as *anterior* (*ante* means "before"). Not shown are two other directions: *lateral* (toward the left or right side) and *medial* (toward the middle). Thus, a neural pathway through the upper sides of the brain might be described as *dorsolateral* (*dorsal* meaning toward the top of the head, and *lateral* meaning toward the side).

medulla is essential to life, controlling such vital physiological functions as heartbeat, circulation, and respiration. Neither humans nor other animals can survive destruction of the medulla.

The medulla is the link between the spinal cord and the rest of the brain. Here, bundles of axons cross over from each side of the body to the opposite side of the brain. As a result, most of the sensations experienced on the right side of the body, as well as the capacity to move the right side, are controlled by the left side of the brain, and vice versa. Thus, if a person has weakness in the left side of the body following a stroke, the damage to the brain was likely on the right side of the brain.

## Cerebellum

The **cerebellum** (Latin for "little cerebrum") is a large structure at the back of the brain. For decades researchers have believed that the cerebellum is exclusively involved in coordinating smooth, well-sequenced movements (such as riding a bike) and in maintaining balance and posture. Staggering and slurred speech after a few too many drinks stem in large part from the effects of alcohol on cerebellar functioning. The cerebellum also takes a pounding when the head is repeatedly snapped back in boxing. Over the span of a boxer's career the damage may be permanent, leading to a movement disorder or slurred speech, particularly if the boxer refuses to retire as his reflexes slow and he takes more punches on the chin. More recently, however, researchers using positron emission tomography (PET) and functional magnetic resonance imaging (fMRI) scans have found the cerebellum to be involved in sensory and cognitive processes as well, such as learning to associate one stimulus (such as a sound) with another (such as a puff of air on the eye, which leads to an eyeblink reflex)(Blaxton et al., 1996; Cabeza et al., 1997).

*Repeated battering of the brain in boxing can lead to damage to the cerebellum.*

▶ ONE STEP FURTHER

### Tracking Down the Functions of the Cerebellum

Some researchers have begun to wonder whether the role of the cerebellum in movement reflects in part its involvement in processing *sensory* information. When people move, they receive constant feedback about the position of their bodies and the objects they are touching. If they did not, they would constantly fall. The question for researchers is how to tell whether the cerebellum is actually involved in movement, in sensory processes that make smooth movement possible, or both.

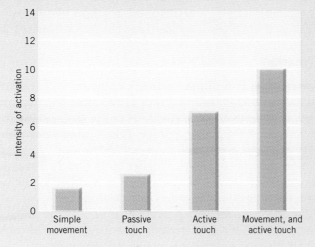

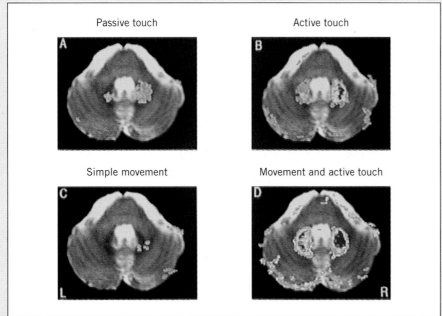

**FIGURE 3.12**
The relation between sensory and motor tasks and activation of the lateral cerebellum. The graph and accompanying photos show the amount of increased activation of the lateral cerebellum for each of four tasks involving sensory and motor processes. The cerebellum was most active when participants had to combine sensory and motor responses. (Data in the chart are for the right hand; the left hand produced similar findings.) In the brain images, the bright green indicates some activation; the yellow, more activation; and the red, high activation.

To try to tease apart these two possibilities, researchers in one study observed the activity of the brain using fMRI while participants performed each of four tasks (Gao et al., 1996). In a passive touch condition, participants did nothing other than observe the feeling of sand paper lightly rubbed against their fingers. In an active touch condition, they were asked to judge whether the sand paper rubbed on each of their hands was equally coarse—a test of sensory discrimination between two stimuli. In a simple movement condition, they were instructed to reach for, grab, and drop an object repeatedly. Finally, in a condition that combined movement and sensory discrimination, they were asked to pick up an object in each hand and judge whether the two objects were the same. The study was intended to assess whether sensory processing, movement, or both lead to activation of the side portions of the cerebellum (the *lateral* cerebellum).

The results are shown in Figure 3.12. As can be seen, simple movement led to slight activation, as did simple sensation (passive touch). However, sensory discrimination—and especially the combination of sensory discrimination plus movement—led to the strongest activation of the cerebellum, suggesting that the cerebellum (or at least its lateral regions) may be involved in combining sensory and motor information.    ◄

### Reticular Formation

The **reticular formation** is a diffuse network of neurons that extends from the lowest parts of the medulla in the hindbrain to the upper end of the midbrain. The reticular formation sends axons to many parts of the brain and to the spinal cord. Its major functions are to maintain consciousness, regulate arousal levels, and modulate the activity of neurons throughout the central nervous system. The reticular formation also appears to help higher brain centers integrate information from different neural pathways (such as sounds and associated images) by calling attention to their simultaneous activation (Munk et al., 1996).

Reticular damage can affect sleep patterns as well as the ability to be alert or attentive. Damage to the reticular formation is a major cause of coma. In fact, humans can lose an entire side (or hemisphere) of the cerebrum—about 50 billion cells—without losing the capacity for consciousness, whereas lesions to the reticular formation can render all the information in the cortex useless (Baars, 1995).

## THE MIDBRAIN

The **midbrain** consists of the tectum and tegmentum. The **tectum** includes structures involved in vision and hearing. These structures largely help humans orient to visual and auditory stimuli with eye and body movements. When higher brain structures are lesioned, people can often still sense the presence of stimuli, but they cannot identify them. The **tegmentum,** which includes parts of the reticular formation and other neural structures, serves a variety of functions. Many are related to movement; the tegmentum includes the substantia nigra, which deteriorates in Parkinson's disease and was apparently destroyed by encephalitis lethargica.

Recent research suggests that these midbrain structures also play an important role in learning to produce behaviors that minimize unpleasant (aversive) consequences and maximize rewards—a kind of learning studied for years by behaviorists (Chapter 5). Neurons deep inside the tectum are part of a system of neurons involved in generating unpleasant feelings and linking them, through learning, to actions that can help the animal escape or avoid them (Brandao et al., 1994). Chemical or electrical activation of these pathways in rats produces "freezing" (a characteristic fear response) and efforts to escape. Other *nuclei* (collections of neurons in a region of the brain that serve a shared function) in the tegmentum are involved in the experience of pleasure or reward, which is crucial to learning to produce actions that lead to positive consequences (Johnson et al., 1996; Nader & van der Kooy, 1997). For example, rats will learn to perform behaviors that lead to morphine injections in regions of their tegmentum (Jaeger & van der Kooy, 1996).

**INTERIM SUMMARY**   The hindbrain includes the **medulla oblongata,** the **cerebellum,** and parts of the **recticular formation.** The medulla regulates vital physiological functions, such as heartbeat, circulation, and respiration, and forms a link between the spinal cord and the rest of the brain. The cerebellum has long been seen as the lowest brain structure involved in movement, but parts of it also appear to be involved in learning and sensory discrimination. The reticular formation is most centrally involved in consciousness and arousal. The midbrain consists of the **tectum** and **tegmentum.** The tectum is involved in orienting to visual and auditory stimuli. The tegmentum is involved, among other things, in movement and arousal. Hindbrain structures are also part of neural circuits that help humans learn to approach or avoid stimuli associated with reward and punishment.

## THE FOREBRAIN

The **forebrain,** which is involved in complex sensory, emotional, cognitive, and behavioral processes, consists of the hypothalamus, thalamus, and cerebrum. Within the cerebrum are the basal ganglia and limbic system, which are called **subcortical** structures (*sub*, or *below*, the cortex). The outer layers of the cerebrum, or cortex, are so complex that we will devote a separate section to them.

### Hypothalamus

Situated in front of the midbrain and adjacent to the pituitary gland is the **hypothalamus.** Although the hypothalamus accounts for only 0.3 percent of the brain's total weight, this tiny structure helps regulate behaviors ranging from eating and sleeping to sexual activity and emotional experience. In nonhuman animals, the hypothalamus is involved in species-specific behaviors, such as responses to predators. For example, electrical stimulation of the hypothalamus in cats can produce rage attacks—filled with hissing, growling, and biting (Bandler, 1982; Lu et al., 1992). The hypothalamus works closely with the pituitary gland and provides a key link between the nervous system and the endocrine system, largely by activating pituitary hormones. When people undergo stressful experiences (such as taking a psychology exam or getting into a heated argument), the hypothalamus activates the pituitary, which in turn puts the body on alert by sending out hormonal messages.

One of the most important functions of the hypothalamus is *homeostasis*—keeping vital processes such as body temperature, blood-sugar (glucose) level, and metabolism (use and storage of energy) within a fairly narrow range. For example, as people ingest food, the hypothalamus detects a rise in glucose level and responds by shutting off hunger sensations. Chemically blocking glucose receptors (cells that detect glucose levels) in cats can produce ravenous eating, as the hypothalamus attempts to maintain homeostasis in the face of misleading information (Batuev & Gafurov, 1993; Berridge & Zajonc, 1991; Katafuchi et al., 1985).

### Thalamus

The **thalamus** is a set of nuclei located above the hypothalamus. Its various nuclei perform a number of functions; one of the most important is to provide initial processing of sensory information and to transmit this information to higher brain centers. In some respects the thalamus is like a switchboard for routing information from neurons connected to visual, auditory, taste, and touch receptors to appropriate regions of the brain. However, the thalamus plays a much more active role than a simple switchboard. Its function is not only to *route* messages to the appropriate structures but also to *filter* them, highlighting some and de-emphasizing others.

The thalamus is ideally situated for performing this function, since it receives *projections* (that is, axons leading to it) from several sensory systems, as well as feedback from higher cortical centers in the brain. Thus, the thalamus can collect information from multiple senses and determine the extent to which information is converging on something important that may require more detailed processing. The thalamus also receives input from the reticular formation, which "highlights" some neural messages. Recent studies using PET and other techniques suggest that the reticular formation and thalamus may be the anatomically "lower" sections of a neural circuit that directs attention and consciousness toward potentially significant events (Kinomura et al., 1996; Newman, 1995).

## The Limbic System

The **limbic system** is a set of structures with diverse functions, including emotion, motivation, learning, and memory. The limbic system includes the septal area, the amygdala, and the hippocampus (Figure 3.13).

The role of the **septal area** is only gradually becoming clear. Early research linked it to the experience of pleasure: Stimulating a section of the septal area proved to be a powerful reinforcer for rats, which would walk across an electrified grid to receive the stimulation (Milner, 1991; Olds & Milner, 1954). More recent research suggests that, like most brain structures, different sections of the septal area likely have distinct, though related, functions. For example, one part of the septal area appears to be involved in relief from pain and other unpleasant emotional states (Yadin & Thomas, 1996). Another part seems to help animals learn to avoid situations that *lead* to aversive experiences, since injection of chemicals that temporarily block its functioning makes rats less able to learn to avoid stimuli associated with pain (Rashidy-Pour et al., 1995). These regions receive projections from midbrain and thalamic nuclei involved in learning.

The **amygdala** is an almond-shaped structure (amygdala is Latin for "almond") involved in many emotional processes, especially learning and remembering emotionally significant events (Aggleton, 1992; LeDoux, 1995; Sarter &

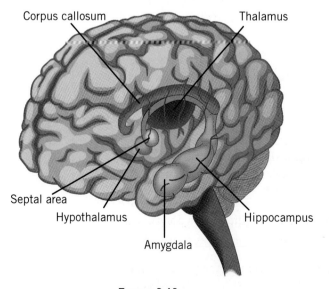

**FIGURE 3.13**

The limbic system. The limbic system, located within the cerebrum, consists of the septal area, amygdala, and hippocampus. The drawing shows the parts of the limbic system, and the photo shows the way it looks using computer imaging.

Markowitsch, 1985). One of its primary roles is to attach emotional significance to events. The amygdala appears to be particularly important in fear responses. Lesioning the amygdala in rats, for example, inhibits learned fear responses; that is, the rats no longer avoid a stimulus they had previously connected with pain (LaBar & LeDoux, 1996).

The amygdala is also involved in recognizing emotion, particularly fearful emotion, in other people. One study using PET technology found that presenting pictures of fearful rather than neutral or happy faces activated the left amygdala and that the amount of activation was strongly correlated with the amount of fear displayed in the pictures (Morris et al., 1996). From an evolutionary perspective, this suggests that humans have evolved particular mechanisms for detecting fear in others and that these "fear detectors" are anatomically connected to neural circuits that *produce* fear. This makes sense, since fear in others is likely a signal of danger to oneself. In fact, infants as young as 9 to 12 months show distress when they see distress on their parents' faces (Campos et al., 1993).

The **hippocampus** is particularly important in memory (see, e.g., Schachter, 1992, 1996; Squire, 1991). This was demonstrated dramatically in a famous case study by Brenda Milner and her colleagues (Milner et al., 1968; Scoville & Milner, 1957). A man identified as H. M. underwent surgery to control life-threatening epileptic seizures. The surgeon removed sections of his cortex and some underlying structures. Unfortunately, one of those structures was the hippocampus, and although H. M. was now free of seizures, he was also "free" of the capacity to remember new information.

Actually, that is only half the story, and the other half has, in the last 15 years, changed our understanding of memory. H. M. *did* lose his memory in the sense that psychologists and laypeople alike have traditionally understood memory. For example, every time he met Dr. Milner, who studied him over 20 years, he had to be reintroduced; invariably, he would smile politely and tell her it was a pleasure to make her acquaintance. But as we will see in Chapter 6, we now know that certain kinds of memory do not involve the hippocampus, and H. M. retained those capacities. For example, on one occasion H. M.'s father took him to visit his mother in the hospital. Afterward, H. M. did not remember anything of the visit, but he "expressed a vague idea that something might have happened to his mother" (Milner et al., 1968, p. 216). His capacity to form associations (such as the connection between his mother and a sense of unease) was intact, even though he could not recall the events that led to those associations.

### The Basal Ganglia

The **basal ganglia** are a set of structures located near the thalamus and hypothalamus that are involved in movement. Damage to the basal ganglia can cause changes in posture and muscle tone or various kinds of abnormal movements. The basal ganglia have been implicated in Parkinson's disease and in the epidemic of encephalitis lethargica that struck millions early in the twentieth century. The dopamine-rich neurons of the substantia nigra (in the midbrain) normally project to the basal ganglia. When these neurons die, as in Parkinson's, they stop sending signals to the basal ganglia, which in turn cease functioning properly to regulate movement. Some neural circuits involving the basal ganglia appear to inhibit movement, whereas others initiate it, since lesions in different sections of the basal ganglia can either release movements (leading to twitches or jerky movements) or block them.

Damage to the basal ganglia can also lead to mood and memory disorders, as higher regions of the brain fail to receive necessary activation (see Federoff et al., 1992; Krishnan, 1993; Lopez-Villegas et al., 1996). In addition, at least one neural pathway in the basal ganglia is part of a circuit involved in memory that leads from the cerebellum to the cerebral cortex (Cabeza et al., 1997).

INTERIM SUMMARY    The forebraim consists of the **hypothalamus, thalamus,** the **subcortial** structures of the **cerebrum** (the limbic system and basal ganglia), and the **cerebral cortex.** The hypothalamus is involved in regulating a wide range of behaviors, including eating, sleeping, sexual activity, and emotional experience. Among its other functions, the thalamus provides initial processing of sensory information and transmits this information to higher brain centers. The **limbic system** includes the **septal area, amygdala,** and **hippocampus.** The precise functions of the septal area are unclear, although it appears to be involved in learning to act in ways that avoid pain and produce pleasure. The amygdala is crucial to the experience of emotion. **Basal ganglia** structures are involved in the control of movement and also play a part in mood and memory.

## THE CEREBRAL CORTEX

Although many components of normal behaviors are produced below the cortex—in the spinal cord and medulla up through the limbic system and basal ganglia—the cerebral cortex coordinates and integrates these components. The cortex consists of a three-millimeter-thick layer of densely packed interneurons; it is grayish in color and highly convoluted (that is, filled with twists and turns). The convolutions appear to serve a purpose: Just as crumpling a piece of paper into a tight wad reduces its size, the folds and wrinkles of the cortex allow a relatively large area of cortical cells to fit into a compact region within the skull. The hills of these convolutions are known as **gyri** (plural of **gyrus**) and the valleys as **sulci** (plural of **sulcus**).

In humans, the cortex performs three functions. First, it allows the flexible construction of sequences of voluntary movements involved in activities such as changing a tire or playing a piano concerto. Second, it permits subtle discriminations among complex sensory patterns; without a cerebral cortex, the words *gene* and *gem* would be indistinguishable. Third, the cortex makes possible symbolic thinking—the ability to use symbols such as words or pictorial signs (like a flag) to represent an object or concept with a complex meaning. The capacity to think symbolically enables people to have conversations about things that do not exist or are not presently in view; it is the foundation of human thought and language.

### Primary and Association Areas

The cortex consists of regions specialized for different functions, such as vision, hearing, and body sensation. Each of these areas can be divided roughly into two zones, called primary and association cortex. The **primary areas** process raw sensory information or (in one section of the brain, the frontal lobes) initiate movement. The **association areas** are involved in complex mental processes such as forming perceptions, ideas, and plans. They were given this name in the nineteenth century because of the belief that higher mental functioning revolves around the association of one idea with another.

The primary areas are responsible for the initial cortical processing of sensory information. Neurons in these zones receive sensory information, usually via the thalamus, from sensory receptors in the ears, eyes, skin, and muscles. When a person sees a safety pin lying on her dresser, the primary or sensory areas receive the simple visual sensations that make up the contours of the safety pin. Activation of circuits in the visual association cortex enables the person to recognize the object as a safety pin rather than a needle or a formless shiny object.

Neurons in the primary areas tend to have more specific functions than neurons in association cortex. Many of these neurons are genetically wired to register very basic, and very specific, attributes of a stimulus. For example, some neurons in the primary visual cortex respond to horizontal lines but not to vertical lines;

other neurons respond only to vertical lines (Hubel & Wiesel, 1963). Some neurons in the association cortex are equally specific in their functions, but many develop their functions through experience. The brain may be wired from birth to detect the contours of objects like safety pins, but a person must learn what a safety pin is and does. From an evolutionary perspective, this combination of "hard-wired" and "flexible" neurons guarantees that we have the capacity to detect features of *any* environment that are likely to be relevant to adaptation but can also learn the features of the *specific* environment in which we find ourselves.

### Lobes of the Cerebral Cortex

The cerebrum is divided into two roughly symmetrical halves, or **cerebral hemispheres,** which are separated by the **longitudinal fissure.** (A fissure is a deep sulcus, or valley.) A band of neural fibers called the **corpus callosum** connects the **right** and **left hemispheres.** Each hemisphere consists of four regions, or **lobes:** occipital, parietal, frontal, and temporal. Thus, a person has a right and left occipital lobe, a right and left parietal lobe, and so forth (Figure 3.14). Once again, it is important to bear in mind that nature did not create clearly bounded cortical regions and rope them off from one another; the functions of adjacent cortical regions tend to be related, even if some cells are called "occipital" and others "temporal."

The Occipital Lobes   The **occipital lobes,** located in the rear portion of the cortex, are specialized for vision. Primary areas of the occipital lobes receive visual input from the thalamus. The thalamus, in turn, receives information from the receptors in the retina via the optic nerve. The primary areas respond to relatively simple features of a visual stimulus, and the association areas organize these simple characteristics into more complex maps of features of objects and their position in space. Damage to the primary areas leads to partial or complete blindness.

The visual association cortex, which actually extends into neighboring lobes, projects (that is, sends axons carrying messages) to several regions throughout the cortex that receive other types of sensory information, such as auditory or tactile (touch). Areas that receive information from more than one sensory system are called **polysensory areas.** The existence of polysensory areas at various levels of

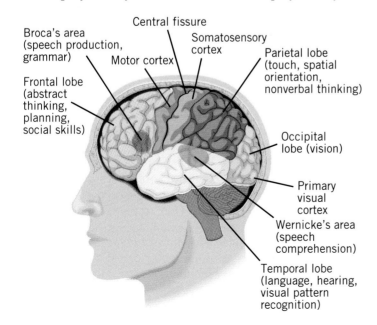

**FIGURE 3.14**
The lobes of the cerebral cortex. The cortex has four lobes, each specialized for different functions and each containing primary and association areas.

the brain (including subcortical levels) helps us, for example, to associate the sight of a car stopping suddenly with the sound of squealing tires.

**The Parietal Lobes**   The **parietal lobes** are located in front of the occipital lobes. They are involved in several functions, including the sense of touch, detection of movement in the environment, locating objects in space, and the experience of one's own body as it moves through space. A person with damage to the primary area of the parietal lobes may be unable to feel a thimble on her finger, whereas damage to the association area could render her unable to recognize the object she was feeling as a thimble or to understand what the object does.

The primary area of the parietal lobe, called the **somatosensory cortex,** lies directly behind the **central fissure,** which divides the parietal lobe from the frontal lobe. Different sections of the somatosensory cortex receive information from different parts of the body (Figure 3.15). Thus, one section registers sensations from the hand, another from the foot, and so forth. The parietal lobes are also involved in complex visual processing, particularly the posterior (back) regions nearest to the occipital lobes.

**The Frontal Lobes**   The **frontal lobes** are involved in a number of functions, including movement, attention, planning, social skills, abstract thinking, memory, and some aspects of personality (see Goldman-Rakic, 1995; Russell & Roxanas, 1990; Stuss & Benson, 1984). Figure 3.15 shows the **motor cortex,** the primary zone of the frontal lobe. Through its projections to the basal ganglia, cerebellum, and spinal cord, the motor cortex initiates voluntary movement. The motor cortex and the adjacent somatosensory cortex send and receive information from the same parts of the body.

As the figure indicates, the amount of space devoted to different parts of the body in the motor and somatosensory cortexes is not directly proportional to their size. Parts of the body that produce fine motor movements or have particularly dense and sensitive receptors take up more space in the motor and somatosensory cortexes. These body parts tend to serve important or complex functions and thus require more processing capacity. In humans, the hands, which are crucial to exploring objects and using tools, occupy considerable territory, whereas a section of the back of similar size occupies only a fraction of that space. Other species have different cortical "priorities"; in cats, for example, input from the whiskers receives considerably more space than input from "whiskers" on the face of human males.

In the frontal lobes, the primary area is motor rather than sensory. The association cortex is involved in planning and putting together sequences of behavior. Neurons in the primary areas then issue specific commands to motor neurons throughout the body.

Damage to the frontal lobes can lead to a wide array of problems, from paralysis to difficulty thinking abstractly, focusing attention efficiently, coordinating complex sequences of behavior, and adjusting socially (Damasio, 1994; Grattan & Eslinger, 1991). Lesions in other parts of the brain that project to the frontal lobes can produce similar symptoms if the frontal lobes fail to receive normal activation. For example, the victims of encephalitis lethargica could not initiate movements even though their frontal lobes were intact because projections from the basal ganglia that normally activate the frontal lobes were impaired by dopamine depletion.

In most individuals, the left frontal lobe is also involved in language. **Broca's area,** located in the left frontal lobe at the base of the motor cortex, is specialized for movements of the mouth and tongue necessary for speech production. It also plays a pivotal role in the use and understanding of grammar. Damage to Broca's area causes **Broca's aphasia,** in which a person may have difficulty speaking, putting together grammatical sentences, and articulating words, even though he

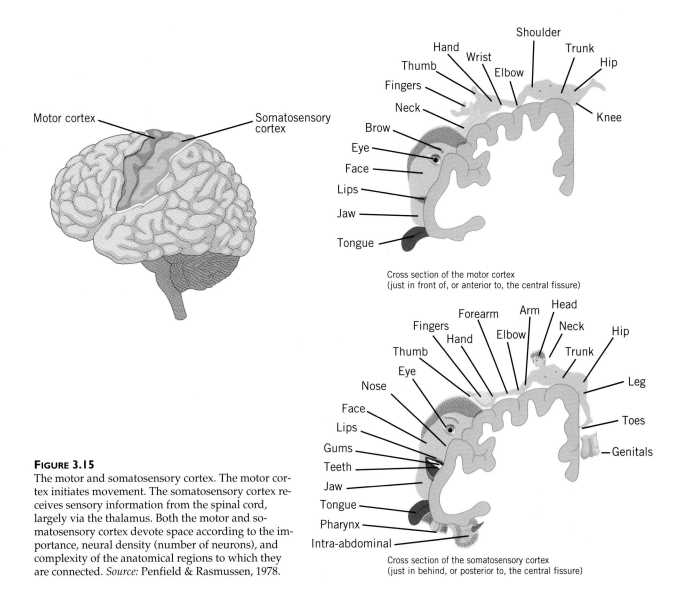

**FIGURE 3.15**
The motor and somatosensory cortex. The motor cortex initiates movement. The somatosensory cortex receives sensory information from the spinal cord, largely via the thalamus. Both the motor and somatosensory cortex devote space according to the importance, neural density (number of neurons), and complexity of the anatomical regions to which they are connected. *Source:* Penfield & Rasmussen, 1978.

may remain able to comprehend language. Individuals with lesions to this area occasionally have difficulty comprehending *complex* sentences if subjects and objects cannot be easily recognized from context. For example, they might have difficulty decoding the sentence, "The cat, which was under the hammock, chased the bird, which was flying over the dog."

The Temporal Lobes    The **temporal lobes,** located in the lower side portions of the cortex, are particularly important in audition (hearing) and language. The connection between hearing and language makes evolutionary sense because language, until relatively recently, was always spoken (rather than written). The primary cortex receives sensory information from the ears, and the association cortex breaks the flow of sound into meaningful units (such as words). Cells in the primary cortex respond to particular frequencies of sound (that is, to different tones) and are arranged anatomically from low (toward the front of the brain) to high frequencies (toward the back).

For most people the left hemisphere of the temporal lobe is specialized for language, although some linguistic functions are shared by the right hemisphere. **Wernicke's area,** located in the left temporal lobe, is important in language comprehension. Damage to Wernicke's area may produce **Wernicke's aphasia,** characterized by difficulty understanding what words and sentences mean. Patients with Wernicke's aphasia often produce "word salad": They may speak fluently and expressively, as if their speech were meaningful, but the words are tossed together so that they make little sense. In contrast, right temporal damage typically results in nonverbal deficits, such as difficulty recognizing songs, faces, or paintings.

Although psychologists once believed that hearing and language were the primary functions of the temporal lobes, more recent research suggests that the temporal lobes have more than one region and that these different regions serve different functions (Rodman, 1997). For example, one region is comprised of visual association cortex involved in identifying objects. As demonstrated in lesion studies with monkeys and humans, neurons toward the back (posterior regions) of the brain adjacent to the occipital lobes are involved in discriminating qualities of objects such as their shape and size. Toward the front of the brain (anterior), temporal neurons are more involved in memory for objects seen previously.

**INTERIM SUMMARY**    The **cerebral cortex** includes **primary areas,** which usually process raw sensory data (except in the frontal lobes), and **association areas,** which are involved in complex mental processes such as perception and thinking. The cortex consists of two hemispheres, each of which has four lobes. The **occipital lobes** are involved in vision. The **parietal lobes** are involved in the sense of touch and in perception of movement and space. The **frontal lobes** serve a variety of functions, such as coordinating and initiating movement, attention, planning, social skills, abstract thinking, memory, and aspects of personality. Sections of the **temporal lobes** are important in hearing, language, and visual object recognition.

## FROM MIND TO BRAIN

### THE IMPACT OF FRONTAL AND TEMPORAL LOBE DAMAGE ON PERSONALITY

If damage to the brain can affect such specific functions as language, what can it do to the complex patterns of emotion, thought, and behavior that constitute an individual's personality? Psychologists define personality much as laypeople do, as both a person's reputation (the way people tend to perceive him) and the enduring psychological attributes (mental processes) that create this reputation. Personality thus includes an individual's characteristic ways of feeling, of thinking about himself and the world, and of behaving. We hold people responsible for their personalities and tend to associate personality more with the "mind" or the "soul" than with the brain. We condemn people for aspects of their personality or character in a way that we do not for mental retardation or physical handicaps.

But is personality really so independent of the brain that serves as its biological substrate? Can a damaged brain create a damaged soul for which a person bears no more responsibility than for paralysis caused by an automobile accident? In fact, damage to parts of the brain can alter personality so that someone literally becomes a different person. Lesions to the frontal and temporal lobes provide striking examples.

Patients with frontal damage often make tactless comments and are described as callous, grandiose, boastful, and unable to understand other people's perspectives. They are also prone to lewd, bawdy, or childish joking (Ron, 1989; Russell & Roxanas, 1990; Stuss et al., 1992). A famous early report of such symptoms was the case of a construction worker named Phineas Gage. In 1848 an explosion sent a metal bar of more than an inch in diameter through Gage's skull, damaging association areas of his frontal lobes. Previously known as a decent, conscientious man, Gage was described following the accident as childish and irreverent. He was also unable to control his impulses and was constantly devising plans that he would abandon within moments (Blumer & Benson, 1984; Damasio, 1994). According to his doctor, the accident disrupted the balance between Gage's intellect and his "animal propensities."

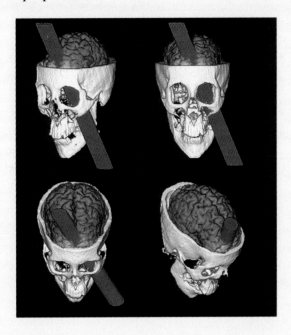

*Computerized images from four angles reconstruct the likely path of the rod through Phineas Gage's frontal lobes.*

Another broad class of personality alterations associated with frontal lobe lesions includes indifference, apathy, and loss of motivation. A 46-year-old man suffered a skull fracture in a car accident and consequently had a portion of his left frontal lobe removed. Although his physical and cognitive abilities returned to normal, his personality changed dramatically. Prior to the accident, his friends described him as friendly, active in the community, talkative, animated, and happy. He was a warm, loving father and husband and a successful salesperson. After his injury, he became quiet, spent most of his time alone smoking, and spoke only in response to questions. His altered behavior makes sense neuropsychologically, since the frontal lobes are involved in initiating activity. The patient spoke in an intelligent but very "matter of fact" manner, and he was completely indifferent to his wife and children, who eventually stopped seeing him (Blumer & Benson, 1984).

Another type of brain pathology associated with specific types of personality change is temporal lobe epilepsy, a seizure disorder characterized by abnormal electrical activity in the brain that begins in the temporal lobe. A 43-year-old businessman began to experience seizures and personality changes after he suffered a head injury in a car accident. After his injury he became excessively verbose and preoccupied with irrelevant details; he could literally spend hours discussing small, tangential details before returning to the point he was trying to make. (No, he did not become a professor or textbook author.) His inability to maintain a fluent conversation, as well as his short temper, eventually led to a breakdown in communication with his wife and periods of marital separation (Blumer & Benson, 1984).

These cases challenge the way most of us intuitively understand ourselves and other people, particularly in the West, where cultural beliefs emphasize personal responsibility and the separation of mind and body. How does a person respond to a once loving spouse or father who no longer seems to care? Is he the same husband or father, or does the same body now house a different person? Is he accountable for the way he behaves?

The courts were faced with just such a dilemma in sentencing children who survived encephalitis lethargica, some of whom developed sexual perversions and became sex offenders (Cheyette & Cummings, 1995). As we will see in Chapter 12, the moral and philosophical issues become even more complex in the face of evidence that personality is partly innate and that some people are born with a tendency to behave antisocially or indifferently to other people.

### Cerebral Lateralization

We have seen that the left frontal and temporal lobes tend to play a more important role in speech and language than their right-hemisphere counterparts. This raises the question of whether other cortical functions are **lateralized,** that is, localized on one or the other side of the brain, and if so, how extensively.

Global generalizations require caution because most functions that are popularly considered to be lateralized are actually represented on both sides of the brain in most people. However, some division of labor between the hemispheres does exist, with each side **dominant** for (that is, in more control of) certain functions. In general, at least for right-handed people, the left hemisphere tends to be dominant for language, logic, complex motor behavior, and aspects of consciousness (particularly verbal aspects). Many of these left-hemisphere functions are analytical, breaking down thoughts and perceptions into component parts and analyzing the relations among them.

*Drawing by Sidney Harris.*

The right hemisphere tends to be dominant for nonlinguistic functions such as forming visual maps of the environment. Studies indicate that it is involved in the recognition of faces, places, and nonlinguistic sounds such as music. The right hemisphere's specialization for nonlinguistic sounds also seems to hold in nonhuman animals: Japanese macaque monkeys, for example, process vocalizations from other macaques on the left but other sounds in their environment on the right (Petersen et al., 1984). Recent research indicates that the region of the brain that constitutes Wernicke's area of the left temporal lobe in humans may have special significance in chimpanzees as well, since this region is larger in the left than right hemisphere in chimps as in humans (Gannon et al., 1998).

**Split-Brain Studies**    A particularly important source of information about cerebral lateralization has been case studies of **split-brain** patients—individuals whose corpus callosum has been surgically cut, blocking communication between the two hemispheres. Severing this connective tissue is a radical treatment for severe epileptic seizures that spread from one hemisphere to another and cannot be controlled by other means.

In their everyday behavior, split-brain patients generally appear normal (Sperry, 1984). However, their two hemispheres can actually operate independently, and each may be oblivious to what the other is doing. Under certain experimental circumstances, the disconnection between the two minds housed in one brain becomes apparent. To understand the results of these experiments, bear in mind that the left hemisphere, which is dominant for most speech functions, receives information from the right visual field and that the right hemisphere receives information from the left. Normally, whether the right or left hemisphere receives the information makes little difference because once the message reaches the brain, the two hemispheres freely pass information between them. Severing the corpus callosum, however, blocks this sharing of information (Gazzaniga, 1967).

Figure 3.16a depicts a typical split-brain experiment. A split-brain patient is seated at a table, and the surface of the table is blocked from view by a screen so the individual cannot see objects on it. The experimenter asks the person to focus on a point in the center of the screen. A word (here, *key*) is quickly flashed on the left side of the screen. When information is flashed for only about 150 milliseconds, the eyes do not have time to move, ensuring that the information is sent to only one hemisphere. The patient is unable to identify the word verbally because the information never reached his left hemisphere, which is dominant for speech. He can, however, select a key with his left hand from an array of objects hidden behind the screen because the left hand receives information from the right hemisphere, which "saw" the key. Thus, the right hand literally does not know what

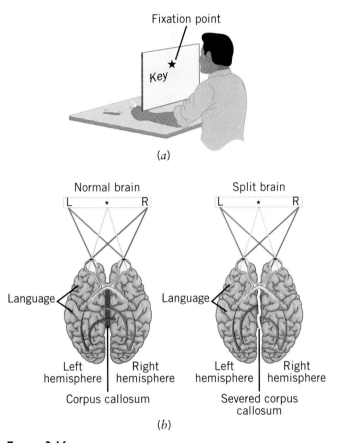

**FIGURE 3.16**

A split-brain study. In a typical split-brain study (*a*), a patient with a severed corpus callosum sees the word *key* flashed on the left portion of the screen. Although he cannot name what he has seen, as speech is lateralized to the left hemisphere, he is able to use his left hand to select the key from a number of objects because the right hemisphere, which has "seen" the key, controls the left hand and has *some* language skills. Part (*b*) illustrates the way information from the left and right visual fields is transmitted to the brain in normal and split brains. When participants focus their vision on a point in the middle of the visual field (such as the star in the diagram), anything on the left of this fixation point (for instance, point L) will be sensed by receptors on the right half of each eye. These receptors are located in the retina, at the back of the eye. This information is subsequently processed by the right hemisphere. Conversely, receptors in the left part of each eye's retina register information from the right visual field and pass this information along to the left hemisphere. In the normal brain, information is readily transmitted via the corpus callosum between the two hemispheres. In the split-brain patient, the severed neural route means the right and left hemispheres "see" different things. *Source:* Part (*a*) adapted from Gazzaniga, 1967.

the left hand is doing, and neither does the left hemisphere. Figure 3.16*b* illustrates the way visual information from the left and right visual fields is transmitted to the brain in normal and split-brain patients.

This research raises an intriguing question: Can a person with two independent hemispheres be literally of two minds, with two centers of conscious awareness, like Siamese twins joined at the cortex? Consider the case of a 10-year-old boy with a split brain (LeDoux et al., 1977). In one set of tests, the boy was asked about his sense of himself, his future, and his likes and dislikes. The examiner asked the boy questions in which a word or words were replaced by the word *blank*. The missing words were then presented to one hemisphere or the other. For example, when the boy was asked, "Who _____?" the missing words *are you* were projected to the left or the right hemisphere. Not surprisingly, the boy could only answer verbally when inquiries were made to the left hemisphere. The right hemisphere could, however, answer by spelling out words with letter tiles with the left hand (because the right hemisphere is usually not entirely devoid of language) when the question was flashed to the right hemisphere. Thus, the boy could describe his feelings or moods with both hemispheres.

Many times the views expressed by the right and left hemispheres overlapped, but not always. One day, when the boy was in a pleasant mood, his hemispheres tended to agree (both, for example, reporting high self-esteem). Another day, when the boy seemed anxious and behaved aggressively, the hemispheres were in disagreement. In general, his right-hemisphere responses were consistently more negative than those of the left, as if the right hemisphere tended to be in a worse mood. Researchers using other methods have also reported that the two hemispheres differ in their processing of positive and negative emotions and that these differences may exist at birth (Davidson, 1995; Fox, 1991). Left frontal regions are generally more involved in processing positive feelings that motivate approach toward objects in the environment, whereas right frontal regions are more related to negative emotions that motivate avoidance or withdrawal. One of my own patients received frontal damage in a horseback-riding accident and has unsuccessfully undergone every form of treatment for a severe and deadening depression possible, thus far to no avail. The damage was actually in the right hemisphere and appears to have destroyed inhibitory mechanisms that normally *control* right frontal emotional activation.

**Sex Differences in Lateralization**   Psychologists have long known that females typically score higher on tests of verbal fluency, perceptual speed, and manual dexterity than males, whereas males tend to score higher on tests of mathematical ability and spatial processing, particularly geometric thinking (Bradbury, 1989; Casey et al., 1997; Maccoby & Jacklin, 1974). In a study of students under age 13 with exceptional mathematical ability (measured by scores of 700 or above on the SAT), boys outnumbered girls 13 to 1 (Benbow & Stanley, 1983). On the other hand, males are much more likely than females to develop learning disabilities with reading and language comprehension. Although these sex differences are not particularly large (Caplan et al., 1997; Hyde, 1990), they have been documented in several countries and have not consistently decreased over the last two decades despite social changes encouraging equality of the sexes (see Bradbury, 1989; Randhawa, 1991). Psychologists have thus debated whether such discrepancies in performance might be based in part on innate differences between the brains of men and women.

Some data suggest that women's and men's brains may indeed differ in ways that affect cognitive functioning. At a hormonal level, research with human and nonhuman primates indicates that the presence of testosterone and estrogen in the bloodstream early in development influences aspects of brain development (Clark & Goldman-Rakic, 1989; Gorski & Barraclough, 1963). One study found that level of exposure to testosterone during the second trimester of pregnancy predicted the speed with which children could rotate mental images in their minds at age 7 (Grimshaw et al., 1995). Some evidence even suggests that women's spatial abilities on certain tasks are lower during high-estrogen periods of the menstrual cycle, whereas motor skills, on which females typically have an advantage, are superior during high-estrogen periods (Kimura, 1987).

Perhaps the most definitive data on gender differences in the brain come from recent research using fMRI technology (Shaywitz et al., 1995). In males, a rhyming task led to activation of Broca's area in the left frontal lobe. The same task in females produced frontal activation in *both* hemispheres (Figure 3.17). Thus, in females, language appears less lateralized.

Cultural factors appear to play a significant role in shaping the skills and interests of males and females as well. Parents tend to talk to little girls more, and they encourage boys to play with mechanical objects and discourage them from many verbal activities such as writing poetry. Furthermore, despite efforts to remove gender biases from textbooks, a study comparing high school chemistry textbooks from the early 1970s with their current editions found that males are still shown three times more often in illustrations and examples than females, subtly perpetuating the view of chemistry as a male discipline (although the ratio had dropped from 5 to 1) (Bazler & Simonis, 1991). Some of the most interesting evidence of the impact of culture comes from a study that followed girls from ages 11 to 18 (Newcombe & Dubas, 1992). The best predictors of spatial ability at age 16 were two psychological attributes at age 11: wishing to be a boy and having a more stereotypically masculine view of what they would like to be. To what extent these psychological attributes themselves could be influenced by biology, however, is unknown.

**INTERIM SUMMARY**    Some psychological functions are **lateralized,** or processed primarily by one hemisphere. In general, the left hemisphere is more verbal and analytic, and the right is specialized for nonlinguistic functions. Although the differences tend to be relatively small, males and females tend to differ in cognitive strengths, which appears to be related in part to differences between their brains, including in the extent of lateralization of functions such as language.

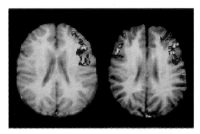

**FIGURE 3.17**
Gender differences in cortical activation during a rhyming task. The photo on the left shows that for males, rhyming activated only Broca's area in the left frontal lobe. For females (right photo), this task activated the same region in both hemispheres. (From the angle at which these images were taken, left activation appears on the right.) *Source:* B. A. Shaywitz, et al., 1995. NMR/Yale Medical School.

## A GLOBAL VISTA

### ENVIRONMENT, CULTURE, AND THE BRAIN

The issue of how, and in what ways, cultural practices and beliefs influence cognitive abilities raises an intriguing question: Since all abilities reflect the actions of neural circuits, can environmental and cultural factors actually affect the circuitry of the brain?

We have little trouble imagining that *biological* factors can alter the brain. **Tumors,** or abnormal tissue growths, can damage regions of the brain by putting pressure on them, leading to symptoms as varied as blurred vision, searing headaches, or explosive emotional outbursts. High blood pressure or diseases of the blood vessels can lead to **strokes,** in which blood flow to regions of the brain is interrupted. If the interruption occurs for more than about 10 minutes, the cells in that area die, leading to changes in psychological functioning such as paralysis, loss of speech, or even death if the stroke destroys neural regions vital for life support such as the medulla or hypothalamus. Trauma to the nervous system caused by automobile accidents, blows to the head, or falls that break the neck can have similar effects, as can infections caused by viruses, bacteria, or parasites.

But what about psychological blows to the head, or, conversely, experiences that enrich the brain or steer it in one direction or another? As we saw in Chapter 2, monkeys separated from their mothers for long periods of time develop abnormal electroencephalograms (EEGs), suggesting that social and environmental processes can indeed alter the structure of the brain. A fascinating line of research indicates that early sensory enrichment or deprivation can affect the brain in fundamental ways that may be relevant to the experience of children in different social and cultural environments (Heritch et al., 1990; Rosenzweig et al., 1972). In one series of studies, young male rats were raised in one of two conditions: an enriched environment, with 6 to 12 rats sharing an open-mesh cage filled with a variety of toys; or an impoverished one, in which rats lived alone without toys or companions (Cummins et al., 1977). Days or months later, the experimenters sacrificed the rats and weighed their forebrains. The brains of enriched rats tended to be heavier than those of the deprived rats, indicating that different environments can alter the course of neural development.

Is the same true of humans? And can cultural differences become translated into neurological differences? The human brain triples in weight in the first two years and quadruples to its adult weight by age 14 (Winson, 1985). This means that social, cultural, and other environmental influences can become *built into* the brain (Shore, 1995), particularly into the more evolutionarily recent cortical regions involved in complex thought and learning (Damasio, 1994). For instance, many native Asian language speakers have difficulty distinguishing *la* from *ra* because Asian languages do not distinguish these units of sound. One study found that Japanese people who heard sound frequencies between *la* and *ra* did not hear them as *either la or ra*, as do Americans (Goto, 1971). If children do not hear certain linguistic patterns in the first few years of life (such as the *la–ra* distinction, the French *r*, or the Hebrew *ch*), they may lose the capacity to do so. Thus, these patterns may have to be laid down with different and much less efficient neural machinery later on (Lenneburg, 1967).

*This schoolboy from Shanghai may be using somewhat different neural circuits than a schoolchild across the globe who writes in a language that is not pictographic.*

Many Asian languages also differ from languages derived from Latin (such as French, English, and Spanish) in that they are *tone languages*, which means that intonation—the rising and falling of the voice—is used to distinguish otherwise identical words. In Mandarin Chinese, for example, saying the word *mao* with a rising tone means "cat" and with a falling tone, "hat." The processing of tone, like music, is typically more lateralized to the right hemisphere in the West. A study of Chinese subjects suffering from Broca's aphasia, however, suggests that being a native Chinese speaker may shift this function to the left hemisphere. These patients, with documented left-hemisphere damage, had considerable difficulty producing tone (Packard, 1986). Another study found similar evidence for left-hemisphere processing of tone in Norwegian, a non-Asian language that uses tone as well (Moen, 1993). In this study, which focused on normal individuals without brain damage, participants were better able to discriminate tone with their right ear than their left, suggesting a left-hemisphere superiority for tone processing. As we will see in later chapters, cultures shape not only language but also fundamental ways of thinking and feeling, which themselves rely on, and shape the connections among, billions of neurons. Thus, mind, brain, and culture may not be so easily divisible.

## MIND, BRAIN, AND GENE

Having described the structure and function of the nervous system, we conclude with a brief discussion of the influence of genetics on psychological functioning. Few people would argue with the view that hair and eye color are heavily influenced by genetics or that genetic vulnerabilities contribute to heart disease, cancer, and diabetes. Yet, as we saw in Chapter 1, as soon as one suggests genetic roots to human behaviors or to differences between individuals, clouds of controversy begin to collect. In part, the controversy reflects realistic concerns about branding certain people or races as genetically inferior. In part, though, a resistance to genetic explanations is based in strongly held cultural beliefs that "all men are created equal" and that anyone can do almost anything with hard work and perseverance.

### GENETICS

Psychologists interested in genetics study the influence of genetic blueprints—**genotypes**—on observable psychological attributes or qualities—**phenotypes.** The phenotypes that interest psychologists are characteristics such as quickness of thought, extroverted behavior, and the tendency to become anxious or depressed. The **gene** is the unit of hereditary transmission. Although a single gene may control eye color, genetic contributions to most complex phenomena, such as intelligence or personality, reflect the action of many genes.

Genes are encoded in the DNA (deoxyribonucleic acid) contained within the nucleus of every cell in the body. Genes are arranged along **chromosomes**—strands of paired DNA that spiral around each other (Figure 3.18). Human cells have 46 chromosomes, except sperm cells in males and egg cells in females, each of which has 23. The union of a sperm and an egg creates a cell with 46 chromo-

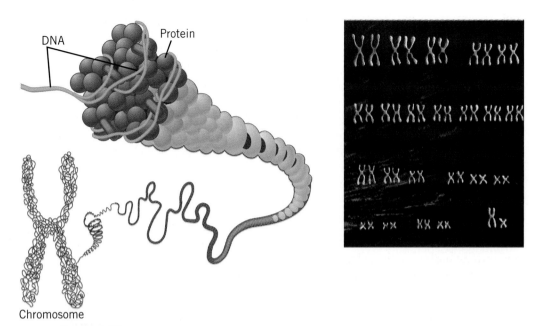

**FIGURE 3.18**
Human chromosomes. A drawing and magnified photograph of human chromosomes.

somes, half from the mother and half from the father. Children receive a somewhat random selection of half the genetic material of each parent, which means that the probability of sharing any particular gene with a parent is 1 out of 2, or .50. This number represents the **degree of relatedness** between parent and offspring.

Because children and their parents are related by .50 and parents and *their* parents are related by .50, the degree of relatedness between grandchildren and grandparents is .25, or $.5 \times .5$. In other words, a grandmother passes on half of her genes to her daughter, who passes on half of those genes to her child; the likelihood that the grandchild receives any particular gene from her maternal grandmother through her mother is thus .25. Siblings are also related by .50 because they have a .25 chance of sharing a gene from their mother and a .25 chance from their father; added together, this means that they are related by .50 on the average. Table 3.2 shows the degree of relatedness for various relatives.

The fact that relatives differ in degree of relatedness enables researchers to tease apart the relative contributions of heredity and environment to phenotypic differences between individuals. If the similarity between relatives on attributes

**TABLE 3.2    DEGREE OF RELATEDNESS AMONG SELECTED RELATIVES**

| RELATION | DEGREE OF RELATEDNESS |
|---|---|
| Identical (MZ) twin | 1.0 |
| Fraternal (DZ) twin | .50 |
| Parent/child | .50 |
| Sibling | .50 |
| Grandparent/grandchild | .25 |
| Half-sibling | .25 |
| First cousin | .125 |
| Nonbiological parent/adopted child | 0 |

such as intelligence or conscientiousness varies with their degree of relatedness, this suggests genetic influence, especially if the relatives did not share a common upbringing (such as siblings adopted into different families). Particularly important for research on the genetic basis of behavioral differences are identical and fraternal twins. **Monozygotic (MZ, or identical) twins** develop from the union of the same sperm and egg. They share the same genetic makeup, so their degree of genetic relatedness is 1.0. In contrast, **dizygotic (DZ, or fraternal) twins** develop from the union of two sperm with two separate eggs. Like other siblings, their degree of relatedness is .50, since they have a 50 percent chance of sharing the same gene for any characteristic.

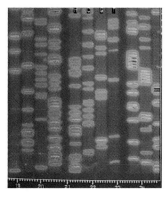

*Data from the Human Genome Project, an international collaborative effort to map the genetic structure of all 46 human chromosomes.*

## BEHAVIORAL GENETICS

A relatively new field called behavioral genetics has produced rapid advances in our understanding of the relative roles of genetics and environment in shaping mental processes and behavior. Recent evidence suggests that genetic influences are far greater than once believed in a number of domains, including personality, intelligence, and mental illness (Fuller & Thompson, 1978; Gottesman, 1991; Kendler & Diehl, 1993; McGue et al., 1993; Plomin et al., 1997). Studies of twins provide psychologists a golden opportunity to examine the role of genetics because MZ and DZ twins typically share similar environments but differ in their degree of genetic relatedness. If a psychological attribute is genetically influenced, MZ twins should be more likely than DZ twins and other siblings to share it. This method is not free of bias; identical twins may receive more similar treatment than fraternal twins, since they look the same. Thus, behavioral geneticists also compare twins reared together in the same family with twins who were adopted separately and reared apart (Bouchard et al., 1991; Loehlin, 1989, 1992; Lykken et al., 1992; Tellegen et al., 1988).

The findings from these studies have allowed psychologists to estimate the extent to which differences among individuals on psychological dimensions such as intelligence and personality are **heritable,** or determined by genetic factors. A **heritability coefficient** quantifies the extent to which variation in the trait across individuals (such as high or low levels of conscientiousness) can be accounted for by genetic variation. A coefficient of 0 indicates no heritability at all, while a coefficient of 1.0 indicates that a trait is completely heritable.

An important point, but one that is often misunderstood, is that heritability refers to genetic influences on *variability among individuals*; it says nothing about the extent to which a trait is genetically determined. An example should make this clear. The fact that humans have two eyes is genetically determined. For all practical purposes, however, humans show no variability in the expression of the trait of two-eyedness because virtually all humans are born with two eyes. Thus, the heritability of two-eyedness is 0; genetic variability is not correlated with phenotypic or observed variability because virtually no variability exists. In contrast, the trait of eye *color* has a very high degree of heritability (approaching 1.0) in a heterogeneous population. Thus, heritability refers to the proportion of variability among individuals on an observed trait (phenotypic variance) that can be accounted for by variability in their genes (genotypic variance).

Several studies of the personality characteristics of twins have produced heritability estimates from .15 to .50 (that is, up to 50 percent heritability) on a broad spectrum of traits, including conservatism, neuroticism, nurturance, assertiveness, and aggressiveness (Plomin et al., 1997). Some findings have been very surprising and counterintuitive. For example, identical twins reared apart, who may never have even met each other, tend to have very similar vocational interests and levels of job satisfaction (Arvey et al., 1989; Moloney et al., 1991). Researchers have even found a genetic influence on religious attitudes, beliefs, and values

*Jerry Levey and Mark Newman, separated at birth, met when a colleague did a double-take at a firefighters' convention.*

(Waller et al., 1990). Remarkably, the likelihood of *divorce* is influenced by genetics, since personality traits such as the tendency to be unhappy are partly under genetic control and influence life events such as divorce (Jockin et al., 1996). Heritability estimates for IQ are over .50.

In interpreting findings such as these, however, some caveats are in order. First, as emphasized by leading behavioral geneticists but too readily forgotten, heritability in the range of 50 percent means that environmental factors are equally important—they account for the other 50 percent (Plomin & Rende, 1991). Second, estimates of heritability depend in part on who one includes in the sample. Children who are severely malnourished may show less heritability of IQ than others because malnutrition can place constraints on intellectual potential that can suppress the impact of hereditary differences. In contrast, excluding diverse populations from a sample can lead to the mistaken conclusion that cultural or environmental factors make little difference. Including Bosnian and North American participants in a study of the relative roles of heredity and environment in shaping feelings of mistrust would likely yield much stronger estimates of environmental impact than studying only North Americans because of the recent turmoil, civil war, and genocide in Bosnia. As we will see throughout the book, in most domains, psychologists have become less interested in parceling out the relative roles of genes and environment than in understanding the way genetic and environmental variables *interact*.

**INTERIM SUMMARY**   Psychologists interested in genetics study the influence of genetic blueprints **(genotypes)** on observable qualities **(phenotypes).** Research in behavioral genetics suggests that a surprisingly large percent of the variation among individuals on psychological attributes such as intelligence and personality reflects genetic influences, which interact with environmental variables in very complex ways. **Heritability** refers to the proportion of variability among individuals on an observed characteristic (phenotypic variance) that can be accounted for by genetic variability (genotypic variance).

## SOME CONCLUDING THOUGHTS

When I entered the field as a graduate student less than 20 years ago, a person could be a competent psychologist in many areas of research without being terribly well informed about the brain or genetics. To be sure, knowing more was better than knowing less. Understanding the brain's hierarchical organization was useful in understanding motivation, just as knowing about medications that impact the brain was important in working with patients with severe psychiatric disorders.

But 20 years ago a cognitive psychologist with minimal knowledge about the brain could develop hypotheses and design important experiments—because we knew so little about the function of the hippocampus in memory or the role of the frontal lobes in attention and problem solving. When researchers debated whether people use mental images of verbal propositions to solve spatial problems, they had to design very clever experiments that might test the advantages of one explanation over the other. (Now, we ask participants to rotate mental images in their minds and scan their brains to see where they show the most activation relative to control tasks such as simply looking at pictures.)

Today, things are very different. As we will see throughout this book, scarcely an area of research in psychology has been left untouched by the explosion of new information about the brain, biology, and behavioral genetics. We now know that different memory systems reflect different neural pathways, and we can no longer study "memory" as if it were one system. We know that pleasant and unpleasant feelings occur through the activation of separate neural pathways that rely on different neurotransmitters, so we can no longer view happiness and sadness as opposite ends of a continuum. And we know that genetic factors contribute substantially to success in school, work, and marriage. Thus, if we discover, for example, that children of divorce are more likely themselves to have problems sustaining long-term relationships, we must at least consider the possibility that *genetic* vulnerabilities—to sadness or anxiety, for example—might render them, like their parents, less able to sustain a relationship.

Does this mean that psychological experiences are nothing but biological events dressed up in cognitive or emotional clothing? No. The grief of losing a parent or lover is not adequately explained as the activation of neural circuits in the hypothalamus, amygdala, and cortex. And the most sophisticated brain-scanning techniques yield little of value if psychologists cannot associate what is happening in the brain with psychologically meaningful processes. For example, if we do not understand how people think and feel as they make moral decisions, we will have no idea what tasks to have them perform while scanning their brains to learn about the neural underpinnings of morality.

Thus, psychologists are increasingly focusing on *brain–behavior relationships*. To study the biological side of human nature is not to commit oneself to an image of a disembodied brain divorced from its psychological, social, and cultural context. An understanding of the biological underpinnings of human mental life and behavior should not *reduce* its richness; it should *add to* it. We will never comprehend the complexities of motivation, personality, development, or social interaction simply by "looking under the hood" of our skulls or of our genes. But as the explosion of research that has come at the end of the millenium has shown, we will never again understand these phenomena *without* looking under the hood. We have reached a new level of self-understanding, and we can never turn back.

## SUMMARY

### NEURONS: BASIC UNITS OF THE NERVOUS SYSTEM

1. The firing of billions of nerve cells provides the physiological basis for psychological processes.

2. **Neurons,** or nerve cells, are the basic units of the nervous system. **Sensory neurons** carry sensory information from sensory receptors to the central nervous system. **Motor neurons** transmit commands from the brain to the glands and muscles of the body. **Interneurons** connect neurons with one another.

3. A neuron typically has a **cell body, dendrites** (branchlike extensions of the cell body), and an **axon** that carries information to other neurons. Axons are often covered with **myelin** for more efficient electrical transmission. Located on the axons are **terminal buttons,** which contain **neurotransmitters,** chemicals that transmit information across the **synapse** (the space between neurons through which they communicate).

4. The "resting" voltage at which a neuron is not firing is called the **resting potential.** When a neuron stimulates another neuron, it either **depolarizes** the membrane (reducing its polarization) or **hyperpolarizes** it (increasing its polarization). The spreading voltage changes that occur when the neural membrane receives signals from other cells are called **graded potentials.** If enough depolarizing graded potentials accumulate to cross a threshold, the neuron will **fire.** This **action potential,** or nerve impulse, leads to the release of **neurotransmitters** (such as glutamate, GABA, dopamine, serotonin, and acetylcholine). These chemical messages are received by **receptors** in the cell membrane of other neurons, which in turn can excite or inhibit those neurons. *Neuromodulators* can increase or reduce the impact of other neurotransmitters released into the synapse.

## THE ENDOCRINE SYSTEM

5. The **endocrine system** is a collection of glands that control various bodily functions through the secretion of **hormones.** The endocrine system complements the cell-to-cell communication of the nervous system by sending global messages through the bloodstream.

## THE PERIPHERAL NERVOUS SYSTEM

6. The **peripheral nervous system (PNS)** consists of neurons that carry messages to and from the central nervous system. The peripheral nervous system has two subdivisions: the somatic nervous system and the autonomic nervous system. The **somatic nervous system** consists of the sensory neurons that receive information through sensory receptors in the skin, muscles, and other parts of the body, such as the eyes, and the motor neurons that direct the action of skeletal muscles. The **autonomic nervous system** controls basic life processes such as the beating of the heart, workings of the digestive system, and breathing. It consists of two parts, the **sympathetic nervous system** (which is activated in response to threats) and the **parasympathetic nervous system** (which returns the body to normal and works to maintain the body's energy resources).

## THE CENTRAL NERVOUS SYSTEM

7. The **central nervous system (CNS)** consists of the brain and spinal cord. It is hierarchically organized, with an overall structure that follows its evolution. Evolutionarily more recent centers regulate many of the processes that occur at lower levels.

8. Aside from carrying out reflexes, the **spinal cord** transmits sensory information to the brain and transmits messages from the brain to the muscles and organs.

9. Several structures comprise the **hindbrain.** The **medulla oblongata** controls vital physiological functions, such as heartbeat, circulation, and respiration,

and forms a link between the spinal cord and the rest of the brain. The **cere-bellum** appears to be involved in a variety of tasks, including learning, discriminating stimuli from one another, and coordination of smooth movements. The **reticular formation** maintains consciousness and helps regulate activity and arousal states throughout the central nervous system, including sleep cycles.

10. The **midbrain** consists of the tectum and tegmentum. The **tectum** includes structures involved in orienting to visual and auditory stimuli as well as others involved in linking unpleasant feelings to behaviors that can help the animal escape or avoid them. The **tegmentum** includes parts of the reticular formation and other nuclei with a variety of functions, of which two are particularly important: movement and the linking of pleasure to behaviors that help the animal obtain reward.

11. The **forebrain** consists of the hypothalamus, thalamus, and cerebrum. The **hypothalamus** is involved in regulating a wide range of behaviors, including eating, sleeping, sexual activity, and emotional experience. The **thalamus** is a complex of nuclei that perform a number of functions; one of the most important is to provide initial processing of sensory information and transmit this information to higher brain centers.

12. The **cerebrum** includes a number of **subcortical** structures as well as an outer layer, or **cortex.** The subcortical structures are the limbic system and the basal ganglia. Structures of the **limbic system** (the **septal area, amygdala,** and **hippocampus**) are involved in emotion, motivation, learning, and memory. **Basal ganglia** structures are involved in the control of movement; they also appear to play a part in mood and memory.

13. In humans, the **cerebral cortex** allows the flexible construction of sequences of voluntary movements, enables people to discriminate complex sensory patterns, and provides the capacity to think symbolically. The **primary areas** of the cortex receive sensory information and initiate motor movements. The **association areas** are involved in putting together perceptions, ideas, and plans.

14. The **right** and **left hemispheres** of the cerebral cortex are connected by the **corpus callosum.** Each hemisphere consists of four sections or lobes. The **occipital lobes** are specialized for vision. The **parietal lobes** are involved in a number of functions, including the sense of touch, movement, and the experience of one's own body and other objects in space. The functions of the **frontal lobes** include coordination of movement, attention, planning, social skills, conscience, abstract thinking, memory, and aspects of personality. Sections of the **temporal lobes** are important in hearing, language, and visual object recognition. Some psychological functions are **lateralized,** or primarily processed by one hemisphere.

15. Cultural and environmental factors can modify not only behavior but also the structure of the brain.

## MIND, BRAIN, AND GENE

16. Environment and genes interact in staggeringly complex ways that psychologists are just beginning to understand. Psychologists interested in genetics study the influence of genetic blueprints (**genotypes**) on observable psychological attributes or qualities (**phenotypes).** Studies in **behavioral genetics** suggest that a substantial portion of the variation among individuals on many psychological attributes such as intelligence and personality are **heritable.** Heritability refers to the proportion of variability among individuals on an observed trait (phenotypic variance) that can be accounted for by variability in their genes (genotypic variance).

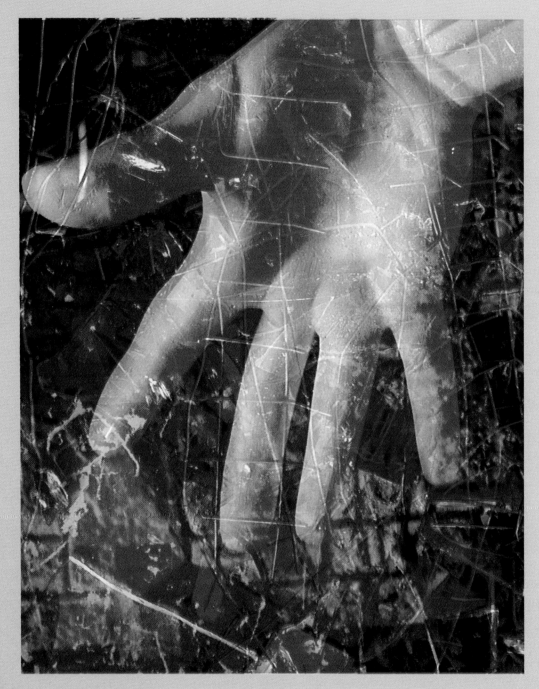

Saul le Boff, Untitled.

CHAPTER *4*

# Sensation and Perception

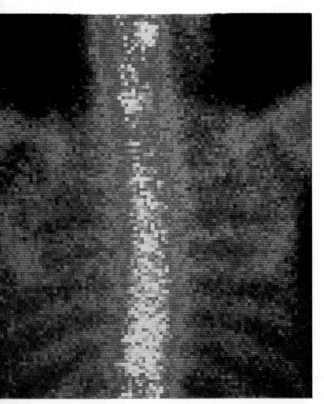

*A* woman in her early twenties damaged her knee in a fall. Following surgery, she experienced sharp, burning pain so excruciating that she could not eat or sleep. The pain ran from her ankle to the middle of her thigh, and the slightest touch—even a light brush with a piece of cotton—provoked a feeling of intense burning. Surgical attempts to relieve her pain gave her no relief or only temporary relief followed by even more severe pain (Gracely et al., 1992). Tragically, her pain persisted indefinitely.

Another case had a happier ending. A 50-year-old man suffering from chronic lower back pain underwent surgery after unsuccessful attempts to treat it with exercise and medication. Like roughly 1 percent of patients who undergo this procedure (Sachs et al., 1990), he, too, developed severe burning pain and extraordinary sensitivity to any kind of stimulation of the skin. Fortunately, however, the pain disappeared after three months of treatment.

These patients suffered from a disorder called *painful neuropathy*, which literally means a painful illness of the neurons. Painful neuropathy can result from either an accident or from surgery. What essentially happens is that the brain interprets signals from receptors in the skin or joints that normally indicate light touch, pressure, or movement as excruciating pain. Researchers are unclear whether the problem lies in the peripheral or the central nervous system. Physical trauma might rewire peripheral nerves, so that they connect with the wrong sensory receptors and transmit an erroneous message to the brain; alternatively, the brain may adapt to nerve damage by becoming hypersensitive to any stimulation of the affected region (Gracely et al., 1992).

Whether the damage is peripheral or central, this syndrome raises some intriguing questions about the way the nervous system translates information about the world into psychological experience. Does the intensity of sensory experience normally mirror the intensity of physical stimulation? In other words, when pain increases or the light in a theater seems extremely bright following a movie, how much does this reflect changes in reality versus changes in our *perception* of reality? And if neurons can become accidentally rewired so that touch is misinterpreted as burning pain, could attaching neurons from the ear to the primary cortex of the occipital lobes produce visual images of sound?

These are some of the central questions underlying the study of sensation and perception. **Sensation** refers to the process by which the sense organs gather information about the environment and transmit this information to the brain for initial processing. **Perception** is the process by which the brain organizes and interprets these sensations. Sensations are immediate experiences of qualities—red, hot, bright, and so forth—whereas perceptions are experiences of objects or events that appear to have form, order, or meaning (Figure 4.1). The distinction between sensation and perception is useful though somewhat artificial, since sensory and perceptual processes form an integrated whole, translating physical reality into psychological reality.

**FIGURE 4.1**
From sensation to perception. Take a careful look at this picture before reading further, and try to figure out what it depicts. The photograph makes little sense until you recognize a Dalmatian, nose to the ground, walking toward a tree in the upper left corner. When people first look at this photo, their eyes transmit information to the brain about which parts of the picture are white and which are black; this is sensation. Sorting out the pockets of white and black into a meaningful picture is perception.

Why do sensation and perception matter? When students first approach this topic, they often think, "Oh, that rods-and-cones stuff I learned when I was ten," and wonder what it has to do with psychology. I was one of those students. What drew me to psychology were questions such as how memory works and why people fall in love. It was only years later that a simple and obvious fact penetrated my thick skull (and my apparently thin cortex): *Sensation and perception are the gateway from the world to the mind.* Memory involves the mental reconstruction of past experience—but what would we remember if we could not sense, perceive, and store images or sounds to re-create in our minds? Or consider love. What would love be if we could not feel another person's skin against ours? Could lovers experience the sense of comfort and security they feel when they mold into each other's arms if the skin were not laden with pressure detectors? (Okay, it isn't Shakespeare, but you get the point.) Without our senses, we are literally senseless—without the capacity to know or feel. And without knowledge or feeling, there is little left to being human.

We begin the chapter with sensation, exploring basic processes that apply to all the senses (or *sensory modalities*—the different senses that provide ways of knowing about stimuli). We then discuss each sense individually, focusing on the two that allow sensation at a distance, vision and hearing (or *audition*), and more briefly exploring smell (*olfaction*), taste (*gustation*), touch, and *proprioception* (the sense of the body's position and motion). Next we turn to perception, beginning with the way the brain organizes and interprets sensations and concluding with the influence of experience, expectations, and needs on the way people make sense of sensations. Does a hamburger taste the same to someone who is starving as to someone who has just eaten? Does an X-ray of a finger look different to a radiologist than to a layperson? And do people *learn* to organize visual sensations into meaningful three-dimensional shapes or are we born with certain processes that organize our experience?

**INTERIM SUMMARY**   **Sensation** is the process by which sense organs gather information about the environment and transmit it to the brain for initial processing; **perception** is the

*Sensation is an active process in which humans, like other animals, focus their senses on potentially important information.*

related process by which the brain selects, organizes, and interprets sensations. Sensation and perception are the gateway from the external world to the mind.

## BASIC PRINCIPLES

Throughout this discussion, three general principles repeatedly emerge. First, *there is no one-to-one correspondence between physical and psychological reality.* What is "out there" is not directly reproduced "in here." Of course, the relation between physical stimuli and our psychological experience of them is not random; as we will see, it is actually so orderly that it can be expressed as an equation. Yet the inner world is not simply a photograph of the outer. The degree of pressure or pain experienced when a pin presses against the skin—even in those of us *without* painful neuropathy—does not precisely match the actual pressure exerted. Up to a certain point, light pressure is not experienced at all, and pressure only feels like pain when it crosses a certain threshold. The inexact correspondence between physical and psychological reality is one of the fundamental findings of **psychophysics,** the branch of psychology that studies the relation between attributes of the physical world and our psychological experience of them.

Second, *sensation and perception are active.* Sensation may seem passive—images are cast on the retina at the back of the eye; pressure is imposed on the skin. Yet sensation is first and foremost an act of translation, converting external energy into an internal version, or *representation,* of it. People also orient themselves to stimuli to capture sights, sounds, and smells that are relevant to them. We turn our ears toward potentially threatening sounds to magnify their impact on our senses, just as we turn our noses toward the smell of baking bread. We also selectively focus our consciousness on parts of the environment that are particularly relevant to our needs and goals (Chapter 9).

Like sensation, perception is an active process, which organizes and interprets sensations. The world as subjectively experienced by an individual—the *phenomenological world*—is a joint product of external reality and the person's creative efforts to understand and depict it mentally. People often assume that perception is like photographing a scene or tape recording a sound and that they need only open their eyes and ears to capture what is "really" there. In fact, perception is probably more like stitching a quilt than taking a photograph. The phenomenological world must be constructed from sensory experience, just as the quilt maker creates something whole from threads and patches.

If perception is a creative, constructive process, to what extent do people perceive the world in the same way? Does red appear to one person as it does to another? If one person loves garlic and another hates it, are the two loving and hating the same taste or does garlic have a different taste to each? To what extent do people see the world the way it really is?

Plato argued that what we perceive is little more than shadows on the wall of a cave, cast by the movement of an unseen reality in the dim light. What does it mean to say that a cup of coffee is hot? Relative to what? Do fish perceive the depths of the ocean as cold? And is grass *really* green? A person who is color blind for green, whose visual system is unable to discriminate certain wavelengths of light, will not see the grass as green. Is greenness, then, an attribute of the object (grass), the perceiver, or some interaction between them? These are philosophical questions at the heart of sensation and perception.

The third general principle is that *sensation and perception are adaptive.* From an evolutionary perspective, the ability to see, hear, or touch is the product of millions of adaptations that left our senses exquisitely crafted to serve functions that

*The world as perceived represents an interaction between the perceiver and the perceived. (George Braque,* Landscape with Houses, *1908-9, oil on canvas, 65.5x54cm. Collection: Art Gallery of New South Wales. ©1998 Artists Rights Society (ARS), New York, ADAGP, Paris. Reproduced with permission.)*

facilitate survival and reproduction (Tooby & Cosmides, 1992). Frogs have "bug detectors" in their visual systems that automatically fire in the presence of a potential meal. Similarly, humans have neural regions specialized for the perception of faces and facial expressions (Adolphs et al., 1996; Phillips et al, 1997). Human infants have an innate tendency to pay attention to forms that resemble the human face, and over the course of their first year they become remarkably expert at reading emotions from other people's faces (Chapter 13). Attending to their parents' facial cues (such as concern or fear) can mean the difference between approaching or escaping a predator, and reading faces is as important for later adjustment and adaptation as reading words is in a literate culture.

The specific ways sensory systems are constructed reflects evolutionary pressures. Consider something we take for granted, like the placement of the eyes (Figure 4.2). Among vertebrates, the eyes can be placed frontally, as in humans, or laterally (on the sides), as in rabbits. Frontal placement is common in predators, who rely on sensory input from two eyes to pinpoint distance. Lateral placement is more common among animals who are frequently prey, for it provides them with an expanded field of vision; if they cannot have eyes in the back of their head, at least they have something close.

**INTERIM SUMMARY**    Three basic principles apply across all the senses: There is no one-to-one correspondence between physical and psychological reality; sensation and perception are active, not passive; and sensory and perceptual processes reflect the impact of adaptive pressures over the cource of evolution.

## SENSING THE ENVIRONMENT

Although each sensory system is attuned to particular forms of energy, all the senses share certain common features. First, they must translate physical stimulation into sensory signals. Second, they all have thresholds below which a person does not sense anything despite external stimulation. Children know this intuitively when they tiptoe through a room to "sneak up" on someone—who may suddenly hear them and turn around. The tiptoeing sounds increase gradually in intensity as the child approaches, but the person senses nothing until the sound crosses a threshold. Third, sensation requires constant decision making, as the individual tries to distinguish meaningful from irrelevant stimulation. We are unaware of most of these sensory "decisions" because they occur so rapidly and unconsciously. Alone at night, people often wonder, "Did I hear something?" Their

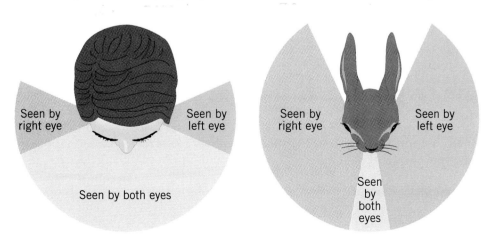

**FIGURE 4.2**
Eye placement and field of vision. Frontal placement of the eyes allows depth perception but reduces the field of vision. Lateral eye placement has the opposite result. Regardless of eye placement, animals expand their range of vision by moving their eyes and heads. *Source:* Adapted from Sekuler & Blake, 1994, pp. 28–29.

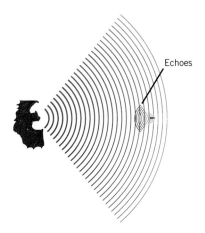

**FIGURE 4.3**
Echolocation in the bat. Bats use echolocation to detect stimuli in the dark, such as insects. They send out pulses of sound waves and home in by sensing the echoes that bounce off their prey. As they prepare to intercept, they send out pulses at a more rapid rate to get the precise coordinates. *Source:* Griffin, 1959, p. 86.

answers depend not only on the intensity of the sound but also on their tendency to attach meaning to small variations in sound. Fourth, sensing the world requires the ability to detect *changes* in stimulation, to notice when a bag of groceries has gotten heavier or a light has dimmed. Finally, efficient sensory processing means "turning down the volume" on information that is redundant; the nervous system tunes out messages that continue without change. We examine each of these processes in turn.

## TRANSDUCTION

Sensation requires converting energy in the world into internal signals that are psychologically meaningful. The more the brain processes these signals—from sensation to perception to cognition—the more meaningful they become.

Sensation typically begins with an environmental stimulus, a form of energy capable of exciting the nervous system. We actually register only a tiny fraction of the energy surrounding us, and different species have evolved the capacity to process different types of information. Honeybees can sense the Earth's magnetic field and essentially relocate important landmarks, such as places they have found food, by their compass coordinates (Collett & Baron, 1994). Bats are nocturnal creatures, but instead of relying on vision in darkness (like cats), they "see with their ears," using a process called echolocation. **Echolocation** enables animals such as bats, whales, and porpoises to obtain information about the size, location, and movement of objects by emitting waves of sound (mechanical energy that causes particles of air or water to vibrate) and sensing the resulting echoes as these waves bounce off objects (Griffin, 1959). The ears and brains of bats evolved to detect very tiny air movements caused by echoes from small flying insects. As the bat approaches its prey, it emits faster pulses of sound to help it locate the insect in space (Figure 4.3). SONAR (the acronym for "sound navigation and ranging") uses similar principles to navigate the ocean. Instruments such as SONAR or Geiger counters for detecting X-ray radiation expand the range of our senses to detect energy for which they lack the sensitivity.

Creating a Neural Code   Specialized cells in the nervous system, called **receptors,** transform energy in the environment into neural impulses that can be interpreted by the brain (Loewenstein, 1960; Miller et al., 1961). Receptors respond to different forms of energy and generate action potentials in sensory neurons adjacent to them. In the eye, receptors respond to particles of light; in the ear, to the movement of molecules of air. The process of converting physical energy or stimulus information into neural impulses is called **transduction.** The brain then interprets the impulses generated by sensory receptors as light, sound, smell, taste, touch, or motion. It essentially reads a neural code—a pattern of neural firing—and translates it into a psychologically meaningful "language."

In 1826, Johannes Müller proposed that whether a neural message is experienced as light, sound, or some other sensation results less from differences in stimuli than from the particular neurons excited by them. Müller's hypothesis, known as the **doctrine of specific nerve energies,** is bolstered by reports of syndromes such as painful neuropathy, in which a cotton ball can produce a sensation of burning instead of a light touch because receptors presumably become rewired to different neural fibers. Extending and revising Müller's doctrine, psychologists now recognize that the nature of a sensation depends on the pathways in the brain it activates. Electrical stimulation of the primary visual cortex produces visual sensations as surely as shining a light in the eye, whereas electrical stimulation of the auditory cortex produces sensations experienced as sound. The stimulus may be the same—electrical current—but the pathways are different.

**Coding for Intensity and Quality of the Stimulus** For each sense, the brain codes sensory stimulation for intensity and quality. The neural code for **intensity,** or strength, of a sensation varies by sensory modality but usually involves the number of sensory neurons that fire, the frequency with which they fire, or some combination of the two. The neural code for **quality,** or nature, of the sensation (such as color, pitch, taste, or temperature) is often more complicated, relying on both the specific type of receptors involved and the pattern of neural impulses generated. For example, some receptors respond to warmth and others to cold, but a combination of both leads to the sensation of extreme heat. Remarkably, the brain synthesizes millions of simple on–off decisions (made by sensory neurons that receive information from receptors and either fire or do not fire) to perceive the lines and shapes of a Cezanne landscape or words on a printed page. It does this so quickly and automatically that we are unaware of anything but the end product.

**INTERIM SUMMARY** Sensation begins with an environmental stimulus; all sensory systems have specialized cells called **receptors** that respond to environmental stimuli and typically generate action potentials in adjacent sensory neurons. This process is called **transduction.** Within each sensory modality, the brain codes sensory stimulation for **intensity** and **quality.**

## ABSOLUTE THRESHOLDS

Even if a sensory system has the capacity to respond to a stimulus, the individual may not experience the stimulus if it is too weak. The minimum amount of physical energy needed for an observer to notice a stimulus is called an **absolute threshold.** One way psychologists measure absolute thresholds is by presenting a particular stimulus (light, sound, taste, odor, pressure) at varying intensities and determining the level of stimulation necessary for the person to detect it about 50 percent of the time. A psychologist trying to identify the absolute threshold for sound of a particular pitch would present subjects with sounds at that pitch, some so soft they would never hear them and others so loud they would never miss them. In between would be sounds they would hear some or most of the time. The volume at which most subjects hear the sound half the time but miss it half the time is defined as the absolute threshold; above this point, people sense stimulation most of the time. The absolute thresholds for many senses are remarkably low, such as a small candle flame burning 30 miles away on a clear night (Table 4.1).

Despite the "absolute" label, absolute thresholds vary from person to person and situation to situation. One reason for this variation is the presence of **noise,** which technically refers to irrelevant, distracting information (not just to loud

| TABLE 4.1 | EXAMPLES OF ABSOLUTE THRESHOLDS |
|---|---|
| **SENSE** | **THRESHOLD** |
| Vision | A candle flame 30 miles away on a dark, clear night |
| Hearing | A watch ticking 20 feet away in a quiet place |
| Smell | A drop of perfume in a six-room house |
| Taste | A teaspoon of sugar in two gallons of water |
| Touch | A wing of a fly falling on the cheek from a height of one centimeter |

*Source:* Adapted from Brown et al., 1962.

*Whether a perceiver interprets an ambiguous stimulus as a meaningful signal or as noise can have extremely important ramifications.*

sounds). Some noise is external; to pick out the ticking of a watch at a concert is far more difficult than in a quiet room. Other noise is internal, created by the random firing of neurons. Psychological events such as expectations, motivation, stress, and level of fatigue can also affect the threshold at which a person can sense a low level of stimulation (see Fehm-Wolfsdorf et al., 1993; Pause et al., 1996). Someone whose home has been burglarized, for example, is likely to be highly attuned to night-time sounds and to "hear" suspicious noises more readily, whether or not they actually occur.

▶ **ONE STEP FURTHER**

### Signal Detection

Is the absolute threshold, then, really absolute? Or perhaps sensation at low levels of stimulation really involves the detection of a stimulus against a background of noise (Greene & Swets, 1966; Swets, 1992). According to **signal detection theory,** sensation is not a passive process that occurs when the amount of stimulation exceeds a critical threshold; rather, experiencing a sensation means making a *judgment* about whether a stimulus is present or absent.

Does a noise downstairs, a blip on a radar screen, or a small irregularity on a brain scan signal something dangerous? According to signal detection theory, two distinct processes are at work in detection tasks of this sort. The first is an initial sensory process, reflecting the observer's **sensitivity** to the stimulus—how well the person sees, hears, or feels the stimulus. The second is a decision process, reflecting the observer's **response bias** (or **decision criterion**), that is, the individual's readiness to report detecting a stimulus when uncertain.

To assess response bias, signal detection researchers present participants with stimuli at low intensities, as in the traditional procedure for measuring absolute thresholds, but they also add trials in which *no* stimulus is presented. What subjects experience on each trial is some mixture of stimulus energy (the signal), which may or may not be present, and noise, which randomly waxes and wanes. Sometimes the noise alone is enough to lead the person to say she heard or saw something because its effect crosses the decision criterion. At other times, the signal is present but too weak to be detected, and the noise level is too low to augment it. (At still other times, noise, when added to a signal, increases the intensity of the signal enough to lead the participant to report a sensation.)

Participants in signal detection experiments can make two kinds of errors. They may respond with a *false alarm*, reporting a stimulus when none was presented, or they may fail to report an actual stimulus (a *miss*). Similarly, they may give two kinds of correct response. They may *hit*, reporting an actual stimulus, or they may provide a *correct negative*, reporting no stimulus when none was presented. Accuracy in sensing a signal involves a trade-off between sensitivity to stimuli that are presented and vulnerability to reporting stimuli that have not been presented. Thus, an observer who tends to overreport sensations will have a high number of hits but also a high number of false alarms. An observer who tends to underreport will have a lower number of hits but also a lower number of false alarms.

Whether a person has a low or high response bias for reporting "yes" depends on many factors. One is expectations: If a patient complains of heart pain, shooting pain in his legs, and shortness of breath, his doctor is more likely to hear an irregular heartbeat. Another factor that influences response bias is motivation. Two neurologists who review the MRI scan of a woman who is experiencing blinding headaches may come to different conclusions about a possible irregularity. The neurologist who recently lost a patient by mistaking a tumor for noise will have a low threshold for reporting "yes" because the psychological cost of setting it higher is too great. The other, who recently performed exploratory surgery when in fact no tumor was present and accidentally left the patient with partial blindness, will have a much higher criterion for reporting a "hit."

To distinguish the relative contributions of sensitivity and response bias, psychologists experimentally manipulate the costs and benefits of over- or underreporting stimulation by paying participants different amounts for different types of correct or incorrect responses (Figure 4.4). These consequences can be described in a payoff matrix, which shows the costs and benefits of each type of response. Researchers then plot the proportion of hits against the proportion of false alarms on a *receiver operating characteristic (ROC)* curve, which literally shows the way the receiver of the signal operates at different signal intensities. This allows the researcher to determine how well the subject can actually sense the stimulus, independent of response bias. ◀

**HERMAN®**

"My mistake! I thought I heard a noise down here."

## DIFFERENCE THRESHOLDS

Thus far, we have focused on absolute thresholds, the lowest level of stimulation required to sense a stimulus. Above this threshold, another kind of threshold is the **difference threshold**—the lowest level of stimulation required to sense that a *change* in stimulation has occurred. In other words, the difference threshold is the difference in intensity between two stimuli necessary to produce a **just noticeable difference** (or **jnd**), such as the difference between two light bulbs of slightly different wattage. (The absolute threshold is actually a special case of the difference threshold, in which the difference is between no intensity and a very weak stimulus.)

The jnd depends not only on the intensity of the new stimulus but also on the level of stimulation already present. The more intense the existing stimulus, the larger the change must be to be noticeable. A person carrying a two-pound backpack will easily notice the addition of a half-pound book, but adding the same book to a 60-pound backpack will not make the pack feel any heavier; that is, it will not produce a jnd.

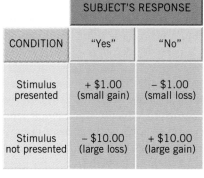

| CONDITION | SUBJECT'S RESPONSE | |
|---|---|---|
| | "Yes" | "No" |
| Stimulus presented | + $10.00 (large gain) | − $10.00 (large loss) |
| Stimulus not presented | − $1.00 (small loss) | + $1.00 (small gain) |

(a) Matrix that will produce a "yes" bias

| CONDITION | SUBJECT'S RESPONSE | |
|---|---|---|
| | "Yes" | "No" |
| Stimulus presented | + $1.00 (small gain) | − $1.00 (small loss) |
| Stimulus not presented | − $10.00 (large loss) | + $10.00 (large gain) |

(b) Matrix that will produce a "no" bias

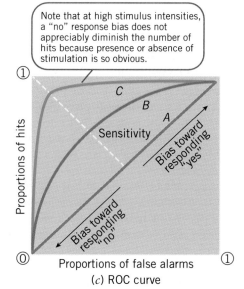

Note that at high stimulus intensities, a "no" response bias does not appreciably diminish the number of hits because presence or absence of stimulation is so obvious.

(c) ROC curve

**FIGURE 4.4**

Signal detection. Two payoff matrices, one that leads to a "yes" bias (a) and the other to a "no" bias (b). To assess sensitivity to a stimulus (c), researchers plot the proportion of hits against the proportion of false alarms on a ROC curve. If the signal is so low that it is imperceptible, the proportion of hits will equal the proportion of false alarms because the receiver's responses are essentially random (diagonal line A). At a somewhat higher stimulus intensity (line B), subjects have a better ratio of hits to false alarms because their responses are influenced by the presence of a detectable signal, so they are no longer just guessing. At very high signal intensities (line C), people rarely give wrong answers. The sensitivity of the observer to different signal intensities (e.g., how well the person can hear) is represented by the dotted line, which shows how far the receiver's ROC curve diverges from the diagonal, which represents random responding.

## Weber's Law

In 1834, the German physiologist Ernst Weber recognized not only this lack of a one-to-one relationship between the physical and psychological worlds but also the existence of a consistent relationship between them. Regardless of the magnitude of two stimuli, the second must differ from the first by a constant proportion—for example, it must be a tenth larger—for it to be perceived as different. This relationship is called **Weber's law** (Figure 4.5a). That constant proportion—the ratio of change in intensity required to produce a jnd compared to the previous intensity of the stimulus—can be expressed as a fraction, called the **Weber fraction.**

The Weber fraction varies depending on the individual, stimulus, context, and sensory modality. For example, the Weber fraction for perceiving changes in heaviness is 1/50. This means that the average person can perceive an increase of one pound if added to a 50-pound bag, two pounds added to 100 pounds, and so forth. The Weber fraction for a sound around middle C is 1/10, which means that a person can hear an extra voice in a chorus of 10 but would require two voices to notice an increase in loudness in a chorus of 20.

## Fechner's Law

Weber's brother-in-law, Gustav Fechner, took the field a noticeable step forward in 1860 with the publication of his *Elements of Psychophysics*. One of his major achievements was to broaden the application of Weber's law by linking the subjective experience of intensity of stimulation with the actual magnitude of a stimulus. In other words, using Weber's law, Fechner was able to estimate precisely how intensely a person would report experiencing a sensation based on the amount of stimulus energy actually present. He assumed that for any given stimulus, all jnds are created equal; that is, each additional jnd feels subjectively like one incremental (additional) unit in intensity. Using Weber's law, he then plotted these subjective units against the actual incremental units of stimulus intensity necessary to produce each jnd (Figure 4.5b). He recognized that at low stimulus intensities, only tiny increases in stimulation are required to produce subjective effects as large as those produced by enormous increases in stimulation at high levels of intensity.

As can be seen from Figure 4.5b, the result was a logarithmic function, which simply means that as one variable (in this case, subjective intensity) increases arithmetically (1, 2, 3, and etc.), the other variable (in this case, objective intensity) increases geometrically (1, 8, 64, etc.). This became known as **Fechner's law.** Fechner's law means, essentially, that people experience only a small percentage of actual increases in stimulus intensity but that this percentage is predictable. Knowing the Weber constant and the intensity of the stimulus, then, a psychologist can actually predict how strong a person's *subjective sensation* will be. This was a remarkable feat, since it demonstrated that aspects of our subjective experience can be predicted mathematically.

## Stevens's Power Law

Fechner's law held up for a century but was modified by S. S. Stevens (1961, 1975) because it did not quite apply to all stimuli and senses. For example, the relation between perceived pain and stimulus intensity is the opposite of most other psychophysical relations: The greater the pain, the *less* additional intensity is required for a jnd. This makes adaptive sense, since increasing pain means increasing danger and therefore demands increased attention. In part on a dare from a colleague (Stevens, 1956), Stevens set out to prove that people can accurately rate subjective intensity on a numerical scale. He instructed participants to listen to a series of tones of differing intensity and asked them simply to assign numbers to the tones to indicate their relative loudness. What he discovered was a lawful relation between self-reports and stimulus intensity across a much wider range of sensory modes and intensities than Fechner's law could accommodate.

According to **Stevens's power law** (Figure 4.5c), as the perceived intensity of a stimulus grows arithmetically, the actual magnitude of the stimulus grows exponentially, that is, by some power (squared, cubed, etc.). The exponent varies, however, for different senses, just as the Weber fraction varies. Where the exponent is less than 1 (for example, for brightness it is .33), the results are generally similar to Fechner's law. Thus, to double the perceived brightness of a light, the physical stimulus has to increase by a factor of 8. Where the exponent is larger than 1, however, as for sensations produced by electric shock (where the exponent is 3.5), the magnitude of sensations grows quite rapidly as stimulation increases. Thus, Stevens's power law can predict subjective experiences of pain intensity as readily as brightness.

Although the formulas have become more precise, the message from Weber, Fechner, and Stevens is fundamentally the same: Sensation bears an orderly, predictable relation to physical stimulation, but psychological experience is not a photograph, tape recording, or wax impression of external reality.

INTERIM SUMMARY   The **absolute threshold** is the minimum amount of energy needed for an observer to notice a stimulus. The **difference threshold** is the lowest level of stimulation required to sense that a change in stimulation has occurred. According to **Weber's**

**law,** regardless of the magnitude of two stimuli, the second must differ by a constant proportion from the first for it to be perceived as different. According to **Fechner's law,** the magnitude of a stimulus grows logarithmically as the subjective experience of intensity grows arithmetically, so that people subjectively experience only a fraction of actual increases in stimulation. According to **Stevens' power law,** subjective intensity increases in a linear fashion as actual intensity grows exponentially.

---

**FIGURE 4.5**
Quantifying Subjective Experience: From Weber to Stevens

**(a) Weber's Law**

**Weber's law** states that regardless of the magnitude of two stimuli, the second must differ from the first by a constant proportion for it to be perceived as different. Expressed mathematically,

$$\Delta I / I = k$$

where $I$ = the intensity of the stimulus, $\Delta I$ = the additional intensity necessary to produce a jnd at that intensity, and $k$ = a constant. To put it still another way, the ratio of change in intensity to initial intensity required to produce a jnd—expressed as a fraction, such as one unit of change for every ten units—is a constant for a given sensory modality. This constant is known as a Weber fraction. This can be seen in the accompanying graph, where the constant is the slope of the line (in this case, 1/10), plotting $\Delta I$ (the $y$-axis) as a function of I (the x-axis).

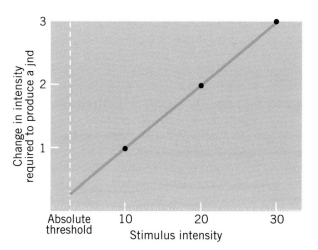

**(b) Fechner's Law**

Starting with Weber's law, Fechner realized that as the experienced sensation increases one unit of perceived intensity at a time, the actual intensity of the physical stimulus is increasing logarithmically. **Fechner's law** thus held that the subjective magnitude of a sensation ($S$) grows as a proportion ($k$) of the logarithm of the objective intensity of the stimulus ($I$), or

$$S = k \log I$$

This can be readily seen in the accompanying graph: Subjective units of sensation ($S1$, $S2$, etc.) increase by increments of one as objective units ($I1$, $I2$, etc.) increase geometrically (that is, by a factor of more than one). This leads to a logarithmic curve.
*Source:* Adapted from Guilford, 1954, p. 38.

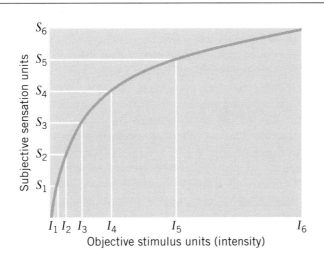

**(c) Stevens' Power Law**

**Stevens' power law** states that subjective intensity ($S$) grows as a proportion ($k$) of the actual intensity ($I$) raised to some power ($b$). Expressed mathematically,

$$S = k \, I^b$$

As the graph below shows, Stevens' power law plots subjective magnitude of stimulation as an exponential function of stimulus magnitude. Here, these functions are shown for brightness (where the exponent is .33), apparent length (where the exponent is 1.0, so the function is linear), and electric shock (where the exponent is 3.5). *Source:* Stevens, 1961, p. 11.

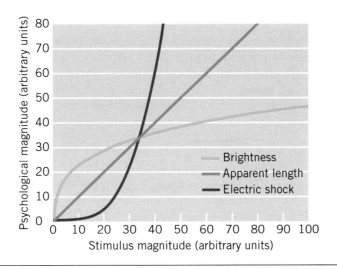

## SENSORY ADAPTATION

A final process shared by all sensory systems is adaptation. You walk into a crowded restaurant, and the noise level is overwhelming, yet within a few minutes, you do not even notice it. Driving into an industrial city, you notice an unpleasant odor that smells like sulfur and wonder how anyone tolerates it; a short time later, you are no longer aware of it. These are examples of **sensory adapta-**

tion—the tendency of sensory receptors to respond less to stimuli that continue without change.

Sensory adaptation makes sense from an evolutionary perspective. Constant sensory inputs provide no new information about the environment, so the nervous system essentially ignores them. Given all the stimuli that bombard an organism at any particular moment, an animal that paid as much notice to constant stimulation as to changes that might be adaptively significant would be at a disadvantage. Sensory adaptation also performs the function of "turning down the volume" on information that would overwhelm the brain, by reducing its perceived intensity to a manageable level.

Although sensory adaptation generally applies across senses, the nervous system is wired to circumvent it in some important instances. For example, the visual system has ways to keep its receptors from adapting; otherwise, stationary objects would disappear from sight. The eyes are constantly making tiny quivering motions, which guarantees that the receptors affected by a given stimulus are constantly changing. The result is a steady flow of graded potentials on the sensory neurons that synapse with those receptors. Similarly, although we may adapt to mild pain, we generally do not adapt to severe pain (Miller & Kraus, 1990), again an evolutionarily sensible design feature of a sensory system that responds to body damage.

**INTERIM SUMMARY**    **Sensory adaptation** is the tendency of sensory systems to respond less to stimuli that continue without change. This makes adaptive sense, since changing stimuli provide more new information than those that are relatively constant.

# VISION

Throughout this chapter we will use vision as our major example of sensory processes because it is the best understood of the senses. We begin by discussing the form of energy (light) transduced by the visual system. We then examine the organ responsible for transduction (the eye) and trace the neural pathways that take raw information from receptors and convert it into sensory knowledge.

## THE NATURE OF LIGHT

Light is just one form of electromagnetic radiation, but it is the form to which the eye is sensitive. That humans and other animals respond to light is no accident, since cycles of light and dark have occurred over the course of five billion years of evolution. These cycles, and the mere presence of light as a medium for sensation, have shaped virtually every aspect of our psychology, from the times of day at which we are conscious to the way we choose mating partners (using visual appearance as a cue). Indeed, light is so useful for tracking prey, avoiding predators, and "checking out" potential mates that a structure resembling the eye has apparently evolved independently over 40 times in different organisms (Fernald, 1996). Other forms of electromagnetic radiation to which humans are blind include infrared, ultraviolet, radio, and X-ray radiation.

Electromagnetic energy travels in waves, created by the patterned movement, or *oscillation*, of electrically charged particles. Different forms of radiation have waves of different lengths, or **wavelengths.** This simply means that their particles oscillate more or less frequently, that is, with higher or lower *frequency*. Some of these wavelengths, such as gamma rays, are as short or shorter than the diameter

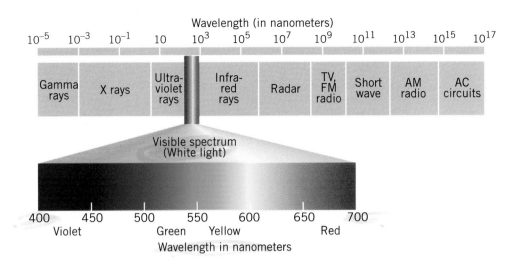

**FIGURE 4.6**
The electromagnetic spectrum. Humans sense only a small portion of the electromagnetic spectrum (enlarged in the figure), light. Light at different wavelengths is experienced as different colors.

of an atom; others are quite long, such as radio waves, which may oscillate once in a mile. Wavelengths are measured in **nanometers (nm),** or billionths of a meter (Figure 4.6).

The receptors in the human eye are tuned to detect only a very restricted portion of the electromagnetic spectrum, from roughly 400 to 700 nm. Other organisms are sensitive to different regions of the spectrum; for example, many insects (such as ants and bees) and some vertebrate animals (such as iguanas and some bird species) see ultraviolet light (Alberts, 1989; Goldsmith, 1994; Newman & Hartline, 1982).

The physical dimension of wavelength translates into the psychological dimension of color, just as the physical *intensity* of light is related to the subjective sensation of brightness. Light is a useful form of energy to sense for a number of reasons (see Sekuler & Blake, 1994). Like other forms of electromagnetic radiation, light travels very quickly (186,000 miles, or roughly 300,000 kilometers, per second), so sighted organisms can see things almost immediately after they happen. Light also travels in straight lines, which means that it preserves the geometric organization of the objects it illuminates; the image an object casts on the retina resembles its actual structure. Perhaps most importantly, light interacts with the molecules on the surface of many objects and is either absorbed or reflected. The light that is reflected reaches the eyes and creates a visual pattern. Objects that reflect a lot of light appear brighter, whereas those that absorb much of the light that hits them appear dark.

## THE EYE

Two basic processes occur in the eyes (Figure 4.7). First, the cornea, pupil, and lens focus light on the retina. Next, the retina transduces this visual image into neural impulses that are relayed to and interpreted by the brain.

### Focusing Light

Light enters the eye through the **cornea,** a tough, transparent tissue covering the front of the eyeball. Under water, people cannot see clearly because the cornea is constructed to bend (or *refract*) light rays traveling through air, not water. That is why a diving mask allows clearer vision: It puts a layer of air between the water and the cornea.

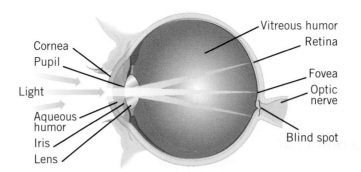

**FIGURE 4.7**
Anatomy of the human eye. The cornea, pupil, and lens focus a pattern of light onto the retina, which then transduces the retinal image into neural signals carried to the brain by the optic nerve.

From the cornea, light passes through a chamber of fluid called *aqueous humor*, which supplies oxygen and other nutrients to the cornea and lens. Unlike blood, which performs this function in other parts of the body, the aqueous humor is a clear fluid, so light can pass through it. Next, light travels through an opening in the center of the **iris** (the pigmented tissue that gives the eye its blue, green, or brown color); this opening is the **pupil.** Muscle fibers in the iris cause the pupil to expand (dilate) or constrict to regulate the amount of light entering the eye. The size of the pupil also changes with different psychological states, such as fear, excitement, interest, and sexual arousal. Experienced gamblers (and perhaps Don Juans) can use pupil size to read other people's emotions (Hess, 1965).

The next step in focusing light occurs in the **lens,** an elastic, disc-shaped structure about the size of a lima bean. Muscles attached to cells surrounding the lens alter its shape to focus on objects at various distances. The lens flattens for distant objects and becomes more rounded or spherical for closer objects, a process known as **accommodation.** The light is then projected through the *vitreous humor* (a clear, gelatinous liquid) onto the **retina,** a light-sensitive layer of tissue at the

*The size of the pupils changes in different emotional states, which means that a skilled gambler may literally be able to read his opponents' hands from their eyes, although he may have no awareness of the mechanisms by which he can do this.*

back of the eye. The retina receives a constant flow of images as people turn their heads and eyes or move through space.

Abnormalities in the eye sometimes make accommodation difficult, affecting **visual acuity,** or sharpness of the image. Since light waves normally spread out over a distance, the eye has to focus them on a single point in the retina to produce a clear image. **Nearsightedness** (or **myopia**) occurs when the cornea and lens focus this image in front of the retina; by the time rays of light reach the retina, they have begun to cross, leading to a blurred image (Figure 4.8). The opposite effect occurs in **farsightedness** (or **hyperopia**): The eye focuses light on a point beyond the retina, leading to decreased acuity at close range. Both abnormalities are common at all ages and usually are readily corrected with lenses that alter the optics of the eye. With advancing age, however, losses in visual acuity become more pronounced (Curcio and Drucker, 1993; Fukada et al., 1990; Matjucha and Katz, 1994). The lens becomes more opaque and loses some of its ability to accommodate, and the diameter of the pupil shrinks so that less light reaches the retina. Cataracts, which are common in older people, occur when the lens becomes so cloudy that the person may become almost blind. As a result of age-related changes, the retina of a normal 65-year-old receives only about one-third as much light as that of a 20-year-old (Kline & Schieber, 1985).

## The Retina

The eye is like a camera, insofar as it has an opening to adjust the amount of incoming light, a lens to focus the light, and the equivalent of photosensitive film—

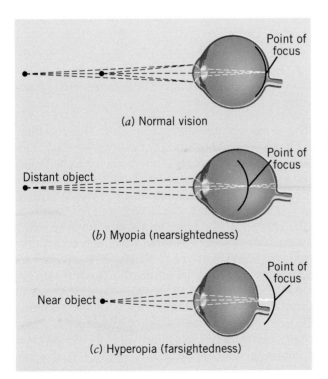
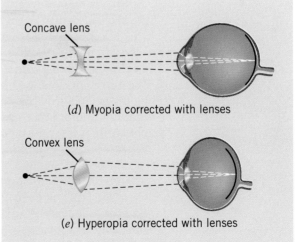

**FIGURE 4.8**

Normal vision (*a*), nearsightedness (*b*), and farsightedness (*c*). In (*a*), the cornea and lens focus the image on the retina, producing normal vision. The shape of the lens, of course, differs for optimal focus on objects nearby or at a distance. In (*b*), the image is focused in front of the retina (myopia), whereas in (*c*), it is focused behind the retina (hyperopia). In (*d*), a concave lens corrects vision by spreading out the light rays from distant objects. In (*e*), a convex lens has the opposite effect, bending light rays toward each other to focus them on the retina instead of behind it.

Light

Ganglion cell axons

Ganglion cells

Bipolar cells

Retina

Rod

Cone

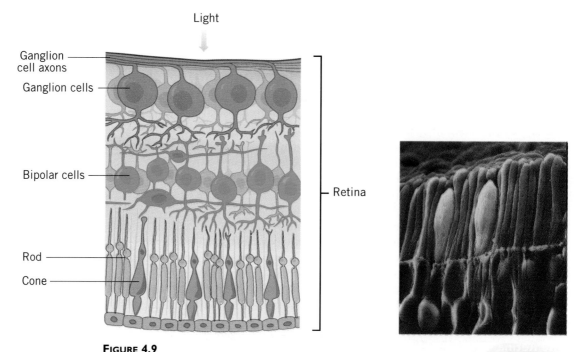

**FIGURE 4.9**

The retina. Light passes through layers of neurons to reach photoreceptors, called rods and cones, which respond to different wavelengths of light. These receptors in turn connect to bipolar cells, which pass information to the ganglion cells, whose axons form the optic nerve. The photo shows rods and cones magnified thousands of times. Above them are bipolar cells.

the retina. (The analogy is incomplete, of course, because the eye, unlike a camera, works best when it is moving.) The retina transduces light energy from illuminated objects into neural impulses, transforming a pattern of light reflected off objects into psychologically meaningful information.

**Structure of the Retina**    The retina is a multilayered structure about as thick as a sheet of paper (Figure 4.9). The innermost layer (at the back of the retina) contains two types of light receptors, or **photoreceptors** ("photo" is from the Greek word for light), called **rods** and **cones,** which were named for their distinctive shapes. Each retina contains approximately 120 million rods and 8 million cones. When a rod or cone absorbs light energy, it generates an electrical signal, stimulating the neighboring **bipolar cells.** These cells combine the information from many receptors and produce graded potentials on **ganglion cells,** which integrate information from multiple bipolar cells. The long axons of these ganglion cells bundle together to form the **optic nerve,** which carries visual information to the brain.

The central region of the retina, the **fovea,** is most sensitive to small detail, so vision is sharpest for stimuli directly in sight. In contrast, the point on the retina where the optic nerve leaves the eye, called the **optic disk** (or **blind spot**), has no receptor cells. People are generally unaware of their blind spots for several reasons. Different images usually fall on the blind spots of the two eyes, so one eye sees what the other does not. In addition, the eyes are always moving, providing information about the missing area. To avoid perceiving an empty visual space, the brain also automatically uses visual information from the rest of the retina to fill in the gap. (To see the effects of the blind spot in action, see Figure 4.10.)

**Rods and Cones**    Rods and cones have distinct functions. Rods are more sensitive to light than cones, allowing vision in dim light. Rods only produce visual sensations in black, white, and gray. Cones are, evolutionarily speaking, a

**FIGURE 4.10**
The blind spot. Close your left eye, fix your gaze on the plus, and slowly move the book toward and away from you. The circle will disappear when it falls in the blind spot of the right retina.

more recent development than rods and respond to color as well as black and white. They require more light to be activated, however, which is why we see little or no color in dim light. Nocturnal animals such as owls have mostly rods, whereas daytime animals and most other birds have mostly cones (Schiffman, 1996). Humans see both in black and white and in color, depending on the amount of light available.

Rods and cones also differ in their distribution on the retina and in their connections to bipolar cells. Rods are concentrated off the center of the retina. Thus, in dim light, objects are seen most clearly by looking slightly away from them. (You can test this yourself tonight by looking at the stars. Fix your eyes directly on a bright star and then focus your gaze slightly off to the side of it. The star will appear brighter when the image is cast away from the fovea.) Several rods may also provide input to a single bipolar cell. Since the bipolar cell can be activated by many different rods or combinations of them, it cannot transmit fine details to the brain. On the other hand, the sum of the energy collected by many rods can easily cause an action potential in sensory neurons excited by them, so these cells can fire in very dim light.

In contrast, cones are concentrated in the center of the retina in the fovea, although they are also found in smaller proportions in the periphery. Thus, in bright light an object is seen best if looked at directly, focusing the image on the fovea. Further, a single cone may connect with a single bipolar cell. This allows perception of fine detail, since precise information from each cone is preserved and passed on for higher processing.

**Transforming Light into Sight**    Both rods and cones contain photosensitive pigments that change chemical structure in response to light (Rushton, 1962; Wald, 1968). This process is called **bleaching** because the pigment breaks down when exposed to light, leading the photoreceptors to lose their characteristic color. When photoreceptors bleach, they create graded potentials in the bipolar cells connected to them, which may then fire.

Bleaching must be reversed before a photoreceptor is restored to full sensitivity. Pigment regeneration takes time, which is why people often have to feel their way around the seats when entering a dark theater on a bright day. Adjusting to a dimly illuminated setting is called **dark adaptation.** The cones adapt relatively quickly, usually within about five minutes, depending on the duration and intensity of light to which the eye was previously exposed. Rods, in contrast, take about 15 minutes to adapt. Since they are especially useful in dim light, vision may remain less than optimal in the theater for some time. **Light adaptation,** the process of adjusting to bright light after exposure to darkness, is much faster; readapting to bright sunlight upon leaving a theater takes only about a minute (Matlin, 1983).

Receptive Fields    Once the rods and cones have responded to patterns of light, the nervous system must somehow convert these patterns into a neural code to allow the brain to reconstruct the scene. This is truly a remarkable process: Waves of light reflected off, say, your friend's face, pass through the eye to the rods and cones of the retina. The pattern of light captured by those receptor cells translates your friend's face into a pattern of nerve impulses that the brain can "read" with such precision that you know precisely who you are seeing.

This process begins with the ganglion cells. Each ganglion cell has a *receptive field*. A **receptive field** is a region within which a neuron responds to appropriate stimulation (that is, in which it is *receptive* to stimulation), (Hartline, 1938). Neurons at higher levels of the visual system (in the brain) also have receptive fields, which means that at higher and higher levels of processing, the visual system keeps creating maps of the scenes the eye has observed. The same basic principles apply in other sensory systems, as when neurons from the peripheral nervous system all the way up through the cortex map precisely where a mosquito has landed on the skin.

Psychologists have learned about receptive fields in ganglion cells through a technique called single-cell recording. In **single-cell recording,** researchers insert a tiny electrode into the brain or retina of an animal, close enough to a neuron to detect when it fires. Then, holding the animal's head still, they flash light to different parts of the visual field to see what kind of stimulation leads the ganglion cell to fire. By placing electrodes in many places, psychologists can map the receptive fields of the ganglion cells of the retina.

Using this method, researchers discovered that the receptive fields of some ganglion cells have a center and a surrounding area, like a target (Figure 4.11). Presenting light to the center of the receptive field turns the cell "on" (that is, excites the cell), whereas presenting light within the receptive field but outside the center turns the cell "off." For other ganglion cells the pattern is just the opposite:

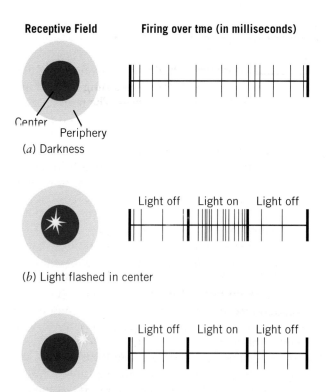

**FIGURE 4.11**

Single-cell recording. In (*a*), the neuron spontaneously fires (indicated by the thin vertical lines) randomly in darkness. In (*b*), it fires repeatedly when light is flashed to the center of its receptive field. In (*c*), firing stops when light is flashed in the periphery of its receptive field; that is, light outside the center inhibits firing. *Source:* Adapted from Sekuler & Blake, 1994, p. 68.

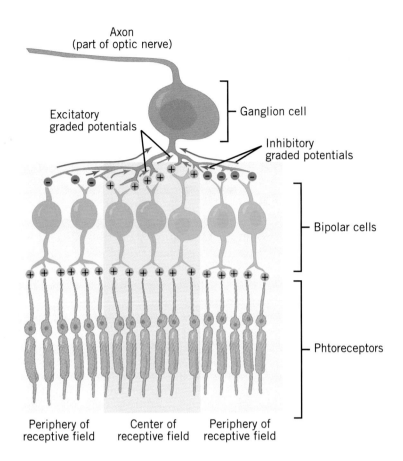

Axon
(part of optic nerve)

Excitatory
graded potentials

Ganglion cell

Inhibitory
graded potentials

Bipolar cells

Phtoreceptors

Periphery of
receptive field

Center of
receptive field

Periphery of
receptive field

**FIGURE 4.12**
Excitation and inhibition in receptive fields of a ganglion cell. In this example of a center-on/periphery-off ganglion cell, the process of transduction begins as photoreceptors that respond to light in the center of the ganglion cell's receptive field excite bipolar cells, which in turn generate excitatory graded potentials (represented here by a +) on the dendrites of the ganglion cell. Photoreceptors that respond to light in the periphery of the ganglion cell's receptive field excite bipolar cells that generate *inhibitory* action potentials (represented by a –). If enough light is present in the center, and little enough in the periphery, of the receptive field, the excitatory graded potentials will depolarize the ganglion cell membrane. The axon of the ganglion cell is part of the optic nerve, which will then transmit information about light in this particular visual location to the brain.

Light in the center inhibits neural firing, whereas light in the periphery excites the neuron. The process by which adjacent visual units inhibit or suppress each other's level of activity is called **lateral inhibition.** Figure 4.12 illustrates the way excitatory and inhibitory graded potentials from bipolar cells may be involved in this process.

Why do receptive fields have this concentric circular organization, with on and off regions that inhibit each other? As described at the beginning of the chapter, our sensory systems are attuned to changes and differences. The targetlike organization of ganglion cells allows humans and other animals to perceive edges and changes in brightness and texture that signal where one surface ends and another begins. A neuron that senses light in the center of its receptive field will fire rapidly if the light is bright and covers much of the center. To the extent that light is also present in the periphery of the receptive field, however, neural firing will be inhibited, essentially transmitting the information that the image is continuous in this region of space, with no edges.

Lateral inhibition appears to be responsible in part for the phenomenon seen in **Hermann grids** (Figure 4.13), in which the intersections of white lines in a dark grid appear gray and the intersections of black lines in a white grid appear gray (Spillman, 1994). Essentially, white surrounded by white on all four sides appears darker than white surrounded by black on two sides, and vice versa. The receptive fields of neurons in the fovea tend to be very small, allowing for high visual acuity, whereas receptive fields increase in size with distance from the center of the retina (Wiesel & Hubel, 1960). This is why looking straight at the illusory patches of darkness or lightness in Hermann grids makes them disappear: Receptive fields of neurons in the fovea can be so small that the middle of each line is surrounded primarily by the same shade regardless of whether it is at an intersection.

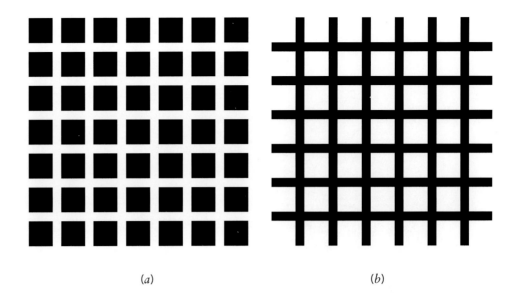

**FIGURE 4.13**
Hermann grids. White lines against a black grid appear to have gray patches at their intersections (*a*), as do black lines against a white grid (*b*).

(*a*)                    (*b*)

INTERIM SUMMARY    Two basic processes occur in the eyes: light is focused on the **retina** by the **cornea, pupil,** and **lens;** and the retina transduces this visual image into a code that the brain can read. The retina includes two kinds of photoreceptors: **rods** (which produce sensations in black, white, and gray and are very sensitive to light) and **cones** (which produce sensations of color). Rods and cones excite **biopolar cells,** which in turn excite or inhibit **ganglion cells,** whose axons constitute the **optic nerve.** Ganglion cells, like sensory cells higher up in the nervous system, have **receptive fields,** in which sensory information can inhibit or excite them.

## NEURAL PATHWAYS

Transduction in the eye, then, starts with the focusing of images onto the retina. When photoreceptors bleach, they excite bipolar cells, which in turn affect the firing of ganglion cells with particular receptive fields. The axons from these ganglion cells comprise the optic nerve, which transmits information from the retina to the brain.

### From the Eye to the Brain

Impulses from the optic nerve first pass through the **optic chiasm** (*chiasm* comes from the Greek word for "cross"), where the optic nerve splits (Figure 4.14*a*). Information from the left half of each retina (which comes from the right visual field) goes to the left hemisphere, and vice versa. Once past the optic chiasm, combined information from the two eyes travels to the brain via the **optic tracts,** which are simply a continuation of the axons from ganglion cells that constitute the optic nerve. From there, visual information flows along two separate pathways within each hemisphere. (Figure 4.14*a*).

One small pathway projects to a clump of neurons in the midbrain known as the **superior colliculus,** which in humans is involved in controlling eye movements. Its neurons respond to the presence or absence of visual stimulation in parts of the visual field but cannot identify specific objects. Neurons in the superior colliculus also integrate input from the eyes and the ears, so that weak stimulation from the two senses together can orient the person toward a region in space that neither sense alone could detect (Stein & Meredith, 1990).

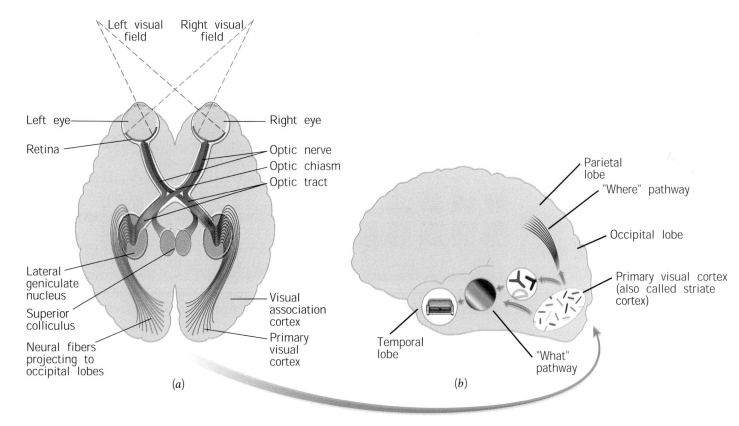

**FIGURE 4.14**
Visual pathways. The optic nerve carries visual information from the retina to the optic chiasm, where the optic nerve splits. The brain processes information from the right visual field in the left hemisphere and vice versa because of the way some visual information crosses and some does not cross over to the opposite hemisphere at the optic chiasm. At the optic chiasm, the optic nerve becomes the optic tract (because bundles of axons within the brain itself are called tracts, not nerves). A small pathway from the optic tract carries information simultaneously to the superior colliculus. The optic tract then carries information to the lateral geniculate nucleus of the thalamus, where neurons project to the primary visual cortex.

The second pathway projects to the **lateral geniculate nucleus** of the thalamus and then to the primary visual cortex in the occipital lobes. Neurons in the lateral geniculate nucleus preserve the map of visual space in the retina. That is, neighboring ganglion cells transmit information to thalamic neurons next to each other, which in turn transmit this retinal map to the cortex. Neurons in the lateral geniculate nucleus have the same kind of concentric (targetlike) receptive fields as retinal neurons. They also receive input from the reticular formation, which means that the extent to which an animal is attentive, aroused, and awake may modulate the transmission of impulses from the thalamus to the visual cortex (Burke & Cole, 1978; Munk et al., 1996).

The presence of two visual pathways from the optic nerve to the brain appears to be involved in an intriguing phenomenon known as **blindsight**, in which individuals are unaware of their capacity to see (Weiskrantz et al., 1974, 1997). Pursuing observations made by neurologists in the early part of the 20th century, researchers have studied patients with lesions to the primary visual cortex, which receives input from the second visual pathway (through the lateral geniculate nucleus). These patients are, for all intents and purposes, blind: If shown an object, they deny that they have seen it. Yet if asked to describe its geometrical form (e.g., triangle or square) or give its location in space (to the right or left, up or down),

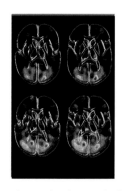

*The primary visual cortex in the occipital lobes lights up on a PET scan when people actively view words, in contrast to when their eyes are closed or they stare continuously at a black dot.*

they do so with accuracy far better than chance—frequently protesting all the while that they cannot do the task because they cannot see! Visual processing in the superior colliculus, and perhaps at the level of the lateral geniculate nucleus, apparently leads to visual experiences outside of awareness.

## Visual Cortex

From the lateral geniculate nucleus, then, visual information travels to the primary visual cortex in the occipital lobes. The primary visual cortex is sometimes called the *striate cortex* because of its striped appearance; visual pathways outside the striate cortex to which its neurons project are thus called *extrastriate* cortex (because they are outside, or extra to, the striate cortex).

Primary Visual Cortex   The size of a brain region that serves a particular function (in this case, vision) is a rough index of the importance of that function to the organism's adaptation over the course of evolution. Once again this simply reflects the "logic" of natural selection: If vision was particularly useful for survival and reproduction in our primate ancestors, those animals with larger visual processing centers would be at an adaptive advantage, and larger and more sophisticated visual "modules" would be likely to evolve over time. In fact, in many monkey species whose visual systems resemble those of humans, over half the cortex is devoted to visual processing (Van Essen et al., 1992). Within a sensory system, such as the visual system, the same principle also holds true. For example, in humans as in other primates, the primary visual cortex does not give "equal time" to all regions of the person's visual field. Much of the striate cortex is devoted to information from the fovea (Drasdo, 1977), just as the somatosensory cortex in the parietal lobes overrepresents regions such as the hands, which have many receptors and transmit especially important information (Chapter 3).

The striate cortex is the "first stop" in the cortex for all visual information. Neurons in this region begin to "make sense" of visual information, in large measure through the action of neurons known as feature detectors. **Feature detectors,** discovered by Nobel Prize winners David Hubel and Thorsten Wiesel (1959, 1979), are neurons that fire only when stimulation in their receptive field matches a very specific pattern or orientation. **Simple cells** are feature detectors that respond most vigorously to lines of a particular orientation, such as horizontal or vertical, in an exact location in the visual field (Figure 4.15). **Complex cells** are feature detectors that generally cover a larger receptive field and respond when a stimulus of the proper orientation falls anywhere within their receptive field, not just at a particular location. They may also fire only when the stimulus moves in a particular direction. Still other cells, called **hypercomplex cells,** require that a stimulus be of a specific size or length to fire. Other neurons in the primary visual cortex respond selectively to color, contrast, and texture (Engel et al., 1997; Livingstone & Hubel, 1988).

The What and the Where Pathways   From the primary visual cortex, visual information appears to flow along two pathways, or *processing streams* (Figure 4.14*b*) (Shapley, 1995; Ungerleider & Haxby, 1994; Van Essen et al., 1992). Much of what we know about these pathways comes from the study of macaque monkeys, although recent imagining studies using PET and fMRI have confirmed researchers' suspicion that the neural pathways underlying visual perception in the human and the macaque are very similar. Researchers have labeled these visual streams the "what" and the "where" pathways.

The **what pathway,** which runs from the striate cortex in the occipital lobes through the lower part of the temporal lobes (or the *inferior temporal cortex*), is involved in determining *what* an object is. In this pathway, primitive features from

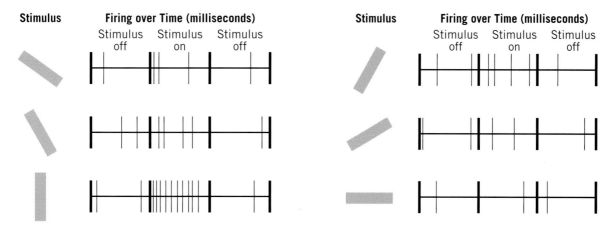

**FIGURE 4.15**
Feature detectors. A simple cell that responds to vertical lines will show more rapid firing the closer a visual image in its receptive field matches its preferred orientation. *Source:* Sekuler & Blake, 1994, p. 119.

the striate cortex (such as lines) are integrated into more complex combinations (such as cones or squares). At other locations along the pathway, the brain processes features of the object such as color and texture. All of these processes occur simultaneously, as the striate cortex routes shape information to a shape-processing module, color information to a color-processing module, and so forth. Although some "cross-talk" occurs among these different modules, each appears to create its own map of the visual field, such as a shape map and a color map. Not until the information has reached the front, or anterior, sections of the temporal lobes does a fully integrated percept appear to exist. At various points along the stream, however, polysensory areas bring visual information in contact with information from other senses. For example, when a person shakes hands with another person, he not only sees the other's hand but also feels it, hears the person move toward him, and feels his own arm moving through space. This requires integrating information from all of the lobes of the cortex. The second stream, the **where pathway,** is involved in locating the object in space, following its movement, and guiding movement toward it. This pathway runs from the striate cortex through the middle and upper (superior) regions of the temporal lobes and up into the parietal lobes.

Lesions that occur along these pathways produce disorders that would seem bizarre without understanding the neuroanatomy. For example, patients with lesions at various points along the what pathway show a variety of disorders, such as an inability to recognize or name objects, to recognize colors, or to recognize familiar faces (prosopagnosia). Patients with lesions in the where pathway, in contrast, typically have little trouble recognizing or naming objects, but they may constantly bump into things, have trouble grasping nearby objects, or fail to respond to objects in a part of their visual field, even including their own limbs (a phenomenon called *visual neglect*). Interestingly, this neglect may occur even when they are picturing a scene from memory: When asked to draw a scene, patients with neglect may simply leave out an entire segment of the scene and have no idea that it is missing.

Anatomically, the location of these two pathways makes sense as well. Recognition of objects ("what") is performed by modules in the temporal lobes directly below those involved in language, particularly in *naming* objects. Knowing where objects are in space and tracking their movements, on the other hand, is important for guiding one's own movement toward or away from them. The position of one's *own* body in space appears to be represented in the parietal lobes, adjacent to the "where" pathway.

*The colors we perceive in a bouquet of flowers depend on the wavelengths of light the flowers reflect into our eyes.*

**INTERIM SUMMARY**    From the optic nerve, visual information travels along two pathways. One is to a midbrain region called the **superior colliculus,** which in humans is particularly involved in eye movements. The other is to the **lateral geniculate nucleus** in the thalamus and on to the visual cortex. **Feature detectors** in the primary visual cortex respond only when stimulation in their receptive field matches a particular pattern or orientation. Beyond the primary visual cortex, visual information flows along two pathways, the **"what" pathway** (involved in determining what an object is) and the **"where" pathway** (involved in locating the object in space, following its movement, and guiding movement toward it).

## PERCEIVING IN COLOR

"Roses are red, violets are blue." Well, not exactly. Color is a psychological property, not a quality of the stimulus. Grass is not green to a cow because cows lack color receptors; in contrast, most insects, reptiles, fish, and birds have excellent color vision (Nathans, 1987). As Sir Isaac Newton demonstrated in research with prisms in the sixteenth century, white light (such as sunlight and light from common indoor lamps) is composed of all the wavelengths that constitute the colors in the visual spectrum. A rose appears red because it absorbs certain wavelengths and reflects others, and humans have receptors that detect electromagnetic radiation in that range of the spectrum.

Actually, color has three psychological dimensions: hue, saturation, and lightness (Sewall & Wooten, 1991). **Hue** is what people commonly mean by color, that is, whether an object appears blue, red, violet, and so on. **Saturation** is a color's purity (the extent to which it is diluted with white or black or "saturated" with its own wavelength, like a sponge in water). **Lightness** is the extent to which a color is light or dark.

People of all cultures appear to perceive the same colors or hues, although cultures vary widely in the number of their color labels (Chapter 7). In the West, color also appears to be gendered (i.e., to differ between the two genders): Few men would pass a test requiring them to distinguish colors such as bone, taupe, and magenta, despite their mastery of the English language. (Males appear to improve considerably, however, after a few trips to the shoe store with a woman.)

### Retinal Transduction of Color

How does the visual system translate wavelength into the subjective experience of color? The first step occurs in the retina, where cones with different photosensitive pigments respond to varying degrees to different wavelengths of the spectrum. In 1802, a British physician named Thomas Young proposed that human color vision is *trichromatic,* that is, the colors we see reflect blends of three colors to which our retinas are sensitive. Developed independently 50 years later by Hermann von Helmholtz, the **Young–Helmholtz (or trichromatic) theory of color** holds that the eye contains three types of receptors, each maximally sensitive to wavelengths of light that produce sensations of blue, green, or red.

Another century later, Nobel Prize winner George Wald and others confirmed the existence of three different types of cones in the retina (Brown & Wald, 1964; Dartnall et al., 1983; Schnapf et al., 1989). Each cone responds to a range of wavelengths but responds most persistently to waves of light at a particular point on the spectrum (Figure 4.16). Short-wavelength cones *(S-cones)* are most sensitive to wavelengths of about 420 nm, which are perceived as blue. Middle-wavelength cones *(M-cones),* which produce the sensation of green, are most sensitive to wavelengths of about 535 nm. Long-wavelength cones *(L-cones),* which produce red sensations, are most sensitive to wavelengths of about 560 nm (Brown & Wald, 1964). Mixing these three primary colors of light—red, green, and blue— produces the thousands of color shades humans can discriminate and identify.

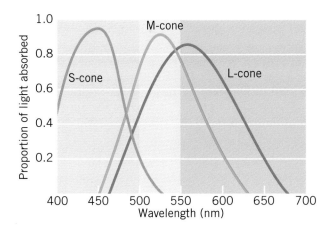

**FIGURE 4.16**
Cone response curves. All three kinds of cones respond to a range of frequencies—that is, they absorb light waves of many lengths, which contributes to bleaching—but they are maximally sensitive at particular frequencies and thus produce different color sensations.

This list of primary colors differs from the list of primary colors children learn in elementary school from mixing paints (blue, red, and yellow). The reason is that mixing paint and mixing light alter the wavelengths perceived in different ways, one *subtracting* and the other *adding* parts of the spectrum. Mixing paints is called **subtractive color mixture** because each new paint added actually blocks out, or subtracts, wavelengths reflected onto the retina. For example, yellow paint appears yellow because its pigment absorbs most wavelengths and reflects only those perceived as yellow; the same is true of blue paint. When blue and yellow paints are mixed, only the wavelengths not absorbed by *either* the blue or yellow paint reach the eye; the wavelengths left are the ones we perceive as green.

Subtractive color mixture, then, mixes wavelengths of light before they reach the eye. In contrast, **additive color mixture** takes place in the eye itself, as light of differing wavelengths simultaneously strikes the retina and thus expands (adds to) the perceived section of the spectrum. Newton discovered additive color mixture by using two prisms to funnel two colors simultaneously into the eye. Color television works on an additive principle. A television picture is composed of tiny blue, green, and red dots, which the eye blends from a distance. When struck by an electron beam inside the set, the spots light up. From a distance, the spots combine to produce multicolored images, although the dots can be seen at very close range.

## Processing Color in the Brain

The trichromatic theory accurately predicted the nature of retinal receptors, but it was not a complete theory of color perception. For example, the physiologist

*The primary colors children learn in elementary school are not the same as the primary colors of the trichromatic theory—although learning the former tends to be more fun.*

*The Impressionists made heavy use of additive color mixture, as in this painting of Venice by the French painter Paul Signac.*

Ewald Hering noted that trichromatic theory could not alone explain a phenomenon that occurs with **afterimages,** visual images that persist after a stimulus has been removed. Hering (1878, 1920) wondered why the colors of the afterimage were different in predictable ways from those of the original image (Figure 4.17). He proposed a theory, modified substantially by later researchers, known as opponent-process theory (DeValois, 1975; Hurvich & Jameson, 1957). **Opponent-process theory** argues that all colors are derived from three antagonistic color systems: black–white, blue–yellow, and red–green. The black–white system contributes to brightness and saturation; the other two systems are responsible for hue.

**FIGURE 4.17**
Afterimage. Stare at the yellow and red globe for three minutes, centering your eyes on the white dot in the middle, and then look at the white space on the page to the left of it. The afterimage is the traditional blue and green globe, reflecting the operation of antagonistic color-opponent cells in the lateral geniculate nucleus.

Hering proposed his theory in opposition to trichromatic theory, but subsequent research suggests that the two theories are actually complementary. Trichromatic theory applies to the retina, where cones are, in fact, particularly responsive to red, blue, or green. Opponent-process theory applies at higher visual centers in the brain. Researchers have found that some neurons in the lateral geniculate nucleus of monkeys, whose visual system is similar to that of humans, are **color-opponent cells,** excited by wavelengths that produce one color but inhibited by wavelengths of the other member of the pair (DeValois & DeValois, 1975). For example, some red–green neurons increase their activity when wavelengths experienced as red are in their receptive fields and decrease their activity when exposed to wavelengths perceived as green; others are excited by green and inhibited by red. The pattern of activation of several color-opponent neurons together determines the color the person senses (Abramov & Gordon, 1994).

Opponent-process theory neatly explains afterimages. Recall that in all sensory modalities the sensory system adapts, or responds less, to constant stimulation. In the visual system, adaptation begins with bleaching in the retina. Photoreceptors take time to resynthesize their pigments once they have bleached and thus cannot respond continuously to constant stimulation. During the period in which their pigment is returning, they cannot send inhibitory signals; this facilitates sensation of the opponent color. The afterimage of yellow therefore appears blue (and vice versa), red appears green, and black appears white.

Opponent-process and trichromatic theory together explain another phenomenon that interested Hering: *color blindness* (or, more accurately, *color deficiency*). Few people are entirely blind to color; those who are (because of genetic abnormalities that leave them with only one kind of cone) can only detect brightness, not color. Most color-deficient people confuse red and green (Figure 4.18). Red–green color blindness is sex linked, over ten times more prevalent in males than females. It generally reflects a deficiency of either M-cones or L-cones, which makes red–green distinctions impossible at higher levels of the nervous system (Vollrath et al., 1988; Weale, 1982; Wertenbaker, 1981).

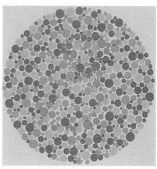

**FIGURE 4.18**
Color blindness. In this common test for color blindness, a green 3 is presented against a background of orange and yellow dots. The pattern of stimulation normally sent to the lateral geniculate nucleus by S-, M-, and L-cones allows discrimination of these colors. People who are red-green color blind see only a random array of dots.

**INTERIM SUMMARY** Two theories together explain what is known about color vision. According to the **Young-Holmholtz,** or **trichromatic, theory,** the eye contains three types of receptors, which are most sensitive to wavelengths experienced as red, green, or blue. According to **opponent-process theory,** the colors we experience (and the afterimages we perceive) reflect three antagonistic color systems—a blue-yellow, red-green, and black-white system. Trichromatic theory is operative at the level of the retina, and opponent-process theory is more applicable at higher neural levels.

## How the World Becomes Represented in the Mind

The processes by which objects in the external world become translated into an "internal" portrait of them in the mind should now be growing clear. At the lowest level of the nervous system, neurons collect highly specific information from receptor cells that would, by itself, be meaningless. At each subsequent stage, through the thalamus to the most complex modules in the cortex, information is combined to provide a progressively richer, more integrated picture of the bits and pieces of knowledge collected at the prior stage. Through this process, isolated units of stimulus energy gradually undergo a remarkable metamorphosis, in which the brain weaves sensory threads into complex and meaningful perceptual tapestries. As we will see, however, perceptions are not woven *exclusively* from sensory input, that is, from the simple threads. Our beliefs, expectations, and needs also exert an influence on what we perceive, so that knowledge is, from the very start, an interaction between an active perceiver and an environment that never stands still.

*People see fireworks from a distance before they hear them because light travels faster than sound.*

# HEARING

If a tree falls in a forest, does it make a sound if no one hears it? To answer this question requires an understanding of hearing, or **audition,** and the physical properties it reflects. Like vision, hearing allows sensation at a distance and is thus of tremendous adaptive value. Hearing is also involved in the richest form of communication, spoken language. As with our discussion of vision, we begin by considering the stimulus energy underlying hearing—sound. Next we examine the organ that transduces it, the ear, and the neural pathways for auditory processing.

## THE NATURE OF SOUND

When a tree falls in the forest, the crash produces vibrations in adjacent air molecules, which in turn collide with one another. A guitar string being plucked, a piece of paper rustling, or a tree falling to the ground all produce sound because they create vibrations in the air. Like ripples on a pond, these rhythmic pulsations of acoustic energy (sound) spread outward from the vibrating object as **sound waves.** Sound waves grow weaker with distance, but they travel at a constant speed, roughly 1130 feet (or 340 meters) per second.

Sound differs from light in a number of respects. Sound travels more slowly, which is why thunder often appears to follow lightening, or why fans in center field sometimes hear the crack of a bat *after* seeing the batter hit the ball; at close range, however, the difference between the speed of light and the speed of sound is imperceptible. Unlike light, sound also travels through most objects, which explains why sound is more difficult to shut out. Like light, sound waves can be reflected off or absorbed by objects in the environment, but the impact on hearing is different from the impact on vision. When sound is reflected off an object, it produces an echo; when it is absorbed by an object, such as carpet, it is muffled. Everyone sounds like the great Italian tenor Luciano Pavarotti in the shower (or like Bruce Springsteen if they have a sore throat) because tile absorbs so little sound, creating echoes and resonance that give fullness to even a mediocre voice.

### Frequency

Acoustic energy has three important properties: frequency, complexity, and amplitude. When a person hits a tuning fork, the prongs of the fork move rapidly inward and outward, putting pressure on the air molecules around them, which collide with the molecules next to them. Each round of expansion and contraction of the distance between molecules of air is known as a **cycle.**

The number of cycles per second determines the sound wave's frequency. **Frequency** is just what it sounds like—a measure of how often (that is, how *frequently*) a wave cycles. Frequency is expressed in **hertz,** or **Hz** (named after the German physicist Heinrich Hertz). One hertz equals one cycle per second, so a 1500-Hz tone has 1500 cycles per second. The frequency of a simple sound wave corresponds to the psychological property of **pitch** (the quality of a tone, from low to high). Generally, the higher the frequency, the higher the pitch. When frequency is doubled—that is, when the number of cycles per second is twice as frequent—the pitch perceived is an octave higher.

The human auditory system is sensitive to a wide range of frequencies. Young adults can hear frequencies from about 15 to 20,000 Hz, but as with most senses, capacity diminishes with aging. Frequencies used in music range from the lowest note on an organ (16 Hz) to the highest note on a grand piano (over 4000 Hz). Human voices range from about 100 Hz to about 3500 Hz, and our ears are most sensitive to sounds in that frequency range. Other species are sensitive to different ranges. Dogs hear frequencies ranging from 15 to 50,000 Hz, which is why they are responsive to "silent" whistles whose frequencies fall above the range humans can sense. Elephants can hear ultralow frequencies over considerable distances.

So, does a tree falling in the forest produce a sound? It produces sound *waves*, but the waves only become perceptible as "a sound" if creatures in the forest have receptors tuned to them.

## Complexity

Sounds rarely consist of waves of uniform frequency. Rather, most sounds are a combination of sound waves, each with a different frequency. The **complexity** of a sound wave—the extent to which it is composed of multiple frequencies—corresponds to the psychological property of **timbre**, or texture of the sound. People recognize each other's voices, as well as the sounds of different musical instruments, from their characteristic timbre. Timbre allows people to distinguish the middle C of a piano from the same pitch played on a flute. The dominant part of each wave produces the predominant pitch (in this case, middle C), but overtones (additional frequencies) give the instrument its distinctive sound. Synthesizers imitate conventional instruments by electronically adding the right overtones to pure frequencies (Hilts, 1980). Much of the music on popular radio stations today is synthesized; many of the sounds are actually played on a keyboard and mixed with special computer software. Adding instrumentation is as easy as saying, "Let's try adding some strings here."

The sounds instruments produce, whether in a rock band or a symphony, are music to our ears because we learn to interpret particular temporal patterns and combinations of sound waves as music. What people hear as music and as random auditory noise depends on their culture. The scales and harmonic structures that are standard in contemporary jazz would have been musically incomprehensible to Mozart, just as rock and roll was denounced by parents of teenagers in the 1960s as senseless noise.

## Amplitude

In addition to frequency and complexity, sound waves have amplitude. **Amplitude** refers to the height and depth of a wave, that is, the difference between its maximum and minimum pressure level (Figure 4.19). The amplitude of a sound wave corresponds to the psychological property of **loudness**; the greater the amplitude, the louder the sound. Amplitude is measured in **decibels (dB)**. Zero decibels is the absolute threshold above which most people can hear a 1000-Hz tone.

Like the visual system, the human auditory system has an astonishing range, handling energy levels that can differ by a factor of 10 billion or more (Bekesy & Rosenblith, 1951). The decibel scale is logarithmic, condensing a huge array of intensities into a manageable range, just as the auditory system does. A loud scream is 100,000 times more intense than a sound at the absolute threshold, but it is only 100 dB different. Conversation is usually held at 50 to 60 dB. Most people experience sounds over 130 dB as painful, and prolonged exposure to sounds over about 90 dB, such as subway cars rolling into the station or amplifiers at a rock concert, can produce permanent hearing loss or ringing in the ears (Figure 4.20).

**INTERIM SUMMARY**    Sound travels in **waves**, which occur as a vibrating object sets air particles in motion. The sound wave's **frequency**, which is experienced as **pitch**, refers to the number of times those particles oscillate per second. Most sounds are actually composed of waves with many frequencies, which gives them their characteristic texture, or **timbre.** The loudness of a sound reflects the height and depth, or **amplitude**, of the wave.

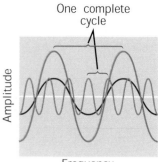

— High frequency, low amplitude (soft tenor or soprano)
— Low frequency, low amplitude (soft bass)
— Low frequency, high amplitude (loud bass)

**FIGURE 4.19**
Frequency and amplitude. Sound waves can differ in both frequency (pitch) and amplitude (loudness). A cycle can be represented as the length of time or distance between peaks of the curve.

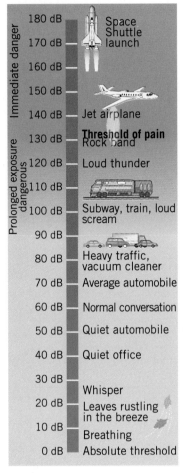

**FIGURE 4.20**
Loudness. Loudness of various common sounds at close range, in decibels.

## THE EAR

Transduction of sound occurs in the ear, which consists of an outer, middle, and inner ear (Figure 4.21). The outer ear collects and magnifies sounds in the air; the middle ear converts waves of air pressure into movements of tiny bones; and the inner ear transforms these movements into waves in fluid that generate neural signals.

### Transduction

The hearing process begins in the outer ear, which consists of the pinna and the auditory canal. Sound waves are funneled into the ear by the **pinna,** the skin-covered cartilage that protrudes from the sides of the head. The pinna is not essential for hearing, but its irregular shape is useful for locating sounds in space, which bounce off its folds differently when they come from various locations (Batteau, 1967). Just inside the skull is the **auditory canal**, a passageway about an inch long. As sound waves resonate in the auditory canal, they are amplified by up to a factor of 2.

   **The Middle Ear**   At the end of the auditory canal is a thin, flexible membrane known as the **eardrum, or tympanic membrane.** The eardrum marks the outer boundary of the middle ear. When sound waves reach the eardrum, they set it in motion. The movements of the eardrum are extremely small—0.00000001 centimeter, or about the width of a hydrogen molecule, in response to a whisper (Sekuler & Blake, 1994). The eardrum essentially reproduces the cyclical vibration of the object that created the noise, on a microcosmic scale. It is only able to do so, however, if air pressure on both sides of it (in the outer and middle ear) is roughly the same. When an airplane begins its descent and a person's head is blocked by a head cold, the pressure is greater on the inside, which blunts the vibrations of the eardrum. The normal mechanism for equalizing air pressure is the *Eustachian tube,* which connects the middle ear to the throat but can become blocked by mucous.

   When the eardrum vibrates, it sets in motion three tiny bones in the middle ear, called **ossicles.** These bones, named for their distinctive shapes, are called the *malleus, incus,* and *stapes,* which translate from the Latin into hammer, anvil, and

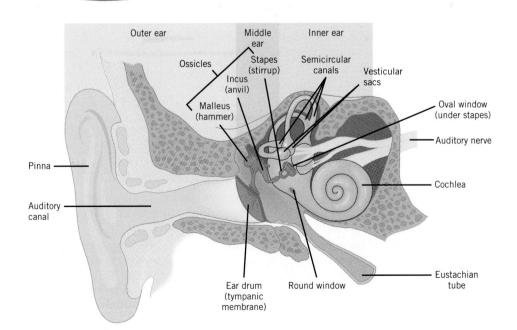

**FIGURE 4.21**
The ear. The ear consists of outer, middle, and inner sections, which direct the sound, amplify it, and turn mechanical energy into neural signals.

stirrup, respectively. The ossicles further amplify the sound two or three times before transmitting vibrations to the inner ear. The stirrup vibrates against a membrane called the **oval window,** which forms the beginning of the inner ear.

    **The Inner Ear**   The inner ear consists of two sets of fluid-filled cavities hollowed out of the temporal bone of the skull: the semicircular canals (involved in balance) and the cochlea (involved in hearing). The temporal bone is the hardest bone in the body and serves as natural soundproofing for its vibration-sensitive cavities. Chewing during a meeting sounds louder to the person doing the chewing than to those nearby because it rattles the temporal bone and thus augments the sounds from the ears.

    The **cochlea** (Figure 4.22) is a three-chambered tube shaped like a snail. When the stirrup vibrates against the oval window, the oval window vibrates, causing pressure waves in the cochlear fluid. These waves disturb the **basilar membrane,** which separates two of the cochlea's chambers. Attached to the basilar membrane are the ear's 15,000 receptors for sound, called **hair cells** (because they terminate

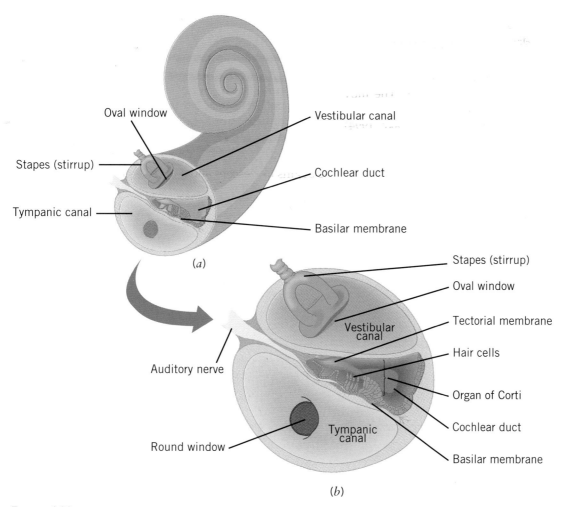

**FIGURE 4.22**

The cochlea. (*a*)The cochlea's chambers (the vestibular canal, the cochlear duct, and the tympanic canal) are filled with fluid. When the stirrup vibrates against the oval window, it vibrates, causing pressure waves in the fluid of the vestibular canal. These pressure waves spiral up the vestibular canal and down the tympanic canal, flexing the basilar membrane and, to a lesser extent, the tectorial membrane. (*b*)Transduction occurs in the organ of Corti, which includes these two membranes and the hair cells sandwiched between them. At the end of the tympanic canal is the round window, which pushes outward to relieve pressure when the sound waves have passed through the cochlea.

in tiny bristles, or **cilia**). Above the hair cells is another membrane, the **tectorial membrane,** which also moves as waves of pressure travel through the cochlear fluid. The cilia bend as the basilar and tectorial membranes move in different directions. This triggers action potentials in sensory neurons forming the **auditory nerve,** which transmits auditory information to the brain. Thus, mechanical energy—the movement of cilia and membranes—is transduced into neural energy.

Sensory deficits in hearing, as in other senses, can arise from problems either with parts of the sense organ that channel stimulus energy or with the receptors and neural circuits that convert this energy into psychological experience. Failure of the outer or middle ear to conduct sound to the receptors in the hair cells is called *conduction loss;* failure of receptors in the inner ear or of neurons in any auditory pathway in the brain is referred to as *sensorineural loss.* The most common problems with hearing result from exposure to noise or reflect changes in the receptors with aging; similar age-related changes occur in most sensory systems (Chapter 13). A single exposure to an extremely loud noise, such as a firecracker, an explosion, or a gun firing at close range, can permanently damage the hair cell receptors in the inner ear.

### Sensing Pitch

Precisely how does auditory transduction transform the physical properties of sound frequency and amplitude into the psychological experiences of pitch and loudness? Two theories, both proposed in the nineteenth century and once considered opposing explanations, together appear to explain the available data. The first, called **place theory,** holds that different areas of the basilar membrane are maximally sensitive to different frequencies (Bekesy, 1959, 1960; Helmholtz, 1863). Place theory was initially proposed by Herman von Helmholtz (of trichromatic color fame), who had the wrong mechanism but the right idea. A Hungarian scientist named Georg von Bekesy discovered the mechanism a century after Helmholtz by recognizing that when the stapes hits the oval window, a wave travels down the basilar membrane like a carpet being shaken at one end (Figure 4.23). Shaking a carpet rapidly (i.e., at high frequency) produces an early peak in

**FIGURE 4.23**
Place theory. The frequency with which the stapes strikes the oval window affects the location of peak vibration on the basilar membrane. The lower the tone, the farther the maximum displacement on the membrane is from the oval window. *Source:* Sekuler & Blake, 1994, p. 315.

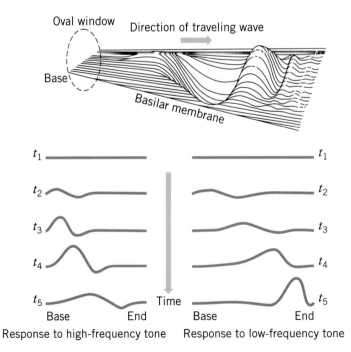

the wave of the carpet, whereas shaking it slowly produces a peak in the wave toward the other end of the carpet. Similarly, high-frequency tones, which produce rapid strokes of the stapes, produce the largest displacement of the basilar membrane close to the oval window, whereas low-frequency tones cause a peak in basilar movement toward the far end of the membrane. Peak vibration leads to peak firing of hair cells at a particular location. Hair cells at different points on the basilar membrane thus transmit information about different frequencies to the brain, just as rods and cones transduce electromagnetic energy at different frequencies.

Place theory has one major problem. At *very* low frequencies the entire basilar membrane vibrates fairly uniformly; thus, for very low tones, location of maximal vibration cannot account for pitch. The second theory of pitch, **frequency theory,** overcomes this problem, proposing that the more frequently a sound wave cycles, the more frequently the basilar membrane vibrates and its hair cells fire. Thus, pitch perception is probably mediated by two neural mechanisms: a place code at high frequencies and a frequency code at low frequencies. Both mechanisms likely operate at intermediate frequencies (Goldstein, 1989).

## NEURAL PATHWAYS

Neurons in the auditory system are similar in many respects to those in the visual system. Firing depends on input from several hair cells, just as firing in ganglion cells reflects the total activity of many photoreceptors. Neurons comprising the auditory nerve also carry information specifying stimulus quality (pitch), as do fibers in the optic nerve (color). Thus, a neuron will respond to a range of frequencies if the sound is intense enough, but it will most readily respond to a characteristic frequency to which it is tuned. Neurons activated by hair cells near the oval window respond to high frequencies, whereas those activated by hair cells on the other end of the basilar membrane fire more readily for low tones. At each pitch, some neurons respond to relatively low intensities of sound, whereas others fire more at high sound levels. As with light, more intense sounds also cause more neurons to fire.

Information transmitted by the ears along the two auditory nerves ultimately finds its way to the auditory cortex in the temporal lobes, but it makes several stops along the way (Figure 4.24). The auditory nerve from each ear projects to the medulla, where the majority of its fibers cross over to the other hemisphere. (Recall that the medulla is where sensory and motor neurons cross from one side of the body to the other). Some information from each ear, however, does not cross over; thus, information from both ears is represented on both sides of the brain.

From the medulla, bundles of axons project to the midbrain (to the *inferior colliculus,* just below the superior colliculus, which is involved in vision) and on to the thalamus (to the *medial geniculate nucleus,* just toward the center of the brain from its visual counterpart, the lateral geniculate nucleus). The thalamus transmits information to the auditory cortex in the temporal lobes, which has sections devoted to different frequencies, much as sites in the primary visual cortex process different parts of the visual field. Some neurons in the auditory cortex also respond to the "movement" of sounds—whether frequency changes, moving up or down—similar to the way some complex cells in the visual cortex respond to movement in space. Just as the cortical region corresponding to the fovea is disproportionately large, so, too, is the region of the primary auditory cortex tuned to sound frequencies in the middle of the spectrum—the same frequencies involved in speech. Indeed, in humans and other animals, some cortical neurons in the left temporal lobe respond exclusively to particular sounds characteristic of the "language" of the species, whether monkey calls or human speech.

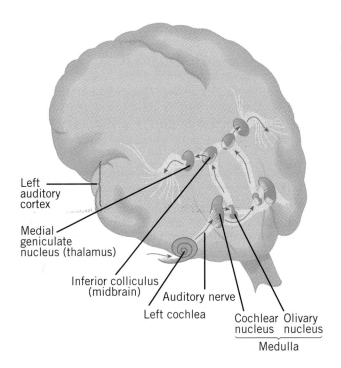

**FIGURE 4.24**
Auditory pathways. Axons from neurons in the inner ear project to the cochlear nucleus in the medulla. From there, most cross over to a structure called the olivary nucleus on the opposite side, although some remain uncrossed. At the olivary nucleus, information from the two ears begins to be integrated. Information from the olivary nucleus then passes to a midbrain structure (the inferior colliculus) and on to the medial geniculate nucleus in the thalamus before reaching the auditory cortex.

Left auditory cortex

Medial geniculate nucleus (thalamus)

Inferior colliculus (midbrain)

Left cochlea

Auditory nerve

Cochlear nucleus  Olivary nucleus

Medulla

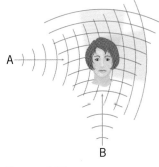

**FIGURE 4.25**
Sound localization. At high frequencies, sounds on one side of the head can be localized by relative intensity in the two ears because the head casts a "sound shadow" on one side but not the other, as in sound *A*. With sound *B*, the shadow is behind the head, so it does not lead to any relative differences between the ears. At low frequencies, the slight difference between the time a sound reaches one ear, as in *A*, provides a cue for sound localization.

## Sound Localization

Neurons in the thalamus and primary cortex are involved in identifying the location of a sound in space, or **sound localization.** In humans, sound localization requires the integration of information from both ears because the brain uses two main cues for localizing sound: differences between the two ears in loudness, and timing of the sound (King & Carlile, 1995; Middlebrooks & Green, 1991; Stevens & Newman, 1934). Particularly for high-frequency sounds, relative loudness in the ear closer to the source provides information about its location because the head blocks some of the sound from hitting the other ear (Figure 4.25).

Loudness is less useful for localizing lower frequency sounds because their waves are so long that the head does not effectively block them. For example, a 900-Hz sound (a relatively low tone) cycles about every 40 centimeters, which is twice the diameter of the average head, so it curves right around the head (Sekuler & Blake, 1994). Localization of sounds at low frequencies relies more on the difference in the arrival time of the sound at the two ears. A sound coming from the left reaches the left ear a split second before reaching the right, particularly if it is moving slowly (that is, at a low frequency). Timing differences are less useful for localizing sounds at high frequencies because they travel so quickly between the two ears. The ability to move the head toward sounds is also crucial for localizing sounds.

Neurologically, the basis for sound localization lies in neurons that respond to relative differences in the signals from the two ears. These *binaural neurons* (i.e., neurons that respond to information from both ears) exist at nearly all levels of the auditory system in the brain, from the brainstem up through the cortex (King & Carlile, 1995). At higher levels of the brain, this information is connected with visual information about the location and distance of objects, which allows a joint mapping of auditory and visual information. Researchers have studied this process extensively in the barn owl, an animal that localizes sound in the inferior colliculus (rather than the cortex) primarily through timing differences between the arrival of the sound at each ear (Feldman et al., 1996; Knudson et al., 1991; Konishi, 1995). When these animals are raised wearing glasses that use prisms to distort the perceived location of objects, their auditory map essentially becomes linked to a visual map with different coordinates.

**INTERIM SUMMARY** Sound waves travel through the **auditory canal** to the **eardrum,** which in turn sets the **ossicles** in motion, amplifying the sound. When the stirrup (one of the ossicles) strikes the **oval window,** it creates waves of pressure in the fluid of the **cochlea. Hair cells** attached to the **basilar membrane** then transduce the sound, triggering firing of the sensory neurons whose axons comprise the **auditory nerve.** Two theories, once considered opposing, explain the psychological qualities of sound. According to **place theory,** which best explains transduction at high frequencies, different areas of the basilar membrane respond to different frequencies. According to **frequency theory,** which best explains transduction at low frequencies, the rate of vibration of the basilar membrane transforms frequency into pitch. From the auditory nerve, sensory information passes through the inferior colliculus in the midbrain and the medial geniculate nucleus of the thalamus on to the auditory cortex in the temporal lobes. Neurons in both the thalamus and primary auditory cortex are involved in **sound localization,** which reflects the action of binaural neurons that respond to relative differences in the loudness and timing of sensory signals transduced by the two ears.

## OTHER SENSES

Vision and audition are the most highly specialized senses in humans, occupying the greatest amount of brain space and showing the most cortical evolution. Our other senses, however, serve important adaptive functions as well. These include smell, taste, the skin senses (pressure, temperature, and pain), and the proprioceptive senses (body position and motion).

### SMELL

Smell **(olfaction)** serves a number of functions in humans. It enables us to detect danger (e.g., the smell of something burning), discriminate palatable and unpalatable or spoiled foods, and recognize familiar others. Smell plays a less important role in humans than in most other animals, who rely heavily on olfaction to mark territory and track other animals. Many species communicate through **pheromones** (Chapter 10), scent messages that regulate the sexual behavior of many animals and direct a variety of behaviors in insects (Carolsfeld et al., 1997; Sorensen, 1996).

We humans, in contrast, often try to "cover our tracks" in the olfactory domain using perfumes and deodorants to mask odors that our mammalian ancestors might have found informative or appealing. Nevertheless, vestiges of this ancient reproductive mechanism remain. Humans appear both to secrete and sense olfactory cues related to reproduction. Experiments using sweaty hands or articles of clothing have shown that people can identify the gender of another person by smell alone with remarkable accuracy (Doty et al., 1982; Russell, 1976; Wallace, 1977). The synchronization of menstrual cycles of women living in close proximity also appears to occur through smell and may reflect ancient pheromonal mechanisms (McClintock, 1971; Preti et al., 1986; Stern & McClintock, 1998).

### Transduction

The environmental stimuli for olfaction are invisible molecules of gas emitted by substances and suspended in the air. The thresholds for recognizing most odors are remarkably low—as low as one molecule per *50 trillion* molecules of air for some molecules (Geldard, 1972). Although the nose is the sense organ for smell, the vapors that give rise to olfactory sensations can enter the **nasal cavities**—the region hollowed out of the bone in the skull that contains smell receptors—through either the nose or the mouth (Figure 4.26). When food is chewed, vapors travel up the back of the mouth into the nasal cavity; this process actually accounts for much of the taste.

Transduction of smell occurs in the **olfactory epithelium,** a thin pair of structures (one on each side) less than a square inch in diameter at the top of the nasal cavities. Chemical molecules in the air become trapped in the mucus of the epithelium, where they make contact with olfactory receptor cells that transduce the stimulus into olfactory sensations. Humans have approximately 10 million olfactory receptors (Engen, 1982), in comparison with dogs, whose 200 million receptors enable them to track humans and other animals with their noses (Marshall & Moulton, 1981). Psychologists have long debated whether a small number of receptors coding different qualities combine to produce complex smells or whether the olfactory epithelium contains hundreds or thousands of receptors that bind only with very specific molecules. Recent research on the genes that produce proteins involved in smell transduction suggests that many receptors are responsive to chemicals with very specific molecular structures (Bartoshuk & Beauchamp, 1994; Breer et al., 1996; Buck & Axel, 1991).

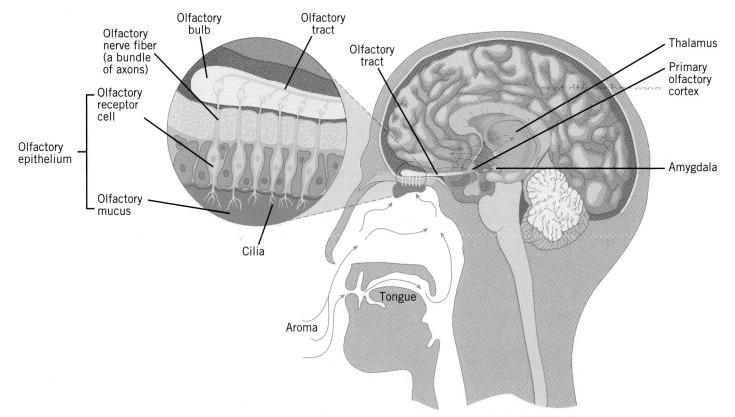

**FIGURE 4.26**

Olfaction. Molecules of air enter the nasal cavities through the nose and throat, where smell is transduced by receptors in the olfactory epithelium. Axons of receptor cells form the olfactory nerve, a relatively short nerve that projects to the olfactory bulb. From there, information passes through the olfactory tract to the primary olfactory cortex. This region connects with the thalamus and amygdala, which in turn connect with higher olfactory centers in a more evolutionarily recent region of the frontal lobe.

## Neural Pathways

The axons of olfactory receptor cells form the **olfactory nerve,** which transmits information to the **olfactory bulbs,** multilayered structures that combine information from receptor cells. Olfactory information then travels to the primary olfactory cortex, a primitive region of the cortex deep in the frontal lobes. Unlike other senses, smell is not relayed through the thalamus on its way to the cortex; however, the olfactory cortex has projections to both the thalamus and the limbic system, so that smell is connected to both taste and emotion.

Many animals that respond to pheromonal cues have a second, or accessory, olfactory system, with its own olfactory bulbs and tracts, that projects directly to the amygdala and on to the hypothalamus, thus contributing to regulation of reproductive behavior. Although the data at this point are conflicting, some studies suggest that humans may have a similar secondary olfactory system, which, if operative, has no links to consciousness and thus influences reproductive behavior without our knowing it (Bartoshuk & Beauchamp, 1994; Stern and McClintock, 1998).

**INTERIM SUMMARY**    The environmental stimuli for smell are gas molecules suspended in the air. These molecules flow through the nose into the **olfactory epithelium,** where they are detected by hundreds of different types of receptors. The axons of these receptor cells comprise the **olfactory nerve,** which transmits information to the **olfactory bulbs** and on to the primary olfactory cortex deep in the front lobes.

## TASTE

The sense of smell is sensitive to molecules in the air, whereas taste **(gustation)** is sensitive to molecules soluble in saliva. At the dinner table, the contributions of the nose and mouth to taste are indistinguishable except when the nasal passages are blocked so that food loses much of its taste. From an evolutionary perspective, taste serves two functions: to protect the organism from ingesting toxic substances and to regulate intake of nutrients such as sugars and salt. For example, toxic substances often taste bitter, and foods high in sugar (which provides the body with energy) are usually sweet. The tendency to reject bitter substances and to ingest sweet ones is present even in newborns, despite their lack of experience with taste (Bartoshuk & Beauchamp, 1994).

Transduction of taste occurs in the **taste buds** (Figure 4.27). Roughly 10,000 taste buds are distributed throughout the mouth and throat (Miller, 1995), al-

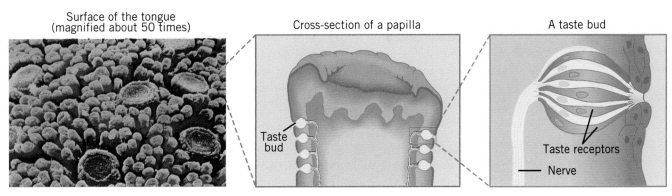

**FIGURE 4.27**
The majority of taste buds are located on the papillae of the tongue. They contain receptor cells that bind with chemicals in the saliva and stimulate gustatory neurons.

though most are located in the bumps on the surface of the tongue called **papillae** (Latin for "pimple"). Soluble chemicals that enter the mouth penetrate tiny pores in the papillae and stimulate the taste receptors. Each taste bud contains between 50 and 150 receptor cells (Margolskee, 1995). Taste receptors, unlike sensory receptors in the eye or ear, wear out and are replaced every ten or 11 days (Graziadei, 1969). Regeneration is essential, or a burn to the tongue would result in permanent loss of taste.

Taste receptors stimulate neurons that carry information to the medulla and pons in the hindbrain. From there, gustatory information travels along one of two pathways. One leads to the thalamus and on to the primary gustatory cortex deep within a region between the temporal and parietal lobes. This pathway allows the identification of tastes. The second pathway, which has no access to consciousness, leads to the limbic system. This pathway allows immediate emotional and behavioral responses to tastes, such as spitting out bitter substances. It also appears to be involved in learned aversions to tastes that become associated through experience with nausea. As in blindsight, people with damage to the first (cortical) pathway cannot identify substances by taste, but they react with appropriate facial expressions to bitter and sour substances if this second, more primitive, pathway is intact.

The gustatory system responds to four basic tastes: sweet, sour, salty, and bitter. Different receptors are most sensitive to one of these tastes, at least at low levels of stimulation. This appears to be cross-culturally universal: People of different cultures diverge in their taste preferences and beliefs about basic flavors, but they vary little in identifying substances as sweet, sour, salty, or bitter (Laing et al., 1993). More than one receptor, however, can produce the same sensation, at least for bitterness. Apparently, as plants and insects evolved toxic chemicals to protect against predation, animals that ate them evolved specific receptors for detecting these substances. The nervous system, however, continued to rely on the same sensation, bitterness, to discourage snacking on them (Bartoshuk & Beauchamp, 1994).

**INTERIM SUMMARY**    Taste occurs as receptors in the **taste buds** transduce chemical information from molecules soluble in saliva into neural information, which is integrated with olfactory sensations in the brain. Taste receptors stimulate neurons that project to the medulla and pons in the hindbrain. From there, the information is carried along two neural pathways, one leading to the primary gustatory cortex, which allows identification of tastes, and the other leading to the limbic system, which allows initial gut-level reactions and learned responses to them. The gustatory system responds to four tastes: sweet, sour, salty, and bitter.

## SKIN SENSES

The approximately 18 square feet of skin covering the human body constitutes a complex, multilayered organ. The skin senses help protect the body from injury, aid in identifying objects, help maintain body temperature, and facilitate social interaction through hugs, kisses, holding, and handshakes. What we colloquially call the sense of touch is actually a mix of at least three qualities: pressure, temperature, and pain. Receptors in the skin respond to different aspects of these qualities, such as warm or cold or light or deep pressure. The human body contains approximately 5 million touch receptors of various types (Figure 4.28). Although receptors are specialized for different qualities, most skin sensations are complex, reflecting stimulation across many receptors (Goldstein, 1989).

As with other sensory systems, several receptors in the skin typically transmit

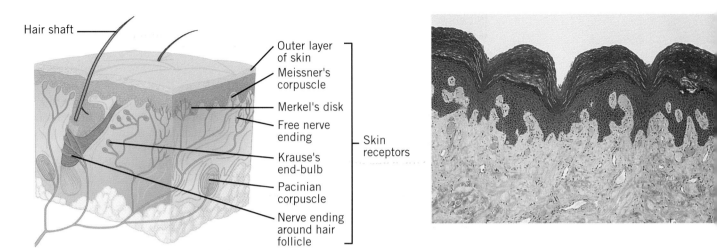

**FIGURE 4.28**

The skin and its receptors. Several different types of receptors transduce tactile stimulation, such as Meissner's corpuscles, which respond to brief stimulation (as when a ball of cotton moves across the skin); Merkel's disks, which detect steady pressure; and the nerve endings around hair follicles, which explain why plucking eyebrows or pulling tape off the skin can be painful.

information to a single sensory neuron, which in turn synapses with other neurons in the spinal cord. The qualities sensory neurons convey to the nervous system (such as soft pressure, warmth, and cold) depend on the receptors to which they are connected. Thus, when receptors reattach to the wrong nerve fibers, as appears to occur in some cases of painful neuropathy, sensory information can be misinterpreted. Like neurons in other sensory systems, those involved in touch also have receptive fields, which distinguish both where and how long the stimulation occurred on the skin.

Sensory neurons synapse with spinal interneurons that stimulate motor neurons, allowing animals to respond with rapid reflex actions. Sensory neurons also synapse with neurons that carry information up the spinal cord to the medulla, where neural tracts cross over. From there, sensory information travels to the thalamus and is subsequently routed to the primary touch center in the brain, the somatosensory cortex. The somatosensory cortex contains a map of the body (Chapter 3); neurons in the somatosensory cortex have receptive fields corresponding to different parts of the body. As in the visual system, the receptive fields of neurons become progressively larger as information passes to higher and higher processing centers. As a result, people can recognize the same shape (such as a pencil) pressing against different regions of the body, even though the stimulation is in entirely different places. Through experience, the brain represents more generalized tactile "pictures" of objects in association areas of the parietal lobes (Johnson et al., 1995).

People store information in this way about parts of their own bodies. People who have had a limb amputated often awaken from the operation disbelieving that the operation has occurred and only begin to believe it when they reach out to touch the missing limb (Katz and Melzack, 1990). Stored experiences of the limb's presence may continue for months or years, although they tend to change over time. For example, the "phantom limb" may begin to feel smaller and smaller, or the foot at the end of an amputated leg may come to feel like it is attached directly to the stump. Although the experience of a phantom limb tends to be most pronounced in people who have more recently lost a limb, phantom experiences of this sort can occur even in people who lost a limb very early in life or were even born without it (Melzack, 1993), suggesting that certain kinds of sensory "expectations" throughout the body may be partly innate. As we will see, phantom limbs may be the site of many "sensations," including intense pain, typically similar to pain experienced prior to amputation.

Each of the skin senses transduces a distinct form of stimulation. Pressure receptors transduce mechanical energy (like the receptors in the ear). Temperature receptors respond to thermal energy (heat). Pain receptors do not directly transform external stimulation into psychological experience; rather, they respond to a range of internal and external bodily states, from strained muscles to damaged skin.

### Pressure

People experience pressure when the skin is mechanically displaced, or moved. Sensitivity to pressure varies considerably over the surface of the body (Weinstein, 1968). The most sensitive regions are the face and fingers; the least sensitive are the back and legs. These disparities in sensitivity are reflected in the amount of space taken by neurons representing these areas in the somatosensory cortex. The hands are the skin's foveas, providing tremendous acuity; they have small receptive fields that allow fine discriminations, and the primary cortex devotes substantial space to them (see Johnson & Lamb, 1981). The hands turn what could be a passive sensory process—responding to indentations produced in the skin by external stimulation—into an active process. As the hands move over objects, pressure receptors register the indentations created in the skin and hence allow perception of texture. Just as eye movements allow people to read written words, finger movements allow blind people to read the raised dots that constitute Braille. In other animals, the somatosensory cortex emphasizes other body zones that provide important information for adaptation, such as whiskers in cats (Kaas, 1987).

### Temperature

When people sense the temperature of an object, they are actually sensing the difference between the temperature of the skin and the object, which is why a pool of 80-degree water feels warm to someone who has been standing in the cold rain but chilly to someone lying on a hot beach. Temperature sensation relies on two sets of receptors, one for cold and one for warmth (see Levine & Shefner, 1991; Spray, 1986). Cold receptors, however, not only detect coolness but are also involved in the experience of extreme temperatures, both hot and cold. Subjects who grasp two pipes twisted together, one containing warm water and the other cold, experience intense heat (Figure 4.29). As with pressure, the pattern of stimulation, rather than the activation of specific receptors alone, creates the sensation.

### Pain

People spend billions of dollars a year fighting pain, but pain serves an important function: preventing tissue damage. Indeed, people who are insensitive to pain because of nerve damage or genetic abnormalities are at serious risk of injury and infection; young children with congenital (inborn) pain insensitivity have reportedly bitten off their tongues, chewed off the tips of their fingers, and been severely burned leaning against hot stoves or climbing into scalding bathwater (Jewesbury, 1951). On the other hand, persistent pain can be debilitating. Some

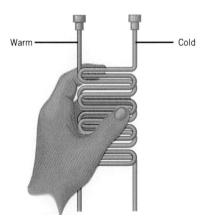

Warm ———————————— Cold

**FIGURE 4.29**
Experiencing intense heat. Warm and cold receptors activated simultaneously produce a sensation of intense heat.

estimates suggest that as many as one-third of North Americans suffer from persistent or recurrent pain. The cost in suffering, lost productivity, and dollars is immense (Miller & Kraus, 1990).

In contrast to other senses, pain has no specific physical stimulus; the skin does not transduce "pain waves." Sounds that are too loud, lights that are too bright, pressure that is too intense, temperatures that are too extreme, and other stimuli can all elicit pain. Although pain transduction is not well understood, the most important receptors for pain in the skin appear to be the *free nerve endings*. According to one prominent theory, when cells are damaged, they release chemicals that stimulate the free nerve endings, which in turn transmit pain messages to the brain (Price, 1988). These chemicals can also activate pain receptors elsewhere in the body, such as in the muscles and teeth and in the spinal nerves that receive input from pain receptors throughout the body (see Cook et al., 1997; Liu et al., 1997; Lynn & Perl, 1996).

One such chemical is a neuropeptide (a string of amino acids that serves as a neurotransmitter) called **substance P** (for pain). In one study, researchers found that pinching the hindpaws of rats led to the release of substance P in the spinal cord (Beyer et al., 1991). The concentration of substance P increased with the amount of painful stimulation and returned to baseline when the stimulation stopped. In another study, rats injected with substance P responded with biting, scratching, and distress vocalizations, all of which are associated with painful stimulation (DeLander & Wahl, 1991).

**Experiencing Pain**   Of all the senses, pain is probably the most affected by beliefs, expectations, and emotional state and the least reducible to level of stimulation (Sternbach, 1968). (The next time you have a headache or a sore throat, try focusing your consciousness on the minute details of the sensation, and you will notice that you can momentarily kill the pain by "reframing" it.) Anxiety can increase pain, whereas intense fear, stress, or concentration on other things can inhibit it (al Absi & Rokke, 1991; Melzack & Wall, 1983). Cultural norms and expectations also influence the subjective experience and behavioral expression of pain (Bates, 1987; Zatzick & Dimsdale, 1990). For example, on the island of Fiji, women of two subcultures appear to experience labor pain quite differently (Morse & Park, 1988). The native Fijiian culture is sympathetic to women in labor and provides both psychological support and herbal remedies for labor pain. In contrast, an Indian subculture on the island considers childbirth contaminating and hence offers little sympathy or support. Interestingly, women from the Indian group rate the pain of childbirth significantly lower than native Fijiians. Apparently, cultural recognition of pain influences the extent to which people can acknowledge it. Similarly, anecdotal evidence in the West suggests that people in subcultures that do not provide support for pain and encourage a "stiff upper lip" show fewer signs of pain and attend less to daily aches and pains than subcultures that dwell on pain.

**Gate Control Theory**   The phenomenological experience of pain is not always initiated by peripheral sensory stimulation. A striking example is phantom limb pain, experienced by a substantial number of amputees. **Phantom limb pain** is pain felt in a limb that no longer exists. The pain does not originate from severed nerves in the stump. Even if the stump is completely anesthetized, the pain persists, and medications that should ease it often fail to do so (Melzack, 1970).

One theory designed to account for phenomena such as phantom limb pain is **gate-control theory,** which emphasizes the role of the central nervous sytem (the brain and spinal cord, rather than the periphery) in regulating pain. According to gate control theory, when sensory neurons transmit information to the back (dor-

*A Japanese boy walks on fire at Mt. Takao. Pain is as much a state of mind as a state of receptors.*

sal region) of the spinal cord, they do not automatically produce pain sensations because their actions can be inhibited or amplified by input from other nearby sensory neurons as well as from messages descending from the brain (Melzack, 1993; Melzack and Wall, 1965).

Gate control theory distinguishes two kinds of neural fibers (axons from sensory neurons) that open and close spinal "gateways" for pain. Large-diameter fibers (called L-fibers), which transmit neural information very quickly, carry information about many forms of tactile stimulation as well as sharp pain. Once they transmit a message, they close the pain gate by inhibiting the firing of the neurons with which they synapse. Small-diameter fibers (S-fibers) synapse with the same neurons, carrying information about dull pain and burning to the brain. Because their small axons transmit neural information more slowly, however, their messages may arrive at a closed gate (or, more accurately, a partially closed gate, since pain does not usually completely disappear) if competing sensory input from L-fibers has inhibited pain transmission. This may explain why rubbing the area around a burn or cut, or even pinching a nearby region of skin, can alleviate pain. These actions stimulate L-fibers, which close the gates to incoming signals from S-fibers. According to gate-control theory, messages from the brain to the spinal cord can also close or open the gates, so that calm or anxious mental states can increase or decrease pain sensations arising from the peripheral nervous system.

Gate-control theory offers one explanation of phantom limb pain (Melzack, 1973, 1995). If L-fibers are destroyed by amputation, the gates remain open, allowing random firing of neurons at the amputation site to trigger action potentials, leading to the experience of pain in the missing limb.

Pain Control   Because mental as well as physiological processes contribute to pain, treatment may require attention to both mind and matter—to both the psychology and neurophysiology of pain. The Lamaze method of childbirth, for example, teaches women to relax through deep breathing and muscle relaxation and to distract themselves by focusing their attention elsewhere. It also teaches the woman's "coach" (her partner) to stimulate L-fibers through gentle massage. These procedures can be quite effective: Lamaze-trained women tend to experience less pain during labor (Leventhal et al., 1989), and they show a general increase in pain tolerance. For example, experiments show that they are able to keep their hands submerged in ice water longer than women without the training, especially if their coach provides encouragement (Whipple et al., 1990; Worthington et al., 1983).

Many other techniques target the cognitive and emotional aspects of pain. Though not a panacea, distraction is generally a useful strategy for increasing pain tolerance (Christenfeld, 1997; McCaul & Malott, 1984; Weisenberg et al., 1995). Health care professionals often chatter away while giving patients injections in order to distract and relax them. Something as simple as a pleasant view can affect pain tolerance in hospitalized patients. In one study, surgery patients whose rooms overlooked lush plant life had shorter hospital stays and required less medication than patients whose otherwise identical rooms looked out on a brick wall (Ulrich, 1984). Environmental psychologists, who apply psychological knowledge to building and landscape design, use such information to help architects design hospitals (Saegert & Winkel, 1990). Hypnosis (Chapter 9) can also be useful in controlling pain (Evans, 1990; Hilgard & Hilgard, 1975). Research suggests that hypnotic procedures can help burn victims tolerate debriding (removing dead tissue and changing dressings on wounds), which can be so painful that patients writhe in agony even on the maximum dosage of medications such as morphine (Patterson et al., 1992).

## FROM MIND TO BRAIN

### PERSONALITY AND PAIN

If mental states can affect pain sensation, are some people vulnerable to chronic pain by virtue of their personalities? Despite long-standing controversy in this area, researchers have identified a personality style that appears to be shared by many chronic pain patients (Keller & Butcher, 1992). These patients often blame their physical condition for all life's difficulties and deny any emotional or interpersonal problems. They tend to have difficulty expressing anger and to be anxious, depressed, needy, and dependent. The difficulty in studying such patients, however, is distinguishing the causes from the effects of chronic pain, since unending pain could produce many of these personality traits (Gamsa, 1990).

A team of researchers addressed this methodological problem by studying patients *at risk* for developing chronic pain before they actually developed it (Dworkin et al., 1992). The patients suffered from herpes zoster (shingles), a viral infection that results from reactivation of chicken pox virus. The nature and duration of pain associated with herpes zoster vary widely, but some patients experience disabling chronic pain. To see if they could predict which patients would develop chronic pain, the investigators gave a sample of recently diagnosed herpes zoster patients a series of questionnaires and tests, including measures of depression, anxiety, life stress, attitudes toward their illness, and pain severity. Physicians provided data on the severity of the patients' initial outbreak of the disease.

The researchers recontacted the patients several times over the next year and distinguished those who reported ongoing pain three months after the acute outbreak from those who did not. Although these two groups did not differ in the initial severity of their symptoms, they did differ significantly on a number of psychological dimensions assessed *at the time of their initial diagnosis*. Fitting the description of the "chronic pain personality," those patients who would later experience continued pain were initially more depressed and anxious and less satisfied with their lives than patients without pain, and they were more likely to dwell on their illness and resist physicians' reassurances.

Chronic pain is by no means "all in the head." In many cases it likely reflects an interaction of psychological factors, physiological vulnerabilities, and disease or injury. But this research suggests that the way people experience themselves and the world affects their vulnerability to their own sensory processes.

INTERIM SUMMARY    Touch includes three senses: pressure, temperature, and pain. Sensory neurons synapse with spinal interneurons that stimulate motor neurons (producing reflexes) as well as with neurons that carry information up the spinal cord to the medulla. From there, nerve tracts cross over, and the information is conveyed through the thalamus to the somatosensory cortex, which contains a map of the body. The function of pain is to prevent tissue damage; the experience of pain is greatly affected by beliefs, expectations, emotional state, and personality.

## PROPRIOCEPTIVE SENSES

Aside from the five traditional senses—vision, hearing, smell, taste, and touch—two additional senses, called **proprioceptive senses,** register body position and movement. The first, the **vestibular sense,** provides information about the position of the body in space by sensing gravity and movement. The ability to sense gravity is a very early evolutionary development, found in nearly all animals. The existence of this sense again exemplifies the way psychological characteristics have evolved to match characteristics of the environment that impact on adaptation. Gravity affects movement, so humans and other animals have receptors to transduce it, just as they have receptors for light.

The vestibular sense organs are in the inner ear, above the cochlea (see Figure 4.21, p. 160). Two organs transduce vestibular information: the semicircular canals and the vestibular sacs. The **semicircular canals** sense acceleration or deceleration in any direction as the head moves. The **vestibular sacs** sense gravity and the position of the head in space. Vestibular receptors are hair cells that register movement, much as hair cells in the ear transduce air movements. The neural pathways for the vestibular sense are not well understood, although impulses from the vestibular system travel to several regions of the hindbrain, notably the cerebellum, which is involved in smooth movement, and to a region deep in the temporal cortex.

The other proprioceptive sense, **kinesthesia,** provides information about the movement and position of the limbs and other parts of the body *relative to* one another. Kinesthesia is essential in guiding every complex movement, from walking, which requires instantaneous adjustments of the two legs, to drinking a cup of coffee. Some of the receptors for kinesthesia are in the joints; these cells transduce information about the position of the bones. Other receptors, in the tendons and muscles, transmit messages about muscle tension that signal body position (Neutra & LeBlond, 1969).

The vestibular and kinesthetic senses work in tandem, sensing different aspects of movement and position. Proprioceptive sensations are also integrated with messages from other sensory systems, especially touch and vision. For example, even when the proprioceptive senses are intact, walking can be difficult if tactile stimulation from the feet is shut off, as when a person's legs "fall asleep." (To see the importance of vision to balance, try balancing on one foot while raising the other foot as high as you can, first with your eyes closed and then with your eyes open.)

*Without the capacity to sense position of the body in space and position of the limbs relative to each other, this skier would be on his way to the hospital rather than the lodge.*

INTERIM SUMMARY   The **proprioceptive senses** register body position and movement. The **vestibular sense** provides information on the position of the body in space by sensing gravity and movement. **Kinesthesia** provides information about the movement and position of the limbs and other parts of the body relative to one another.

# PERCEPTION

The line between sensation and perception is thin, and we probably have already crossed it in discussing the psychology of pain. The hallmarks of perception are organization and interpretation. (Many psychologists consider attention a third aspect of perception, but since attention is also involved in memory, thought, motivation, and emotion, we address it in Chapter 9 on consciousness.) Perception *organizes* a continuous array of sensations into meaningful units. When we speak we produce, on average, a dozen meaningful units of sounds (called phonemes) per second (such as "walk" and "-ing") and are capable of understanding up to *40* phonemes per second (Pinker, 1994). When we listen to a symphony or a popular song, we can easily follow the melody despite the presence of other instruments or voices. This requires organization of sensations. Beyond organization, we must *interpret* the information organized. A scrawl on a piece of paper is not just a set of lines of particular orientation but a series of letters and words. A melodic pattern in the middle of a song or symphony is not just a novel set of notes but a variation on an earlier theme.

In this final section, we again emphasize the visual system, since the bulk of work in perception has used visual stimuli, but the same principles largely hold across the senses. We begin by describing several ways in which perception is organized and then examine the way people interpret sensory experiences.

## ORGANIZING SENSORY EXPERIENCE

If you put this book on the floor, it does not suddenly look like part of the floor; if you walk slowly away from it, it does not seem to diminish in size. These are examples of perceptual organization. **Perceptual organization** integrates sensations into **percepts** (meaningful perceptual units, such as images of particular objects), locates them in space, and preserves their meaning as the perceiver examines them from different vantage points. Here we explore four aspects of perceptual organization: form perception, depth or distance perception, motion perception, and perceptual constancy.

### Form Perception

**Form perception** refers to the organization of sensations into meaningful shapes and patterns. When you look at this book, you do not perceive it as a patternless collection of molecules. Nor do you perceive it as part of your leg even though it may be resting on it or think a piece of it has disappeared simply because your hand or pen is blocking your vision of it.

Gestalt Principles   The first psychologists to study form perception systematically were the **Gestalt psychologists** of the early twentieth century. As noted in Chapter 1, *Gestalt* is a German word that translates loosely to "whole" or "form." Proponents of the Gestalt approach argued that in perception the whole (the percept) is greater than the sum of its sensory parts. Consider the ambiguous picture

**FIGURE 4.30**
An ambiguous figure. Whether the perceiver forms a global image of a young or an old woman determines the meaning of each part of the picture; what looks like a young woman's nose from one perspective looks like a wart on an old woman's nose from another. The perception of the whole even leads to different inferences about the coat the woman is wearing: In one case, it appears to be a stylish fur, whereas in the other, it is more likely to be interpreted as an old overcoat. *Source:* Boring, 1930, p.42.

in Figure 4.30, which some people see as an old woman with a scarf over her head and others see as a young woman with a feather coming out of a stylish hat. Depending on the perceiver's gestalt, or whole view of the picture, the short black line in the middle could be either the old woman's mouth or the young woman's necklace.

Based on experiments conducted in the 1920s and 1930s, the Gestalt psychologists proposed a small number of basic perceptual rules the brain automatically and unconsciously follows as it organizes sensory input into meaningful wholes (Figure 4.31). **Figure–ground perception** refers to the fact that people inherently distinguish between figure (the object they are viewing) and ground (or background), such as words in black ink against a white page. The second Gestalt principle is **similarity:** The brain tends to group similar elements together, such as the circles that form the letter R in Figure 4.31*a*. Another principle, **proximity** (nearness), means that the brain tends to group together objects that are close to one another. In Figure 4.31*b*, the first six lines have no particular organization, whereas the same six lines arranged somewhat differently in the second part of the panel are perceived as three pairs. The Gestalt rule of **good continuation** states that, if possible, the brain organizes stimuli into continuous lines or patterns rather than discontinuous elements. For example, in Figure 4.31*c*, the figure appears to show an X superimposed on a circle, rather than pieces of a pie with lines extending beyond the pie's perimeter. According to the principle of **simplicity,** people tend to perceive the simplest pattern possible. Most people perceive Figure 4.31*d* as a heart with an arrow through it because that is the simplest interpretation. Finally, the rule of **closure** states that, where possible, people tend to perceive incomplete figures as complete. If part of a familiar pattern or shape is missing, perceptual processes complete the pattern, as in the triangle shown in Figure 4.31*e*. The second part of Figure 4.31*e* demonstrates another type of closure (sometimes called *subjective contour*) (Albert, 1993; Kanizsa, 1976). People see two overlapping triangles, but in fact, neither one exists; the brain simply fills in the gaps to perceive familiar patterns. Covering the incomplete black circles reveals that the solid white triangle is entirely an illusion.

Although the Gestalt principles are most obvious with visual perception, they apply to other senses as well. For example, the figure–ground principle applies when people attend to the voice of a waitress in a noisy restaurant; her voice becomes figure and all other sounds, ground. In music perception, good continuation allows people to hear a series of notes as a melody; similarity allows them to

**FIGURE 4.31**
Gestalt principles of form perception. The Gestalt psychologists discovered a set of laws of perceptual organization, including (*a*) similarity, (*b*) proximity, (*c*) good continuation, (*d*) simplicity, and (*e*) closure. *Source:* Part (*e*) adapted from Kanizsa, 1976.

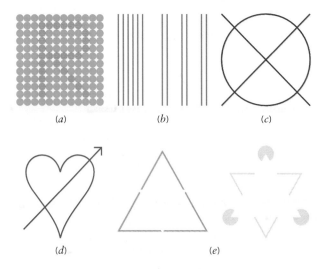

recognize a melody played on a violin while other instruments are playing; and proximity groups notes played together as a chord.

From an evolutionary perspective, the Gestalt principles exemplify the way the brain organizes perceptual experience to reflect the regularities of nature. In nature, the parts of objects tend to be near one another and attached. Thus, the principles of proximity and good continuation are useful perceptual rules of thumb. Similarly, objects often partially block, or occlude, other objects, as when a squirrel crawls up the bark of a tree. The principle of closure leads humans and other animals to assume the existence of the part of the tree that is covered by the squirrel's body.

Combining Features    More recent research has focused on the question of how the brain combines the simple features detected in primary areas of the cortex (particularly primary visual cortex) into larger units that can be used to identify objects. *Object identification* requires matching the current stimulus array against past percepts stored in memory to determine the identity of the object (such as a ball, a chair, or a particular person's face). Findings from imaging studies and research on patients and animals with temporal lobe lesions suggest that this process occurs along the "what" pathway, probably around the border between the occipital and temporal lobes.

One prominent theory of how the brain forms and recognizes images was developed by Irving Biederman (1987, 1990; Bar & Biederman, in press; Kirkpatrick-Steger & Biederman, 1998). Consider the following common scenario. It is late at night, and you are "channel surfing" on the television—rapidly pressing the remote control in search of something to watch. From less than a second's glance, you can readily perceive what most shows are about and whether they might be interesting. How does the brain, in less than a second, recognize a complex visual array on a television screen in order to make such a rapid decision?

Biederman and his colleagues have shown that we do not even need a *half* a second to recognize most scenes; 100 milliseconds—a tenth of a second—will typically do. To explain phenomena such as this, Biederman developed a theory called **recognition-by-components,** which asserts that we perceive and categorize objects in our environment by breaking them down into component parts and then matching the components and the way they are arranged against similar

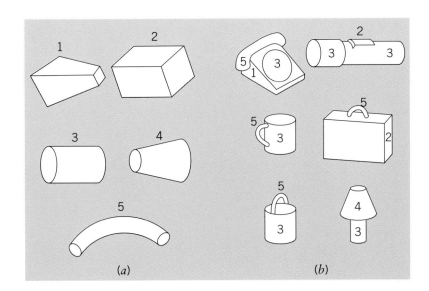
(a)                                    (b)

**FIGURE 4.32**
Recognition by components. The simple geons in (*a*) can be used to create thousands of different objects (*b*) simply by altering the relations among them, such as their relative size and placement. *Source:* Biederman, 1990, p. 49.

"sketches" stored in memory. In other words, the brain combines the simple features extracted by the primary cortex (such as lines of particular orientations) into a small number of elementary geometrical forms (called *geons*, for "geometric ions"). From this geometrical "alphabet" of 20 to 30 geons, Biederman argues, the outlines of virtually any object can be constructed, just as millions of words can be constructed from an alphabet of 26 letters in various combinations and orders. Figure 4.32 presents examples of some of these geons and the way most objects can be identified at a glance using only two or three of them.

Biederman argues that combining primitive visual sensations into geons not only allows rapid identification of objects but also explains why we can recognize objects even when parts of them are blocked or missing. The reason is that the Gestalt principles, such as good continuation, apply to perception of geons. In other words, the brain fills in gaps in a segment of a geon, such as a blocked piece of a circle. The theory predicts that failures in identifying objects should occur if the lines where separate geons connect are missing or ambiguous, so that the brain can no longer tell where one component ends and another begins (Figure 4.33). Experiments have supported this hypothesis: People can identify objects with parts missing only if the parts do not obscure the relations among the geons.

Recognition-by-components is not a complete theory of form perception. It was intended to explain how people make relatively rapid initial determinations

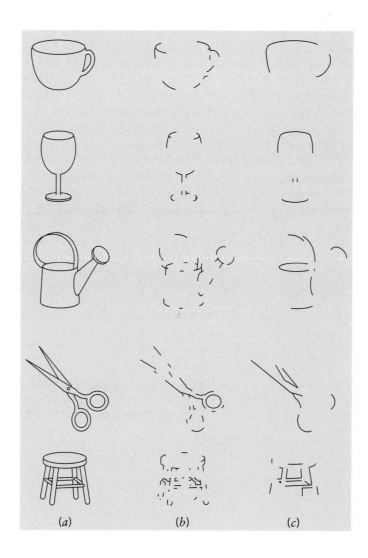

**FIGURE 4.33**
Identifiable and unidentifiable images. People can rapidly identify objects (*a*) even if many parts of them are missing, as long as the relations among their components, or geons, remain clear (*b*). When they can no longer tell where one geon ends and another begins (*c*), the ability to identify the objects will disappear. *Source:* Biederman, 1987, p. 135.

(*a*)          (*b*)          (*c*)

about what they are seeing and what might be worth closer inspection. More subtle discriminations—such as which type of poodle or which five-foot, ten-inch male is in view—require additional analysis of qualities such as color, texture, and characteristic motion (such as the way the dog walks or the man swaggers) (Ullman, 1995). These discriminations take considerably longer than 100 milliseconds because they require integration across a number of mental maps of visual space. Research shows, for example, that if people are asked to find a triangle amidst a large array of geometrical shapes, they can do so extremely quickly, and whether the triangle is in the midst of ten or 50 other shapes makes little difference in the length of time required to find it (Triesman, 1986). In contrast, if they are asked to find the *red* triangle, not only will their response time in finding it increase, but the length of time required to find it will be directly proportional to the number of other geometrical shapes in view. In other words, they will have to scan the objects one by one, which takes much more time. Apparently, making judgments about the *conjunction* of two attributes—in this case, shape and color—requires not only consulting two maps (one of shape and the other of color) but also superimposing one on the other. That we can nonetheless carry out such complex computations in seconds or hundreds of milliseconds is remarkable.

**Perceptual Illusions** Sometimes the brain's efforts to organize sensations into coherent and accurate percepts fail. This is the case with **perceptual illusions,** in which normal perceptual processes produce perceptual misinterpretations. Impossible figures are one such type of illusion, which provide conflicting cues for three-dimensional organization, as illustrated in Figure 4.34. The second part of the figure shows a painting by M. C. Escher, an artist who made explicit use of psychological research on perception in his work (Ernst, 1976). Recognizing the impossibility of these figures takes time because the brain attempts to impose order by using principles such as simplicity on data that allow no simple solution. Each portion of an impossible figure is credible, but as soon as the brain organizes sensations in one way, another part of the figure invalidates it.

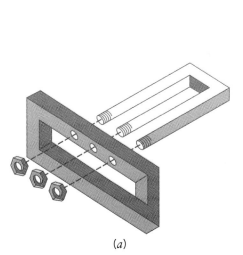

(a)

(b)

**FIGURE 4.34**
Impossible figures. The brain cannot form a stable percept because each time it does, another segment of the figure renders the percept impossible. Escher, who painted the impossible figure in (b), made use of perceptual research.

INTERIM SUMMARY    Perception involves the organization and interpretation of sensory experience. **Form perception** refers to the organization of sensations into meaningful shapes and patterns **(percepts).** The **Gestalt psychologists** described several principles of form perception; more recently, a theory called **recognition-by-components** has argued that people perceive and categorize objects by first breaking them down into elementary units. The brain's efforts to organize percepts can sometimes produce **perceptual illusions.**

## Depth Perception

A second aspect of perceptual organization is **depth** or **distance perception,** the organization of perception in three dimensions. You perceive this book as having height, width, and breadth and being at a particular distance; a skilled athlete can throw a ball 15 yards into a tiny hoop not much bigger than the ball. These three-dimensional judgments arise from a two-dimensional retinal image—and do so with such rapidity that we have no awareness of the computations our nervous system must be making. Although we focus again on the visual system, other sensory systems provide cues for depth perception as well. Auditory cues are particularly important, but so are kinesthetic sensations about the extension of the body while touching an object and other kinesthetic sensations that occur as a person lifts and swivels an object (such as a pencil) held by the hands (Turvey, 1996). Two kinds of visual information provide particularly important information about depth and distance: **binocular cues** (visual input integrated from the two eyes) and **monocular cues** (visual input from one eye).

Binocular Cues    Because the eyes are in slightly different locations, all but the most distant objects produce a different image on each retina, or a **retinal disparity.** To see this in action, hold your finger about six inches from your nose and alternately close your left and right eye. You will note that each eye sees your finger in a slightly different position. Now, do the same for a distant object; you will note only minimal differences between the views. Retinal disparity is greatest for close objects and diminishes with distance.

How does the brain translate retinal disparity into depth perception? Most cells in the primary visual cortex are **binocular cells;** that is, they receive information from both eyes. Some of these cells respond most vigorously when the same input arrives from each eye, whether the input is a vertical line, a horizontal line, or a line moving in one direction. Other binocular cells respond to different sorts of disparities between the eyes. Like many cells receptive to particular orientations, binocular cells require environmental input early in life to assume their normal functions. Researchers have learned about binocular cells by allowing kittens to see with only one eye at a time, covering one eye or the other on alternate days. As adults, these cats are unable to use binocular cues for depth (Blake & Hirsch, 1975; Packwood & Gordon, 1975).

Another binocular cue, convergence, is actually more kinesthetic than visual. When looking at a close object (such as your finger six inches in front of your face), the eyes converge, whereas distant objects require ocular divergence. **Convergence** of the eyes toward each other thus creates a distance cue produced by muscle movements in the eyes.

Monocular Cues    Although binocular cues are extremely important for depth perception, people do not crash their cars whenever an eyelash momentarily gets into one eye because they can still rely on monocular cues. The photograph of the Taj Majal in Figure 4.35 illustrates the main monocular depth cues that arise even when looking at a nonmoving scene. **Interposition** occurs when one object blocks part of another; as a result, the obstructed object is perceived as

**FIGURE 4.35**
Monocular depth cues. The photo of the Taj Majal in India illustrates all of the monocular cues to depth perception: interposition (the trees blocking the sidewalk and the front of the building), elevation (the most distant object seems to be the highest), texture gradient (the relative clarity of the breaks in the walkways closer to the camera), linear perspective (the convergence of the lines of the walkways surrounding the water), shading (the indentation of the arches toward the top of the building), aerial perspective (the lack of the detail of the bird in the distance), familiar size (the person standing on the walkway who seems tiny), and relative size (the diminishing size of the trees as they get further away).

more distant. **Elevation** refers to the fact that objects farther away are higher on a person's plane of view and thus appear higher up toward the horizon. Another monocular cue is **texture gradient:** When looking at textured surfaces, such as cobblestones or grained wood, the pattern or texture appears coarser at close range and finer and more densely packed at greater distances. A similar mechanism is **linear perspective:** Parallel lines appear to converge in the distance. **Shading** also provides monocular depth cues, since two-dimensional objects do not cast shadows. The brain assumes that light comes from above and hence interprets shading differently toward the top or the bottom of an object. Another cue is **aerial perspective:** Since light scatters as it passes through space, and especially through moist or polluted air, objects at greater distances appear fuzzier than those nearby. Two other cues rely on the individual's knowledge of the size of familiar objects. **Familiar size** refers to the tendency to assume an object is its usual size; thus, people perceive familiar objects that appear small as distant. Closely related is **relative size:** When looking at two objects known to be of similar size, people perceive the smaller object as farther away.

Artists working in two-dimensional media rely on monocular depth cues to represent a three-dimensional world. Humans have used interposition and elevation to convey depth for thousands of years. Other cues, however, such as linear perspective, were not discovered until as late as the fifteenth century; as a result, art before that time appears flat to the modern eye (Figure 4.36). Although some monocular cues appear to be innate, cross-cultural research suggests that perceiving three dimensions in two-dimensional drawings is partially learned, influenced by artistic conventions and experience with different kinds of two-dimensional media. Some people in technologically less developed cultures who have never seen photography initially have difficulty recognizing even their own images in two-dimensional form (Berry et al., 1992).

A final monocular depth cue arises from movement. When people move, images of nearby objects sweep across their field of vision faster than objects farther away. This disparity in apparent velocity produces a depth cue called **motion parallax.** The relative motion of nearby versus distant objects is particularly striking when looking out the window of a moving car or train. Nearby trees appear to speed by, whereas distant objects barely seem to move.

*(a)* *(b)*

**FIGURE 4.36**

Artistic use of monocular cues for depth perception has developed tremendously since Giotto's *Flight into Egypt* painted in the fifteenth century *(a)*. In the Cyclorama exhibit in Atlanta *(b)*, which depicts the Battle of Atlanta during the U.S. Civil War, the artists had such mastery of monocular cues for depth perception that visitors cannot easily tell where actual three-dimensional objects (soldiers, trees, etc.) end and a painted background begins.

## Motion Perception

From an evolutionary perspective, just as important as identifying objects and their distance is identifying motion. A moving object is potentially a dangerous object—or, alternatively, a meal, a mate, or a friend or relative in distress. Thus, it is no surprise that humans, like other animals, developed the capacity for **motion perception**—the perception of movement in objects. Motion perception occurs in multiple sensory modes. People can perceive the movement of a fly on the skin through touch, just as they can perceive the fly's trajectory through space by the sounds it makes. We focus here again, however, on the visual system.

Neural Pathways   The visual perception of movement begins in the retina itself, with ganglion cells called **motion detectors** that are particularly sensitive to movement. These cells tend to be concentrated outside the fovea, to respond (and stop responding) very quickly, and to have large receptive fields. These characteristics make adaptive sense. An object in the fovea is one we are already "keeping a close eye on" through attention to it; motion detectors in the periphery of our vision, in contrast, provide an early warning system to turn the head or the eyes toward something potentially relevant. Relatively quick onset and offset of neurons that detect motion is also a useful characteristic; otherwise, many objects could escape detection by moving faster than these neurons could fire. In fact, the eyes cannot detect objects that move either too quickly (which appear blurry or cannot be seen at all) or too slowly (which do not "trip" the motion detectors). Large receptive fields are useful for motion detection because each cell receives input from many bipolar cells; the greater the number of bipolar cells that synapse with the ganglion cell, the greater the potential activation. A wider receptive field also covers more visual terrain in which motion might occur, maximizing the likelihood of detecting it (Schiffman, 1996).

With each new "stop" along the processing stream in the brain, the receptive fields of neurons that detect motion grow larger. Several ganglion cells project to each motion-detecting neuron in the thalamus (in the lateral geniculate nucleus); thus, these neurons are likely to respond to movement in a slightly larger area of space. Several of these thalamic neurons may then synapse with motion-sensitive neurons in the primary visual cortex. From there, information about the movement of objects travels along the "where" pathway through the upper temporal lobes and into the parietal lobes. One important "stop" along the way is a region in the middle of the temporal lobes called *area MT* (for *medial temporal*) (see Barinaga, 1997; Rodman et al., 1989; Tootell et al., 1995). In area MT, receptive fields are even larger than in the primary visual cortex; some neurons respond to movement across a very large part of the visual field or to any movement sensed at all. Like some neurons in the primary visual cortex, many neurons in area MT are also direction sensitive, so that when a human (or monkey) watches an object, these neurons will fire most vigorously only if it is moving in the direction to which the neuron is tuned.

**Two Systems for Processing Movement** Tracking an object's movement is a tricky business because the perceiver may be moving as well; thus, perception requires distinguishing the motion of the perceiver from the motion of the perceived. Consider the perceptual task of a tennis player awaiting a serve. Most tennis players bob, fidget, or move from side to side as they await a serve, which means that the image on their retina is changing every second, even before the ball is in the air. Once the ball is served, its retinal image becomes larger and larger as it approaches, and somehow the brain must compute its distance and velocity as it moves through space. Making matters more complex, the perceiver is likely to be running, all the while trying to keep the ball's image on the fovea. And the brain must integrate these cues—the size of the image on the retina, its precise location on the retina, the movement of the eyes, and the movement of the body—all in a split second.

Two systems appear to be involved in motion perception (Gregory, 1977). The first computes motion from the changing image projected by the object on the retina; the second makes use of commands from the brain to the muscles in the eye that signal eye movements. (A third system, less well understood, likely integrates proprioceptive and other cues to offset the impact of body movements on the retinal image.) The first system operates when the eyes are relatively stable, as when an insect darts across the floor in the person's view so quickly that the eyes cannot move fast enough to track it. In this case, the image of the insect moves across the retina (Figure 4.37a). Motion detectors then fire as adjacent receptors in the retina bleach one after another in rapid succession.

The second system operates when people move their head and eyes to follow an object, as when fans watch a runner sprinting toward the finish line. In this case, the image of the object remains at roughly the same place on the retina; what moves is the position of the eyes (Figure 4.37b). This second system computes movement from a combination of the image on the retina and the movement of eye muscles. If the eyes are moving but the object continues to cast the same retinal image, the object must be moving. Essentially, the brain subtracts out muscle movements before computing movement from the retinal image. Interestingly, the movements of the eye must be intentional for this mechanism to work (although we are not typically conscious of the directives from the brain to the eye muscles). This is readily apparent by performing a simple experiment: Close one eye and then lightly push the other eyeball with your finger. You will perceive movement in the opposite direction in any object in front of you because the brain does not compensate for involuntary shifts in the position of the eye that do not occur through movement of the eye muscles (see Schiffman, 1996).

## Perceptual Constancy

A fourth form of perceptual organization, **perceptual constancy,** refers to the perception of objects as relatively stable despite changes in the stimulation of sensory receptors. As your grandmother walks away from you, you do not perceive her as

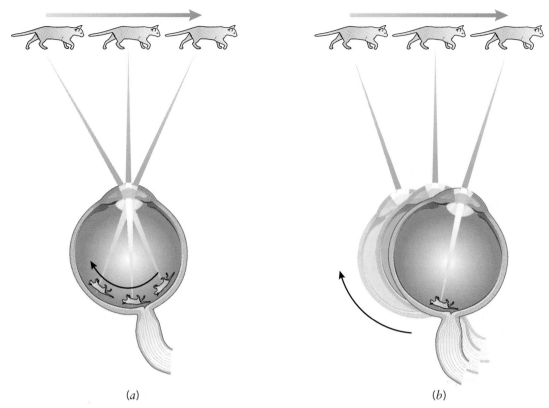

(a)                                              (b)

**FIGURE 4.37**

Two systems for processing movement. In (a), a stationary eye detects movement as an object moves across the person's visual field, progressively moving across the retina. In (b), the eye moves along with the object, which casts a relatively constant retinal image. What changes are the background and signals from the brain that control the muscles that move the eyes. *Source:* Adapted from Gregory, 1973, and Schiffman, 1996.

shrinking, even though the image she casts on your retina is steadily decreasing in size (although you may notice that she has shrunk a little since you last saw her). You similarly recognize that a song on the radio is still the same even though the volume has been turned down. Here we examine three types of perceptual constancy, again focusing on vision: color, shape, and size constancy.

Color Constancy   **Color constancy** refers to the tendency to perceive the color of objects as stable despite changing illumination. An apple appears the same color in the kitchen as it does in the sunlight, even though the light illuminating it is very different. A similar phenomenon occurs with achromatic color (black and white): Snow in moonlight appears whiter than coal appears in sunlight, even though the amount of light reflected off the coal may be greater (Schiffman, 1996). In perceiving the brightness of an object, neural mechanisms essentially adjust for the amount of light illuminating it. For chromatic colors, the mechanism is more complicated, but color constancy does not work if the light contains only a narrow band of wavelengths. Being in a room with only red lightbulbs causes even familiar objects to appear red.

Shape Constancy   A remarkable feat of the engineering of the brain is that we can maintain constant perception of the shape of objects despite the fact that the same object typically produces a new and different impression on the retina (or on the receptors in our skin) every time we encounter it. The brain has to overcome several substantial sources of noise to recognize, for example, that the unkempt beast in the mirror whose hair is pointing in every direction is the same person you happily called "me" the night before. When people see an object for the second time, they are likely to see it from a different position, with different lighting, in a different setting (e.g., against a different background), with different parts of it blocked from view (such as different locks of hair covering the face), and even in an altered shape (such as a body standing up versus on the couch) (see Ullman, 1995).

Recognition-by-components (geon) theory offers one possible explanation: As long as enough of the geons that define the form of the object remain the same, the object ought to be identifiable. Thus, if a person views a bee from one perspective and then from another as it flies around her face, she will still recognize the insect as a bee as long as it still looks like a tube with a little cone at the back and thin waferlike wings flapping at its sides.

Other theorists, however, have argued that this is not likely to be the whole story. Some have proposed that each time we view an object from a different perspective, we form a mental image of it from that point of view. Each new viewpoint provides a new image stored in memory. The next time we see a similar object, we rotate it in our minds so that we can "see" it from a previously seen perspective to determine if it looks like the same object or match it against a generalized image derived from our multiple "snapshots" of it. Recent research suggests, in fact, that the more a scene diverges the perspective from which a person has seen it before (e.g., if the image is 90 versus 15 degrees off from the earlier image), the longer the person will take to recognize it (DeLoache et al., 1997; Tarr et al., 1997; Ullman, 1989). This suggests that shape constancy does, to some extent, rely on the rotation of mental images (probably of both geons and finer perceptual details) and their comparison against perceptual experiences stored in memory.

*Size Constancy*    A third type of perceptual constancy is **size constancy:** Objects do not appear to change in size when viewed from different distances. The closer an object is, the larger an image it casts on the retina; a car ten feet away will cast a retinal image five times as large as the same car 50 feet away. Yet people do not wonder how the car 50 feet away can possibly carry full-sized passengers (Figure 4.38). The reason is that the brain essentially corrects for the size of the retinal image based on cues such as the size of objects in the background.

Helmholtz (1909) was the first to recognize that the brain adjusts for distance when assessing the size of objects, just as it adjusts for color and brightness. He called this process "unconscious inference" because people have no consciousness of the computations involved. Although these computations generally lead to accurate inferences, they can also give rise to perceptual illusions. A classic example is the moon illusion, in which the moon seems larger on the horizon than at its zenith (Figure 4.39). This illusion appears to result from depth cues such as relative size; the moon seems larger against a backdrop of large buildings than against a backdrop of stars that provide no depth cues.

**INTERIM SUMMARY**    **Depth perception** is the organization of perception in three dimensions, which utilizes **binocular** and **monocular visual cues. Motion perception,** the perception of movement, relies on **motion detectors** from the retina through the cortex. It appears to involve two systems, the first of which computes motion from the changing image on the retina, and the second of which uses information from eye muscles about the movements of the eyes. **Perceptual constancy** refers to the organization of changing sensations into percepts that are relatively stable in size, shape, and color. Three types of perceptual constancy are **color, shape,** and **size constancy.**

**FIGURE 4.38**
Size constancy. In (*a*), the man and the pyramids appear to be of normal size because the pyramids are off in the distance. The photo in (*b*) is perceptually confusing because the distance cues have been distorted by doctoring the photo.

(*a*)

(*b*)

**FIGURE 4.39**
The moon illusion. The moon appears larger against a city skyline than high in the sky, where, among other things, no depth cues exist. The retinal image is the same size in both cases, but in one case, depth cues signal that it must be further away.

## A GLOBAL VISTA

### CULTURE AND PERCEPTUAL ILLUSIONS

As this example suggests, size constancy, like other processes of perceptual organization, can sometimes produce perceptual illusions. This is likely the case with the **Müller–Lyer illusion,** in which two lines of equal length appear to differ in size (Figure 4.40). According to one theory, the angled lines provide linear perspective cues that make the vertical line appear closer or farther away (Gregory, 1978). The brain then adjusts for distance, interpreting the fact that the retinal images of the two vertical lines are the same size as evidence that the line on the right is longer.

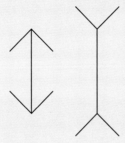

**FIGURE 4.40**
The Müller–Lyer illusion. The line on the right appears longer than the line on the left, when in fact they are exactly the same size.

If the Müller–Lyer illusion relies on depth cues such as linear perspective that are not recognized in all cultures, are people in some cultures more susceptible to the illusion than others? That is, does vulnerability to an illusion depend on culture and experience, or is it rooted entirely in the structure of the brain? Three decades ago, a team of psychologists and anthropologists set out to answer these questions in what has become a classic study (Segall et al., 1966).

Two hypotheses that guided the investigators are especially relevant. The first, called the *carpentered world* hypothesis, holds that the nature of architecture in a culture influences the tendency to experience particular illusions. According to this hypothesis, people reared in cultures lacking roads that join at angles, rectangular buildings, and houses with angled roofs lack experience with the kinds of cues that give rise to the Müller–Lyer illusion and hence should be less susceptible to it. Second, individuals from cultures that do not use sophisticated two-dimensional cues (such as linear perspective) to represent three dimensions in pictures should also be less vulnerable to perceptual illusions of this sort.

The researchers presented individuals from 14 non-Western and three Western societies with several stimuli designed to elicit perceptual illusions. They found that Westerners were consistently more likely to experience the Müller–Lyer illusion than non-Westerners, but they were no more likely to experience other illusions unrelated to angles and sophisticated depth cues. Subsequent studies have replicated these findings with the Müller–Lyer illusion (Pedersen & Wheeler, 1983; Segall et al., 1990). Teasing apart the relative impact of architecture and simple exposure to pictures is difficult, but the available data support both hypotheses (Berry et al., 1992).

(a)

(b)

*People from this African village (a) are less susceptible to illusions involving straight lines than people who live in "carpentered worlds," such as Paris (b), who are familiar with angled buildings and streets.*

**FIGURE 4.41**
The Ponzo illusion. Converging lines lead to the perception of the upper red bar as larger since it appears to be farther away. The bars are actually identical in length.

Size constancy is involved in another famous illusion, the **Ponzo illusion,** which also appears to be influenced by culture and experience (Figure 4.41). Linear perspective cues indicate that the upper bar is larger because it seems farther away. Cross-culturally, people who live in environments in which lines converge in the distance (such as railroad tracks and long, straight highways) appear to be more susceptible to this illusion than people from environments with relatively few converging lines (Brislin & Keating, 1976).

## INTERPRETING SENSORY EXPERIENCE

The processes of perceptual organization we have examined—form perception, depth perception, motion perception, and perceptual constancy—organize sensations into stable, recognizable forms. These perceptions do not, however, tell us what an object *is* or what its emotional or adaptive significance might be. Generating *meaning* from sensory experience is the task of **perceptual interpretation.** The line between organization and interpretation is not, of course, hard and fast. The kind of object identification tasks studied by Biederman, for example, involve both, and in everyday life, organizing perceptual experience is simply one step on the path to interpreting it.

Perceptual interpretation lies at the intersection of sensation and memory, as the brain interprets current sensations in light of past experience. This can occur at a very primitive level—reacting to a bitter taste, recoiling from an object coming toward the face, or responding emotionally to a familiar voice—without either consciousness or cortical involvement. Much of the time, however, interpretation involves classifying stimuli—a moving object is a dog; a pattern of tactile stimulation is a soft caress. In this final section, we examine how experience, expectations, and motivation shape perceptual interpretation.

### The Influence of Experience

To what degree do our current perceptions rely on our past experience? This question leads back to the nature–nurture debate that runs through nearly every domain of psychology. The German philosopher Immanuel Kant argued that humans innately experience the world using certain categories, such as time, space, and causality. For example, when a person slams a door and the door frame shakes, she naturally infers that slamming the door caused the frame to shake. According to Kant, people automatically infer causality, prior to any learning.

**Direct Perception**   In psychology, the theory of **direct perception,** championed by James Gibson (1966, 1979), similarly holds that perceptual meaning requires little prior knowledge. Whereas Kant emphasized the way the mind orders perception of the world, Gibson emphasized the way the world organizes perception, so that we detect the order that exists in nature. Gibson argued that the senses evolved to respond to aspects of the environment relevant to adaptation, so that the meaning of stimuli is often immediate and obvious. An object coming rapidly toward the face is dangerous; food with a sweet taste affords energy; a loud, angry voice is threatening.

Laboratory evidence of direct perception comes from studies using the **visual cliff.** The visual cliff is a clear table with a checkerboard directly beneath it on one side and another checkerboard that appears to drop off like a cliff on the other (Figure 4.42). Infants are reluctant to crawl to the side of the table that looks deep even when they have recently begun crawling and have had little or no relevant experience with falling off of surfaces (E. Gibson & Walk, 1960). Once infants *need* to perceive the meaning of potentially dangerous actions, they rapidly becoming *able* to do so as they interact with the environment (see Bertenthal, 1996).

**Nature and Nurture**   Answers to the nature–nurture question have become more sophisticated as psychologists have come to recognize that the nervous system has certain innate potentials—such as seeing in depth or inferring distance from sound—but that these potentials require environmental input to develop. In one set of studies, researchers reared kittens in darkness for their first five months except for five hours each day, during which time they placed the kittens in a cylinder with either horizontal or vertical stripes (Blakemore & Cooper, 1970). The

**FIGURE 4.42**
The visual cliff. Infants are afraid to crawl over the "cliff" even when they have recently begun to crawl and therefore have little experience leading them to fear it.

**FIGURE 4.43**
Kittens reared in a vertical world lose their "innate" capacity to see horizontal lines.

kittens saw *only* the stripes, since they wore a big collar that kept them from seeing even their own bodies (Figure 4.43). As adults, kittens reared in horizontal environments were unable to perceive vertical lines, and they lacked cortical feature detectors responsive to vertical lines; the opposite was true of kittens reared in a vertical environment. Although these cats were genetically programmed to have both vertical and horizontal feature detectors, their brains adapted to a world without certain features to detect.

Other studies have outfitted infant kittens and monkeys with translucent goggles that allow light to pass through but only in a blurry, diffuse, unpatterned form. When the animals are adults and the goggles are removed, they are able to perform simple perceptual tasks without difficulty, such as distinguishing colors, brightness, and size. However, they have difficulty with other tasks; for example, they are unable to distinguish objects from one another or to track moving objects (Riesen, 1960, 1965; Wiesel, 1982). Similar findings have emerged in studies of humans who were born blind but subsequently obtained sight in adulthood through surgery (Gregory, 1978; Sacks, 1993; von Senden, 1960). Most of these individuals can tell figure from ground, sense colors, and follow moving objects, but many never learn to recognize objects they previously knew by touch and hence remain functionally blind. What these studies suggest, like studies described in Chapter 3, is that the brain has evolved to "expect" certain experiences, without which it will not develop normally.

Early experiences are not the only ones that shape the neural systems underlying sensation and perception. In one study, monkeys who were taught to make fine pitch discriminations showed increases in the size of the cortical regions responsive to pitch (Recanzone et al., 1993). Intriguing research with humans finds that practice at discriminating letters manually in Braille produces changes in the brain. A larger region of the cortex of Braille readers is devoted to the fingertips, with which they read (Pascual-Leone & Torres, 1993). Thus, experience can alter the structure of the brain, making it more or less responsive to subsequent sensory input.

### Bottom-Up and Top-Down Processing

We have seen that experience can activate innate mechanisms or even affect the amount of cortical space devoted to certain kinds of sensory processing. But when we come upon a face that looks familiar or an animal that resembles one we have seen, does our past experience actually alter the way we perceive it, or do we only begin to categorize the face or the animal once we have identified its features? Similarly, does wine taste different to a wine connoisseur—does his knowledge about wine actually alter his perceptions—or does he just have fancier words to describe his experience after the fact?

Psychologists have traditionally offered two opposing answers to questions such as these, which now, as in many classic debates about sensation and perception, appear to be complementary. One view emphasizes the role of sensory data in shaping perception, whereas the other emphasizes the influence of prior experience. **Bottom-up processing** refers to processing that begins "at the bottom" with raw sensory data that feed "up" to the brain. A bottom-up explanation of visual perception argues that the brain forms perceptions by combining the responses of multiple feature detectors in the primary cortex, which themselves integrate input from neurons lower in the visual system. **Top-down processing,** in contrast, starts "at the top," with the observer's expectations and knowledge. Theorists who focus on top-down processing typically work from a cognitive perspective. They maintain that the brain uses prior knowledge to begin organizing and interpreting sensations as soon as the information starts coming in, rather than waiting for percepts to form based on sequential (step-by-step) analysis of

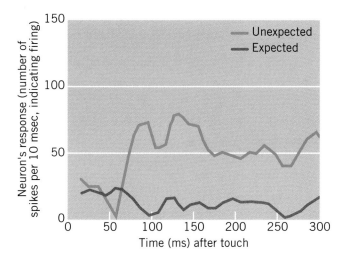

**FIGURE 4.44**
Expectations and neural firing. Expectations modulate the firing of a neuron in the macaque cortex. *Source:* Adapted from Mistlin & Perrett, 1990.

their isolated features. Thus, like Gestalt theorists, these researchers presume that as soon as the brain has detected features resembling eyes, it begins to expect a face and thus to look for a nose and mouth.

    **Studies Demonstrating Bottom-Up and Top-Down Processing**    Both approaches have empirical support. Research on motion perception provides an example of bottom-up processing. Psychologists trained monkeys to report the direction in which a display of dots moved. The researchers then observed the response of individual neurons previously identified as feature detectors for movement of a particular speed and direction while the monkeys performed the task (Newsome et al., 1989). They discovered that the "decisions" made by individual neurons about the direction the dots moved were as accurate as—and sometimes even *more* accurate than—the decisions of the monkeys!

    Perceptual decisions on simple tasks of this sort may require little involvement of higher mental processes. On the other hand, reading these words provides a good example of top-down processing, since reading would be incredibly cumbersome if people had to detect every letter of every word from the bottom up rather than expecting and recognizing patterns. A fascinating study demonstrates how expectations can have a top-down influence on cortical neurons that register sensory stimulation (Mistlin & Perrett, 1990). The researchers were studying a cortical region in macaque monkeys that responds to both visual and tactile stimulation when they noticed that neurons in this region responded differently to expected and unexpected stimuli. So they designed a study to compare the activation level of neurons when the monkey touched a familiar stimulus (part of its chair) or an unfamiliar one (a similar piece of metal not usually there). In both conditions, the monkey's vision was blocked, but its chair was in an expected location. As can be seen in Figure 4.44, touching the expected stimulus produced little neural activity. But when the monkey touched the unexpected object, the neuron fired repeatedly.

    Other evidence of top-down processing has come from recent studies using PET technology while participants generated mental images. In one study, participants in one condition viewed block letters presented in a grid, as in Figure 4.45*a* (Kosslyn et al., in press). Following this, they were shown the same grid without the letter and asked to decide whether the letter would cover an X placed in one of the boxes of the grid. This task required that they create a mental image of the letter in the grid and locate the X on the imaginary letter. Next, they performed the same task, except this time the block letter was actually present in the grid, so they could perceive it instead of having to imagine it. Participants in a control

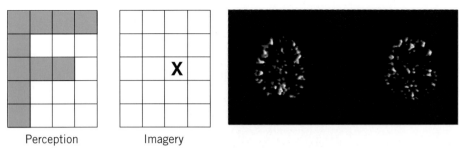

**FIGURE 4.45.**

Visual imagery activates primary visual cortex. Participants viewed one of two stimulus patterns (*a*). In one, they actually saw a letter on a grid along with a black X. In another, they had to imagine the letter to decide whether the X would fall on the letter. In a control condition, they simply looked at the X come and go. The results (*b*) showed activation throughout the visual system in the perception and imagery conditions, notably in the primary visual cortex.

condition performed a simple task that essentially involved viewing the empty grid with and without an X.

The study relied on a "method of subtraction" used in many imaging studies: The investigators measured the amount of neuronal activity in the imagery and perception conditions and subtracted out the amount of brain activity seen in the control condition. The logic is to have the experimental and control conditions differ in as few respects as possible and subtract out the activation that occurs in the control condition; what is left in the computerized image of brain activity after subtraction is a picture of the regions of neural activity uniquely linked to the operation being investigated (in this case, mental imagery and perception).

Predictably, both perception and mental imagery activated many parts of the visual system, such as visual association cortex. However, the most striking finding was that the mental imagery condition activated the same areas of primary visual cortex activated by actual perception of the letters—normally believed to reflect bottom-up processing of sensory information (Figure 4.45*b*). In fact, the primary cortex was even *more* active during mental imagery than during actual perception! Although these findings are controversial (D'Esposito et al., 1997), if they hold up with future replications, they will suggest that when people picture an image in their minds, they actually create a visual image using the same neural pathways involved when they view a visual stimulus—a completely top-down activation of brain regions normally activated by sensory input.

**Resolving the Paradox: Simultaneous Processing in Perception**    Trying to explain perception by either bottom-up or top-down processes alone presents a paradox. You would not be able to identify the shapes in Figure 4.46*a* unless you knew they were part of a dog. Yet you would not recognize Figure 4.46*b* as a dog unless you could process information about the parts shown in the first panel. Without bottom-up processing, external stimuli would have no effect on perception; we would hallucinate rather than perceive. Without top-down processing, experience would have no effect on perception. How, then, do people ever recognize and classify objects?

According to current thinking, both types of processing occur simultaneously (Rumelhart et al., 1986). For example, features of the environment create patterns of stimulation in the primary visual cortex. These patterns in turn stimulate neural circuits in the visual association cortex that represent various objects, such as a friend's face. If the perceiver expects to see that face or if a large enough component of the neural network representing the face becomes activated, the brain essentially forms a "hypothesis" about an incoming pattern of sensory stimulation, even though all the data are not yet in from the feature detectors. It may even

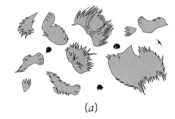

(*a*)

(*b*)

**FIGURE 4.46**

Top-down and bottom-up processing. In isolation (perceiving from the bottom up), the designs in (*a*) would have no meaning. At the same time, the broader design in (*b*), the dog, cannot be recognized without recognizing component parts.

entertain multiple hypotheses simultaneously, which are each tested against new incoming data until one hypothesis "wins out" because it seems to provide the best fit to the data. As we will see in later chapters, some of the most exciting recent research on human cognition suggests that most information processing, from sensation and perception through complex thinking, involves processes of this sort that occur in parallel, rather than one at a time from either the bottom up or the top down.

**INTERIM SUMMARY**    **Perceptual interpretation** means generating meaning from sensory experience. According to the theory of **direct perception,** the meaning or adaptive significance of a percept is often obvious, immediate, and innate. Trying to distinguish the relative roles of nature and nurture in perception may in some ways be asking the wrong question, since the nervous system has innate potentials that require environmental input to develop. Perception simultaneously involves **bottom-up processing,** which begins with raw sensory data that feeds "up" to the brain, and **top-down processing,** which begins with the observer's expectations and knowledge.

## Expectations and Perception

Experience with the environment thus shapes perception by creating perceptual expectations, an important top-down influence on perception. These expectations, called **perceptual set** (i.e., the setting, or context, for a given perceptual "decision"), make certain interpretations more likely. Two aspects of perceptual set are the current context and enduring knowledge structures.

Context    Context plays a substantial role in perceptual interpretation. Consider, for example, how readily you understood the meaning of *substantial role* in the last sentence. Had someone uttered that phrase in a bakery, you would have

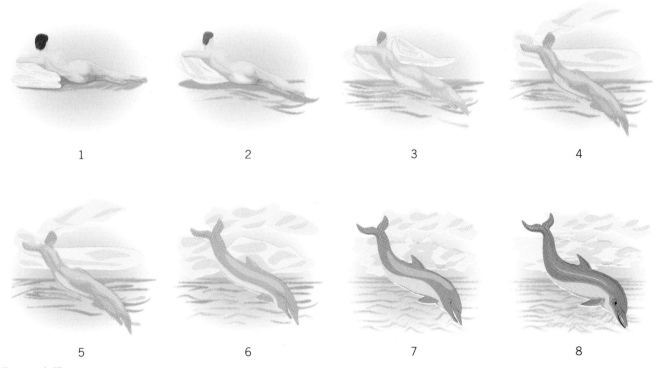

1    2    3    4

5    6    7    8

**FIGURE 4.47**
The impact of context on perception. Look at drawings 1, 2, 3, and 4, in that order (top row, left to right). Now look at drawings 5, 6, 7, and 8, in reverse order (bottom row, right to left). Drawing 4 most likely seems to be a woman's body and drawing 5, a porpoise, yet drawings 4 and 5 are identical. The same pattern of stimulation can be interpreted in many ways depending on context.

assumed they meant "substantial roll," unless the rest of the sentence provided a context suggesting otherwise. Context is just as important with tactile sensations (touch). A hug from a relative or from a stranger may have entirely different meanings and may immediately elicit very different feelings, even though the pattern of sensory stimulation may be identical. Figure 4.47 illustrates the importance of context in the visual mode. Context is especially important in perceiving spoken language (Chapter 7), since even the most careful speaker drops syllables, slurs sounds, or misses words altogether, and many words (such as *role* and *roll*) have the same sound but different meanings.

Schemas    Not only the immediate context but a person's enduring beliefs and expectations affect perceptual interpretation. One way knowledge is organized in memory is in **schemas**—patterns of thinking about a domain that render the environment relatively predictable (Neisser, 1976). We have schemas (organized knowledge) about objects (such as chairs and dogs), people (such as introverts and ministers), and situations (such as funerals and restaurants), which help us behave appropriately. The fact that people generally sit on chairs instead of on other people reflects their schemas about what chairs and people do.

Because schemas allow individuals to anticipate what they will encounter, they increase both the speed and efficiency of perception. For example, people process information extremely quickly when shown photographs of real-world scenes, such as a kitchen, a city street, or a desk top. In one study, subjects could recall almost half the objects in familiar scenes after viewing them for only one-tenth of a second (Biederman et al., 1973). In contrast, subjects who viewed the same scenes cut into six equal pieces and randomly reassembled had difficulty both identifying and remembering the objects in the picture (Figures 4.48a and b). Schemas can also induce perceptual errors, however, when individuals fail to notice what they do not expect to see (Figure 4.48c), such as an unfamiliar pothole on the street (see Biederman et al., 1981, 1982).

## Motivation and Perception

As we have seen, expectations can lead people to see what they expect to see and hear what they expect to hear. But people also frequently hear the words they *want* to hear as well. In other words, motivation, like cognition, can exert a top-

*Schemas produce expectations that can sometimes lead perception astray. Turn the book over and the abnormality in one photo of Bill Clinton is readily apparent.*

*(a)*         *(b)*         *(c)*

**FIGURE 4.48**

Schemas. Subjects had no trouble identifying and remembering objects in (*a*), a photo of a normal Chinatown street, because the scene activates a "city street schema" that guides perception and memory. In contrast, without a schema to help interpret what they were seeing (*b*), they had much more difficulty. Schemas can also lead to perceptual failures. Before reading further, look briefly at (*c*). People rarely notice the unexpected object in the upper right-hand corner (the fire hydrant) because it is incongruent with their activated "restaurant schema."

down influence on perception. This was the argument of a school of perceptual thought in the late 1940s called the *New Look* in perception, which focused on the impact of emotion, motivation, and personality on perception (Dixon, 1980; Erdelyi, 1985; Weinberger, in press). Many of the issues raised by New Look researchers are receiving renewed attention a half century later (see, e.g., Bargh, in press; Bruner, 1992; Uleman & Bargh, 1989).

One classic experiment examined the effects of food and water deprivation on identification of words (Wispe & Drambarean, 1953). The experimenters placed participants in one of three groups. Some went without food for 24 hours prior to the experiment; some ate nothing for ten hours; and others ate just beforehand. The researchers then flashed two kinds of words on a screen so rapidly that they were barely perceptible: neutral words (e.g., *serenade* and *hunch*) and words related to food (e.g., *lemonade* and *munch*). The three groups did not differ in their responses to the neutral words. However, both of the deprived groups perceived the need-related words more readily (i.e., when flashed more briefly) than nondeprived controls. A similar phenomenon occurs outside the laboratory: People are often intensely aware of the aroma of food outside a restaurant when they are hungry but oblivious to it when their stomachs are full.

New Look researchers were also interested in applying psychodynamic ideas to perception. For example, several studies presented participants with words on a screen so quickly that they could not report what they had seen (Broadbent, 1958; Dixon, 1970, 1980; Erdelyi, 1984). They noticed some striking differences when they presented subjects with neutral versus taboo words (such as sexual words). In one study, the researcher exposed participants to neutral and taboo words so quickly that they could barely recognize even a flash of light (Blum, 1954). Yet when asked which stimuli seemed more salient, participants consistently chose the taboo words—even though they had not consciously perceived that they had seen words at all! When similar words were presented at speeds that could just barely allow recognition of them, participants could "see" the neutral words but not the taboo ones. These findings suggest that more emotionally evocative taboo words attract attention even below the threshold of consciousness, but that they are harder to recognize consciously than neutral words. Subsequent research has confirmed and extended these findings (Erdelyi, 1984; Shevrin, 1980; Shevrin et al., 1996; Weinberger, in press).

INTERIM SUMMARY   Expectations, based on both the current context and enduring knowledge structures (schemas), influence the way people interpret ongoing sensory experience. Motives can also influence perception, including motives to avoid perceiving stimuli with uncomfortable content.

# SOME CONCLUDING THOUGHTS

As the examples in this chapter suggest, perception is not independent of our *reasons* for perceiving. Evolution has equipped humans with a nervous system remarkably attuned to stimuli that *matter*. If people did not need to eat or to worry about what they put in their mouths, they would not have a sense of taste. If they did not need to find food, escape danger, and communicate, they would not need to see and hear. And if their skin were not vulnerable to damage, they would not need to feel pain.

Sensation and perception are the gateway to the mind, and they provide much of the raw material for our thought. We think in words we have read and heard; we think in images we have seen. For centuries, philosophers have wondered whether learning, memory, and thought reflect anything *but* the mental manipulation and recombination of sensations—like the novel impressions formed by the turn of a kaleidoscope. In the next few chapters we explore what it means to learn, remember, and think. We then examine the motivational and emotional processes that ultimately provide the impetus for applying the knowledge delivered by our senses.

# SUMMARY

## BASIC PRINCIPLES

1. **Sensation** refers to the process by which sense organs gather information about the environment and transmit it to the brain for initial processing. **Perception** refers to the closely related process by which the brain selects, organizes, and interprets sensations.

2. Three basic principles apply across all the senses. First, there is no one-to-one correspondence between physical and psychological reality. Second, sensation and perception are active, not passive. Third, sensation and perception are adaptive.

## SENSING THE ENVIRONMENT

3. Sensation begins with an environmental stimulus; all sensory systems have specialized cells called **receptors** that respond to environmental stimuli and typically generate action potentials in adjacent sensory neurons. This process is called **transduction.** Within each sensory modality, the brain codes sensory stimulation for intensity and quality.

4. The **absolute threshold** refers to the minimum amount of stimulation needed for an observer to notice a stimulus. The **difference threshold** refers to the lowest level of stimulation required to sense that a *change* in stimulation has occurred (a **just noticeable difference,** or **jnd**). **Weber's law** states that regardless of the magnitude of two stimuli, the second must differ by a

constant proportion from the first for it to be perceived as different. **Fechner's law** holds that the physical magnitude of a stimulus grows logarithmically as the subjective experience of intensity grows arithmetically; in other words, people only subjectively experience a small percentage of actual increases in stimulus intensity. **Stevens' power law** states that subjective intensity grows as a proportion of the actual intensity raised to some power, that is, that sensation increases in a linear fashion as actual intensity grows exponentially.

5. **Sensory adaptation** is the tendency of sensory systems to respond less to stimuli that continue without change.

## Vision

6. The eyes are sensitive to a small portion of the electromagnetic spectrum called light. In vision, light is focused on the retina by the **cornea, pupil,** and **lens**. **Rods** are very sensitive to light, allowing vision in dim light; **cones** are especially sensitive to particular wavelengths, producing the psychological experience of color. Cones are concentrated at the **fovea,** the region of the retina most sensitive to detail. The **ganglion cells** of the retina transmit visual information via the **optic nerve** to the brain. Ganglion cells, like other neurons involved in sensation, have **receptive fields,** a region of stimulation to which the neuron responds. **Feature detectors** are specialized cells of the primary cortex in the occipital lobes that respond only when stimulation in their receptive field matches a particular pattern or orientation, such as horizontal or vertical lines.

7. From the primary visual cortex, visual information appears to flow along two pathways, or *processing streams*, called the "what" and the "where" pathways. The **what pathway** is involved in determining *what* an object is and runs from the primary visual cortex in the occipital lobes through the lower part of the temporal lobes (or the *inferior temporal cortex*). The second stream, the **where pathway,** is involved in locating the object in space, following its movement, and guiding movement toward it. This pathway runs from the primary visual cortex through the middle and upper regions of the temporal lobes and up into the parietal lobes.

8. The property of light that is transduced into color is **wavelength.** The **Young–Helmholtz,** or **trichromatic, theory** proposes that the eye contains three types of receptors, sensitive to red, green, or blue. **Opponent-process theory** argues for the existence of pairs of opposite primary colors linked in three systems: a blue–yellow system, a red–green system, and a black–white system. Both theories appear to be involved in color perception; trichromatic theory is operative at the level of the retina, and opponent-process theory at higher neural levels.

## Hearing

9. Hearing, or **audition,** occurs as a vibrating object sets air particles in motion. Each round of expansion and contraction of the air is known as a **cycle.** The number of cycles per second determines a sound wave's **frequency,** which corresponds to the psychological property of **pitch. Amplitude** refers to the height and depth of the wave and corresponds to the psychological property of **loudness.** Sound waves travel through the auditory canal to the **eardrum,**

where they are amplified; transduction occurs by way of **hair cells** attached to the **basilar membrane** that respond to vibrations in the fluid-filled **cochlea.** This mechanical process triggers action potentials in the **auditory nerve,** which are then transmitted to the brain.

10. Two theories, once considered opposing, explain the psychological qualities of sound. **Place theory,** which holds that different areas of the basilar membrane respond to different frequencies, appears to be most accurate for high frequencies. **Frequency theory,** which asserts that the basilar membrane's rate of vibration reflects the frequency with which a sound wave cycles, explains sensation of low-frequency sounds.

## OTHER SENSES

11. The environmental stimuli for smell, or **olfaction,** are invisible molecules of gas emitted by substances and suspended in the air. As air enters the nose, it flows into the **olfactory epithelium,** where hundreds of different types of receptors respond to various kinds of molecules, producing complex smells. The axons of olfactory receptor cells constitute the **olfactory nerve,** which transmits information to the **olfactory bulbs** under the frontal lobes and on to the primary olfactory cortex, a primitive region of the cortex deep in the frontal lobes.

12. Taste, or **gustation,** is sensitive to molecules soluble in saliva. Much of the experience of taste, however, is really contributed by smell. Taste occurs as receptors in the **taste buds** on the tongue and throughout the mouth transduce chemical information into neural information, which is integrated with olfactory information in the brain.

13. Touch actually includes three senses: pressure, temperature, and pain. The human body contains approximately 5 million touch receptors of at least seven different types. Sensory neurons synapse with spinal interneurons that stimulate motor neurons, allowing reflexive action, as well as with neurons that carry information up the spinal cord to the medulla, where nerve tracts cross over. From there, sensory information travels to the thalamus and is subsequently routed to the primary touch center in the brain, the somatosensory cortex, which contains a map of the body. Pain is greatly affected by beliefs, expectations, and emotional state. **Gate-control theory** holds that the experience of pain is heavily influenced by the central nervous system, through the action of neural fibers that can "close the gate" on pain, preventing messages from other fibers getting through.

14. The **proprioceptive senses** provide information about the body's position and movement. The **vestibular sense** provides information on the position of the body in space by sensing gravity and movement. **Kinesthesia** provides information about the movement and position of the limbs and other parts of the body relative to one another.

## PERCEPTION

15. The hallmarks of perception are organization and interpretation. **Perceptual organization** integrates sensations into meaningful units, locates them in space, tracks their movement, and preserves their meaning as the perceiver observes them from different vantage points. **Form perception** refers to the organization of sensations into meaningful shapes and patterns **(percepts).**

The Gestalt psychologists described several principles of form perception, including figure–ground perception, similarity, proximity, good continuation, simplicity, and closure. A more recent theory, called **recognition-by-components,** asserts that we perceive and categorize objects in the environment by breaking them down into component parts, much like letters in words.

16. **Depth perception** is the organization of perception in three dimensions. Depth perception organizes two-dimensional retinal images into a three-dimensional world primarily through **binocular** and **monocular visual cues.**

17. **Motion perception** refers to the perception of movement. Two systems appear to be involved in motion perception. The first computes motion from the changing image projected by the object on the retina; the second makes use of commands from the brain to the muscles in the eye that signal eye movements.

18. **Perceptual constancy** refers to the organization of changing sensations into percepts that are relatively stable in size, shape, and color. Three types of perceptual constancy are size, shape, and color constancy, which refer to the perception of unchanging size, shape, and color despite momentary changes in the retinal image. The processes that organize perception leave perceivers vulnerable to **perceptual illusions,** some of which appear to be innate and others of which depend on culture and experience.

19. **Perceptual interpretation** involves generating meaning from sensory experience. Perceptual interpretation lies at the intersection of sensation and memory, as the brain interprets current sensations in light of past experience. Perception is neither entirely innate nor entirely learned. The nervous system has certain innate potentials, but these potentials require environmental input to develop. Experience can alter the structure of the brain, making it more or less responsive to subsequent sensory input.

20. **Bottom-up processing** refers to processing that begins "at the bottom," with raw sensory data that feeds "up" to the brain. **Top-down processing** starts "at the top," from the observer's expectations and knowledge. According to current thinking, perception proceeds in both directions simultaneously. Experience with the environment shapes perceptual interpretation by creating perceptual expectations called **perceptual set.** Two aspects of perceptual set are current context and enduring knowledge structures called **schemas.** Motives, like expectations, can influence perceptual interpretation.

Janet Fish, *Ruth Sewing*, 1983, D.C. More Gallery.

# CHAPTER 5
## *Learning*

An experiment by John Garcia and his colleagues adds a new twist to all the stories ever told about wolves and sheep. The researchers fed a wolf a muttonburger (made of the finest sheep flesh) laced with odorless, tasteless capsules of lithium chloride, a chemical that induces nausea. Displaying a natural preference for mutton, the animal wolfed it down but half an hour later became sick and vomited (Garcia & Garcia-Robertson, 1985; Gustavson et al., 1976).

Several days later, the researchers introduced a sheep into the wolf's compound. At the sight of one of its favorite delicacies, the wolf went straight for the sheep's throat. But on contact, the wolf abruptly drew back. It slowly circled the sheep. Soon it attacked from another angle, going for the hamstring. This attack was as short-lived as the last. After an hour in the compound together, the wolf still had not attacked the sheep—and in fact, the sheep had made a few short charges at the wolf. Lithium chloride seems to have been the real wolf in sheep's clothing.

Although the effects of a single dose of a toxic chemical do not last forever, Garcia's research illustrates the powerful impact of **learning,** which refers to any enduring change in the way an organism responds based on its experience. In humans, as in other animals, learning is central to adaptation because the environment does not stand still; it varies from place to place and from moment to moment. Knowing how to distinguish edible from inedible foods or to distinguish friends from enemies or predators is essential for survival. Although many animal species have natural preferences and aversions that guide their learning, such as young children's attraction to sweets (which provide energy) or fear of strangers, the range of possible foods or threats is simply too great to be prewired into the brain. The social environment, too, is complex and varied, particularly in humans. In some Islamic cultures, a woman who shows her legs may be beaten; in Western cultures, revealing skin can be a way to attract a mate. Even *within* a culture, the standards of appropriate behavior change across situations and over time. A skirt length that is acceptable in one context or during one era may be considered inappropriate or scandalous in another.

Theories of learning tend to share three assumptions. The first is that experience shapes behavior. Particularly in complex organisms such as humans, the vast majority of responses are learned rather than innate. The migration patterns of Pacific salmon may be instinctive, but the migration of college students to Daytona Beach during spring break is not. Second, learning is adaptive. Just as nature eliminates organisms that are not well suited to their environments, the environment naturally selects those behaviors in an individual that are adaptive and weeds out those that are not (Skinner, 1977). Behaviors useful to the organism (such as avoiding fights with larger members of its species) will be reproduced because of their consequences (safety from bodily harm). A third assumption is that careful experimentation can uncover laws of learning, many of which apply to human and nonhuman animals alike.

Learning theory is the foundation of the behaviorist perspective, and the bulk of this chapter explores the behavioral concepts of classical and operant conditioning (known together as *associative learning*). The remainder examines cognitive approaches that emphasize the role of thought and social experience in learning, although at many points we will also consider the links between learning and evolution.

Throughout, several questions are worth keeping in mind. First, to what extent are humans like other animals in the way they learn? To put it another way, how much difference does our expanded cortex really make to basic principles of learning observed across species? Second, what constraints and possibilities has evolution placed on what we can learn? As we saw in Chapter 4, our senses are only attuned to a subset of the physical stimuli around us; we obviously cannot learn to associate danger or reward with sound frequencies dogs can hear if our ears are not tuned to those frequencies. But even within the range of experiences available to our senses, are the possibilities for learning limitless? Or has natural selection "wired" us to learn some things more readily than others? And if so, to what degree can experience override innate tendencies?

Third, how complex must laws of learning be to explain most of human behavior? Twenty-five hundred years ago, Aristotle proposed a set of **laws of association**—conditions under which one thought becomes connected, or associated, with another—to account for learning and memory. The most important was the *law of contiguity*, which proposed that two events will become connected in the mind if they are experienced close together in time (such as thunder and lightning). Another was the *law of similarity*, which states that objects that resemble each other (such as two people with similar faces) are likely to become associated. The philosophical school of thought called *associationism* built upon the work of Aristotle, asserting that the most complex thoughts—which allow humans to create airplanes, understand laws of physics, or write symphonies—are ultimately nothing but elementary perceptions that become associated and then recombined in the mind. As we will see in the next few chapters, principles of association are fundamental to behaviorist theories of learning as well as to cognitive theories of memory, and neuroscientists have now begun to understand their neural basis—all the way down to changes at the synapse. The question, then, is the extent to which a relatively small set of fundamental principles such as these can explain most or all of what we do.

INTERIM SUMMARY   **Learning** refers to any enduring change in the way an organism responds based on its experience. Learning theories assume that experience shapes behavior, that learning is adaptive, and that only systematic experimentation can uncover laws of learning. Principles of **association** are fundamental to most accounts of learning.

# Classical Conditioning

**Classical conditioning** (sometimes called *Pavlovian* or *respondent conditioning*) was the first type of learning to be studied systematically. In the late nineteenth century, the Russian physiologist Ivan Pavlov (1849–1936) was studying the digestive systems of dogs (research for which he won a Nobel Prize). During the course of his work, he noticed a peculiar phenomenon. Like humans and other animals, dogs normally salivate when presented with food, which is a simple reflex. A **reflex** is a behavior that is elicited automatically by an environmental stimulus, such as the knee-jerk reflex elicited by a doctor's rubber hammer. A **stimulus** is something in the environment that elicits a response. Pavlov noticed that if a stimulus, such as a bell or turning fork ringing, repeatedly occurred just as a dog was about to be fed, the dog would start to salivate when it heard the bell, even if food were not presented. As Pavlov understood it, the dog had learned to associate the bell with food, and because food produced the reflex of salivation, the bell also came to produce the reflex.

## Pavlov's Model

An innate reflex such as salivation to food is an unconditioned reflex. **Conditioning** is a form of learning; hence, an **unconditioned reflex** is a reflex that occurs naturally, without any prior learning. The stimulus that produces the response in an unconditioned reflex—in this case, food—is called an **unconditioned stimulus, (UCS).** An unconditioned stimulus activates a reflexive response without any learning having taken place; thus, the reflex is unlearned, or unconditioned. An **unconditioned response (UCR)** is a response that does not have to be learned. In Pavlov's experiment, the UCR was salivation.

Pavlov's basic experimental setup is illustrated in Figure 5.1. Shortly before presenting the UCS (the food), Pavlov presented a *neutral stimulus*—a stimulus (in this case, ringing a bell) that normally does not elicit the response in question. After the bell had been paired with the unconditioned stimulus (the food) several times, the sound of the bell alone came to evoke a conditioned response, salivation (Figure 5.2). A **conditioned response (CR)** is a response that has been

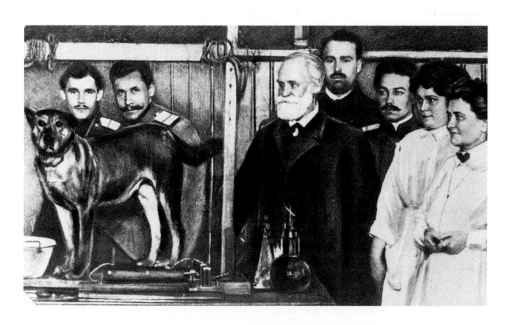

**Figure 5.1**
Pavlov's dogs. Pavlov's research with dogs documented the phenomenon of classical conditioning. Actually, his dogs became conditioned to salivate in response to many aspects of the experimental situation and not just to bells or tuning forks; the sight of the experimenter and the harness, too, could elicit the conditioned response.

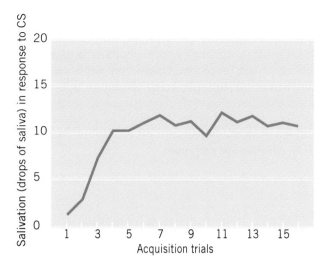

**FIGURE 5.2**
Acquisition of a classically conditioned response. Initially, the dog did not salivate in response to the sound of the bell. By the third conditioning trial, however, the conditioned stimulus (the bell) had begun to elicit a conditioned response (salivation), which was firmly established by the fifth or sixth trial. *Source:* Pavlov, 1927.

learned. By pairing the UCS (the food) with the sound of a bell, the bell became a **conditioned stimulus (CS)**—a stimulus that, through learning, has come to evoke a conditioned response. Figure 5.3 summarizes the classical conditioning process.

Why did such a seemingly simple discovery earn Pavlov a central place in the history of psychology? The reason is that classical conditioning can explain a wide array of learned responses outside the laboratory as well. For example, a house cat that was repeatedly sprayed with flea repellent squinted reflexively as the repellent got in its eyes. Eventually it came to squint and meow piteously (CR) whenever its owner used an aerosol spray (CS). The same cat, like many household felines, also came to associate the sound of an electric can opener with the opening of its favorite delicacies and would dash to the kitchen counter and meow whenever its owner opened any can, whether cat food or green beans. If you are beginning to feel somewhat superior to the poor cat wasting all those meows and squints on cans of deodorant and vegetables, consider whether you have ever been at your desk, engrossed in work, when you glanced at the clock and discovered that it was dinner time. If so, you probably noticed some physiological responses—feeling hungry, or perhaps mouth watering—that had not been present seconds earlier. Through repeated pairings of stimuli associated

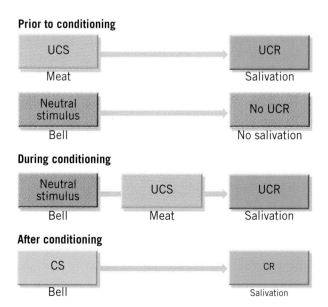

**FIGURE 5.3**
Classical conditioning. In classical conditioning, an initially neutral stimulus comes to elicit a conditioned response.

*Drawing by John Chase*

with a particular time of day and dinner, you have been classically conditioned to associate a time of day indicated on a clock (the CS) with food (the UCS). At the other end of the digestive system, most readers have probably had the experience of needing to go to the bathroom but deciding to wait until they get home. Upon arriving at the front door—and worse still upon entering the bathroom—the intensity of the urge seems to intensify a thousand-fold, requiring considerable self-control. This phenomenon, too, is a straightforward example of classical conditioning: Stimuli associated with entering the house, and especially the bathroom, are CSs that signal an impending eliminatory response.

## CONDITIONED RESPONSES

Pavlov was heavily influenced by Darwin and recognized that the ability to learn new associations is crucial to adaptation. He also saw how learning could produce maladaptive patterns as well (Hollis, 1997; Windholz, 1997). Three cases in which classical conditioning generally fosters adaptation but can also lead to maladaptive responses are conditioned taste aversions, conditioned emotional responses, and conditioned immune responses.

### Conditioned Taste Aversions

The case of the wolf and the muttonburger with which this chapter opened is an example of a *conditioned taste aversion*—a learned aversion to a taste associated with an unpleasant feeling, usually nausea. From an evolutionary perspective, the ability to connect tastes with nausea or other unpleasant visceral ("gut") experiences is crucial to survival; learning to avoid toxic foods can mean the difference between life and death for an animal that forages (that is, scrounges or hunts) for its meals. The capacity to learn taste aversions appears to be hundreds of millions of years old and is present in some very simple invertebrates, like certain species of slugs (Garcia et al., 1985; Schafe & Bernstein, 1996). As further evidence of its ancient roots, conditioned taste aversions do not require cortical involvement in humans or other vertebrates. Rats with their cortex removed can still learn taste aversions, and even animals *completely anesthetized* while nausea is induced can learn taste aversions, as long as they are conscious during presentation of the CS.

Although conditioned taste aversions normally protect the organism from ingesting toxic substances, anyone who has ever developed an aversion to a food eaten shortly before getting the flu knows how irrational these aversions can sometimes be. Cancer patients undergoing chemotherapy often develop aversions to virtually all food—and may lose dangerous amounts of weight—because a common side effect of chemotherapy is nausea. To put this in the language of classical conditioning, chemotherapy is a UCS that leads to nausea, a UCR; the result is an inadvertent association of any food eaten (CS) with nausea (the CR). This conditioned response can develop rapidly, with only one or two exposures to the food paired with nausea (Bernstein, 1991), much as Garcia's wolf took little time to acquire an aversion to the taste of sheep. Some patients even begin to feel nauseous at the sound of a nurse's voice, the sight of the clinic, or the thought of treatment, although acquisition of these CRs generally requires repeated exposure (Bovbjerg et al., 1990).

### Conditioned Emotional Responses

One of the most important ways classical conditioning affects behavior is in the conditioning of emotional responses. Consider the automatic smile that comes to a person's face when hearing a special song or the fear of horses a person may de-

THE FAR SIDE    By GARY LARSON

"Zelda! Cool it! ... The Rothenbergs hear the can opener!"

*Through classical conditioning, little Albert developed a fear of rats and other furry objects—even Santa's face (a disabling phobia for a child, indeed). Courtesy of Benjamin Harris.*

velop after falling off of one. *Conditioned emotional responses* occur when a formerly neutral stimulus is paired with a stimulus that evokes an emotional response (either naturally, as when bitten by an animal, or through prior learning). Conditioned emotional responses are commonplace in everyday life, such as the sweaty palms, pounding heart, and feeling of anxiety that arise after an instructor walks into a classroom and begins handing out a few printed pages of questions.

One of the most famous examples of classical conditioning was the case of little Albert. The study was performed by John Watson, considered the founder of American behaviorism, and his colleague, Rosalie Rayner (1920). The study was neither methodologically nor ethically beyond reproach, but its provocative findings served as a catalyst for decades of research. When Albert was nine months old, Watson and Rayner presented him with a variety of objects, including a dog, a rabbit, a white rat, masks (including a Santa Claus mask), and a fur coat. Albert showed no fear in response to any of these objects; in fact, he played regularly with the rat—a budding behaviorist, no doubt. A few days later, Watson and Rayner tested little Albert's response to a loud noise (the UCS) by banging on a steel bar directly behind his head. Albert reacted by jumping, falling forward, and whimpering.

About two months later, Watson and Rayner selected the white rat to be the CS in their experiment and proceeded to condition a fear response in Albert. Each time Albert reached out to touch the rat, they struck the steel bar, creating the same loud noise that had initially startled him. After only a few pairings of the noise and the rat, Albert learned to fear the rat.

Studies since Watson and Rayner's time have proposed classical conditioning as an explanation for some human **phobias,** that is, irrational fears of specific objects or situations (Merckelbach et al., 1991; Ost, 1991; Wolpe, 1958). For example, many people develop severe emotional reactions (including fainting) to hypodermic needles through exposure to injections in childhood. Knowing as an adult that injections are necessary and relatively painless usually has little impact on the fear, which is elicited automatically. Athletes such as football players often amuse nurses in student health centers with their combination of fearlessness on the field and fainting at the sight of a tiny needle. Many such fears are acquired and elicited through the activation of subcortical neural pathways between the visual system and the amygdala (LeDoux, 1995). Adult knowledge may be of little use in counteracting them because the crucial neural circuits are outside cortical control and are activated before the cortex even gets the message.

## Conditioned Immune Responses

Psychologists have recently discovered that classical conditioning can even impact the **immune system,** the system of cells throughout the body that fight disease (e.g., Ader & Cohen, 1985, 1993). For example, aside from causing nausea, chemotherapy for cancer has a second unfortunate consequence: It decreases the activity of cells in the immune system that normally fight off infection. Can stimuli associated with chemotherapy, then, become CRs that suppress the activity of these cells? One study tested this by comparing the functioning of immune cells from the blood of cancer patients at two different times (Bovbjerg et al., 1990). The first time was a few days prior to chemotherapy. The second time was the morning of the day the patient would be receiving chemotherapy, after checking into the hospital. The investigators hypothesized that exposure to hospital stimuli associated with prior chemotherapy experiences (CS) would suppress immune functioning (CR), just as chemotherapy (UCS) reduces the activity of immune cells (UCR). They were right: Blood taken the morning of hospitalization showed weakened immune functioning when exposed to germs.

Researchers are now trying to see whether they can actually *strengthen* immune functioning using classical conditioning. One of the effects of exposure to potentially threatening substances such as bacteria or viruses is that the body develops *antibodies* for them (proteins that latch onto them and destroy them). To see whether antibody production can be classically conditioned, one research team allowed rats in one condition to drink water with saccharine (a sugar substitute) in it (the CS) just prior to injecting them with a substance (UCS) known to elicit antibodies (UCR) (Alvarez-Borda et al., 1995). Rats in a control condition received only water along with the injection. Several days later, after antibodies to this substance were no longer detectable in the rats' blood, rats in both conditions were given saccharine water, while rats in a third condition received another injection (along with water).

The experimenters hypothesized that rats in the first condition, for whom saccharine (CS) was associated with injection of the substance (UCS), would produce antibodies in response to the saccharine (CR), as would rats reexposed to the substance. In contrast, control rats, for whom saccharine was not a CS, should not show any renewed antibody production. As can be seen in Figure 5.4, this hypothesis was confirmed: Rats exposed to saccharine produced almost as much antibody as those given a fresh injection. Their immune systems seemed to anticipate

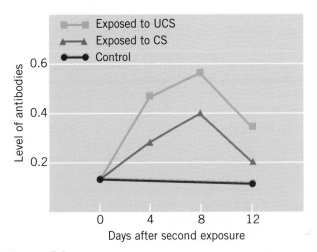

**FIGURE 5.4**

Conditioned immune response. The graph shows the density of antibodies seen in the blood of experimental rats reexposed to the CS (saccharine), rats reexposed to the UCS (injection of a substance that elicits antibody production), and control rats exposed to neither. Rats exposed to the UCS not surprisingly showed the most antibody production, but rats exposed to the CS also showed significant increases in antibodies. The impact of the experimental manipulation peaked for both groups at eight days after reexposure and dropped thereafter. *Source:* Alvarez-Borda et al., 1995.

an injection and prepare for it with antibodies, just as Pavlov's dogs prepared for meat with a mouth full of saliva when they heard a familiar tone.

**INTERIM SUMMARY** In **classical conditioning,** an environmental stimulus leads to a learned response, through pairing of an **unconditioned stimulus** with a previously neutral **conditioned stimulus.** The result is a **conditioned response,** or learned reflex. *Conditioned taste aversions* are learned aversions to a taste associated with an unpleasant feeling (usually nausea). *Conditioned emotional responses* occur when a conditioned stimulus is paired with a stimulus that evokes an emotional response. *Conditioned immune responses* can occur when a conditioned stimulus is paired with a stimulus that evokes a change in the functioning of the **immune system** (the system of cells in the body that fight disease).

## STIMULUS GENERALIZATION AND DISCRIMINATION

Once an organism has learned to associate a CS with a UCS, it may respond to stimuli that resemble the CS with a similar response. This phenomenon, predicted by Aristotle's principle of similarity, is called **stimulus generalization.** For example, you are at a sporting event and you stand for the national anthem. You suddenly well up with pride in your country (which you realize now, of course, is nothing but a classically conditioned emotional response). But the song you have heard, familiar as it may sound, is not *exactly* the same stimulus you heard the last time you were at a game. It is not in the same key, and this time the tenor took a few liberties with the melody. So how do you know to respond with the same emotion? Similarly, in Watson and Rayner's experiment, the pairing of the rat and the loud noise led little Albert to fear not only the rat but also other furry or hairy objects, including the rabbit, the dog, the fur coat, and even Santa's face. In other words, Albert's fear of the rat had *generalized* to other furry objects.

Many years ago researchers demonstrated that the more similar a stimulus is to the CS, the more likely generalization will occur (Hovland, 1937). In a classic study, the experimenters paired a tone (the CS) with a mild electrical shock (the UCS). With repeated pairings, participants produced a conditioned response to the tone known as a **galvanic skin response,** or **GSR**—an electrical measure of the amount of sweat on the skin, associated with arousal or anxiety. The experimenter then presented tones of varying frequencies that had not been paired with shock and measured the resulting GSR. Tones with frequencies similar to the CS evoked the most marked GSR, whereas dissimilar tones evoked progressively smaller responses (Figure 5.5).

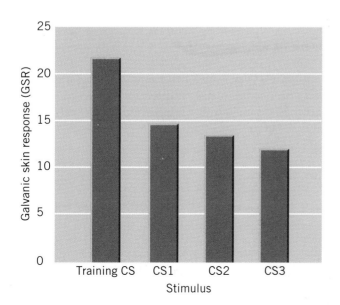

**FIGURE 5.5**
Stimulus generalization. Galvanic skin response (a measure of physiological arousal) varies according to the similarity of the CS to the training stimulus. In this case, the training stimulus was a tone of a particular frequency. CS-1 is most similar to the training stimulus; CS-3 is least similar to it. *Source:* Hovland, 1937.

A major component of adaptive learning is knowing when to generalize and when to be more specific or discriminating. Maladaptive patterns in humans often involve inappropriate generalization from one set of circumstances to others, as when a person who has been frequently criticized by a parent responds negatively to all authority figures. Much of the time, however, people are able to discriminate among stimuli in ways that foster adaptation. **Stimulus discrimination** is the learned tendency to respond to a restricted range of stimuli or only to the stimulus used during training. In many ways, stimulus discrimination is the opposite of stimulus generalization. Pavlov's dogs did not salivate in response to just *any* sound, and people do not get hungry when the clock reads four o'clock even though it is not far from six o'clock. Organisms learn to discriminate between two similar stimuli when these stimuli are not consistently associated with the same UCS.

## EXTINCTION

In the **acquisition,** or initial learning, of a conditioned response, each pairing of the CS and UCS is known as a **conditioning trial.** But what happens later if the CS repeatedly occurs *without* the UCS? What would have happened if Watson and Rayner had, on the second, third, and all subsequent trials, exposed little Albert to the white rat without the loud noise?

Albert's learned fear response would eventually have been *extinguished*, or eliminated, from his behavioral repertoire. **Extinction** in classical conditioning refers to the process by which a CR is weakened by presentation of the CS without the UCS. If a dog has come to associate the sounding of a bell with food, it will eventually stop salivating at the bell tone if the bell rings enough times without the presentation of food. The association is weakened—but not obliterated. If days later the dog once more hears the bell, it is likely to salivate again. This is known as **spontaneous recovery**—the reemergence of a previously extinguished conditioned response. The spontaneous recovery of a CR is typically short-lived, however, and will rapidly extinguish again without renewed pairings of the CS and UCS.

INTERIM SUMMARY    **Stimulus generalization** occurs when an organism learns to respond to stimuli that resemble the CS with a similar response; **stimulus discrimination** occurs when an organism learns to respond to a restricted range of stimuli. **Extinction** occurs when a CR is weakened by presentation of the CS without the UCS.

## FACTORS AFFECTING CLASSICAL CONDITIONING

Classical conditioning does not occur every time a bell rings, a baby startles, or a wolf eats some tainted lamb chops. Several factors influence the extent to which classical conditioning will occur. These include the interstimulus interval, the individual's learning history, and the organism's preparedness to learn (see Chase, 1988; Wasserman & Miller, 1997).

### Interstimulus Interval

The **interstimulus interval** is the time between presentation of the CS and the UCS. Presumably, if too much time passes between the presentation of these two stimuli, the animal is unlikely to associate them, and conditioning is less likely to occur. For most responses, the optimal interval between the CS and UCS is very brief, usually a few seconds or less. The optimal interval depends, however, on the stimulus and tends to bear the imprint of natural selection (Hollis, 1997). A CS that occurs about a half a second before a puff of air blows on the eye will have the maximum power to elicit a conditioned eyeblink response in humans (Ross & Ross, 1971). This makes evolutionary sense because we usually have very little warning between the time we see or hear something and the time debris reaches our eyes. At the other extreme, conditioned taste aversions do not occur when the interstimulus interval is *less than* ten seconds, and learning often occurs with intervals up to several hours (Schafe & Bernstein, 1996). Given that nausea or stomach pain can develop hours after ingestion of a toxic substance, the capacity to associate tastes with feelings in the gut minutes or hours later clearly fosters survival. Just as in perception, our brains appear to be attuned to the patterns that exist in nature.

The temporal order of the CS and the UCS—that is, which one comes first—is also crucial (Figure 5.6). Maximal conditioning occurs when the onset of the CS precedes the UCS—called *forward conditioning*. Less effective is *simultaneous conditioning*, in which the CS and UCS are presented at the same time. A third pattern, *backward conditioning*, is the least effective of all. Here, the CS is presented after the UCS has occurred. These principles, too, make evolutionary sense, since a CS that consistently occurs after a UCS offers little additional information, whereas a CS that precedes a UCS allows the organism to prepare.

## The Individual's Learning History

Another factor that influences classical conditioning is the individual's learning history. An extinguished response is usually easier to learn the second time around, presumably because the stimulus was once associated with the response. A previously extinguished nausea response to the taste of bacon is likely to be easily reinstated—and difficult to extinguish—if bacon and nausea ever occur together again. This suggests that neuronal connections established through learning may diminish in their strength when the environment no longer supports them but do not entirely disappear; later learning can build on old "tracks" that have been covered up but not obliterated.

In other circumstances, prior learning can actually *hinder* learning. Suppose a dog has learned to salivate at the sound of a bell (conditioned stimulus A, or CSA). The researcher now wants to teach the dog to associate food with a flash of light as well (CSB). If the bell continues to sound even occasionally in learning trials pairing the light (CSB) with food (the UCS), the dog is unlikely to produce a conditioned response to the flash of light. This phenomenon is known as blocking. **Blocking** refers to the failure of a stimulus (such as a flash of light) to elicit a CR when it is combined with another stimulus that already elicits the response (Kamin, 1969; Pearce, 1987). If a bell is already associated with food, a flashing light is of little consequence unless it provides additional, nonredundant information. Interestingly, if the CR to the bell (CSA) is subsequently extinguished, the animal will more quickly develop a CR to the CSB (the light) than control animals who have not undergone blocking trials. What this suggests is that the organism was in fact forming *associations* between the blocked CS (CSB) and the CR but that these were never expressed in *behavior* because they were blocked by prior associations (Wasserman & Miller, 1997).

A similar phenomenon occurs in **latent inhibition,** in which repeated exposure to a neutral stimulus without a UCS makes it less likely than a novel stimulus to become a CS; in other words, the familiar stimulus is less likely to produce a CR (Lubow & Gewirtz, 1995). Once again, this makes evolutionary sense, since it reduces the likelihood of accidental associations that do not mirror the natural co-occurrence of events in nature. A person who has drunk from water fountains 999 times and becomes sick two hours after the thousandth time is unlikely to associ-

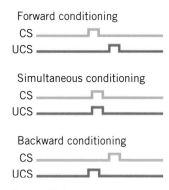

**FIGURE 5.6**

Forward, simultaneous, and backward conditioning. In forward conditioning, the onset of CS occurs before the UCS. In simultaneous conditioning, the CS is presented at the same time as the UCS. In backward conditioning, the CS is presented after the onset UCS.

ate water with nausea. If, however, she *repeatedly* gets sick after drinking from that fountain, she may start to associate water with nausea. Alternatively, she may learn to discriminate this fountain from others or may develop a more complex, compound association: The CSA (water) is associated with nausea only if the CSB (the fountain) precedes presentation of the water (CSA). Complex associations of this sort are extremely important in daily life (e.g., Schmajuk et al., 1998). For example, a child may normally feel happy (a conditioned emotional response) in the presence of her father (CSA) but learn over time to feel afraid (a different conditioned emotional response) if she hears her father slam the door when he enters the house (CSB).

## Preparedness to Learn: An Evolutionary Perspective

A third influence on classical conditioning is the organism's readiness to learn certain associations. Many early behaviorists, such as Watson, believed that the laws of classical conditioning could link virtually any stimulus to any response. Yet subsequent research has shown that some responses can be conditioned much more readily to certain stimuli than to others.

This was demonstrated in a classic study by Garcia and Koelling (1966). The experimenters used three conditioned stimuli: light, sound, and taste (flavored water). For one group of rats, these stimuli were paired all at once with the UCS of radiation, which produces nausea. For the other group, the stimuli were paired with a different UCS, electric shock. The experimenters then exposed the rats to each of the three conditioned stimuli separately, rather than simultaneously, to test the strength of the conditioned response to each.

The results can be seen in Figure 5.7. Rats that experienced nausea after exposure to radiation developed an aversion to the flavored water but not to either the light or sound cues. In contrast, rats exposed to electric shock developed avoidance reactions to the audiovisual stimuli but not to the taste cues. In other words, the rats learned to associate sickness in their stomachs with a taste stimulus, and an aversive tactile stimulus (electrical shock) with audiovisual stimuli.

The phenomenon of **prepared learning**—the biologically wired *preparedness* to learn some associations more easily than others—is not limited to taste aversions (Seligman, 1971). Phobias of spiders, snakes, and similar animals are more common than phobias of flowers or telephones, and many snake phobics, such as people who are terrified of tarantulas, have never seen one up close, let alone been bitten by one (Kirby et al., 1995; Marks, 1969; Ohman et al., 1976; Seligman, 1971).

These findings once again suggest an evolutionary explanation: Natural selection has favored organisms that more readily associate stimuli that tend to be associated in nature and whose association is highly relevant to survival or reproduction. An animal lucky enough to survive after eating a poisonous caterpillar is more likely to survive if it can associate nausea with the right stimulus. For most land-dwelling mammals, taste cues are particularly useful for discriminating

**FIGURE 5.7**
Preparedness to learn. Garcia and Koelling's experiment examined the impact of biological constraints on learning in rats exposed to shock or X-rays. Rats associated nausea with a taste stimulus rather than with audiovisual cues; they associated an aversive tactile event with sights and sounds rather than with taste stimuli. The results demonstrated that animals are prepared to learn certain associations more readily than others in classical conditioning. *Source:* Adapted from Garcia & Koelling, 1966.

| Unconditioned stimulus (ucs) | Conditioned stimulus (cs) | | |
|---|---|---|---|
| | Light | Sound | Taste |
| **Shock** | Avoidance | Avoidance | No avoidance |
| **X-rays** | No avoidance | No avoidance | Avoidance |

toxic from nontoxic substances; a preparedness to connect taste with nausea allows the animal to bypass irrelevant associations to the hundreds of other stimuli it might have encountered between the time it dined on the offending caterpillar and the time it got sick hours later. In contrast, most birds do not have well-developed gustatory systems and thus cannot rely heavily on taste to avoid toxic insects. In support of the evolutionary hypothesis, research on quail and other birds finds that, unlike rats, they are more likely to associate nausea with visual than gustatory stimuli (Hollis, 1997; Wilcoxon et al., 1991). Garcia and colleagues (1985) theorize that vertebrate animals have evolved two defense systems, one attending to defense of the gut (and hence favoring associations between nausea and sensory cues relevant to food) and the other attending to defense of the skin (and usually predisposing the animal to form associations between pain and sights and sounds that signal dangers such as predators).

Humans show some evidence of biological preparedness as well. Readers of this book, for example, are much more likely to have snake or spider phobias than automobile phobias, despite the fact that they are more than 10,000 times more likely to die at the wheel of a car than at the mouth of a spider—and to have experienced a car accident rather than a snakebite. Experimental data suggest that humans may also be biologically predisposed to associate aversive experiences more readily with angry faces than smiling ones (Dimberg, 1990).

Biological preparedness, of course, has its limits, especially in humans, whose associative capacities are *almost* limitless (McNally, 1987). One study, for example, found people equally likely to develop a fear of handguns as of snakes (Honeybourne et al., 1993). Where biological predispositions leave off, learning begins as a way of naturally selecting adaptive responses.

*Snakes strike terror in the human psyche, even though most people have never had unpleasant encounters with them.*

## WHAT DO ORGANISMS LEARN IN CLASSICAL CONDITIONING?

In some ways, contrasting innate with learned responses is setting up a false dichotomy, because the capacity to learn—to form associations—is itself a product of natural selection. Precisely what organisms learn when they are classically conditioned, however, has been a topic of considerable debate. Some behavioral theorists have argued that in classical conditioning the organism learns to associate the CS with the UCS—a *stimulus–stimulus*, or *S–S*, association. Others have argued that what is learned is an association between the CS and the CR—a *stimulus–response*, or *S–R*, association. Both explanations are consistent with Aristotle's proposition that humans learn by associating events that tend to co-occur, and both probably occur in classical conditioning. For example, the S–S association may occur first, through repeated co-occurrence (contiguity) of the two stimuli; shortly thereafter, an S–R association forms as the CS begins to co-occur with the CR.

Pavlov (1927) was influenced by associationism and hypothesized that in classical conditioning the CS essentially becomes a *signal* to an organism that the UCS is about to occur. As a result, the organism responds to the CS as if it *were* the UCS. Pavlov proposed a neurological mechanism for this, hypothesizing that repeated pairings of the UCS and the CS lead to connections between them in the brain; as a result, the two stimuli eventually trigger the same response. Although Pavlov was probably right in broad strokes, subsequent research suggests that the CR and the UCR, though usually similar, are rarely identical. Dogs typically do not salivate as much in response to a bell as to the actual presentation of food, which means that the CS is not triggering the exact same response as the UCS.

Sometimes the CR is even the opposite of the UCR as in **paradoxical conditioning,** where the CR is actually the body's attempt to *counteract* the effects of a stimulus that is about to occur. For example, the sight of drug paraphernalia in heroin addicts can activate physiological reactions that reduce the effect of the heroin they are about to inject (Caggiula et al., 1991; Siegel, 1984). This produces a *conditioned tolerance,* or decreased sensitivity, to the drug with repeated use, as the body counteracts dosages that were previously effective. This conditioned response may be involved in the processes that force addicts to take progressively higher doses of a drug to achieve the same effect. One study of paradoxical conditioning in opiate addicts compared the effects of self-injection, which involved exposure to drug paraphernalia (the CS), with an intravenous injection provided by the researchers, which did not (Ehrman et al., 1992). Only the bodies of addicts who self-injected showed efforts to counteract the drug.

## FROM MIND TO BRAIN

### THE NEURAL BASIS OF CLASSICAL CONDITIONING

Research *has* however, confirmed Pavlov's speculation that classical conditioning alters the action of neurons that link stimuli with responses (Bailey & Kandel, 1995; Martinez & Derrick, 1996; Matthies, 1989). Eric Kandel and his colleagues have studied the cellular basis of learning in the marine snail, *Aplysia,* a simple organism ideally suited to the study of associative learning because reflex learning in *Aplysia* involves a very small number of large neurons. Thus, researchers can actually observe what is happening at all the relevant synapses as *Aplysia* learns. (In humans, in comparison, thousands or millions of neurons may be activated in a simple instance of classical conditioning.)

In *Aplysia,* classical conditioning and similar forms of learning occur through changes at synapses that link sensory neurons (activated by the CS) to neurons that trigger a motor reflex. Changes occur in both the presynaptic neuron, which releases neurotransmitters more readily with additional conditioning trials, and the postsynaptic neuron, which becomes more easily excited with additional trials (Kandel, 1989; Kandel & Schwartz, 1982). A small number of trials produces changes that last for minutes or hours, whereas a larger number of trials can produce changes that last for days.

Kandel and his colleagues have discovered some differences at the cellular level between short-term and longer term learning of this sort. For example, in short-term learning, the presynaptic neuron uses proteins already available within the cell to facilitate release of neurotransmitters. More frequent pairings of the CS and UCS, however, generate *new* proteins that lead to the sprouting of new dendritic connections between the presynaptic and postsynaptic neuron. This strengthens the connections between the two cells, creating a long-lasting neural association.

Other researchers have studied a similar phenomenon called *long-term potentiation (LTP)* in more complex animals (Bliss and Lomo, 1973; Jeffery et al., 1997; Laroche et al., 1995; Martinez & Derrick, 1996; McGaugh et al., 1995; Robertson et al., 1996). Long-term potentiation refers to the tendency of a *group of neurons* to fire more readily after consistent stimulation from other neurons, as presumably occurs in classical conditioning. Its name refers to a heightened potential for neural firing ("potentiation") that lasts much longer than the initial stimulus. Thus, even after the CS is no longer present, cellular changes at the synapse *are.*

Like the work on *Aplysia,* research on LTP supports a hypothesis proposed by the neurologist Donald Hebb (1949) years before the technologies existed to test it: "When an axon of cell A is near enough to excite cell B and repeatedly or persistently take part in firing it, some . . . process . . . takes

*The marine snail,* Aplysia, *has afforded researchers the opportunity to study the molecular basis of learning.*

place in one or both cells such that A's efficiency, as one of the cells firing B, is increased." In other words, when the activation of one set of neurons repeatedly leads to activation of another, the strength of the connection between the two neurons increases—a neural translation of the principles of association first formulated by Aristotle. The evidence linking LTP to learning and memory is not yet complete (see Eichenbaum, 1996). Nevertheless, in many respects LTP parallels processes seen in *Aplysia*, although it occurs in much larger networks of neurons.

**INTERIM SUMMARY**    Several factors influence classical conditioning, including the **interstimulus interval** (the time between presentation of the CS and the UCS), the individual's learning history (such as prior associations between the stimulus and other stimuli or responses), and **prepared learning** (the evolved tendency of some associations to be learned more readily than others). Precisely what organisms learn in classical conditioning is a matter of debate. Research on the marine snail Aplysia and on long-term potentiation in more complex animals suggests that learning occurs through changes in the strength of connections between neurons.

## OPERANT CONDITIONING

In 1898, Edward Thorndike placed a hungry cat in a box with a mechanical latch and then placed food in full view just outside the box. The cat meowed, paced back and forth, and rubbed against the walls of the box. In so doing, it happened to trip the latch. Immediately, the door to the box opened, and the cat gained access to the food. Thorndike repeated the experiment, and with continued repetitions the cat became more adept at tripping the latch. Eventually, it was able to leave its cage almost as soon as food appeared.

Thorndike proposed a law of learning to account for this phenomenon, which he called the **law of effect:** An animal's tendency to reproduce a behavior depends on that behavior's effect on the environment and the consequent effect on the animal. If tripping the latch had not helped the cat reach the food, the cat would not have learned to keep brushing up against the latch. More simply, the law of effect states that *behavior is controlled by its consequences.*

The behavior of Thorndike's cats exemplifies a second form of conditioning, known as instrumental or operant conditioning. Thorndike used the term *instru-*

*"Oh, not bad. The light comes on, I press the bar, they write me a check. How about you?"*

*mental conditioning* because the behavior is instrumental to achieving a more satisfying state of affairs. B. F. Skinner, who spent years experimenting with and systematizing the ways in which behavior is controlled by the environment, called it **operant conditioning,** which means learning to operate on the environment to produce a consequence.

Although the lines between operant and classical conditioning are not always hard and fast, the major distinction between them is that in classical conditioning an environmental stimulus initiates a response, whereas in operant conditioning a *behavior* (or operant) produces an environmental response. **Operants** are behaviors that are emitted (spontaneously produced) rather than elicited by the environment. Thorndike's cat spontaneously emitted the behavior of brushing up against the latch, which resulted in an effect that conditioned future behavior. Skinner emitted the behaviors of experimenting and writing about his results, which brought him the respect of his colleagues and hence influenced his future behavior. Had his initial experiments failed, he would likely have been less likely to persist, just as Thorndike's cats did not continue emitting behaviors with neutral or aversive environment effects. In operant conditioning—whether the animal is a cat or a psychologist—the behavior *precedes* the environmental event that conditions future behavior. By contrast, in classical conditioning, an environmental stimulus (such as a bell) precedes a response.

The basic idea behind operant conditioning, then, is that behavior is controlled by its consequences. In this section, we explore two types of environmental consequence that produce operant conditioning: **reinforcement,** which increases the probability that a response will occur, and **punishment,** which diminishes its likelihood.

## REINFORCEMENT

Reinforcement means just what the name implies: Something in the environment fortifies, or reinforces, a behavior. A **reinforcer** is an environmental consequence that occurs after an organism has produced a response and makes the response more likely to recur. Psychologists distinguish two kinds of reinforcement, positive and negative.

### Positive Reinforcement

**Positive reinforcement** is the process whereby presentation of a stimulus (a reward or payoff) after a behavior makes the behavior more likely to occur again.

*Old Psychological Testing Center*

(a)

(b)

**FIGURE 5.8**
Apparatus for operant conditioning: (*a*) a pigeon is placed in a cage with a target on one side, which can be used for operant conditioning; (*b*) B. F. Skinner experiments with a rat placed in a Skinner box, with a similar design, in which pressing a bar may result in reinforcement.

For example, in experimental procedures pioneered by B. F. Skinner (1938, 1953), a pigeon was placed in a cage with a target mounted on one side (Figure 5.8). (Pigeons and rats were Skinner's favorite—that is, most reinforcing—subjects.) The pigeon spontaneously pecked around in the cage. This behavior was not a response to any particular stimulus; pecking is simply innate avian behavior. If, by chance, the pigeon pecked at the target, however, a pellet of grain dropped into a bin. If the pigeon happened to peck at the target again, it was once more rewarded with a pellet. The pellet is a **positive reinforcer**—an environmental consequence that, when presented, strengthens the probability that a response will recur. The pigeon would thus start to peck at the target more frequently since this operant became associated with the positive reinforcer.

Positive reinforcement is not limited to pigeons. In fact, it controls much of human behavior as well. Students learn to exert effort studying when they are reinforced with praise and good grades, salespeople learn to appease obnoxious customers and laugh at their jokes because doing so yields them commissions, and people learn to go to work each day because they receive a paycheck.

### Negative Reinforcement  *removal*

*Eliminating* something aversive can itself be a reinforcer or reward. This is known as **negative reinforcement**—the process whereby termination of an aversive stimulus makes a behavior more likely to occur. Just as the presentation of a positive reinforcer rewards a response, the removal of an aversive stimulus rewards a response. **Negative reinforcers,** then, are aversive or unpleasant stimuli that strengthen a behavior by their removal. Hitting the snooze button on an alarm clock is negatively reinforced by the termination of the alarm; cleaning the kitchen is negatively reinforced by the elimination of unpleasant sights and smells.

Negative reinforcement occurs in both escape learning and avoidance learning. In **escape learning,** a behavior is reinforced by the elimination of an aversive state of affairs that already exists; that is, the organism escapes an aversive situation. For example, a rat presses a lever and terminates an electric shock; an overzealous sunbather applies lotion to her skin to relieve sunburn pain; or a child cleans his room to stop his parents from nagging. **Avoidance learning** occurs as an organism prevents an *expected* aversive event from happening. In this case, avoidance of a potentially aversive situation reinforces the operant. For example, a rat presses a lever when it hears a tone that signals that a shock is about

*"I would share my cookies, but I'm afraid I'll set up a cycle of dependency."*

to occur; the sunbather puts on sunscreen before going out in the sun to avoid a sunburn; or the child cleans his room to avoid nagging.

## PUNISHMENT

Reinforcement is one type of environmental consequence that controls behavior through operant conditioning; the other is punishment (Figure 5.9). Whereas reinforcement always *increases* the likelihood of a response, either by the presentation of a reward or the removal of an aversive stimulus, punishment *decreases* the probability that a response will recur. Thus, if Skinner's pigeon received an electric shock each time it pecked at the target, it would be less likely to peck again because this operant resulted in an aversive outcome. Parents intuitively apply this behavioral technique when they "ground" a teenager for staying out past curfew. The criminal justice system also operates on a system of punishment, attempting to discourage illicit behaviors by imposing penalties.

Like reinforcement, punishment can be positive or negative. ("Positive" and

*Reinforcement strengthens behavior—such as hard work and practice in sports.*

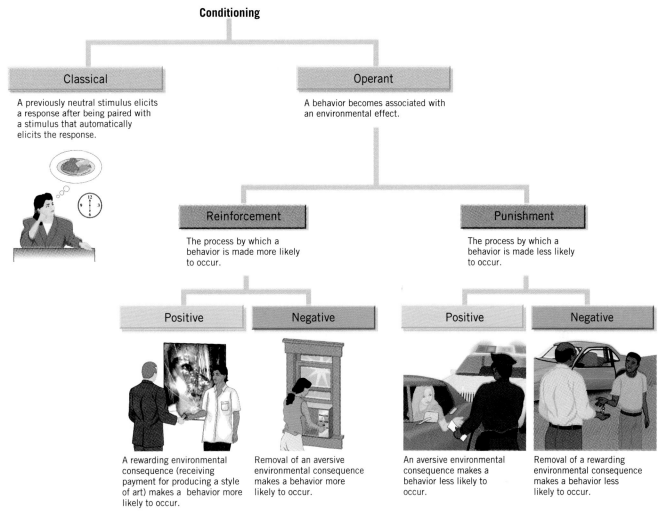

**Conditioning**

**Classical**

A previously neutral stimulus elicits a response after being paired with a stimulus that automatically elicits the response.

**Operant**

A behavior becomes associated with an environmental effect.

**Reinforcement**

The process by which a behavior is made more likely to occur.

**Punishment**

The process by which a behavior is made less likely to occur.

**Positive**

A rewarding environmental consequence (receiving payment for producing a style of art) makes a behavior more likely to occur.

**Negative**

Removal of an aversive environmental consequence makes a behavior more likely to occur.

**Positive**

An aversive environmental consequence makes a behavior less likely to occur.

**Negative**

Removal of a rewarding environmental consequence makes a behavior less likely to occur.

**FIGURE 5.9**
Conditioning processes. Behaviorists distinguish two kinds of conditioning, classical and operant. In operant conditioning, the environment influences behavior through reinforcement and punishment.

"negative" here do not refer to the feelings of the participants, who rarely consider punishment a positive experience. Positive simply means something is presented, whereas negative means something is taken away.) In positive punishment, such as spanking, exposure to an aversive event following a behavior reduces the likelihood of the operant recurring. Negative punishment involves losing, or not obtaining, a reinforcer as a consequence of behavior, as when an employee fails to receive a pay increase because of frequent lateness or absenteeism.

Punishment is commonplace and essential in human affairs, since reinforcement alone is not likely to inhibit many undesirable behaviors, but it is frequently applied in ways that render it ineffective (Chance, 1988; Laub & Sampson, 1995; Newsom et al., 1983; Skinner, 1953). One common problem in using punishment with animals and young children is that the learner may have difficulty distinguishing which operant is being punished. People who yell at their dog for coming after it has been called several times are actually punishing good behavior—coming when called. The dog is more likely to associate the punishment with its action than its inaction—and is likely to adjust its behavior accordingly, by becoming even less likely to come when called. A second and related problem associated with punishment is that the learner may come to fear the person meting out the punishment (via classical conditioning) rather than the action (via operant conditioning). A child who is harshly punished by his father may become afraid of his father instead of changing his behavior.

Third, people who rely heavily on punishment often fail to recognize that punishment may not eliminate existing rewards for a behavior. In nature, unlike the laboratory, a single action may have multiple consequences, and behavior can be controlled by any number of them. A teacher who punishes the class clown may not have much success if the behavior is reinforced by classmates. Sometimes, too, punishing one behavior (such as stealing) may inadvertently reinforce another (such as lying).

Fourth, people typically use punishment when they are angry, which can lead both to poorly designed punishment (from a learning point of view) and to the potential for abuse. An angry parent may punish a child for misdeeds just discovered but that occurred a considerable time earlier. The time interval between the child's action and the consequence may render the punishment ineffective because the child does not adequately connect the two events. Parents also frequently punish depending more on their mood than on the type of behavior they want to discourage, which can prevent the child from learning what behavior is being punished, under what circumstances, and how to avoid it.

Finally, aggression that is used to punish behavior often leads to further aggression. The child who is beaten typically learns a much deeper lesson: that problems can be solved with violence. In fact, the more physical punishment parents use, the more aggressively their children tend to behave at home and at school (Dodge et al., 1995, 1997; Kaplan, 1996; Larzelere, 1986; Larzelere et al., 1996; Weiss et al., 1993). Correlation does not, of course, prove causation; aggressive children may provoke punitive parenting. Nevertheless, the weight of evidence suggests that violent parents tend to create violent children. There is no evidence that the use of belts or paddles augments the painful effects of a swat with the hand of an adult who usually outweighs a child by a factor of at least 3 or 4. If parents who use such devices aim to teach their children self-control, they would do better to learn it themselves, since beating children tends to make them more likely as adults to have *less* self-control, lower self-esteem, more troubled relationships, and more depression and to be more likely to abuse their own children and spouses (Rohner, 1975, 1985; Straus & Kantor, 1994).

Punishment tends to be most effective when it is accompanied by reasoning—even in 2- and 3-year-olds (Larzelere et al., 1996)—and when the person being punished is also reinforced for an alternative, acceptable behavior. Explaining helps a child correctly connect an action with a punishment. Having other positively reinforced behaviors to draw on allows the child to generate alternative responses.

## EXTINCTION

As in classical conditioning, learned operant responses can be extinguished. Extinction occurs if enough conditioning trials pass in which the operant is not followed by the consequence previously associated with it. A child may reduce effort in school if hard work no longer leads to reinforcers (such as "good work!" written on homework), just as a corporate executive may choose to stop producing a product that is no longer bringing in profits.

Knowing how to extinguish behavior is important in everyday life, particularly for parents. Consider the case of a 21-month-old boy who had a serious illness requiring around-the-clock attention (Williams, 1959). After recovering, the child continued to demand this level of attention, which was no longer necessary. His demands were especially troublesome at bedtime, when he screamed and

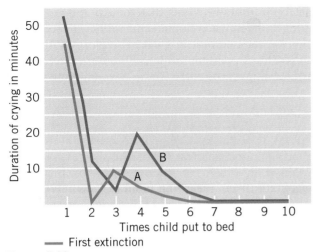

FIGURE 5.10

Extinction of tantrum behavior in a 21-month-old child. As shown in curve *A*, the child initially cried for long periods of time, but very few trials of nonreinforced crying were required to extinguish the behavior. In curve *B*, the behavior was again quickly extinguished following its spontaneous recovery. *Source:* Williams, 1959, p. 269.

cried unless a parent sat with him until he fell asleep, which could take up to two hours.

Relying on the principle that unreinforced behavior will be extinguished, the parents, with some help from a psychologist, began following a new bedtime regimen. In the first trial of the extinction series, they spent a relaxed and warm good-night session with their son, closed the door when they left the room, and refused to respond to the wails and screams that followed. After 45 minutes, the boy fell asleep, and he fell asleep immediately on the second trial (Figure 5.10). The next several bedtimes were accompanied by tantrums that steadily decreased in duration, so that by the tenth trial, the parents fully enjoyed the sounds of silence.

As in classical conditioning, spontaneous recovery (in which a previously learned behavior recurs without renewed reinforcement) sometimes occurs. In fact, the boy cried and screamed again one night when his aunt attempted to put him to bed. She inadvertently reinforced this behavior by returning to his room; as a result, his parents had to repeat their extinction procedure.

INTERIM SUMMARY    **Operant conditioning** means learning to operate on the environment to produce a consequence. **Operants** are behaviors that are emitted rather than elicited by the environment. **Reinforcement** refers to a consequence that increases the probability that a response will recur. **Positive reinforcement** occurs when the environmental consequence (a reward or payoff) makes a behavior more likely to occur again. **Negative reinforcement** occurs when termination of an aversive stimulus makes a behavior more likely to recur. Whereas reinforcement increases the probability of a response, **punishment** decreases the probability that a response will recur. Punishment is commonplace in human affairs but is frequently applied in ways that render it ineffective. Extinction in operant conditioning occurs if enough condition trials pass in which the operant is not followed by the consequence previously associated with it.

## OPERANT CONDITIONING OF COMPLEX BEHAVIORS

Thus far we have discussed relatively simple behaviors controlled by their environmental consequences—pigeons pecking, rats pressing, and people showing up at work for a paycheck. In fact, operant conditioning offers one of the most comprehensive explanatory accounts of the range of human and animal behavior ever produced. We will now ratchet up the complexity level by exploring four phenomena that substantially increase the breadth of the behaviorist account of learning: schedules of reinforcement, discriminative stimuli, context, and characteristics of the learner.

### Schedules of Reinforcement

In the examples described so far, an animal is rewarded or punished every time it performs a behavior. This situation, in which the consequence is the same each time the animal emits a behavior, is called a **continuous reinforcement schedule** (because the behavior is *continuously* reinforced). A child reinforced for altruistic behavior on a continuous schedule of reinforcement would be praised every time she shares, just as a rat might receive a pellet of food each time it presses a lever. Such consistent reinforcement, however, rarely occurs in nature or in human life. More typically, an action sometimes leads to reinforcement but other times does not. Such reinforcement schedules are known as **partial** or **intermittent schedules of reinforcement** because the behavior is reinforced only part of the time, or intermittently. (These are called schedules of *reinforcement,* but the same principles apply with punishment.)

Intuitively, one would think that continuous schedules would be more effective. Although this tends to be true during the initial learning (acquisition) of a response (presumably because continuous reinforcement renders the connection between the behavior and its consequence clear and predictable), partial reinforcement is usually superior for maintaining learned behavior. For example, suppose you have a relatively new car, and every time you turn the key the engine starts. If one day, however, you try to start the car ten times and the engine will not turn over, you will probably give up and call a towing company. In contrast, if you are the proud owner of a rusted-out 1972 Chevy and are accustomed to ten turns of the ignition before the car finally cranks up, you may try 20 or 30 times before enlisting the help of a mechanic. Thus, behaviors maintained under partial schedules are usually more resistant to extinction.

Behaviorist researchers, notably Skinner and his colleagues, have categorized intermittent reinforcement schedules as either ratio schedules or interval schedules (Ferster & Skinner, 1957; Skinner, 1938). In **ratio schedules,** payoffs are tied to the number of responses emitted; only a fraction of "correct" behaviors receive reinforcement (such as one out of every five, for a ratio of 1 : 5). In **interval schedules,** rewards are delivered only after some interval of time. The organism can produce a response as often as it wants, but the response will only be reinforced (or punished) after a certain amount of time has elapsed.

Reinforcement schedules are often studied with a **cumulative response recorder,** an instrument that tallies the number of times a subject produces a response, such as pressing a bar or pecking a target. Figure 5.11 illustrates typical cumulative response recordings for the four reinforcement schedules we will now describe: fixed ratio, variable ratio, fixed interval, and variable interval.

Fixed-Ratio Schedules    In a **fixed-ratio (FR) schedule** of reinforcement, an organism receives reinforcement for a fixed proportion of the responses it emits. Piecework employment uses a fixed-ratio schedule of reinforcement: A person receives payment for every bushel of apples picked (an FR-1 schedule) or for every ten scarves woven (an FR-10 schedule). Workers weave the first nine scarves without reinforcement; the payoff occurs when the tenth scarf is completed. As shown in Figure 5.11, FR schedules are characterized by rapid responding, with a brief pause after each reinforcement.

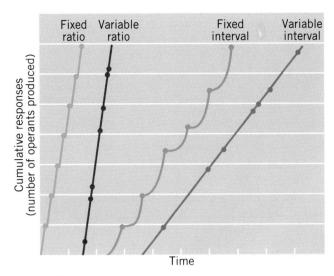

**FIGURE 5.11**
Schedules of reinforcement. The figure shows cumulative response records for fixed-ratio, variable-ratio, fixed-interval, and variable-interval reinforcement schedules. A cumulative response record graphs the total number of responses that have been emitted at any point in time. Different schedules of reinforcement produce different patterns of responding.

**Variable-Ratio Schedules**    In **variable-ratio (VR) schedules,** the individual receives a reward for some percentage of responses, but the number of responses required before reinforcement is unpredictable (that is, variable). Variable-ratio schedules specify an *average* number of responses that will be rewarded. Thus, a pigeon on a VR-5 schedule may be rewarded on its fourth, seventh, 13th, and 20th responses, averaging one reward for every five responses. Variable-ratio schedules generally produce rapid, constant responding and are probably the most common in daily life. People cannot predict that they will be rewarded or praised for every fifth good deed, but they do receive occasional, irregular social reinforcement, which is enough to reinforce altruistic behavior in most people. Similarly, students may not receive a good grade each time they study hard for an examination, but many study nonetheless because they learn that the *average* rate of reinforcement is higher than if they do not study. The power of variable-ratio schedules can be seen in gambling, in which people may gradually lose their shirts if they are intermittently—and very irregularly—reinforced.

**Fixed-Interval Ratios**    In a **fixed-interval (FI) schedule,** an animal receives reinforcement for its responses only after a fixed amount of time. For example, a rat that presses a bar is reinforced with a pellet of food every ten minutes. The rat may press the bar 100 times or one time during that ten minutes; doing so does not make a difference in the delivery of the pellet, just as long as the rat presses the bar at some point during each ten-minute interval.

An animal on an FI schedule of reinforcement will ultimately learn to stop responding except toward the end of each interval, producing the scalloped cumulative response pattern shown in Figure 5.11. Fixed-interval schedules affect human performance in the same way. For example, workers whose boss comes by only at two o'clock are likely to relax the rest of the day. Schools rely heavily on FI schedules; as a result, some students procrastinate between exams and pull "all-nighters" when reinforcement (or punishment) is imminent. Politicians, too, seem to resemble rats in their response patterns (Figure 5.12). Periodic adjournment of Congress on a fixed interval appears to reinforce bill passing (the congressional equivalent of bar pressing), producing precisely the same scalloped response record (Waldrop, 1972).

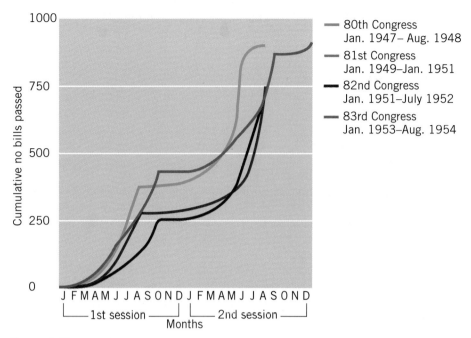

**FIGURE 5.12**

The effects of a fixed-interval schedule on the U.S. Congress. Adjournment serves as a powerful reinforcer for members of the U.S. House of Representatives, who seem to respond to this fixed-interval schedule of reinforcement with a flurry of last-minute activity before being reinforced. As the graph shows, the pattern looked the same over several years investigated. The scalloped curve is remarkably similar to the fixed-interval cumulative response recording derived from studying rats and pigeons in Figure 5.11. *Source:* Weisberg & Waldrop, 1972, p. 23.

**Variable-Interval Schedules**   A **variable interval (VI) schedule,** like a fixed-interval schedule, ties reinforcement to an interval of time after which the individual's response leads to reinforcement. In a VI schedule, however, the animal cannot predict how long that time interval will be. Thus, a rat might receive reinforcement for bar pressing, but only at five, six, 20, and 40 minutes (a VI-10 schedule).

Variable-interval schedules are more effective than fixed-interval schedules in maintaining consistent performance. Random, unannounced governmental inspections of working conditions in a plant are much more effective in getting management to maintain safety standards than inspections at fixed intervals. In the classroom, pop quizzes make similar use of VI schedules.

### Discriminative Stimuli

In everyday life, then, rarely does a response receive continuous reinforcement in a given situation, such as work or school. Making matters even *more* complicated for learners is that a single behavior can lead to different effects in different situations. Professors receive a paycheck for lecturing to their classes, but if they lecture new acquaintances at a cocktail party, the environmental consequences will not be the same. Similarly, domestic cats learn that the dining room table is a great place to stretch out and relax—except when their owners are home.

In some situations, then, a connection might exist between a behavior and a consequence (called a response *contingency*, because the consequence is dependent, or *contingent*, on the behavior). In other situations, however, the contingencies might be different, so the organism needs to be able to discriminate circumstances under which different contingencies apply. A stimulus that signals the presence of particular contingencies of reinforcement is called a **discriminative stimulus (S$^D$).** In other words, an animal learns to produce certain actions only in the presence of the discriminative stimulus. For the professor, the classroom situation signals that lecturing behavior will be reinforced; for the cat on the dinner table, the presence of humans is a discriminative stimulus signaling punishment. In an experimental demonstration, rats were rewarded for turning clockwise when they were placed in one chamber and turning counterclockwise when placed in another; the chamber was the discriminative stimulus signaling different contingencies of reinforcement (Richards et al., 1990).

Stimulus discrimination is one of the keys to the complexity and flexibility of human and animal behavior. Behavior therapists, who apply behaviorist principles to maladaptive behaviors (Chapter 16), use the concept of stimulus discrimination to help people recognize and alter some very subtle triggers for maladaptive responses, particularly in relationships (Kohlenberg & Tsai, 1994). For example, one couple was on the verge of divorce because the husband complained that his wife was too passive and indecisive and the wife complained that her husband was too rigid and controlling. A careful analysis of their interactions suggested some complex contingencies controlling their behavior. The couple often engaged in mutually enjoyable conversation, in which each felt comfortable and relatively spontaneous. At times, however, the woman would detect a particular "tone" in her husband's voice (an S$^D$) that she had associated with his getting angry; upon hearing this tone, she would "shut down" and become more passive and quiet. Her husband, however, found her passivity (an S$^D$ for him) infuriating and would then begin to push her for answers and decisions, which only intensified her "passivity" and his "controlling" behavior. She was not, in fact, always passive, and he was not always controlling. Easing the tension in the marriage thus required isolating the discriminative stimuli that controlled each of their responses.

**INTERIM SUMMARY**    In everyday life, **continuous schedules of reinforcement** (in which the consequence is the same each time an animal emits a behavior) are far less common than **intermittent schedules of reinforcement** (in which reinforcement occurs in some ratio or after certain intervals). A **discriminative stimulus** is a stimulus that signals that particular contingencies of reinforcement are in effect, so that the organism only produces the behavior in the presence of the discriminative stimulus.

## Context

Thus far, we have treated operants as if they were isolated behaviors, produced one at a time in response to specific consequences. In fact, however, learning usually occurs in broader context (see Herrnstein, 1970; Premack, 1965).

**The Costs and Benefits of Obtaining Reinforcement**    In real life, reinforcement is not infinite, and attainment of one reinforcer may affect both its future availability and the availability of other reinforcers. Researchers studying the way animals forage in their natural habitats have noted that reinforcement schedules change because of the animal's own behavior: By continually eating fruit from one tree, an animal may deplete the supply, so that remaining fruit must be obtained with more work (Stephens & Krebs, 1986). Psychologists have simulated this phenomenon by changing contingencies of reinforcement based on the number of times rats feed from the same "patch" (Aparicio & Baum, 1997; Collier et al., 1998; Shettleworth, 1988). Thus, a rat may find that the more it presses one lever, the less reward it receives at that lever but not at another. Researchers using this kind of experimental procedure have found that rats make "choices" about how long to stay at a patch depending on variables such as its current rate of reinforcement, the average rate of reinforcement they could obtain elsewhere, and the amount of time required to get to a new "patch."

Obtaining one reinforcer may also adversely affect the chances of obtaining another. An omnivorous animal merrily snacking on some foliage must somehow weigh the benefits of its current refreshments against the cost of pursuing a source of protein it notices scampering nearby. Similarly, a person at a restaurant must choose which of many potential reinforcers to pursue, knowing that each has a cost and that eating one precludes eating the others. This recognition of the cost–benefit analysis involved in operant behavior has led to an approach called *behavioral economics*, which weds aspects of behavioral theory with economics (Bickel et al., 1995; Green & Freed, 1993; Rachlin et al., 1976). For example, some reinforcers, such as two brands of soda, are relatively substitutable for each other, so that as the cost of one goes down, its consumption goes up and the consumption of the other decreases. Other reinforcers are complementary, such as bagels and cream cheese, so that if the cost of bagels skyrockets, consumption of cream cheese will decrease.

Psychologists have studied principles of behavioral economics in some ingenious ways in the laboratory using rats and other animals as subjects. For example, they put animals on a "budget" by only reinforcing them for a certain number of lever presses per day; thus, the animals had to "conserve" their lever presses to purchase the "goods" they preferred (Rachlin et al., 1976). Decreasing the "cost" of Tom Collins mix (by reducing the number of bar presses necessary to obtain it) led rats to shift their natural preference from root beer to Tom Collins—a finding the liquor industry would likely find heartening. In contrast, decreasing the cost of food relative to water had much less effect on consumption. In the language of economics, the demand for water is relatively "inelastic"; that is, it does not change much, regardless of the price.

**The Social and Cultural Context**    We have spoken thus far as if reinforcement and punishment were unilateral techniques, in which one person (a trainer) conditions another person or animal (a learner). In fact, in human social interactions, each partner continuously uses operant conditioning techniques to mold the behavior of the other. When a child behaves in a way his parents find upsetting, the parents are likely to punish the child. But the parents' behavior is itself being conditioned: The operant of punishing the child will be *negatively reinforced* if it causes the child's bad behavior to cease. Thus, the child is negatively reinforcing the parents' use of punishment just as the parents are punishing the child's behavior. From this point of view, people give each other reinforcement and punishment in nearly all their interactions (Homans, 1961).

The reliance on different operant procedures varies considerably cross-culturally. In part, this reflects the dangers that confront a society. The Gusii of Kenya, with a history of tribal warfare, face threats not only from outsiders but also from natural forces, including wild animals. Gusii parents tend to rely more on punishment and fear than on rewards in conditioning social behavior in their children. Caning, food deprivation, and withdrawing shelter and protection are common forms of punishment. One Gusii mother warned her child, "If you don't stop crying, I shall open the door and call a hyena to come and eat you!" (LeVine & LeVine, 1963, p. 166). Death from wild animals is a real fear, so this threat gains compliance from Gusii children.

In contrast, the Mixtecan Indians of Juxtlahuaca, Mexico, are a highly cohesive community, with little internal conflict and social norms (expectations of appropriate behavior) that encourage cooperation. The Mixtecans do not generally impose fines or jail sentences or use physical punishment to deter aggression in either adults or children. They are more likely to rely on soothing persuasion. An anthropologist reported an incident of aggression that occurred among a group of Mixtecan males in which one man assaulted several others while intoxicated (Romney, 1963). Instead of retaliating, the victims worked together to calm him down. Social ostracism is the most feared punishment in Mixtecan culture, and social ties within the community are strong, so responses that reinforce these ties are effective in maintaining social order.

## Characteristics of the Learner

An additional set of factors that increase the complexity of operant conditioning have to do less with the environment than with the learner. Current environmental contingencies operate on an animal that already has behaviors in its repertoire, enduring ways of responding, and species-specific learning patterns.

*Shaping can introduce some unusual behaviors into an animal's repertoire.*

### Capitalizing on Past Behaviors: Shaping and Chaining

The range of behaviors humans and other animals can produce is made infinitely more complex by the fact that existing behaviors often serve as the raw material for novel ones. This occurs as the environment subtly refines them or links them together into sequences. For example, circus animals (and gymnasts) learn to do backflips and perform other behaviors not usually seen in their natural habitats. How does this occur?

A procedure used by animal trainers, called **shaping,** produces novel behavior by reinforcing closer and closer approximations to the desired response. Skinner (1951) described a shaping procedure that can be used to teach a dog to touch its nose to a cupboard door handle. The first step is to bring a hungry dog (in behavioral terms, a dog that has been deprived of food for a certain number of hours or until its body weight is a certain percent below normal) into the kitchen and immediately reward him with food any time he happens to face the cupboard; the dog will soon face the cupboard most of the time. The next step is to reward the dog whenever it moves toward the cupboard, then to reward it when it moves its head so that its nose comes closer to the cupboard, and finally to reward the dog only for touching its nose to the cupboard handle. This shaping procedure should take no more than five minutes, even for a beginner.

The same shaping techniques can be used to teach more complex behaviors. The key, as a trainer, is to begin by reinforcing a response the animal can readily produce. Gradually, the trainer reinforces only certain ways of performing the desired behavior, so that the animal eventually produces a very specific operant. With humans, shaping is common in all kinds of teaching. A tennis instructor may at first praise a student any time he holds the racquet in a way that resembles a good grip and gets the ball over the net. Gradually, however, the instructor compliments only proper form and well-placed shots, progressively shaping the student's behavior. Shaping does not require instruction and often occurs naturally as well. A tennis player may evolve a particular grip on the racket as his behavior is progressively reinforced toward a grip that originally would have felt completely unnatural and would never have been spontaneously produced.

Whereas shaping leads to the progressive modification of a specific behavior to produce a new response, **chaining** involves putting together a *sequence* of existing responses in a novel order. When I was a child, my brother Marc displayed a natural gift for applying a variant of this operant technique. Marc would awaken at four o'clock in the morning (who knows why), and while everyone else slept soundly, he devised a way to train the family cat to wake me by licking my face. This trick does not come naturally to most felines and required several steps to accomplish. The cat already knew how to climb, jump, and lick. Marc's goal was to get the cat to perform these behaviors in a particular sequence. First, Marc placed pieces of cat food on the stairs leading up to my bedroom. After several trials, the cat learned to climb the stairs on its own. The next step was to reinforce the operant of jumping onto my bed; again, a few judiciously placed bits of cat food did the trick. The same reward, placed gently in the proper location, was enough to train the cat to lick me on the face. Once this occurred enough times, the cat seemed to be reinforced simply by licking my cheek. (Marc seemed quite amused and was apparently reinforced for his little foray into behaviorism as well.)

**Enduring Characteristics of the Learner**   Not only do prior learning experiences influence operant conditioning, but so, too, do enduring characteristics of the learner. In humans as in other species, individuals differ in the ease with which they can be conditioned (Corr et al., 1995; Eysenck, 1990; Hooks et al., 1994). Individual rats vary, for example, in their tendency to behave aggressively or to respond with fear or avoidance in the face of aversive environmental events (e.g., Ramos et al., 1997). Rats can also be selectively bred for their ability to learn mazes (Innis, 1992; van der Staay & Blokland, 1996).

The role of the learner was especially clear in an experiment that attempted to teach three octopi (named Albert, Bertram, and Charles) to pull a lever in their saltwater tanks to obtain food (Dews, 1959). The usual shaping procedures worked successfully on Albert and Bertram, who were first rewarded for approaching the lever, then for touching it with a tentacle, and finally for tugging at it. With Charles, however, things were different. Instead of *pulling* the lever to obtain food, Charles tugged at it with such force that he broke it. Charles was generally a surly subject, spending much of his time "with eyes above the surface of the water, directing a jet of water at any individual who approached the tank" (p. 62).

Humans differ in their "conditionability" as well. Many individuals with antisocial personality disorder, who show a striking disregard for society's standards, tend to be relatively unresponsive to punishment (Eysenck, 1967, 1990; Magnusson, 1996). Their lack of anxiety when confronted with potential punishment renders them less likely to learn to control selfish, aggressive, or impulsive behaviors that other people learn to inhibit (Chapter 15). Similarly, genetic and environmental factors lead to differences among individuals in the ability to solve problems quickly and efficiently (Chapter 8).

**Species-Specific Behavior and Preparedness**   Operant conditioning is influenced not only by characteristics of the individual but also by characteristics of the species. Just as some stimulus–response connections are easier to acquire in classical conditioning, certain behaviors are more readily learned by some species in operant conditioning—or may be emitted despite learning to the contrary. This was vividly illustrated in the work of Keller and Marian Breland (1961), who learned operant conditioning techniques while working with Skinner. The Brelands went on to apply these procedures in their own animal training business but initially with mixed success. In one case, they trained pigs to deposit wooden coins in a large "piggy bank" in order to obtain food (p. 683):

> Pigs condition very rapidly. . . . [T]hey have ravenous appetites (naturally), and in many ways are among the most tractable animals we have worked with. However, this particular problem behavior developed in pig after pig, usually after a period of weeks or months, getting worse every day. At first the pig would eagerly pick up one dollar, carry it to the bank, run back, get another, carry it rapidly and neatly, and so on. . . . Thereafter, over a period of weeks the behavior would become slower and slower. He might run over ea-

gerly for each dollar, but on the way back, instead of carrying the dollar and depositing it simply and cleanly, he would repeatedly drop it, root it [nuzzle it with his snout], drop it again, root it along the way, pick it up, toss it up in the air, drop it, root it some more, and so on.

The Brelands observed that the pigs' "rooting" behavior eventually replaced the conditioned behavior of depositing coins in the bank so much that the hungry pigs were not getting enough food. The Brelands had similar experiences with porpoises that swallowed the balls they were supposed to manipulate, cats that would stalk their food slots, and raccoons that tried to wash the tokens they were supposed to deposit in banks. All these operants were more closely related to instinctive, species-specific behaviors than the operants the Brelands were attempting to condition. Species-specific behavior also influences the way animals respond to negative reinforcement. Conditioning a rat to press a lever to avoid an electric shock may be difficult because a rat's natural response to shock is either to crouch and freeze or to run away, both of which interfere with bar pressing. Species-specific behavioral tendencies, like prepared learning in classical conditioning, make sense from an evolutionary perspective: Pigs' rooting behavior normally allows them to obtain food, and a "frozen" rat is less likely to be noticed by a predator than a frenzied one searching for levers to press (Seligman, 1970, 1971).

**INTERIM SUMMARY**   Learning occurs in a broader context than one behavior at a time. Humans and other animals learn that attaining one reinforcer may affect attainment of others. Cultural factors also influence operant conditioning, since different cultures rely on different operate procedures. Characteristics of the learner influence operant conditioning, such as prior behaviors in the animal's repertoire, enduring characteristics of the learner (such as the tendency to respond with fear or avoidance in the face of aversive environmental events), and species-specific behavior (the tendency of particular species to produce particular responses).

## SIMILAR PROCESSES IN CLASSICAL AND OPERANT CONDITIONING

As this discussion of preparedness in operant conditioning suggests, operant and classical conditioning share many features. Just as the interstimulus interval influences learning in classical conditioning, the interval between the operant and its environmental consequences is important as well. Parents intuitively recognize the advantage of shorter intervals: When a child misbehaves at the grocery store, parents rarely wait until the next day to address the problem. Concepts of discrimination and generalization also apply to operant conditioning. Animals can learn to make some surprisingly subtle discriminations and generalizations when access to food is at stake. For example, in one study, pigeons in one condition received access to a container of seed if they pecked at a pecking key when presented with paintings by Monet (projected from slides) (Watanabe et al., 1995). Pigeons in a second condition received reinforcement instead if they pecked at Picassos. Remarkably, the pigeons in each condition learned to peck at novel paintings (paintings they had not previously seen) by the same painter (stimulus generalization) but not at paintings by the other painter (stimulus discrimination). They even generalized from Monet to other impressionists (such as Cezanne) and from Picasso to other cubists (such as Matisse)! Apparently, pigeons can become impressive connoisseurs of art—if the price is right.

Further, just as humans and other animals can develop phobias by forming idiosyncratic associations, they can also erroneously associate an operant and an environmental event, a phenomenon Skinner (1948) labeled **superstitious behavior.**

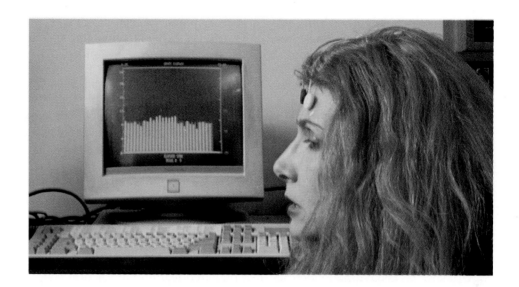

*Biofeedback allows patients to gain operant control of autonomic processes.*

In one study, he placed pigeons on a schedule in which grain was delivered at regular time intervals, no matter what behavior the pigeons happened to perform. As a result, each pigeon developed its own idiosyncratic response. One turned counterclockwise about the cage, another repeatedly thrust its head in an upper corner of the cage, and a third tossed its head as if lifting an invisible bar (1948, p. 168). Skinner compared these behaviors to human actions such as wearing a lucky outfit to a basketball game or tapping home plate three times when up to bat in baseball. According to Skinner, such behaviors develop because the delivery of a reinforcer strengthens whatever behavior an organism is engaged in at the time.

Are operant and classical conditioning really distinct processes? In some ways, yes. As we have seen, in classical conditioning the organism's behavior follows an environmental event (the stimulus), whereas in operant conditioning the environmental event (reinforcement or punishment) follows the behavior (operant). Furthermore, operant conditioning typically involves voluntary behavior, whereas classical conditioning involves involuntary behavior usually controlled by the autonomic nervous system.

The distinction is not, however, always so clear. In **biofeedback,** psychologists feed information back to patients about their biological processes, allowing them to gain operant control over autonomic responses such as heart rate, body temperature, and blood pressure (Nakao et al., 1997; Stroebel, 1985). As patients monitor their physiological processes on an electronic device or computer screen, they receive reinforcement for changes such as decreased muscle tension or heart rate. Biofeedback can help patients reduce or eliminate problems such as high blood pressure, headaches, and chronic pain (Arena & Blanchard, 1996; Gauthier, Ivers, & Carrier, 1996; Nakao et al., 1997). In one study, patients treated for chronic back pain with biofeedback showed substantial improvement in comparison to control subjects (Flor et al., 1986). They maintained these benefits at follow-up over two years later, reporting less need for treatment, less life disruption from pain, and fewer pain-related thoughts (Table 5.1).

In everyday life, operant and classical conditioning are often equally difficult to disentangle because most learned behavior involves both processes (Mowrer, 1947). A person who has a car accident, for instance, may develop a conditioned fear response to riding in cars, an example of classical conditioning. This typically leads to the operant response of avoiding cars, since doing so is negatively reinforced by avoidance of an aversive event (anxiety).

**TABLE 5.1 THE EFFECTS OF BIOFEEDBACK ON CHRONIC BACK PAIN**

| (A) COMPARISONS OF BIOFEEDBACK AND CONTROL CONDITIONS AT END OF TREATMENT | | | (B) CHANGES BETWEEN PRETREATMENT AND 2-YEAR FOLLOW-UP RATINGS FOR PARTICIPANTS WHO RECEIVED BIOFEEDBACK | | |
|---|---|---|---|---|---|
| DOMIAN DISRUPTED BY PAIN | BIOFEEDBACK CONDITION | CONTROL CONDITION | PAIN RATINGS | PRETREATMENT | 2-YEAR FOLLOW-UP |
| Sex | 2.0 | 45.0 | Hours in pain per day | 15.5[b] | 8.7[b] |
| Work | 19.9 | 48.6 | Interference with life | 35.0 | 15.0 |
| Life in General | 14.3[a] | 38.9[a] | Negative pain-related thoughts | 40.7 | 29.0 |

*Source:* Adapted from Flor et al., 1986, pp. 198–199.

*Note:* Prior to and after treatment, patients made a number of ratings, such as the extent to which back pain interfered with their lives. As can be seen in (a), pain treated with biofeedback interfered substantially less in the lives of experimental subjects than in untreated controls. At follow-up (b), patients in the biofeedback condition continued to show substantial gains as compared with their initial pain reports prior to treatment.

---

**INTERIM SUMMARY**   Operant and classical conditioning share many features (such as extinction, prepared learning, discrimination, generalization, and the possibility of irrational associations) and are often intertwined in daily life.

▶ **ONE STEP FURTHER**

## Why Are Reinforcers Reinforcing?

Behaviorists aim to formulate general *laws of behavior* that link behaviors with events in the environment. Skinner and others who called themselves "radical behaviorists" were less interested in theorizing about the mechanisms that produced these laws, since these mechanisms could not be readily observed. Other theorists within and without behaviorism, however, have asked, "What makes a reinforcer reinforcing or a punisher punishing?" No answer has achieved widespread acceptance, but three are worth considering.

### Reinforcers as Drive Reducers

One theory relies on the concept of **drive**, a state that impels, or "drives," the organism to act. Clark Hull (1943, 1952) used the term to refer to unpleasant tension states caused by deprivation of basic needs such as food and water. He proposed a **drive-reduction theory**, which holds that stimuli that reduce drives are reinforcing. This theory makes intuitive sense and explains why an animal that is not hungry will not typically work hard to receive food as reinforcement. However, it requires additional principles to explain why behaviors related to basic needs may be learned even when drives are not currently activated. Lions can learn to hunt in packs, and humans to manipulate numbers on a computer, even when their stomachs are full (Smith, 1984). In fact, optimal learning does not typically occur under intense arousal.

## Primary and Secondary Reinforcers

Drives help explain why some stimuli such as food, sex, and water are reinforcing. Hull and others called such stimuli **primary reinforcers** because they innately reinforce behavior without any prior learning. A **secondary reinforcer** is an originally neutral stimulus that becomes reinforcing by being paired repeatedly with a primary reinforcer. For example, children often hear phrases like "good girl!" while receiving other forms of reinforcement (such as hugs), so that the word "good" becomes a secondary reinforcer. Smiles are reinforcing in all cultures.

Most secondary reinforcers are culturally defined. Good grades, gold medals for athletic performance, thank-you notes, and cheering crowds are all examples of secondary reinforcers in many cultures. Children learn to associate coins and bills with *many* reinforcers in cultures that use money. In noncash economies, alternative forms of "currency" acquire secondary reinforcement value. In the Gusii community in Kenya, for example, cattle and other livestock are the primary form of economic exchange. Cattle, rather than cash, are thus associated with marriage, happiness, and social status (LeVine & LeVine, 1963), and the smell of the barnyard carries very different connotations than for most Westerners.

*Gold medals are secondary reinforcers that reward skilled performance.*

## The Role of Feelings

A third explanation of reinforcement stresses the role of feelings. Consider the example of a student who cheats on a test and is lavishly praised for his performance by his unaware teacher. The more she praises him, the guiltier he feels. Paradoxically, the student may be *less* likely to cheat again following this apparent reinforcement. Why?

This third explanation harkens back to Thorndike's law of effect. It holds that feelings—including emotions such as sadness or joy as well as sensory experiences of pleasure or pain—provide a basis for operant conditioning (see Dollard & Miller, 1950; Mowrer, 1960; Wachtel, 1977; Westen, 1985, 1994). An operant that is followed by a pleasurable feeling will be reinforced, whereas one followed by unpleasant feelings will be less likely to recur. From this approach, the teacher's praise—normally a positive reinforcer—was punishing because it evoked guilt, which in turn decreased the probability of future cheating. This theory is incompatible with the goal of many behaviorists to avoid mentalistic explanations, but it fits with an intuitive understanding of operant conditioning: Positive reinforcement occurs because a consequence *feels good*, negative reinforcement occurs because termination of an unpleasant event *feels better*, and punishment occurs because a consequence *feels bad*.

Neuropsychological data support the proposition that feelings play a central role in operant conditioning. Gray (1987, 1990) has demonstrated the role of anatomically distinct pathways in the nervous system, each related to distinct emotional states, which lead to approach and avoidance (Figure 5.13). The **behavioral approach system (BAS)** is associated with pleasurable emotional states and is responsible for approach-oriented operant behavior. This system appears to be primarily involved in positive reinforcement. The **behavioral inhibition system (BIS)** is associated with anxiety and is involved in negative reinforcement and punishment. Dopamine is the primary neurotransmitter involved in transmitting information along BAS pathways (see also Schultz et al., 1997), whereas norepinephrine (known to be related to fear and anxiety) plays a more important role in the synapses involved in the BIS. (Gray also describes a third, more evolutionarily primitive system, the **fight–flight system**, which is related to rage and terror and leads to species-specific responses such as freezing in rats.)

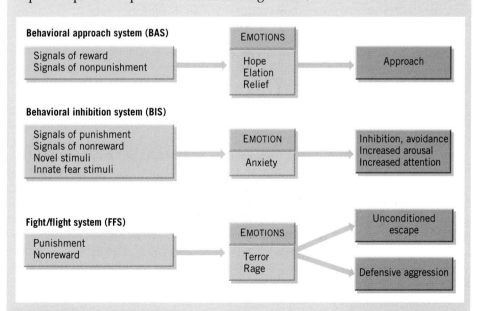

**FIGURE 5.13**

Gray's three behavioral systems. The behavioral approach system (BAS) orients the person (or animal) to stimuli associated with reward; approach is motivated by the positive emotions of hope, elation, and relief. The behavioral inhibition system (BIS) orients the person to avoidance and vigilance against threat. The BIS addresses potential dangers and involves anxiety. The fight–flight system (FFS) is a more evolutionarily primitive system that orients the person to escape currently punishing stimuli. It is associated with terror and rage. *Source:* Adapted from Gray, 1988, pp. 278–279.

Supporting this theory are studies showing that chemicals that reduce norepinephrine activity (and hence reduce anxiety) lead to poorer performance in avoidance learning tasks, that is, failure to learn from negative reinforcement. For example, dogs given antianxiety medications are less able to avoid behaviors associated with electric shock than dogs in control conditions (Scott, 1980), presumably because decreased fear leads to decreased behavioral inhibition. Further evidence for distinct pathways comes from experiments using EEG to measure electrical activity in the frontal lobes (Davidson, 1995; Sutton & Davidson, 1997). Left frontal activation tends to be more associated with pleasurable feelings and behavioral approach, whereas right frontal activation tends to be associated with unpleasant feelings and behavioral inhibition.

Psychodynamic conceptions have largely been aversive stimuli to learning theorists, but someday we may have an integrated account of learning that includes some psychodynamic concepts as well (Dollard & Miller, 1950; Wachtel, 1997). For example, one psychotherapy patient was unable to recall any events within a four-year period surrounding her parents' divorce, a phenomenon psychodynamic psychologists would call repression. A conditioning explanation would suggest that these memories are associated with emotions such as anxiety and sadness, so that recalling them elicits a conditioned emotional response. This CR is so unpleasant that it evokes avoidance or escape responses, one of which is to avoid retrieving the memories. If this mental "operant" reduces unpleasant emotion, it will be negatively reinforced—strengthened by the removal of an aversive emotional state—and hence likely to be maintained or used again. Similar ideas have recently been proposed by leading behavioral researchers to account for the "emotional avoidance" of unpleasant feelings (Hayes & Wilson, 1994).    ◄

## COGNITIVE-SOCIAL THEORY

By the 1960s, many researchers and theorists had begun to wonder whether a psychological science could be built strictly on observable behaviors without reference to thoughts. Most agreed that learning is the basis of much of human behavior, but some were not convinced that classical and operant conditioning could explain *everything* people do. From behaviorist learning principles thus emerged **cognitive-social theory** (sometimes called *cognitive social learning* or *cognitive-behavioral theory*), which incorporated concepts of conditioning but added two new features: a focus on cognition and a focus on social learning.

### LEARNING AND COGNITION

According to cognitive-social theory, the way an animal *construes* the environment is as important to learning as actual environmental contingencies. That is, humans and other animals are always developing mental images of, and expectations about, the environment that influence their behavior.

### Latent Learning

Some of the first research to question whether a science of behavior could completely dispense with thought was conducted by the behaviorist Edward Tolman.

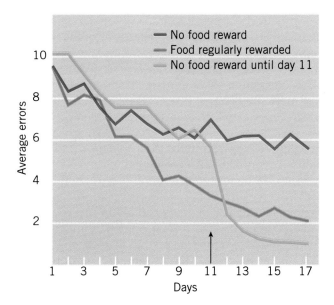

**FIGURE 5.14**
Latent learning. Rats that were not rewarded until the 11th trial immediately performed equally with rats that had been rewarded from the start. This suggests that they were learning the maze prior to reinforcement and were forming a cognitive map that allowed them to navigate it as soon as they received reinforcement. *Source:* Tolman & Honzik, 1930, p. 267.

In a paper entitled "Cognitive Maps in Rats and Men" (1948), Tolman described learning that occurred when rats were placed in a maze without any reinforcement, similar to the kind of learning that occurs when people learn their way around a city while looking out the window of a bus. In one experiment, Tolman let rats wander through a maze in ten trials on ten consecutive days without any reinforcement (Tolman & Honzik, 1930). A control group spent the same amount of time in the maze, but these rats received a food reinforcement on each trial.

The rats that were reinforced learned quite rapidly to travel to the end of the maze with few errors; not surprisingly, the behavior of the unreinforced rats was less predictable. On the 11th day, however, Tolman made food available for the first time to the previously unreinforced rats and recorded the number of errors they made. As Figure 5.14 shows, his findings were striking: These rats immediately took advantage of their familiarity with the maze and were able to obtain food just as efficiently as the rats who had previously received reinforcement. A third group of rats who still received no reinforcement continued to wander aimlessly through the maze.

To explain what had happened, Tolman suggested that the rats who were familiar with the maze had formed **cognitive maps**—mental representations or images—of the maze, even though they had received no reinforcement. Once the rats were reinforced, their learning became observable. Tolman called learning that has occurred but is not currently manifest in behavior **latent learning**. To cognitive-social theorists, latent learning was evidence that knowledge or beliefs about the environment are crucial to the way animals behave. And so began the effort to look inside the black box that lies between behaviors and environmental events while still maintaining a scientific, experimental approach to behavior.

### Conditioning and Cognition

Many learning phenomena have been reinterpreted from a cognitive perspective. For example, in classical conditioning, why does an organism respond to a previously neutral stimulus (such as a particular taste) with a conditioned response (such as nausea)? A cognitive explanation suggests that the presence of the CS alerts the animal to prepare for a UCS that is likely to follow. In other words, the CS *predicts* the presence of the UCS. If a CS does *not* routinely predict a UCS, it will not likely draw a CR. In fact, experimental data show that when a UCS (such as electric shock) frequently occurs in the absence of a CS (a tone), rats are unlikely to develop a conditioned fear response to the CS, regardless of the number of times the CS has been paired with the UCS (Rescorla, 1988; Rescorla & Holland, 1982; Rescorla & Wagner, 1972). In cognitive language, rats will not become afraid of a stimulus unless it is highly predictive of an aversive event. This does not imply that rats are *conscious* of these predictions; it simply means that their nervous systems are making them. This was, in fact, an argument offered by Pavlov himself, who described these predictions as "unconscious" (see excerpts of Pavlov, 1997). From a cognitive point of view, stimulus discrimination and generalization similarly reflect an animal's formation of a concept of what "counts" as a particular type of stimulus, which may be relatively general (any furry object) or relatively specific (a white rat).

Operant conditioning phenomena can also be reinterpreted from a more cognitive framework. Consider the counterintuitive finding that intermittent reinforcement is more effective than continuous reinforcement in maintaining behavior. From a cognitive standpoint, exposure to an intermittent reinforcement schedule (such as an old car that starts after five or ten turns of the ignition) produces the expectation that reinforcement will only come intermittently. As a result, lack of reinforcement over several trials does not signal a change in environmental contingencies. In contrast, when the owner of a new car suddenly finds the engine will not turn over, he has reason to stop trying after only three or four attempts because he has come to *expect* continuous reinforcement.

## Expectancies

Cognitive-social theory proposes that the expectations, or **expectancies,** an individual forms about the consequences of a behavior are what render the behavior more or less likely to occur. If a person expects a behavior to produce a reinforcing consequence, she is likely to perform it, as long as she has the competence or skill to do so (Mischel, 1973). Julian Rotter (1954), one of the earliest cognitive-social theorists, distinguished expectancies that are specific to concrete situations ("If I ask this professor for an extension, he will refuse") from those that are more generalized ("You can't ask people for anything in life—they'll always turn you down"). Rotter was particularly interested in **generalized expectancies** that influence a broad spectrum of behavior. He used the term **locus of control of reinforcement** (or simply **locus of control**) to refer to the generalized expectancies people hold about whether or not their own behavior can bring about the outcomes they seek (Rotter, 1954, 1990). Individuals with an **internal locus of control** believe they are the masters of their own fate; people with an **external locus of control** believe their lives are determined by forces outside (external to) themselves. Figure 5.15 shows some of the items included in Rotter's questionnaire for assessing locus of control. People who believe they control their own destiny are more likely to learn to do so, in part simply because they are more inclined to make the effort.

## Learned Helplessness and Explanatory Style

The powerful impact of expectancies on the behavior of nonhuman animals was dramatically demonstrated in a series of studies by Martin Seligman (1975). Seligman harnessed dogs so that they could not escape electric shocks. At first the dogs howled, whimpered, and tried to escape the shocks, but eventually they gave up; they would lie on the floor without struggle, showing physiological stress responses and behaviors resembling human depression. A day later Seligman placed the dogs in a shuttlebox from which they could easily escape the shocks.

**I more strongly believe that**

| | | |
|---|---|---|
| 1. Promotions are earned through hard work and persistence. | **OR** | Making a lot of money is largely a matter of getting the right breaks. |
| 2. In my experience I have noticed that there is usually a direct connection between how hard I study and the grades I get. | **OR** | Many times the reactions of teachers seem haphazard to me. |
| 3. I am the master of my fate. | **OR** | A great deal that happens to me is probably a matter of chance. |

**FIGURE 5.15**
Items from Rotter's locus-of-control questionnaire, called the Internal–External Scale. The scale presents subjects with a series of choices between two responses, one of which is internal and the other external. *Source:* Rotter, 1971.

Unlike dogs in a control condition who had not been previously exposed to inescapable shocks, the dogs in the experimental condition made no effort to escape and generally failed to learn to do so even when they occasionally *did* escape. The dogs had come to expect that they could not get away; they had learned to be helpless. **Learned helplessness** consists of the expectancy that one cannot escape aversive events and the motivational and learning deficits that result from this belief.

Seligman argued that learned helplessness is central to human depression as well. In humans, however, learned helplessness is not an automatic outcome of uncontrollable aversive events. Seligman and his colleagues observed that some people have a positive, active coping attitude in the face of failure or disappointment, whereas others become depressed and helpless (Peterson & Seligman, 1984). They demonstrated in dozens of studies that **explanatory style**—the way people make sense of bad events—plays a crucial role in whether or not they become, and remain, depressed. Individuals with a depressive or **pessimistic explanatory style** blame themselves for the bad things that happen to them; in the language of helplessness theory, pessimists believe the causes of their misfortune are *internal* rather than external, leading to lowered self-esteem. They also tend to see these causes as *stable* (unlikely to change) and *global* (broad, general, and widespread in their impact). When a person with a pessimistic style does poorly on a biology exam, he may blame it on his own stupidity—an explanation that is internal, stable, and global. Most people, in contrast, would offer themselves explanations that permit hope and encourage further effort, such as "I didn't study hard enough," "The exam was ridiculous," or "I just had a bad day."

Whether optimists or pessimists are more *accurate* in these inferences is a matter of debate. Several studies suggest that pessimistic people are actually more accurate than optimists in recognizing when they lack control over outcomes; people who maintain *positive illusions* about themselves and their ability to control their environment are less accurate but tend to be happier and report fewer psychological symptoms such as depression and anxiety (Taylor, 1992; Taylor & Brown, 1988). Other researchers have challenged these findings, however, showing that people who deny their problems or substantially overestimate their positive qualities tend to be more poorly adjusted socially than people who see themselves as others see them (Colvin et al., 1995; Colvin & Block, 1995; Shedler et al., 1993). Optimism and positive illusions about the self are probably useful up to a point, since confidence can spur action. However, when optimism verges on denial of obvious realities, it is likely to be neither healthy nor useful.

Whether or not pessimists are more accurate in their beliefs, they clearly pay a price for their explanatory style: Numerous studies document that pessimists have a higher incidence of depression and lower achievement in school than optimists (Peterson & Seligman, 1984). As we will see (Chapter 11), pessimists are also more likely to become ill and to die earlier than those who do not attribute negative events to stable, internal, and global factors.

INTERIM SUMMARY    **Cognitive-social theory** incorporated concepts of conditioning from behaviorism but added a focus on cognition and on social learning. Many learning phenomena can be reinterpreted from a cognitive perspective. One example of this is the counterintuitive finding that intermittent reinforcement is more effective than continuous reinforcement, by considering the expectations, or **expectancies,** humans and other animals develop.

## A GLOBAL VISTA

### OPTIMISM, PESSIMISM, AND EXPECTANCIES OF CONTROL IN CROSS-CULTURAL PERSPECTIVE

Optimism and pessimism occur within a social and cultural context. Cultural belief systems offer individuals ways of interpreting experience that influence their reactions to unpleasant events. For example, in the United States, people from fundamentalist religious backgrounds (both Christian and Jewish) tend to have more optimistic explanatory styles than nonfundamentalists (Sethi & Seligman, 1993). They tend to believe their fate is in God's hands and that God will do what is right for them. This can be extremely comforting in the face of unpleasant events such as death or disease.

People who live in a society also share common experiences that lead to shared beliefs and expectancies. We often speak of "culture" as if it were a single variable; however, cultural beliefs and practices only influence individual thought and action through specific experiences (Matthews & Moore, in press; Sapir, 1949; Shore, 1995; Strauss & Quinn, 1998). For example, studies comparing people from East and West Berlin before the fall of the Berlin Wall have provided a window to understanding the impact of social, political, and cultural factors on expectancies of control and optimism (Oettingen & Seligman, 1990; Oettingen, Little, Lindenberger, & Baltes, 1994). Individuals from these two cities shared a common culture until 1945, at which point contact between them ceased. After 1945, the people of West Berlin lived in an affluent, thriving country, in which individual initiative was rewarded through free enterprise. Those in the East lived under Soviet domination, were much poorer, had fewer freedoms, and lived under the weight of inefficient bureaucracies that controlled many aspects of their lives, from the clothes that were available to the books they were allowed to read.

These realities were reflected in a more pessimistic explanatory style and more external locus of control among East Berliners. These patterns could be observed as early as the school years, probably reflecting not only the broader sociopolitical climate but also specific features of the school environment (Oettingen et al., 1994). In East Berlin, school curricula were much more rigid and lacked any room for tailoring learning to the individual child's strengths and weaknesses. The ideology taught to children also de-emphasized individualism, and feedback on school performance was largely delivered publicly, in front of peers, rather than privately on a report card.

Expectations of control and explanatory style differ cross-culturally in ways that reflect long-standing cultural differences as well. A classic study in the early 1960s examined value orientations in five North American groups: white Texans, Mormons, Hispanics, Zuni Indians, and Navaho Indians (Kluckhohn & Strodtbeck, 1961). The researchers presented subjects with short stories that posed a problem or dilemma and asked them to indicate which of several solutions was most appropriate. Individuals differed, of course, within each group; white Texans are not all alike, and neither are Hispanic or Navajo individuals. Nevertheless, some broad patterns emerged. For example, Hispanic participants, like members of most cultures in human history, tended to believe that humans should not tamper with nature. Most Navajo similarly did not view control over nature as a dominant value; rather, they tended to stress peaceful coexistence between humans and their natural environment.

In contrast, the white Texans, like most people in the West (that is, people from cultures of European descent—not the Wild West, although that heritage may have had an influence as well) preferred mastery over nature. For them, control was a core value, and lack of control would be associated with frustration and a sense of helplessness and failure. This value system makes sense in a highly competitive, individualistic, technologically advanced, capitalist society in which individual initiative is rewarded and mastery over nature—turning ores in the ground into metals for manufacturing, predicting earthquakes, and sending people to the moon—is commonplace. It is also adaptive for people who cannot count on help from others in the ways they did even a century ago, when most people in the West lived and died in small towns near family and close neighbors.

More recent studies document substantial cultural differences in the way people make sense of positive and negative events. One study compared explanatory style in white-American, Chinese-American, and mainland Chinese college students (Lee & Seligman, 1997). The mainland Chinese were much more pessimistic than white Americans; Chinese Americans were intermediate between the other two groups. White Americans tended to attribute their successes to themselves and their failures to others—a way of interpreting events that bolsters self-confidence but probably at the cost of accuracy. Mainland Chinese, in comparison, tended to attribute both positive and negative events to forces outside their control.

Some of the differences between white Americans and mainland Chinese may, like the differences between East and West Berliners, reflect the more recent history of mainland China, in which the communist government has actively promoted communal values and created communal work settings. However, the fact that Chinese Americans, who have grown up in the United States but share elements of culture with the mainland Chinese, showed similarities to both of the other groups suggests the impact of more long-standing cultural differences as well. For hundreds of years of Chinese history, people have lived with their families in densely populated agricultural areas. In such environments, as elsewhere in Asia, excessive pride and self-centeredness are disruptive and discouraged. Attributing successes to one's personal characteristics is likely to be neither adaptive nor accurate, since much of labor in agricultural societies is communal, and families and villagers tend to share much of their fate.

*Much of human behavior reflects social learning processes such as modeling.*

## SOCIAL LEARNING

As this discussion suggests, learning does not occur in an interpersonal vacuum. Cognitive-social theory proposes that individuals learn many things from the people around them, with or without reinforcement, through **social learning** mechanisms other than classical and operant conditioning.

A major form of social learning is **observational learning**—learning by observing the behavior of others. The impact of observational learning in humans is enormous, from learning how to give a speech, to learning how to feel and act when someone tells an inappropriate joke, to learning what kind of clothes, haircuts, or foods are fashionable. Albert Bandura (1967), one of the major cognitive-social theorists, provides a tongue-in-cheek example of observational learning in the story of a lonesome farmer who bought a parrot to keep him company. The farmer spent many long hours trying to teach the parrot to repeat the phrase, "Say uncle," but to no avail. Even hitting the parrot with a stick whenever it failed to respond correctly had no effect. Finally, the farmer gave up; in disgust, he relegated the parrot to the chicken coop. Not long afterward, the farmer was walking by the chicken coop when he heard a terrible commotion. Looking in, he saw his parrot brandishing a stick at the chickens and yelling, "Say uncle! Say uncle!" The moral of the story is that the lesson intended in observational learning is not always the lesson learned.

Observational learning in which a human or other animal learns to reproduce behavior exhibited by a model is called **modeling** (Bandura, 1967). The most well-known modeling studies were done by Bandura and his colleagues on children's aggressive behavior (1961, 1963). In these studies, children observed an adult model interacting with a large inflatable doll named Bobo. One group of children watched the model behave in a subdued manner, while other groups observed the model verbally and physically attack the doll in real life, on film, or in a cartoon. A control group observed no model at all. Children who observed the model acting aggressively displayed nearly twice as much aggressive behavior as those who watched the nonaggressive model or no model at all (Figure 5.16).

The likelihood that a person will imitate a model depends on a number of factors, such as the model's prestige, likeability, and attractiveness. Whether an individual actually *performs* modeled behavior also depends on the behavior's likely outcome. This outcome expectancy is, itself, often learned through an observational learning mechanism known as vicarious conditioning. In **vicarious conditioning,** a person learns the consequences of an action by observing its consequences for someone else. For example, adolescents' attitudes toward high-risk behaviors such as drinking and having sex without a condom are influenced by their perceptions of the consequences of their older siblings' risk taking behavior (D'Amico and Fromme, 1997).

In a classic study of vicarious conditioning, Bandura and his colleagues (1963) had nursery school children observe an aggressive adult model named Rocky. Rocky took food and toys that belonged to someone named Johnny. In one condition, Johnny punished Rocky; in the other, Rocky packed all of Johnny's toys in a sack, singing, "Hi ho, hi ho, it's off to play I go" as the scene ended. Later, when placed in an analogous situation, the children who had seen Rocky punished displayed relatively little aggressive behavior. In contrast, those who had seen Rocky rewarded behaved much more aggressively. Because Rocky's aggressive behavior exemplified what the children had previously learned was bad behavior, however, even those who followed his lead displayed some ambivalence when they saw his behavior rewarded. One girl voiced strong disapproval of Rocky's behavior but then ended the experimental session by asking the researcher, "Do you have a sack?" More recent research shows that people who are empathic and

*In Bandura's classic Bobo studies, children learned by observation.*